Readings in the
Arts and Sciences

Readings in the Arts and Sciences

ELAINE P. MAIMON *Department of English*

GERALD L. BELCHER *Department of History*

GAIL W. HEARN *Department of Biology*

BARBARA F. NODINE *Department of Psychology*

FINBARR W. O'CONNOR *Department of Philosophy*

Beaver College

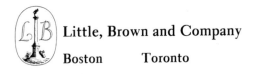

Little, Brown and Company

Boston   Toronto

Library of Congress Cataloging in Publication Data

Main entry under title:

Readings in the arts and sciences.

   1. College readers. 2. English language—Rhetoric.
I. Maimon, Elaine P.
PE1417.R425 1983   808'.0427   83-19913
ISBN 0-316-54422-1

Library of Congress Catalog Card Number 83-19913

ISBN 0-316-54422-1

9 8 7 6 5 4 3 2

HAL
Published simultaneously in Canada
by Little, Brown & Company (Canada) Limited

Printed in the United States of America

Contents

General Introduction   1

Reading to Learn in the Arts and Sciences   5

1. The Composition of the Declaration of Independence   6

   Jefferson's assignment   6
   Getting started   7
   First draft and peer review   8
   The "Rough Draft"   9
   Revision   16
   The "Committee of Five" Draft   17
   Audience considerations   24
   The Final Draft   26
   QUESTIONS AND EXERCISES   31

2. Reading Textbooks   33

   THE SOCIAL SCIENCES
   "Supply and Demand: The Bare Elements" PAUL SAMUELSON
   from *Economics*   34
   QUESTIONS AND EXERCISES   50

   THE NATURAL SCIENCES
   "Hormonal Regulation in Females" HELENA CURTIS from
   Biology   51
   QUESTIONS AND EXERCISES   60

   THE HUMANITIES
   "What Is Buddhism?" RICHARD PAUL JANARO and THELMA C.
   ALTSHULER from *The Art of Being Human*   61
   QUESTIONS AND EXERCISES   73

3. Reading to Understand Liberal Learning   74

"The Cave" PLATO from *The Republic*   76
QUESTIONS AND EXERCISES   80

Selection from *Leviathan* THOMAS HOBBES   81
QUESTIONS AND EXERCISES   88

"The Search for Certainty" RENÉ DESCARTES from *Discourse on Method*   90
QUESTIONS AND EXERCISES   103

Selection from *Vindication of the Rights of Woman* MARY WOLLSTONECRAFT   105
QUESTIONS AND EXERCISES   110

Selection from *On Liberty* JOHN STUART MILL   111
QUESTIONS AND EXERCISES   129

"Struggle for Existence" CHARLES DARWIN from *On the Origin of Species*   130
QUESTIONS AND EXERCISES   140

"Autobiographical Notes" ALBERT EINSTEIN from *Albert Einstein: Philosopher-Scientist*, Paul Arthur Schilpp, Ed.   141
QUESTIONS AND EXERCISES   150

"Letter from Birmingham Jail" MARTIN LUTHER KING, JR.   151
QUESTIONS AND EXERCISES   167

Reading in the Academic Disciplines   171

The Arts and Humanities   172

4. Readings in the Arts and Humanities   174

Fiction   174

"Araby" JAMES JOYCE from *Dubliners*   174
QUESTIONS AND EXERCISES   180

Hard Times, Chapters 1 and 2 CHARLES DICKENS   181
QUESTIONS AND EXERCISES   187

Essays of Analysis and Contemplation   189

"The Rhetoric of *Hard Times*" DAVID LODGE from *Language of Fiction*   189
QUESTIONS AND EXERCISES   205

"Restoring Charles II" ANTONIA FRASER from *The New Republic*   206
QUESTIONS AND EXERCISES   211

"All Animals Are Equal" PETER SINGER from *Philosophic Exchange* 212
QUESTIONS AND EXERCISES 224

Selection from *Man's World, Woman's Place* ELIZABETH JANEWAY 225
QUESTIONS AND EXERCISES 230

"Climates of Opinion" CARL BECKER from *The Heavenly City of the Eighteenth-Century Philosophers* 231
QUESTIONS AND EXERCISES 234

"The Myth of Mental Illness" THOMAS S. SZASZ from *American Psychologist* 235
QUESTIONS AND EXERCISES 245

Five Articles on Justice and Discrimination from *Analysis* 246
QUESTIONS AND EXERCISES 259

The Sciences

261

5. Readings in the Social Sciences 265

"The Nature of Social Science" BERNARD MAUSNER from *A Citizen's Guide to the Social Sciences* 265
QUESTIONS AND EXERCISES 278

"Running a Fencing Business: Wheelin' and Dealin'" CARL KLOCKARS from *The Professional Fence* 279
QUESTIONS AND EXERCISES 288

Selection from *Love Is Not Enough* BRUNO BETTELHEIM 289
QUESTIONS AND EXERCISES 292

"Sanity in Bedlam" from *Newsweek* 293

"On Being Sane in Insane Places" DAVID L. ROSENHAN from *Science* 293
QUESTIONS AND EXERCISES 312

"Visual Thinking in Overview" RUDOLF ARNHEIM from *Perception and Pictorial Representation*, eds. Calvin F. Nodine and Dennis F. Fisher 313
QUESTIONS AND EXERCISES 319

6. Readings in the Natural Sciences 321

"Sounder Thinking Through Clearer Writing" F. PETER WOODFORD from *Science* 321
QUESTIONS AND EXERCISES 328

"Experiments" VINCENT C. DETHIER from *To Know a Fly* 329
QUESTIONS AND EXERCISES 332

"Germs" LEWIS THOMAS from *Lives of a Cell*   334
QUESTIONS AND EXERCISES   344

The Songs of the Whales: A Study of Scientific Writing for Various Audiences   348

"A Whale of a Singer" from *Newsweek*   349
QUESTIONS AND EXERCISES   350

"Songs of Humpback Whales" ROGER S. PAYNE AND SCOTT MC VAY from *Science*   350
QUESTIONS AND EXERCISES   359

"Humpbacks, Their Mysterious Songs" ROGER PAYNE from *National Geographic*   360
QUESTIONS AND EXERCISES   362

"A Whale of a Song" JULIE ANN MILLER from *Science News*   363
QUESTIONS AND EXERCISES   366

"Sound Playback Experiments with Southern Right Whales (Eubalaena australis)" CHRISTOPHER W. CLARK AND JANE M. CLARK from *Science*   367
QUESTIONS AND EXERCISES   376

Appendix: Acknowledging a Community of Colleagues   378

Preface to the Instructor

Readings in the Arts and Sciences is informed by our philosophy of liberal learning. We see the composition course as an introduction to liberal learning, and the role of the composition instructor as native informant, initiating students to academic conversation. When students come to college, they encounter a conversation already in progress. Professors and more advanced students seem caught up in a world of knowledge and cross-references unfamiliar to the newcomer. Everyone else, it seems, knows the names and the in jokes. Every printed page makes references to many other unknown pages in a bewildering progression. Even the most confident newcomer might be cowed into silent retreat. The purpose of *Readings in the Arts and Sciences* is to help students enter the conversation.

Participation in the academic conversation means more than attaining a diploma. Learning how to articulate ideas for oneself and then for others prepares students for public discourse in the society at large. Such articulate participation is essential in the United States, since democracy itself depends, as Jefferson said, upon an educated citizenry. Historically, in Europe, a university was intended to be a training ground for the religious and secular ruling classes. In the United States, Jeffersonian democracy makes all citizens members of the ruling classes. Each person in a democracy has a vote; each person should have a voice.

Writing enfranchises by giving people access to their own thoughts. Then, if they choose, they can make their ideas accessible to others by writing. Writing is the sign and the privilege of the educated person.

If they do not understand the vital connections between themselves as struggling writers and those absent demigods who have produced the printing in their textbooks, students may be intimidated by writing or may find it artificial "make-work." In this anthology we link the work of scholars and the work of students into a continuum of academic conversation. In the introductions we frequently present information about the original situation that motivated the writer to compose the article. We want readers to see that each document did not emerge as polished prose directly from the mind of the writer. We hope that these introductions will help students to feel greater kinship as writers with the individuals who produce books and articles.

In the exercises that follow each selection we offer students opportunities to write several different sorts of responses to the readings: writing in a private journal; writing to prepare for or report from small group discussions; writing for a public, usually of classmates and instructor.

The journal assignments reflect our belief that the impulse to write comes from the representation of a problem in a person's own mind, the problem itself deriving from a confrontation between the mind of the writer and the world outside. The expressive writing that we suggest in some of the exercises is meant to help students make personal discoveries, to move from an outsider's confrontation with a topic to an insider's struggle with a problem.

Before students can make intellectual problems their own, they often need to share ideas informally with friends. We are committed to the idea that learning at all levels is enhanced through exchange within small groups. We provide several exercises for this small group exchange, and we suggest that you set aside some class time to accustom students to the experience. We have found that many students are secretive about their ideas, as if someone else might deplete their supply. Small group work can help students to understand that writing is a social activity. This textbook encourages students to behave like experienced writers, most of whom compare notes with a community of peers.

In each section of exercises we also suggest public projects, which we expect will grow naturally from the journal writing and small group work. We hope that whenever students sit down to draft something, they will have notes to read over and friends to call upon.

We ourselves called upon many friends during the composition of this book. We acknowledge their help, as we hope you will ask your students formally to acknowledge the assistance that they receive on work in progress. More than that, we give witness to our membership through conversation in the community of people whom we gratefully acknowledge.

This project began under the guidance of Paul O'Connell, English editor at Bobbs-Merrill. In 1977, as president and English editor at Winthrop, he was willing to take a risk on two books imagined by five coauthors, all from different disciplines. At a time when composition textbooks were more trendy than rigorous, he shared our vision of a composition course that would introduce students to their intellectual heritage.

Because the concept of this book was new, Winthrop and then in its turn, Winthrop's purchaser Little, Brown invited three stages of review. Carolyn Potts, English editor at Little, Brown, has patiently and wisely guided the evolution of the text in its later stages. We thank her, Julia Winston, Pat Torelli, Lauren Green, Virginia Pye, Patricia Gross, and Sarah Clark for work on the production of the book. We thank the following readers, some of whom, true practitioners of writing and reviewing as processes of learning, read the manuscript in more than one avatar: John Bean, Patricia Bizzell, Robin L. Jeffers, Paula Johnson, Richard Larson, Leah Masiello, and K. Jay Wilson.

Our longstanding thanks go to Richard Larson, who advised us early on that *Readings in the Arts and Sciences* might be a happy partner for *Writing in the Arts and Sciences*, although we should create in each text the autonomy necessary for any healthy marriage. We have a special debt of gratitude to Patricia Bizzell, whose intelligent and prolific commentary on two stages of the manuscript established for us the nurturing dialogue that makes revision creative. Some of the ideas for exercises are hers, and many gaps in the text were filled through her perspicacity.

The conversation that created this book extends beyond those officially assigned to be our reviewers. From the beginning, we have been inspired by Mina Shaughnessy's expectation that the complexities of higher education are best made accessible through thinking systematically about fundamentals, not through oversimplification. James Kinneavy has taught us to look first at the aim of discourse and only then at the mode chosen to achieve that aim. Kenneth Bruffee has served as a sustaining collaborator during the evolution of this project. The metaphor of "conversation" comes from his suggestion that we read Richard Rorty. But more than that, Bruffee has taught us by his scholarship, his teaching, and his example that writing and learning are social activities.

The social nature of learning is promoted through many activities of the National Endowment for the Humanities. We have an immense debt to that agency for two program grants which have connected our work to the larger intellectual community. Individual staff members at NEH have been particularly helpful, not only in guiding Beaver College's internal and external programs of faculty development, but also in their advice as scholars and friends. We thank Blanche Premo, Lynn Maxwell White, Gene Moss, and Janice Litwin.

Other scholars and friends listened on the telephone, advised over lunch, suggested during dinner. We thank Harvey Wiener, Donald McQuade, Nancy Sommers, Edward P. J. Corbett, John R. Hayes, Abe Edel, Betty Flower, Charles Long, Winifred Horner, Frederick Crews, Richard Lanham, Harriet Sheridan, Richard Young, Claire Gaudiani, and Robert Lucid.

Our colleagues at Beaver College have, over the years, lived and worked with the ideas in this book. Myra Jacobsohn and Carol Schilling created one of the exercises. Jack Davis has kept us aware of visual literacy. Beaver's librarians, Marion Green, Josephine Charles, Joan Allen, and Peg Hibbs, have cheerfully aided us at every stage of the project. Janice Haney-Peritz, Jo Ann Bomze, Peggy Horodowich, and the rest of the composition staff have classroom-tested the manuscript while it was still in an unwieldy, photocopied form. Bette Landman and David Gray, through their leadership in the college administration, have created an atmosphere in which people can function at their best and in which instructors in different disciplines can work productively together.

For research and clerical assistance we thank four students, Carolyn Daly, Linda Bobrin, Susan Mills, and Lili Velez. Margaret Belcher has proved that you can type and pasteup a manuscript for your husband's "second family" and still maintain a happy marriage. Marie Lawrence, woman of many talents, has coordinated our research assistants, organized our permissions, typed, pasted, photocopied, and telephoned. Above all, she has understood the manuscript and its coeditors. Her affectionate care is evident on every page.

As the five of us grew into a special sort of family, our primary families have shown extraordinary understanding and patience. We thank Mort, Cal, Peter, Marg, Eric, Craig, Renée, Linda, Ricky, Jody, Gillian and Alan for their understanding and help. Mort Maimon was our special consultant on style, and Cal Nodine on reading and learning in the social sciences.

Finally, we acknowledge a continuing debt for the five-way conversation which has promoted our growth as scholars, teachers, and friends.

Readings in the
Arts and Sciences

General Introduction

Readings in the Arts and Sciences presents opportunities for you to practice the kinds of reading and writing assignments you will encounter in your college courses. Such broad participation in reading and writing fills an immediate need, success in college. Writing, reading, and conversing are the activities fundamental to all courses across the curriculum. This anthology will help you to read, write, and converse in different disciplinary contexts.

Success in college means more than passing your courses — it means gaining membership in the community of educated people. Academic reading and writing prepare you for the analytic thinking and clarity of expression that allow full participation in educated conversation. Much of that conversation, outside the classroom as well as within, is carried on in writing. Electronic advances like the computer and word processor have accelerated rather than diminished the production of written material.

As members of the educated community, all of you will be writers. You may have once believed that writers are only those people who publish stories and articles. According to our definition, however, writers are those who write something that is important to themselves and to others. You are a writer when you record your thinking in a private journal, when you write a letter that must strike just the right tone, or when you write a memo that must accomplish a task. In your personal or professional life, all of you will be required to write something that matters, and in that sense you will be writers.

Academic reading and writing enable you to participate in academic conversation inside the classroom and educated conversation in the wider public forum. This anthology can serve as an initiation into that general conversation and as an introduction to the more specialized exchanges typical in various disciplines. Some assignments are apprentice versions of writing you will do later in your careers. Social workers, for example, will write case studies like the pieces by Klockars and Bettelheim. Chemists and engineers will write research reports that are similar in form to the reports by Roger Payne and the Clarks. Literary critics and historians will write essays that may resemble the work of David Lodge and Carl Becker.

All these published writers belong to smaller communities within the larger community of educated people. In our introductions we provide some information about the intellectual communities to which these published writers belong. Writers converse with a group much larger than their immediate circle of friends. In effect, writers know how to carry on conversations with other selected writers, living and dead. The writer working alone in his or her study is not alone at all. People "work together," writes Robert Frost, "whether they work together or apart."[1] The writer is carrying on a conversation with other writers represented in the books on his shelves and the books in his head. Our introductions attempt to explain the background of this conversation. Academic writing may be difficult for you to read. One reason is that this writing is not merely about the world of experience but always about other pieces of writing — material that many students will not have read. When Thomas Jefferson, for example, wrote the Declaration of Independence, he was writing not only about the grievances of the American colonists; he was writing also about the philosophy of John Locke.

Besides providing this needed context, our introductions often present information about some feature of the author's composing process. For example, we write about how Thomas Hobbes worked out a way to begin writing, how Mary Wollstonecraft developed a sense of audience for *Vindication of the Rights of Women,* how René Descartes composed, and how John Stuart Mill revised. The introduction to Carl Becker's *The Heavenly City of the Eighteenth Century Philosophers* quotes parts of an essay that he wrote on the importance of writing as a means of self-discovery. In the introductions to the selections by Elizabeth Janeway, Carl Klockars, and Christopher and Jane Clark, we include letters in which the authors explain their methods of composition. In the introduction to Bernard Mausner's essay, we present an interview with the writer.

Beyond stimulating your thinking and writing abilities, the selections in this anthology are designed also to introduce you to the types of writing that you will encounter in college. We have included examples of academic writing from most of the major disciplines. Studying these selections in a composition course should help you to read more critically and write more effectively in all the academic subjects you study.

The book is divided into two major sections. In the first, "Reading to Learn in the Arts and Sciences," we emphasize reading and writing as ways to discover ideas and to learn concepts. Because of our belief in the interdependence of writing and reading, we begin with an introduction to the composing process as illustrated in the writing of the Declaration of Independence.

1. From "A Tuft of Flowers," in Louis Untermeyer, ed., *Modern American Poetry* (N.Y.: Harcourt, Brace, 1950), p. 184.

We then proceed to the most frequent kind of reading assigned to students: the textbook. We present excerpts from three very commonly used texts, each representing one of the three major academic divisions: the social sciences, the natural sciences, and the humanities. As you study this subsection, you will have a chance to compare three basic disciplinary approaches in the arts and sciences.

The eight selections that compose the next group of readings appear under the title, "Reading to Understand Liberal Learning." These eight are a sampling of some of the great ideas that have contributed to liberal learning in western society. The general topics include truth, human nature, knowledge, equality, liberty, evolution, creativity, and justice. The authors, of course, are not making definitive statements on these topics, but they are saying something fundamental, something with which anyone subsequently writing on the same topic ought to be conversant. Again, our emphasis is on joining an ongoing conversation.

The second half of the anthology, "Reading in the Academic Disciplines," prepares you to participate in the more specialized conversation that occurs as you move from course to course. The selections, divided by academic disciplines, provide a survey of the types of writing that you will be asked to read in college. These range from short fiction to scientific research reports, from speculative essays in philosophy to case study papers in criminology. These works not only introduce you to the nature of inquiry and writing in different fields, they also represent models for students writing in these disciplines.

We divide this second major section into "The Arts and Humanities" and "The Sciences." In "The Arts and Humanities," we include fiction, literary criticism, and philosophical and historical analyses. We divide "The Sciences" into social and natural sciences. In the social sciences, we start with a general article entitled, "The Nature of Social Science" and then proceed to case studies, theoretical articles, and reports of research. In the natural sciences we reprint an article on scientific writing, two articles written for an educated public (one on germs, the other on experiments), and a series of articles about humpback whales. The articles about whales, each of which written for a different audience — from the general public to practicing scientists — are presented so that we can include at least one example of the condensed and specialized form used by scientists to pass on new knowledge to other scientists. We do not expect you necessarily to enter that technical conversation, but the more accessible articles that we reprint earlier in that section will at least give you enough background to eavesdrop on the forms of scientific conversation.

We hope that *Readings in the Arts and Sciences* will help you to join in the educated conversation of our culture. Reading and writing enable you to find and to use your voice in our civilization. Education leads you out of the confines of immaturity to full participation in the wider community.

ociei

cat

als

But

ges

th

rity

ainst the King's C

urt vs. the count

ouse of Commons

ss, which include

hat seemed to the

erties. They didr

ere directed again

kes, dissolved his

ers. An angry and

Reading to Learn
in the Arts
and Sciences

1

The Composition of the Declaration of Independence

Draft 1

We hold these truths to be sacred & undeniable; that all men are created equal & independent; that from that equal creation they derive in rights inherent & inalienable, among which are the preservation of life, & liberty, & the pursuit of happiness . . .

Draft 2

We hold these truths to be self-evident; that all men are created equal, that they are endowed by their creator with inherent & inalienable rights; that among these are life, liberty, & the pursuit of happiness . . .

Draft 3

We hold these truths to be self-evident, that all men are created equal, that they are endowed by their Creator with certain unalienable Rights, that among these are Life, Liberty and the pursuit of Happiness. . . .

The Declaration of Independence, that venerable parchment document enclosed in glass in The National Archives, was humbly born from notes and rough drafts. Thomas Jefferson, the principal author, struggled to bring his composition to maturity, just as you may write and rewrite your own assignments.

Jefferson's assignment

Following months of war with Great Britain, the American colonists had begun by the spring of 1776 to talk of independence. The Continental Congress, meeting in Philadelphia, received its first resolution to that effect on June 7. Because the leaders believed that the members were not ready to make so momentous a decision, they postponed the vote on the resolution until July. In preparation for that vote, they appointed on June 11, a Committee of Five (Thomas Jefferson, John Adams, Benjamin Franklin, Roger Sherman, and Robert R. Livingston) to draft a declaration that would justify the necessity for political independence. The June 7 resolution, which had been introduced by Richard Henry Lee, read:

> That these United Colonies are, and of right ought to be, free and independent states, that they are absolved from all allegiance to the British Crown, and that all political connection between them and the State of Great Britain is, and ought to be, totally dissolved.

The Committee's assignment was to defend that statement, should it be passed, and to explain why it was passed. The Committee met after the eleventh to discuss the general form of the declaration. They apparently came to some agreements and gave the task of composing a draft to Jefferson. Adams later said that he asked Jefferson to write the working draft because, among other reasons, "you write ten times better than I can."[1]

Getting started

Jefferson's interpretation of his assignment was that he was

> not to find out new principles, or new arguments never before thought of, not merely to say things which had never been said before; but to place before mankind the common sense of the subject, in terms so plain and firm as to command their assent, and to justify ourselves in the independent stand we are compelled to take.[2]

So Jefferson regarded his task as writing a common-sense argument based on ideas that would be persuasive because they already had a wide acceptance. The principle of independence would be justified by existing political theory. This justification required research.

If Jefferson wrote from notes, we do not have them. Consequently, historians still debate the problem of his sources. Some believe that he relied heavily on the English philosopher John Locke, whose *Second Treatise on Government* had justified the English revolution of 1688.[3] Another historian argues that Jefferson's ideas were derived not from England, but from the radical Scottish theorists Thomas Reid, David Hume, and especially Francis Hutchison.[4] Even though historians may disagree on the exact

1. As quoted in Carl Becker, *The Declaration of Independence: A Study of the History of Political Ideas* (New York: Alfred A. Knopf, 1956), p. 135.

2. Dumas Malone, *Jefferson: The Virginian* (New York: Little, Brown, and Co., 1948), p. 220.

3. In addition to Becker, *Declaration* and Malone, *Jefferson*, see Julian Boyd, *The Declaration of Independence: The Evolution of the Text* (Princeton: Princeton University Press, 1945).

4. Garry Wills, *Inventing America: Jefferson's Declaration of Independence* (New York: Vintage Press, Random House, 1979), pp. 167–255.

nature of his sources, they all agree that in his famous introduction Jefferson drew heavily from the writings of earlier defenders of revolution.

To write the body of the paper — the charges against King George III and England — Jefferson relied on some of his own documents and the writings of other colonists. This list of eighteen grievances is the longest part of the declaration, and all but five of the charges were compiled from existing documents. The sources from Jefferson's writings were the list of grievances that he had just incorporated into the Virginia Constitution, the *Summary View of the Rights of British Americans*, and the *Declaration of the Causes and Necessity for Taking up Arms*; the other sources were the 1774 Bill of Rights passed by the Congress and the 1774 Congressional Petition to the King of England.[5] These sources provided all but five of the charges that appear in his first draft. These grievances all dealt with the way George had conducted the war, which had been going on since April 1775.

First draft and peer review

Only seventeen days elapsed between the time Congress gave the assignment and the Committee's submission of a revised draft. In that short time the paper went through at least two, and possibly three drafts, and at least two peer review sessions.

Jefferson was able to produce a first draft in a matter of days not only because he was so familiar with his sources, but also because he wrote swiftly. In fact, the month before, he had written three drafts of the Virginia Constitution in only thirteen days. As a rule he revised and corrected his prose as he wrote; within a few days he had a draft to show to Benjamin Franklin and John Adams. They apparently suggested corrections informally. Writing about the event forty-seven years later, Jefferson remembered that "their alterations were two or three only, and merely verbal."[6] It is probable that their changes were more extensive, however, because Jefferson seems to have written another draft to submit to the entire Committee of Five.

This draft, reproduced below, is commonly known as the "Rough Draft." It is probably the second draft. Jefferson, again writing from a distance of a half century, recalled that after Franklin and Adams looked at his first draft, he "wrote a fair copy, reported it to the Committee, and from there, unaltered, to the Congress."[7] As you can see, it did not make it through the Committee unaltered. Altogether, they made twenty-three changes in wording and phrasing, mostly in the introduction, and added three paragraphs. These are not extensive changes and seem to indicate

5. This list is taken from Wills, *Inventing America*, pp. 68–72.
6. As quoted in Becker, *Declaration*, p. 136.
7. *Ibid.*

that the Committee had reached broad areas of agreement during their planning.

The draft below is adapted from Carl Becker's book *The Declaration of Independence*.[8] The original represents what Jefferson probably wrote. The circled corrections are those made by Jefferson, Franklin, and Adams before the draft was submitted to the Committee. The Committee's deletions are represented by the crossed-out lines, and their additions are given in italics.

The "Rough Draft"
as it was presented to and revised
by the Committee of Five

A DECLARATION BY THE REPRESENTATIVES OF THE

UNITED STATES OF AMERICA, IN GENERAL

CONGRESS ASSEMBLED.

When in the course of human events it becomes nec-   1
    one   *dissolve the political bands which have con-*
sary for a ∧ people to ∧ ~~advance from that subordination in~~   2
nected them with another, and to
~~which they have hitherto remained, & to~~ assume among   3
      separate and equal
the powers of the earth the ∧ ~~equal & independent~~ station   4

to which the laws of nature & of nature's god entitle them,   5

a decent respect to the opinions of mankind requires that   6
        the sep-
they should declare the causes which impel them to ∧ ~~the~~   7
aration
~~change.~~   8

       (self-evident)

We hold these truths to be ∧ ~~sacred & undeniable;~~ that   9
       they are endowed by their
all men are created equal ~~& independent;~~ that ∧ ~~from that~~   10
creator with ~~equal rights, some of which are~~   *rights; that*
~~equal creation they derive in rights~~ inherent & inalienable ∧   11
    these
among ~~which~~ ∧ are ~~the preservation of~~ life, & liberty, &   12
      rights
the pursuit of happiness; that to secure these ∧ ~~ends,~~   13

governments are instituted among men, deriving their   14

just powers from the consent of the governed; that   15

8. *Ibid.*, pp. 160–171.
From Carl Becker, *The Declaration of Independence: A Study of the History of Political Ideas*, © copyright 1956 Alfred A. Knopf, Inc. Reprinted by permission of the publisher.

whenever any form of government ~~shall~~ becomes de- 16

structive of these ends, it is the right of the people to 17

alter or to abolish it, & to institute new government, 18

laying it's foundation on such principles & organizing 19

it's powers in such form, as to them shall seem most likely 20

to effect their safety & happiness. prudence indeed will 21

dictate that governments long established should not be 22

changed for light & transient causes: and accordingly all 23

experience hath shewn that mankind are more disposed to 24

suffer while evils are sufferable, than to right themselves 25

by abolishing the forms to which they are accustomed. 26

but when a long train of abuses & usurpations, begun 27

at a distinguished period, & pursuing invariably the 28

same object, evinces a design to ~~subject~~ reduce them 29
under absolute Despotism

ʌ ~~to arbitrary power,~~ it is their right, it is their duty, to 30

throw off such government & to provide new guards 31

for their future security. such has been the patient 32

sufferance of these colonies; & such is now the necessity 33

which constrains them to expunge their former systems 34
the   king of Great Britain
of government. the history of ~~his~~ present ʌ ~~majesty~~ is a 35

history of unremitting injuries and usurpations, among 36
appears no solitary fact
which ʌ ~~no one fact stands single or solitary~~ to contradict 37
but all
the uniform tenor of the rest, ~~all of which~~ ʌ have in 38

direct object the establishment of an absolute tyranny 39

over these states. to prove this, let facts be submitted 40

to a candid world, for the truth of which we pledge 41

a faith yet unsullied by falsehood. 42

he has refused his assent to laws the most wholesome and 43

    necessary for the public good: 44

he has forbidden his governors to pass laws of immediate 45

    & pressing importance, unless suspended in their opera- 46

tion till his assent should be obtained; and when so 47

suspended, he has neglected utterly to attend to them. 48

he has refused to pass other laws for the accomodation 49

of large districts of people unless those people would 50

relinquish the right of representation ∧ *in the legislature*, a right inesti- 51

mable to them & formidable to tyrants only: 52

he has called together legislative bodies at places unusual, 53

uncomfortable & distant from the depository of their 54

public records for the sole purpose of fatiguing them into 55

compliance with his measures: 56

he has dissolved, Representative houses repeatedly & con- 57

tinually, for opposing with manly firmness his invasions 58

on the rights of the people: 59

~~he has dissolved~~ he has refused for a long ~~space of time~~ ∧ *time after such dissolutions* 60

to cause others to be elected, whereby the legislative 61

powers, incapable of annihilation, have returned to the 62

people at large for their exercise, the state remaining in 63

the meantime exposed to all the dangers of invasion 64

from without, & convulsions within: 65

he has endeavored to prevent the population of these 66

states; for that purpose obstructing the laws for natural- 67

ization of foreigners; refusing to pass others to en- 68

courage their migrations hither; & raising the conditions 69

of new appropriations of lands: 70

he has suffered the administration of justice totally to 71

cease in some of these ∧ *states* ~~colonies,~~ refusing his assent to 72

laws for establishing judiciary powers: 73

he has made our judges dependent on his will alone, 74

for the tenure of their offices, and ∧ *the* amount ∧ *and payment* of their 75

salaries: 76

he has erected a multitude of new offices by a self- 77

assumed power, & sent hither swarms of officers to   78

harrass our people & eat out their substance: 79

he has kept among us in times of peace ∧ standing armies &   80
without our consent (struck through)

the
without ~~our~~ _consent. of our legislatures_
ships of war ∧:   81

he has effected to render the military, independent of &   82

superior to the civil power: 83

he has combined with others to subject us to a jurisdiction   84

foreign to our constitutions and unacknoleged by our   85
acts of
laws; giving his assent to their ∧ pretended ~~acts of~~ legis-   86

lation,   87

    for quartering large bodies of armed troops among   88

    us;   89

    for protecting them by ~~a mock~~-trial from punish-   90
       (which)
    ment for any murders ∧ they should commit on   91

    the inhabitants of these states;   92

    for cutting off our trade with all parts of the world;   93

    for imposing taxes on us without our consent;   94

    for depriving us of the benefits of trial by jury;   95

    for transporting us beyond seas to be tried for   96

    pretended offenses;   97

   for abolishing the free system of English laws in a neigh-   98

    boring province, establishing therein an arbitrary gov-   99

    ernment, and enlarging it's boundaries so as to render   100

    it at once an example & fit instrument for introducing   101

    the same absolute rule into these ~~_colonies_~~ _states;_   102
                 valuable
       abolishing our most ~~_important_~~ _laws_
    for taking away our charters, ∧ & altering funda-   103

    mentally the forms of our governments;   104

    for suspending our own legislatures & declaring   105

    themselves invested with power to legislate for   106

    us in all cases whatsoever: 107

he has abdicated government here, withdrawing his gov- 108

ernors, & declaring us out of his allegiance & protection: 109

he has plundered our seas, ravaged our coasts, burnt our 110

towns & destroyed the lives of our people: 111

he is at this time transporting large armies of foreign 112

mercenaries to compleat the works of death, desolation 113

& tyranny, already begun with circumstances of cruelty 114

& perfidy unworthy the head of a civilized nation: 115

he has endeavored to bring on the inhabitants of our 116

frontiers the merciless Indian savages, whose known 117

rule of warfare is an undistinguished destruction of 118

all ages, sexes, & conditions of existence: 119

he has incited treasonable insurrections of our fellow- 120

citizens, with the allurements of forfeiture & confisca- 121

tion of our property: 122

he has constrained others ∧ ^{taken captives} ~~falling into his hands,~~ *on the* 123

high seas to bear arms against their country ~~& to destroy~~ 124

~~& be destroyed by the brethren whom they love,~~ *to become* 125

the executioners of their friends & brethren, or to fall 126

themselves by their hands. 127

he has waged cruel war against human nature itself, 128

violating it's most sacred rights of life & liberty in the 129

persons of a distant people who never offended him, 130

captivating & carrying them into slavery in another 131

hemisphere, or to incur miserable death in their 132

transportation thither. this piratical warfare, the 133

opprobrium of *infidel* powers, is the warfare of the 134

Christian king of Great Britain. *determined to keep* 135

open a market where MEN should be bought & sold, he 136

has prostituted his negative for suppressing every legis- 137

lative attempt to prohibit or to restrain this execrable 138

~~determining to keep open a market where MEN should be bought & sold~~

commerce ∧ and that this assemblage of horrors might   139

want no fact of distinguished die, he is now exciting   140

those very people to rise in arms among us, and to   141

purchase that liberty of which *he* has deprived them,   142

by murdering the people upon whom *he* also obtruded   143

them; thus paying off former crimes committed   144

against the *liberties* of one people, with crimes which he   145

urges them to commit against the *lives* of another.   146

in every stage of these oppressions we have petitioned for   147

redress in the most humble terms; our repeated petitions   148

have been answered ∧ *only* by repeated injury a prince whose   149

character is thus marked by every act which may define   150

a tyrant, is unfit to be the ruler of a people who mean to   151

be free. future ages will scarce believe that the hardiness   152

of one man, adventured within the short compass of   153

to ~~lay~~ *build* a foundation so broad & undisguised for tyranny

twelve years only, ∧ ~~on so many acts of tyranny without~~   154

~~a mask,~~ over a people fostered & fixed in principles of   155

~~liberty.~~ *freedom.*   156

Nor have we been wanting in attentions to our British   157

brethren. we have warned them from time to time of   158

attempts by their legislature to extend a jurisdiction over   159

these our states. we have reminded them of the cir-   160

cumstances of our emigration & settlement here, no one   161

of which could warrant so strange a pretension: that   162

these were effected at the expence of our own blood &   163

treasure, unassisted by the wealth or the strength of   164

Great Britain: that in constituting indeed our several   165

forms of government, we had adopted one common king,   166

thereby laying a foundation for perpetual league & amity   167 with them: but that submission to their parliament was 168

no part of our constitution, nor ever in idea if history may 169

be credited: and we appealed to their native justice & 170

magnanimity as well as to the ties of our common kindred 171

to disavow these usurpations which were likely to interrupt 172

our ∧ correspondence & connection. they too have been 173

connection &

deaf to the voice of justice & of consanguinity, & when 174

occasions have been given them, by the regular course 175

of their laws, of removing from their councils the dis- 176

turbers of our harmony, they have by their free election 177

re-established them in power. at this very time too they 178

are permitting their chief magistrate to send over not 179

only soldiers of our common blood, but Scotch & foreign 180

destroy us

mercenaries to invade & ∧ deluge us in blood. these facts 181

have given the last stab to agonizing affection, and manly 182

spirit bids us to renounce forever these unfeeling brethren. 183

we must endeavor to forget our former love for them, and 184

to hold them as we hold the rest of mankind, enemies in 185

war, in peace friends. we might have been a free & a 186

great people together; but a communication of grandeur 187

& of freedom it seems is below their dignity. be it so, 188

& to glory

since they will have it: the road to glory & happiness ∧ 189

apart from them

is open to us too; we will climb it ∧ in a separately state 190

de

and acquiesce in the necessity which pronounces our 191

everlasting adieu! eternal separation! 192

    We therefore the representatives of the United States of 193

America in General Congress assembled do, in the name 194

& by authority of the good people of these states, reject 195

and renounce all allegiance & subjection to the kings of 196

Great Britain & all others who may hereafter claim by, 197

through, or under them; we utterly dissolve & ~~break off~~ ^{have} 198

all political connection which may ~~have~~ heretofore ∧ sub- 199

sisted between us & the people or parliament of Great 200

Britain; and finally we do assert and declare these 201

colonies to be free and independent states, and that as 202

free & independent states they ~~shall hereafter~~ have∧ (full) 203

power to levy war, conclude peace, contract alliances, 204

establish commerce, & to do all other acts and things 205

which independent states may of right do. And for the 206

support of this declaration we mutually pledge to each 207

other our lives, our fortunes, & our sacred honour. 208

Revision

On June 28, the Committee of Five submitted its draft to the entire Congress. The Congress, however, was not ready to consider the document because they had not yet voted on the issue of independence. It was not until July 2 that Lee's resolution was removed from the table, voted on, and passed. Then it became necessary to consider the document. From July 2 to July 4 the Congress debated the substance and language of the Declaration. It was during these discussions that the document was revised.

This stage in the writing process produced many more changes than in earlier stages. While the Committee of Five had mainly altered the phrasing of the introduction, the Congress barely touched the opening, making only six changes, mostly deletions. Neither the body of the paper (the grievances) nor the conclusion fared so well.

The debates were often heated. We do not have notes from these three days, but we know that the greatest controversy came during the revising of the list of grievances. Altogether, the Congress made twenty-four changes, deleting, in the process, over three hundred words.[9] The most explosive issues involved changes in two key paragraphs: one begins with the strong statement about George that "He has waged cruel war against human nature itself . . ." and indicts him for not putting an end to the slave trade; the other is part of the long denunciation of Englishmen as "unfeeling brethren," whom the colonists had to "renounce." We will return to a discussion of these passages later.

9. Boyd, *The Declaration,* pp. 32–33.

Lastly, the Congress drastically edited out much of the concluding passages and substituted the wording of the original resolution that Lee had introduced on June 7.

A reconstruction of the Committee of Five's draft appears below. Congress's deletions are indicated by crossed-out words; their additions appear in italics.[10]

The "Committee of Five" Draft
as it was presented to and revised by
the Congress July 2–4, 1776

A Declaration by the Representatives of the

UNITED STATES OF AMERICA in General

Congress assembled.

When in the course of human events it becomes neces-   1

sary for one people to dissolve the political bands which   2

have connected them with another, and to assume among   3

the powers of the earth the separate and equal station   4

to which the laws of nature and of nature's god entitle   5

them, a decent respect to the opinions of mankind re-   6

quires that they should declare the causes which impel   7

them to the separation.   8

We hold these truths to be self-evident; that all men   9

are created equal; that they are endowed by their   10

Creator with ~~inherent and~~ _{certain un}alienable rights; that   11

among these are life, liberty, and the pursuit of happiness;   12

that to secure these rights, governments are instituted   13

among men, deriving their just powers from the consent   14

of the governed; that whenever any form of government   15

becomes destructive of these ends, it is the right of the   16

people to alter or to abolish it, and to institute new govern-   17

10. Becker, *Declaration*, pp. 174–184.

From Carl Becker, *The Declaration of Independence: A Study of the History of Political Ideas,* © copyright 1956 Alfred A. Knopf, Inc. Reprinted by permission of the publisher.

ment, laying it's foundation on such principles, and organ- 18

izing it's powers in such form as to them shall seem most 19

likely to effect their safety and happiness. prudence 20

indeed will dictate that governments long established 21

should not be changed for light & transient causes. and 22

accordingly all experience hath shewn that mankind are 23

more disposed to suffer, while evils are sufferable, than to 24

right themselves by abolishing the forms to which they 25

are accustomed. but when a long train of abuses and usur- 26

pations, ~~begun at a distinguished period &~~ pursuing in- 27

variably the same object, evinces a design to reduce them 28

under absolute despotism, it is their right, it is their duty, 29

to throw off such government, & to provide new guards 30

for their future security. such has been the patient 31

sufferance of these colonies, & such is now the necessity 32

which constrains them to ~~expunge~~ ^*alter*^ their former systems 33

of government. the history of the present king of Great 34

Britain is a history of ~~unremitting~~ ^*repeated*^ injuries and usur- 35

pations, ~~among which appears no solitary fact to con-~~ 36

~~tradict the uniform tenor of the rest, but~~ all have ^*having*^ in 37

direct object the establishment of an absolute tyranny 38

over these states. to prove this let facts be submitted 39

to a candid world, ~~for the truth of which we pledge a~~ 40

~~faith yet unsullied by falsehood.~~ 41

He has refused his assent to laws the most wholesome and 42

   necessary for the public good. 43

he has forbidden his governors to pass laws of immediate 44

   & pressing importance, unless suspended in their opera- 45

   tion till his assent should be obtained; and when so 46

   suspended, he has ^*utterly*^ neglected ~~utterly~~ to attend to them. 47

he has refused to pass other laws for the accomodation of 48

 large districts of people, unless those people would 49

 relinquish the right of representation in the legislature; 50

 a right inestimable to them, & formidable to tyrants 51

 only. 52

he has called together legislative bodies at places unusual, 53

 uncomfortable, & distant from the depository of their 54

 public records, for the sole purpose of fatiguing them 55

 into compliance with his measures. 56

he has dissolved Representative houses repeatedly ~~& con~~ 57

~~tinually,~~ for opposing with manly firmness his invasions 58

 on the rights of the people. 59

he has refused for a long time after such dissolutions to 60

 cause others to be elected whereby the legislative 61

 powers, incapable of annihilation, have returned to 62

 the people at large for their exercise, the state remain- 63

 ing in the meantime exposed to all the dangers of in- 64

 vasion from without, & convulsions within. 65

he has endeavored to prevent the population of these 66

 states; for that purpose obstructing the laws for nat- 67

 uralization of foreigners; refusing to pass others to 68

 encourage their migrations hither; & raising the 69

 conditions of new appropriations of lands. 70

he has ~~suffered~~ ⟨obstructed⟩ the administration of justice ~~totally to~~ 71

~~cease in some of these states,~~ ⟨by⟩ refusing his assent to 72

 laws for establishing judiciary powers. 73

he has made ~~our~~ judges dependent on his will alone, for 74

 the tenure of their offices, and the amount & paiment 75

 of their salaries. 76

he has erected a multitude of new offices ~~by a self assumed~~ 77

~~power,~~ & sent hither swarms of officers to harrass our   78

people, and eat out their substance.   79

he has kept among us, in times of peace, standing armies   80

~~and ships of war,~~ without the consent of our legislatures.   81

he has affected to render the military independent of, &   82

superior to, the civil power.   83

he has combined with others to subject us to a jurisdiction   84

foreign to our constitutions and acknoleged by   85

our laws; giving his assent to their acts of pretended   86

legislation for quartering large bodies of armed troops   87

among us;   88

for protecting them by a mock-trial from punishment   89

for any murders which they should commit on the   90

inhabitants of these states;   91

for cutting off our trade with all parts of the world;   92

for imposing taxes on us without our consent;   93

for depriving us ∧ of the benefits of trial by jury;   94
in many cases

for transporting us beyond seas to be tried for pre-   95

tended offenses;   96

for abolishing the free system of English laws in a   97

neighboring province, establishing therein an arbi-   98

trary government, and enlarging it's boundaries so   99

as to render it at once an example & fit instrument   100

for introducing the same absolute rule into these   101

states;   102

for taking away our charters, abolishing our most   103

valuable laws, and altering fundamentally the forms   104

of our governments;   105

for suspending our own legislatures, & declaring them-   106

selves invested with power to legislate for us in all   107

cases whatsoever.   108

he has abdicated government here, ~~withdrawing his~~

       by

~~governors, &~~ ∧ declaring us out of ~~his allegiance and~~

and waging war against us

protection ∧.

he has plundered our seas, ravaged our coasts, burnt our

towns, & destroyed the lives of our people.

he is at this time transporting large armies of foreign

mercenaries, to compleat the works of death, desola-

tion & tyranny, already begun with circumstances of

scarcely paralleled in the most barbarous ages and totally

cruelty & perfidy ∧ unworthy the head of a civilized

nation.

      excited domestic insurrection amongst us and has

he has ∧ endeavored to bring on the inhabitants of our

frontiers the merciless Indian savages, whose known

rule of warfare is an undistinguished destruction of

all ages, sexes, & conditions ~~of existence.~~

~~he has incited treasonable insurrections of our fellow~~

~~citizens, with the allurements of forfeiture & con-~~

~~fiscation of property.~~

      our fellow citizens

he has constrained ∧ ~~others,~~ taken captives on the high

seas to bear arms against their country, to become the

executioners of their friends & brethren, or to fall

themselves by their hands.

~~he has waged cruel war against human nature itself,~~

~~violating it's most sacred rights of life & liberty in the~~

~~persons of a distant people, who never offended him,~~

~~captivating and carrying them into slavery in another~~

~~hemisphere, or to incur miserable death in their trans-~~

~~portation thither. this piratical warfare, the oppro-~~

~~brium of *infidel* powers, is the warfare of the *Christian*~~

~~king of Great Britain. determined to keep open a~~

~~market where MEN should be bought & sold, he has~~

~~prostituted his negative for suppressing every legisla-~~

109
110
111
112
113
114
115
116
117
118
119
120
121
122
123
124
125
126
127
128
129
130
131
132
133
134
135
136
137
138
139

~~tive attempt to prohibit or to restrain this execrable~~ 140

~~commerce: and that this assemblage of horrors might~~ 141

~~want no fact of distinguished die, he is now exciting~~ 142

~~those very people to rise in arms among us, and to~~ 143

~~purchase that liberty of which *he* has deprived them,~~ 144

~~by murdering the people upon whom *he* also obtruded~~ 145

~~them: thus paying off former crimes committed~~ 146

~~against the *liberties* of one people, with crimes~~ 147

~~which he urges them to commit against the *lives* of~~ 148

~~another.~~ 149

In every stage of these oppressions, we have petitioned for 150

redress in the most humble terms; our repeated petitions 151

have been answered only by repeated injury. a prince 152

whose character is thus marked by every act which may 153

define a tyrant, is unfit to be the ruler of a ∧ people ~~who~~ 154

free

~~mean to be free. future ages will scarce believe that the~~ 155

~~hardiness of one man adventured within the short compass~~ 156

~~of twelve years only to build a foundation, so broad and~~ 157

~~undisguised, for tyranny over a people fostered and fixed~~ 158

~~in principles of freedom.~~ 159

    Nor have we been wanting in attentions to our British 160

brethren. we have warned them from time to time of 161

attempts by their legislature to extend ~~a~~ ∧ jurisdiction 162

an unwarrantable

over ∧ ~~these our states.~~ we have reminded them of the 163

circumstances of our emigration and settlement here, ~~no~~ 164

~~one of which could warrant so strange a pretension:~~ 165

~~that these were effected at the expence of our own blood~~ 166

~~and treasure, unassisted by the wealth or the strength~~ 167

~~of Great Britain: that in constituting indeed our several~~ 168

~~forms of government, we had adopted one common king,~~ 169

~~thereby laying a foundation for perpetual league and amity~~ 170

~~with them: but that submission to their parliament was~~ 171

~~no part of our constitution, nor ever in idea, if history~~ 172

              have
~~may be credited: and~~ we ∧ appealed to their native justice 173

        and we have conjured them by
& magnanimity, ~~as well as to~~ ∧ the tyes of our common 174

kindred, to disavow these usurpations, which ~~were likely~~ 175

would inevitably
~~to~~ ∧ interrupt our connection^s ∧ & correspondence. they too 176

have been deaf to the voice of justice and of consan- 177

guinity; ~~and when occasions have been given them,~~ 178

~~by the regular course of their laws, of removing from their~~ 179

~~councils the disturbers of our harmony, they have by~~ 180

~~their free election re-established them in power. at this~~ ~~181~~

~~very time too, they are permitting their chief magistrate~~ 182

~~to send over not only soldiers of our common blood, but~~ 183

~~Scotch and foreign mercenaries to invade and destroy~~ 184

~~us. these facts have given the last stab to agonizing~~ 185

~~affection; and manly spirit bids us to renounce forever~~ 186

                 therefore
~~these unfeeling brethren.~~ we must ∧ ~~endeavor to forget our~~ 187

~~former love for them, and to hold them as we hold the~~ 188

~~rest of mankind, enemies in war, in peace friends. we~~ 189

~~might have been a free & a great people together; but~~ 190

~~a communication of grandeur and freedom, it seems, is~~ 191

~~below their dignity. be it so, since they will have it~~ 192

~~the road to happiness and to glory is open to us too;~~ 193

~~we will climb it apart from them, and~~ acquiesce in the 194

             and hold them, as we hold the rest
necessity which denounces our ~~eternal~~ separation ∧ ! 195
of mankind, enemies in war, in peace friends.
We therefore the Representatives of the United states 196
appealing to the supreme judge of the world for the rectitude of our intentions
of America in General Congress assembled, ∧ do, in the 197
                      colonies, solemnly
name & by authority of the good people of these ∧ ~~states,~~ 198
publish and declare, that these united colonies are and of right ought
~~reject and renounce all allegiance and subjection to the~~ 199
to be free and independent states; that they are absolved from all allegi-
~~kings of Great Britain, & all others who may hereafter~~ 200
ance to the British Crown, and that
~~claim by, through, or under them; we utterly dissolve~~ 201

all political connection ~~which may heretofore have sub-~~ 202

~~sisted~~ between ~~us~~ _them_ ∧ and the ∧ _state_ ~~people or parliament~~ of Great 203
is & ought to be totally dissolved;

Britain ∧ ; ~~and finally we do assert and declare these~~ 204

~~colonies to be free and independent states,~~ & that as 205

free & independent states, they have full power to levy 206

war, conclude peace, contract alliances, establish com- 207

merce, & to do all other acts and things which independent 208

states may of right do. And for the support of this dec- 209
with a firm reliance on the protection of divine providence,

laration, ∧ we mutually pledge to each other our lives, 210

our fortunes, and our sacred honor. 211

Like many authors, Thomas Jefferson reacted negatively to both the nature and the extent of the changes made in his draft. He regarded the deletions as "mutilations."[11] Not only did he suffer through the debates, he spent his evenings fighting against the changes. At the end of the second day of debate, July 3, he copied "his" draft — actually the one sent by the Committee of Five — at least twice to send it to friends[12] so that they would know that the "inferior" Congressional version was not his. He copied the whole document at least five more times immediately after Congress passed the Declaration.[13] Seven years later he was still advocating his version when he sent both Declarations to James Madison "side by side with changes noted."[14]

Audience considerations

Part of Jefferson's response may have been hurt pride, but part of the problem was the confusion over the intended audience for the document. You will remember that Jefferson took his assignment to be "to justify ourselves" before "mankind." That is a rather broad sense of audience. It seems that Congressional leaders had a secondary audience in mind at the time of the assignment, the government of France.

On June 7, when Lee introduced his resolution for independence, he also put forward two other related resolutions. One was to organize the colonies into a confederation to prosecute the war; the other was to work

11. Fawn M. Brodie, _Thomas Jefferson: An Intimate History_ (New York: W. W. Norton, 1974), p. 122.

12. Wills, _Inventing America_, p. 307.

13. _Ibid._, p. 66.

14. _Ibid._, p. 307.

toward the establishment of foreign alliances. If these three motions are related, then it may well have been that the Declaration of Independence was intended primarily to establish the circumstances in which the other two more practical resolutions could be carried out. At least one historian considered the Declaration to be "a propaganda overture, addressed primarily to France,"[15] who would not help the Americans as long as they were part of England.

Jefferson himself believed that the most significant changes were made so as not to offend other audiences. The strongly worded passage on slavery was removed because it gave offense to the southern colonies, who were only lukewarm to the cause of independence. Attempts to organize the colonies into a confederation would have suffered, apparently, if the document condemned slavery. Jefferson also claimed that the Congress removed all passages which "conveyed censures of the people of England . . . lest they should give them offense."[16] The colonists and the English politicians were expected to read the document and, since the declaration was directed at George III, it was probably considered unwise to offend possible friends.

One recent historian has argued that Jefferson's subconscious conception of the audience for the Declaration was himself. This provocative theory argues that Jefferson clung to his own draft so vehemently because the independence he was declaring was his own.[17] His domineering mother had died in March and, this historian argues, Jefferson's intense personalizing of the Declaration was part of a larger pattern of strange behavior in the three months that followed.[18] To accept this theory one has to accept George III and the English as symbols for Jefferson's mother, and the rage he directs against them as intended for her. Such an interpretation holds that the Congressional deletions were made, not for political reasons alone, but because the language was too intemperate, too intense, and too exaggerated to be credible. The following phrases are examples of such language: "He has waged cruel war against human nature itself, violating its most sacred rights of life and liberty . . ."; "manly spirit bids us to renounce forever these unfeeling brethren. we must endeavor to forget our former love for them . . ."; and "the road to happiness and to glory is open to us. . . ."

We will never know Jefferson's exact sense of his audience. What we do know is that the Congress had to consider international and domestic politics in making its changes, and the situation dictated that the document be credible as well as eloquent.

15. *Ibid.*, p. 333.
16. As quoted in Becker, *Declaration*, p. 171.
17. Brodie, *Thomas Jefferson*, pp. 114–118.
18. *Ibid.*, p. 116.

Evaluation

American colonists generally supported the assertion of independence, the French entered the war against England, and the British politicians turned against King George. We do not know whether the Declaration played a significant role in persuading these diverse audiences to take stands that made independence possible. It is, however, generally agreed that the document's revisions did not in any way dilute Jefferson's essential message. In fact, according to a recent writer on the subject, "most critics think that Congress — with the possible exception of the paragraph on slavery — improved his draft, sharpened its meaning, trimming nothing but the rhetorical excess or exaggerated claims."[19] Jefferson's triumph over his defensiveness finally allowed him to listen to his readers and to use their suggestions to improve his composition. Despite the additions, deletions, and changes in wording that it went through, the Declaration is still Jefferson's writing. And despite his frequent complaints about what others were doing to his work, he remained proud of his authorship until his dying day — prouder, in fact, than he was of being the third President of the United States. On his tombstone at Monticello he is described as he wished to be remembered: as the founder of the University of Virginia, and as the author of the Virginia statute for religious freedom and of the Declaration of Independence.

Following is the final draft as it was approved on July 4, 1776. What is your opinion?

The Final Draft
as approved on July 4, 1776

THE UNANIMOUS DECLARATION OF THE THIRTEEN UNITED

STATES OF AMERICA.

When in the Course of human events, it becomes	1
necessary for one people to dissolve the political bands,	2
which have connected them with another, and to assume	3
among the powers of the earth, the separate and equal	4
station to which the Laws of Nature and of Nature's	5
God entitle them, a decent respect to the opinions of	6

19. Wills, *Inventing America*, p. 305.
From Carl Becker, *The Declaration of Independence: A Study of the History of Political Ideas*, © copyright 1956 Alfred A. Knopf, Inc. Reprinted by permission of the publisher.

mankind requires that they should declare the causes 7

which impel them to the separation. — We hold these 8

truths to be self-evident, that all men are created equal, 9

that they are endowed by their Creator with certain 10

unalienable Rights, that among these are Life, Liberty 11

and the pursuit of Happiness. — That to secure these 12

rights, Governments are instituted among Men, deriving 13

their just powers from the consent of the governed, — 14

That whenever any Form of Government becomes destruc- 15

tive of these ends, it is the Right of the People to alter 16

or to abolish it, and to institute new Government laying 17

its foundation on such principles and organizing its powers 18

in such form, as to them shall seem most likely to effect 19

their Safety and Happiness. Prudence, indeed, will 20

dictate that Governments long established should not 21

be changed for light and transient causes; and accordingly 22

all experience hath shewn, that mankind are more dis- 23

posed to suffer, while evils are sufferable, than to right 24

themselves by abolishing the forms to which they are 25

accustomed. But when a long train of abuses and usur- 26

pations, pursuing invariably the same Object evinces a 27

design to reduce them under absolute Despotism, it is 28

their right, it is their duty, to throw off such Government, 29

and to provide new Guards for their future security. — 30

Such has been the patient sufferance of these Colonies; 31

and such is now the necessity which constrains them to 32

alter their former Systems of Government. The history 33

of the present King of Great Britain is a history of re- 34

peated injuries and usurpations, all having in direct 35

object the establishment of an absolute Tyranny over 36

these States. To prove this, let Facts be submitted to 37

a candid world. — He has refused his Assent to Laws, 38

the most wholesome and necessary for the public good. — 39

He has forbidden his Governors to pass Laws of immediate 40

and pressing importance, unless suspended in their opera- 41

tion till his Assent should be obtained; and when so sus- 42

pended, he has utterly neglected to attend to them. — 43

He has refused to pass other Laws for the accommodation 44

of large districts of people, unless those people would 45

relinquish the right of Representation in the Legislature, 46

a right inestimable to them and formidable to tyrants 47

only. — He has called together legislative bodies at 48

places unusual, uncomfortable, and distant from the 49

depository of their public Records, for the sole purpose 50

of fatiguing them into compliance with his measures. — 51

He has dissolved Representative Houses repeatedly, for 52

opposing with manly firmness his invasions on the rights 53

of the people. — He has refused for a long time, after such 54

dissolutions, to cause others to be elected; whereby the 55

Legislative powers, incapable of Annihilation, have re- 56

turned to the People at large for their exercise; the State 57

remaining in the meantime exposed to all the dangers of 58

invasion from without, and convulsions within. — He has 59

endeavoured to prevent the population of these States; 60

for that purpose obstructing the Laws for Naturalization 61

of Foreigners; refusing to pass others to encourage their 62

migrations hither, and raising the conditions of new 63

Appropriations of Lands. — He has obstructed the Admin- 64

istration of Justice, by refusing his Assent to Laws for 65

establishing Judiciary powers. — He has made Judges 66

dependent on his Will alone, for the tenure of their   67

offices, and the amount and payment of their salaries. —   68

He has erected a multitude of New Offices, and sent   69

hither swarms of Officers to harrass our people, and   70

eat out their substance. — He has kept among us, in   71

times of peace, Standing Armies without the Consent of   72

our legislatures. — He has affected to render the Military   73

independent of and superior to the Civil power. — He   74

has combined with others to subject us to a jurisdiction   75

foreign to our constitution, and unacknowledged by our   76

laws; giving his Assent to their Acts of pretended Legis-   77

lation. — For quartering large bodies of armed troops   78

among us: — For protecting them, by a mock Trial,   79

from punishment for any Murders which they should   80

commit on the Inhabitants of these States: — For cutting   81

off our Trade with all parts of the world: — For imposing   82

Taxes on us without our Consent: — For depriving us   83

in many cases, of the benefits of Trial by Jury: —   84

For transporting us beyond Seas to be tried for pretended   85

offenses: — For abolishing the free System of English   86

Laws in a neighboring Province, establishing therein an   87

Arbitrary government, and enlarging its Boundaries so   88

as to render it at once an example and fit instrument for   89

introducing the same absolute rule into these Colonies: —   90

For taking away our Charters, abolishing our most valu-   91

able Laws, and altering fundamentally the Forms of our   92

Governments: — For suspending our own Legislatures,   93

and declaring themselves invested with power to legislate   94

for us in all cases whatsoever. — He has abdicated Govern-   95

ment here, by declaring us out of his Protection and waging   96

War against us. — He has plundered our seas, ravaged 97
our Coasts, burnt our towns, and destroyed the lives 98
of our people. — He is at this time transporting large 99
Armies of foreign Mercenaries to compleat the works of 100
death, desolation and tyranny, already begun with cir- 101
cumstances of Cruelty & perfidy scarcely paralleled in 102
the most barbarous ages, and totally unworthy the Head 103
of a civilized nation. — He has constrained our fellow 104
Citizens taken Captive on the high Seas to bear Arms 105
against their Country, to become the executioners of 106
their friends and Brethren, or to fall themselves by their 107
Hands. — He has excited domestic insurrections amongst 108
us, and has endeavoured to bring on the inhabitants of 109
our frontiers, the merciless Indian Savages, whose known 110
rule of warfare, is an undistinguished destruction of all 111
ages, sexes and conditions. In every stage of these 112
Oppressions We have Petitioned for Redress in the most 113
humble terms: Our repeated Petitions have been an- 114
swered ∧ by repeated injury. A Prince whose character 115
     only
is thus marked by every act which may define a Tyrant, 116
is unfit to be the ruler of a free people. Nor have We 117
been wanting in attentions to our Brittish brethren. We 118
have warned them from time to time of attempts by their 119
legislature to extend an unwarrantable jurisdiction over 120
us. We have reminded them of the circumstances of 121
our emigration and settlement here. We have appealed 122
to their native justice and magnanimity, and we have 123
conjured them by the ties of our common kindred to dis- 124
avow these usurpations, which would inevitably interrupt 125
our connections and correspondence. They too have 126

been deaf to the voice of justice and of consanguinity.   127

We must, therefore, acquiesce in the necessity, which de-   128

nounces our Separation, and hold them, as we hold the   129

rest of mankind, Enemies in War, in Peace Friends. —   130

    We, therefore, the Representatives of the united States   131

of America, in General Congress, Assembled, appealing to   132

the Supreme Judge of the world for the rectitude of our   133

intentions do, in the Name, and by Authority of the good   134

People of these Colonies, solemnly publish and declare,   135

That these United Colonies are, and of Right ought to   136

be Free and Independent States; that they are Absolved   137

from all Allegiance to the British Crown, and that all   138

political connection between them and the State of Great   139

Britain, is and ought to be totally dissolved: and that as   140

Free and Independent States, they have full Power to   141

levy War, conclude Peace, contract Alliances, establish   142

Commerce, and to do all other Acts and Things which   143

Independent States may of right do. — And for the sup-   144

port of this Declaration, with a firm reliance on the   145

protection of divine Providence, we mutually pledge to   146

each other our Lives, our Fortunes and our sacred Honor.   147

Questions and Exercises

1. As you study the "Rough Draft," on pp. 9–16, you will see many suggested changes in wording. List at least five that interest you. Why, for example, did Franklin and Adams suggest changing, "We hold these truths to be sacred and undeniable" to "We hold these truths to be self-evident"? You may want to consult the *Oxford English Dictionary* for the eighteenth-century meanings of key words.

2. Look at the "Committee of Five" draft on pp. 17–24. Congress convinced Jefferson to change the word "inherent" on line 11 to "certain." How does that change affect the meaning of the line? Again, check the *Oxford English Dictionary* and record your thoughts.

3. In two or three sentences, summarize Jefferson's ideas on the relation-ship between the people and their government.

4. List instances from the early drafts of exaggerated language later deleted. Record your thoughts and feelings about these deletions.

5. Read the passage on slavery in the "Rough Draft," pp. 13–14, lines 128–146. Now read the final document, from which that long passage has been deleted. Record your views on Jefferson's agreement to delete the slavery passage. You may also want to record your thoughts and feelings in general on the possible conflict between the advice of read-ers and the integrity of the writer. Meet in small groups and discuss Jefferson's deletion of the slavery passage as well as the general issue of taking or rejecting readers' advice. One of the members should take notes and report on the small group's views to the class as a whole.

6. As you read the final document, note instances where you believe the French are appealed to. Meet in small groups to compare notes and to reach consensus on these instances. A member should report the group's views to the class.

7. Rewrite the last paragraph of the final draft in modern prose — that is, in your own words — without losing the meaning of the paragraph. Read your paragraphs to each other.

8. You are Jefferson. Write a letter to the Congress protesting, as persua-sively as you can, its revisions of the "Committee of Five" draft. What changes do you object to the most? Why?

9. You are the last editor of the Declaration of Independence, and the printer says that the document has to be trimmed by about 10 percent. Without worrying about actual percentages, identify the cuts you would make and write a letter justifying them to Jefferson.

10. Check the sources mentioned in our footnotes. Draft a short research paper intended for your classmates on one of the following questions:
    a) How did the French react to the Declaration of Independence?
    b) How did the people of England react?
    c) How did Parliament respond specifically to this document?
    d) What was George III's response?

11. How has the Declaration of Independence influenced later documents? Look, for example, at the Seneca Falls Declaration (1848) on women's rights. Compare the Declaration of Independence to that document or to other manifestos, including those from the women's movement, from the movement for black rights, or from other colonies who declared their independence from a mother country.

2
Reading Textbooks

Textbooks are designed to provide the first stage of the initiation process into a discipline or, in more advanced courses, to guide you into more sophisticated levels of disciplinary conversation. Textbooks are like friendly and generous individuals who take you aside when you enter a new social group and explain the puzzling names and references. You are already familiar with the means employed by most textbooks to guide you into active exchange: the careful ordering of chapters to show you a plan of development in the subject matter, the subheadings within chapters, the marginal notes, the visual representations, the section summaries, the words written in *italics*, and the questions and exercises. The textbook prompts you in these ways to respond and participate.

Since you will probably purchase the textbooks for each class, you have the luxury of making these books your own indeed by writing notes and brief summaries in the margins. Your goal should be to prepare for a quick review of the material. A maze of underlinings or a sunburst of highlighted material will hardly remind you later of the meaning that you constructed several weeks before. Taking brief notes in the text, on the other hand, makes you an active participant in your own reading and will remind you of early conversations when you search for larger patterns in preparation for examinations.

When you complete a textbook chapter, you may wish to construct an outline to represent the overall organization of the material. Check this outline with the subheadings in the text. You might also try writing a brief summary of each chapter. Refer to your own marginal notes and then write a single sentence that crystallizes your understanding of the chapter. Then record explanations and illustrations of that major idea. Through these means you are saying: "Here is what I think is going on. How does that sound?"

The following selections come from textbooks in three different disciplines: economics, biology, and comparative religion — representing the social sciences, the natural sciences, and the humanities. The structure, format, and tone of each selection illustrate pertinent features of the discipline in question. The textbook author, in each case, has one major goal in mind: to welcome you into the disciplinary conversation.

THE SOCIAL SCIENCES

Supply and Demand: The Bare Elements

PAUL SAMUELSON

from *Economics*

We begin this section on textbooks with a chapter from one of the most successful and widely read textbooks in America. Now in its eleventh edition, Paul Samuelson's *Economics* has introduced that subject to college students since 1955. We have reproduced below the fourth chapter, which discusses the concepts and mechanics of supply and demand.

"Supply" and "demand," as the epigraph to the chapter points out, are the two fundamental words in the conversation of economists. Samuelson guides you into this conversation with a full range of aids. The summary at the end of the chapter can help you review key points but can also be read first to provide context. The ten main headings mark off manageable sections, each of about one page in length. As you finish each section, write a sentence or two to summarize the main idea. Samuelson underlines words and phrases, through the use of a darker type or italics, to identify for you the special vocabulary of economists or to emphasize an example. On p. 36, for instance, Samuelson in effect speaks more emphatically to say, *"That raises the price of meat and cuts the price of potatoes."*

Five times in this chapter Samuelson takes you aside to show you a visual representation. Tables, graphs, charts, maps, and photographs allow you to approach a complex idea from another perspective, literally to *see* what Samuelson is talking about. Samuelson carefully discusses Figures 4–1 through 4–4; Figure 4–5 involves you in problems of interpretation and application.

Active involvement with Samuelson's presentation will introduce you to the questions and general approaches that typify the community of economists. With all the unfamiliar terminology confronting you in this chapter, your temptation may be to memorize definitions before you understand them. You will probably find that your memory will not work effectively when you do not understand. More important, however, rote memorization might allow you to parrot the economist's vocabulary but will not help you to see the world the way an economist sees it.

4
SUPPLY AND DEMAND: THE BARE ELEMENTS

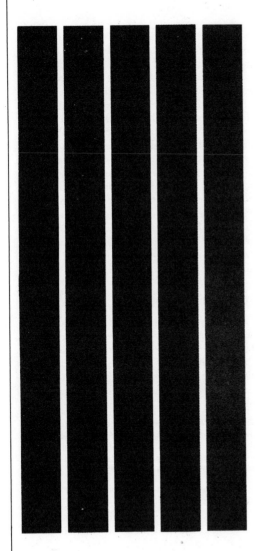

You can make even a parrot into a learned political economist—all it must learn are the two words "supply" and "demand."

ANONYMOUS

Every short statement about economics is misleading (with the possible exception of my present one).

ALFRED MARSHALL

Chapters 2 and 3 introduced the three basic problems every economy must face:

1. WHAT shall be produced of the great variety of possible goods and services, and in precisely what quantities?

2. How shall society combine its different productive factors—land, labor, machinery—to produce each good?

3. FOR WHOM shall goods be produced—that is, how shall the national product be distributed among the different people with their different labor skills and ownerships of land and capital goods?

Chapter 2 showed that a variety of systems can be thought of to solve these three problems. WHAT, HOW, and FOR WHOM might be determined by custom, instinct, or by collective command. But Chapter 3 indicated that the modern mixed economy relies primarily on none of these to solve its basic problems. Instead, it relies on a system of markets and prices.

The consumer, so it is said, is the king. Or rather, with everyone a king, all are voters who use their money as votes to get done what they want done. Your votes must compete with my votes; and the people with the most votes end up with the most influence on what gets produced and on where goods go.

Now our task is to see just how this spending of money votes—this system of "consumer sovereignty"—takes place under the checks and balances of economic competition.

The Market Mechanism

Let us take an example. You wake up this morning with an urge for a new pair of shoes. You would not think of saying, "I'll go down to the city hall and vote for the mayor most likely to give me a new pair of shoes. Of course, I mean a new pair of size 9, soft-leather, dark brown shoes."

Or, to take an actual case from history, suppose we begin to get prosperous enough to afford meat every day and no longer have to fill up on potatoes. How does our desire to substitute meat for potatoes get translated into action? What politicians do we tell? What orders do they in turn give to farmers to move from Maine to Texas? How much extra rent do they decide will be needed to bribe landlords to transfer land from potato production to cattle grazing? And how do they ensure that we people get what we want of pork and lamb as well as beef? And who is to get the choice cuts?

Why belabor the obvious? Everyone knows things don't work out that way at all. What happens is this. Consumers begin to buy fewer potatoes and more meat. *That raises the price of meat and cuts the price of potatoes.* So there soon result losses to the potato growers and gains to the ranchers. Ranch labor finds it can hold out for higher wages, and many potato diggers quit their jobs for better-paying work elsewhere. In time, the higher meat prices coax out larger productions of beef, pork, and lamb. And the different parts of the cow—its horns, hide, liver, kidneys, choice tenderloin, and tough ribs—get auctioned off for what each part will bring.

To show that it is not some important government bureaucrat or businesshead who sets relative prices, see what actually happened when science discovered that liver was good for anemia. Kidneys used to be dearer than liver. Now go to the butcher shop: price liver and, if you can find any, also price kidneys. A veritable revolution has taken place: the price of liver has risen greatly relative to the price of kidneys, so as to *ration* the limited supply of liver among the eager demanders for it—all through the *impersonal* workings of supply and demand.

A System of Prices   Similar revolutions are taking place in the economic marketplace all the time. As people's desires and needs change, as engineering methods change, as supplies of natural resources and other productive factors change, the marketplace registers changes in the prices and the quantities sold of commodities and productive services—of tea, sugar, and beef; of land, labor, and machines. There exists a *system of rationing by prices*, a concept that is far from obvious.

The purpose of this chapter is to show how supply and demand work themselves out in the competitive market *for one particular good*. We shall define a demand curve and then a supply curve. Finally, we shall see how the market price reaches its competitive equilibrium where these two curves intersect—where the forces of demand and supply are just in balance.

The Demand Schedule

Let us start with demand. It is commonly observed: The quantity of a good that people will buy at any one time depends on price. The *higher* the price charged for an article, the *less* the quantity of it people will be willing to buy. And, other things being equal, the lower its market price, the more units of it will be demanded.

Thus there exists at any one time a definite relation between the market price of a good (such as wheat) and the quantity demanded of that good. This relationship between price and quantity bought is called the "demand schedule," or the "demand curve."

The table of Fig. 4-1 gives on the next page an example of a hypothetical demand schedule. At any price, such as $5 per bushel, there is a definite quantity of wheat that will be demanded by all the

DEMAND SCHEDULE FOR WHEAT

	(1) PRICE ($ per bu) P	(2) QUANTITY DEMANDED (million bu per month) Q
A	$5	9
B	4	10
C	3	12
D	2	15
E	1	20

FIG. 4-1
A downward-sloping demand curve relates quantity to price
At each market price, there will be at any time a definite quantity of wheat that people will want to demand. At a lower price, the quantity demanded will go up—as more people substitute it for other goods and feel they can afford to gratify their less important wants for wheat. Compare table's Q and P at A, B, C, D, E.
In the figure, prices are measured on the vertical axis and quantities demanded on the horizontal axis. Each pair of Q, P numbers from the table is plotted here as a point, and a smooth curve passed through the points gives us the demand curve. The fact that dd goes downward and to the right illustrates the "law of downward-sloping demand."

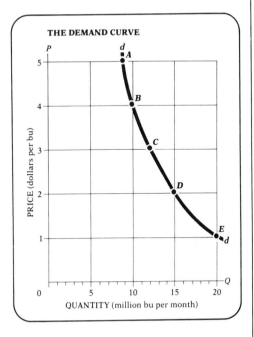

THE DEMAND CURVE

consumers in the market—in this case 9 (million) bushels per month.

At a lower price, such as $4, the quantity bought is even greater, being 10 (million) units. At lower P of $3, quantity demanded is even greater still—namely 12 (million). By lowering P enough, we could coax out sales of more than 20 (million) units. From Fig. 4-1's table we can determine the *quantity demanded at any price*, by comparing Column (2) with Column (1).

The Demand Curve

The numerical data can also be given a graphic interpretation. The vertical scale in Fig. 4-1 represents the various alternative prices of wheat, measured in dollars per bushel. The horizontal scale measures the quantity of wheat (in terms of million bushels) that will be demanded per month by consumers.

A city corner is located as soon as we know its street and avenue. A ship's position is located as soon as we know its latitude and longitude. Similarly, to plot a point on this diagram, we must have two coordinate numbers: a price and a quantity. For our first point, A, corresponding to $5 and 9 million bushels, we move upward 5 units and then over to the right 9 units.

To get the next dot, at B, we go up only 4 units and over to the right 10 units. The last dot is shown by E. Through the dots we draw a smooth orange curve, marked dd.

This picturization of the demand schedule is called the "demand curve." Note that quantity and price are *inversely* related, Q going up when P goes down. The curve slopes downward, going from northwest to southeast. This important property is given a name: the *law of downward-sloping demand*. This law is true of practically all commodities: wheat, electric razors, oil or coal, Kellogg's cornflakes, and theater tickets.

The law of downward-sloping demand: When the price of a good is raised (at the same time that all other things are held constant), less of it is demanded. Or, what is the same thing: If a greater quantity of a good is put on the market, then—other things being equal—it can be sold only at a lower price.

Reasons for the Law of Downward-Sloping Demand

This law is in accordance with common sense and has been known in at least a vague way since the beginning of recorded history. The reasons for it are not hard to identify. When the price of wheat is sky-high, only the rich will be able to afford it. The poor will have to make do with rice or coarse rye bread, just as they still must do in poorer lands. When the price of wheat is still high but not quite so high as it was before, persons of moderate means who also happen to have an especially great liking for white bread will now be coaxed into buying some wheat.

Thus a first reason for the validity of the law of downward-sloping demand comes from the fact that *lowering prices brings in new buyers.*

Not quite so obvious is a second, equally important, reason for the law's validity; namely, each reduction of price may coax out some *extra purchases by each of the good's consumers;* and—what is the same thing—a rise in price may cause any of us to buy less. Why does my quantity demanded tend to fall as price rises? For two main reasons. When the price of a good rises, I naturally try to *substitute* other goods for it (for example, rye for wheat or coal for oil). Second, when a price goes up, I find myself really poorer than I was before; and I will naturally cut down on my consumption of most normal goods when I feel poorer and have less real *income.*

Here are further examples of cases where I buy more of a good as it becomes more plentiful and its price drops. When water is very dear, I demand only enough of it to drink. Then when its price

drops, I buy some to wash with. At still lower prices, I resort to still other uses. Finally, when it is really very cheap, I water flowers and use it lavishly for any possible purpose. (Note once again that people poorer than I will probably begin to use water to wash their cars only at a lower price than that at which I buy water for that purpose. Since market demand is the sum of all different people's demands, what does this mean? It means that even after *my* quantity demanded stops expanding very much with price decreases, the *total* bought in the market may still expand as new uses by new people come into effect.)

To confirm your understanding of the demand concept, imagine that there is an increase in demand for wheat brought about by a boom in people's incomes. Show that this *shifts* the whole demand curve in Fig. 4-1 rightward, and hence upward; pencil in such a new orange curve and label it $d'd'$ to distinguish it from the old dd curve. Note that such an increase in demand means that more will now be bought at each price—as can be verified by carefully reading off points from the new curve and filling in a new Q column for Fig. 4-1's table. (Test yourself: Will a warm winter shift the dd curve for heating oil leftward or rightward? Why this leftward and downward shift?)

The Supply Schedule

Let us now turn from demand to supply. The demand schedule related market prices and the amounts *consumers* wish to buy. How is the "supply schedule" defined?

By the *supply schedule,* or *curve,* is meant the relation between market prices and the amounts of the good that *producers* are willing to supply.

The table of Fig. 4-2 shows, on the next page, the supply schedule for wheat, and the diagram plots it as a supply curve. Unlike the falling demand curve, the ss supply curve for wheat *normally rises upward and to the right,* from southwest to northeast.

At a higher price of wheat, farmers will take

SUPPLY SCHEDULE FOR WHEAT

	(1) POSSIBLE PRICES ($ per bu) P	(2) QUANTITY SELLERS WILL SUPPLY (million bu per month) Q
A	$5	18
B	4	16
C	3	12
D	2	7
E	1	0

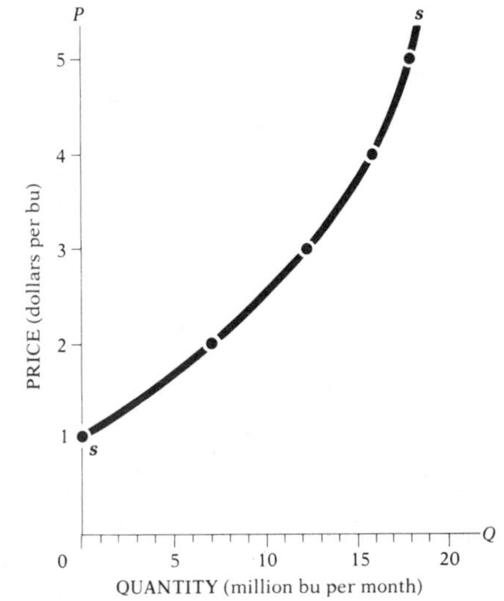

FIG. 4-2
The supply curve relates price to the quantity produced
The table lists, for each price, the quantity that producers will want to bring to market. The diagram plots the (P, Q) pair of numbers taken from the table as the indicated black points. A smooth curve passed through these points gives the black upward-sloping supply curve, ss.

SUPPLY CURVE FOR WHEAT

acres out of corn cultivation and put them into wheat. In addition, each farmer can now afford the cost of more fertilizer, more labor, more machinery, and can now even afford to grow extra wheat on poorer land. All this tends to increase output at the higher prices offered.

As will be seen in Part Three, our old friend the law of diminishing returns provides one strong reason why the supply curve would slope upward. If society wants more wine, then more and more labor will have to be added to the same limited hill sites suitable for producing wine grapes. Even if this industry is too small to affect the general wage rate, each new worker will—according to the law of diminishing returns—be adding less and less extra product; and hence, the necessary cost to coax out

additional product will have to rise. (Cost and returns are opposite sides of the same coin, as will be shown later.[1])

How shall we depict an increase in supply? An increase in supply means an increase in the amounts that will be supplied *at each different price*. Now if you pencil the new supply curve into Fig. 4-2, you will see that it has shifted *rightward*. For an upward-sloping supply curve, this change means the new *s's'* curve will have shifted rightward and *downward* (not rightward and upward as in the case of a shifted downward-sloping demand curve). To verify that *s's'* does depict an increase in supply, fill in a new column in the table by reading off points from your new diagram care-

[1] Although exceptions to the law of downward-sloping demand are few enough to be unimportant in practice, Part Three gives an interesting exception to the upward-sloping supply curve. Thus, suppose that a family farmer produces wheat and its price rises so much as to bring in a much higher income.

With wheat so lucrative, the farmer is at first tempted to *substitute* some leisure time in order to produce more. But won't there reasonably come a time when the family feels comfortably enough off at the *higher income* to be able to afford to take things easier, work less, and supply less Q?

SUPPLY AND DEMAND SCHEDULES FOR WHEAT			
(1)	(2) QUANTITY DEMANDED (million bu per month)	(3) QUANTITY SUPPLIED (million bu per month)	(4)
POSSIBLE PRICES ($ per bu)			PRESSURE ON PRICE
A $5	9	18	Downward
B 4	10	16	Downward
C 3	12	12	Neutral
D 2	15	7	Upward
E 1	20	0	Upward

FIG. 4-3

Equilibrium price is at the intersection point where supply and demand match

Only at the equilibrium price of $3, shown in the orange third row, will the amount supplied just match the amount demanded.

In the diagram, at the C equilibrium intersection (shown by the dot), the amount supplied just matches the amount demanded. At any lower P, the excess amount demanded will force P back up; and at any P higher than the equilibrium, P will be forced back down to it.

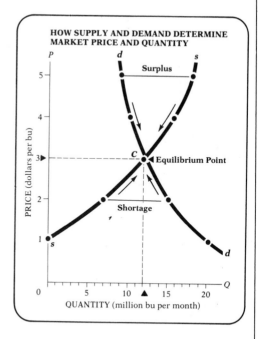

HOW SUPPLY AND DEMAND DETERMINE MARKET PRICE AND QUANTITY

fully. TEST: An invention promotes recovery of oil from abandoned wells. Show that it shifts oil's *ss* rightward and downward.)

Equilibrium of Supply and Demand

Let us now combine our analysis of demand and supply to see how competitive market price is determined. This is done in Fig. 4-3's table.

Thus far, we have been considering all prices as possible. We have said, "If price is so and so, *Q* sales will be so and so; if *P* is such and such, *Q* will be such and such; and so forth." But to which level will price *actually* go? And how much will then be produced and consumed? The supply schedule alone cannot tell us. Neither can the demand schedule alone.

Let us do what an auctioneer would do, i.e., proceed by trial and error. Can situation *A* in the table, with wheat selling for $5 per bushel, prevail for any period of time? The answer is a clear "No." At $5, the producers will be supplying 18 (million) bushels to the market every month [Column (3)].

But the amount demanded by consumers will be only 9 (million) bushels per month [Column (2)]. *As stocks of wheat pile up, competitive sellers will cut the price a little.* Thus, as Column (4) shows, price will tend to fall downward. But it will not fall indefinitely to zero.

To understand this better, let us try the point *E* with price of only $1 per bushel. Can that price persist? Again, obviously not—for a comparison of Columns (2) and (3) shows that consumption will exceed production *at that price.* Storehouses will begin to empty, *disappointed demanders who can't get wheat will tend to bid up the too-low price.* This upward pressure on *P* is shown by Column (4)'s rising arrow.

We could go on to try other prices, but by now the answer is obvious:

The equilibrium price, i.e., the only price that can last, is that at which the amount *willingly* supplied and amount *willingly* demanded are equal. Competitive equilibrium must be *at the intersection point* of supply and demand curves.

Only at point *C*, with a price of $3, will the

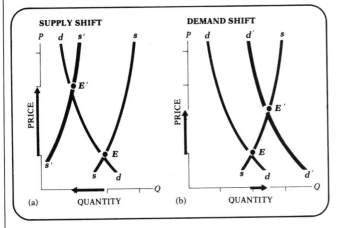

SUPPLY SHIFT

DEMAND SHIFT

(a) QUANTITY

(b) QUANTITY

FIG. 4-4
When either supply or demand curve shifts, equilibrium price changes
(a)   If supply shifts leftward for any reason, the equilibrium-price intersection will travel up the demand curve, giving higher *P* and lower *Q*.
(b)   If demand increases, the equilibrium will travel up the supply curve. *P* rises, and *Q* is also shown to rise.

amount demanded by consumers, 12 (million) bushels per month, exactly equal the amount supplied by producers, 12 (million). Price is at equilibrium, just as an olive at the bottom of a cocktail glass is at equilibrium, because there is no tendency for it to rise or fall. (Of course, this stationary price may not be reached at once. There may have to be an initial period of trial and error, of oscillation around the right level, before price finally settles down in balance.)

Figure 4-3's diagram shows the same equilibrium in pictorial form. The supply and demand curves, superimposed on the same diagram, cross at only one intersection point. This emphasized point *C* represents the equilibrium *P* and *Q*.

At a higher price, the black bar shows the *surplus* of amount supplied over amount demanded. The arrows point downward to show the direction in which price will move because of the competition of excess *sellers*. At a price lower than the $3 equilibrium price, the black bar shows a *shortage*. Now the amount demanded exceeds amount supplied. Consequently, the eager bidding of excess *buyers* requires us to point the arrow indicators upward to show the pressure that they are exerting on price. Only at the point *C* will there be a balancing of forces and a stationary maintainable price.

Such is the essence of the doctrine of supply and demand.

Effect of a Shift in Supply or Demand

Now we can put the supply-and-demand apparatus to work. Gregory King, an English writer of the seventeenth century, noticed that when the harvest was bad, food rose in price. When it was plentiful, farmers got a lower price. Let us try to explain this common-sense fact by what happens in our diagrams.

Figure 4-4(a) shows how a spell of bad growing weather *reduces* the amount that farmers will supply at each and every market price and thereby raises the equilibrium point *E*. The *ss* curve has shifted to the left and has become *s's'*. The demand curve has not changed. Where does the new supply curve *s's'* intersect *dd?* Plainly at *E'*, the new equilibrium price where demand and the new reduced supply have again come into balance. Naturally, *P* has risen. And, because of the law of downward-sloping demand, *Q* has gone down.

Suppose the supply curve, because of good weather and cheaper fertilizers, had *increased*, instead. Draw in a new black equilibrium *E''* with lower *P* and higher *Q*.

Our apparatus will help us also analyze the

effect of an increase in demand. Suppose that rising family incomes make everyone want more wheat. Then at each unchanged P, greater Q will now be demanded. The demand curve will shift rightward to $d'd'$. Figure 4-4(b) shows the resulting travel up the supply curve as enhanced demand raises competitive price to the E' intersection.

Two Stumbling Blocks

It is well to pause here to consider two minor sources of possible confusion concerning supply and demand. These have puzzled students of economics in all generations. The first point deals with the important fact that in drawing up a demand schedule or curve, one always insists that "other things must be equal." The second deals with the exact sense in which demand and supply are equal in equilibrium.

"Other Things Equal"   To draw up a demand schedule for wheat, we vary its price and observe what would happen to its quantity bought *at any one period of time in which no other factors are allowed to change so as to becloud our experiment.*

Specifically, this means that, as we change wheat's P, we must not at the same time change family income; or change the price of a competing product such as corn; or do anything else that would tend to *shift* the demand schedule for wheat. Why? Because, like any scientist who wants to isolate the effects of one causal factor, we must try to vary only *one* thing at a time. True enough, in economics we cannot perform controlled experiments in a laboratory. We can rarely hold other things constant in making statistical observations of economic magnitudes. This limitation on our ability to experiment empirically in economics makes it all the more important *to be clear in our logical thinking,* so that we may hope to recognize and evaluate important *tendencies—* such as the effect of P on Q demanded—when *other* tendencies are likely to be impinging on the situation at the same time.

The case of demand shift back in Fig 4-4(b) can illustrate a common fallacy based upon a failure to respect the following rule: Other things must be held equal in defining a demand curve.

Suppose that the supply curve shifts little or not at all. But suppose the demand curve shifts up to $d'd'$ in good times when jobs are plentiful and people have the incomes to buy more wheat. And suppose in the more depressed phase of the business cycle, demand always shifts down to dd. Now take a piece of graph paper and plot what would actually be recorded in the statistics of the wheat market.

In boom times, you would record the equilibrium point shown at black E', and in bad times, the equilibrium point E. Take a ruler and join the black points E and E' in Fig. 4-4(b). The fallacy to be avoided like the plague is expressed as follows: "I have disproved the law of downward-sloping demand; for note that when P was high, so too was Q—as shown by E'. And when P was lowered, instead of that change increasing Q, it actually lowered Q—as shown by E. My straight line joining E and E' represents an upward-sloping, not a downward-sloping, demand curve; so I have refuted a basic economic law."

Being alerted beforehand, one detects the fallacy in this argument. For at the same time that P went up, other things were *not* held constant; rather, income was also raised. The tendency for a rise in P to choke off purchases was more than masked by the countertendency of rising income to raise purchases. Instead of testing our economic law by moving *along* the demand curve, the beginner has measured changes that result from the *shift* of the demand curve.

Why is this bad scientific method? Because it leads to absurd results such as this: "On the basis of my revolutionary refutation of the alleged law of downward-sloping demand, I predict that, in the years when the harvest is especially big, wheat will sell for a higher rather than a lower price." Not only will such reasoning lead to absurd predictions that would lose fortunes for a speculator or a miller, but it also fails to recognize other important economic relationships—such as the fact that when family incomes go up, demand curves for goods such as wheat tend to shift upward and rightward.

Meaning of Equilibrium   The second stumbling block is a more subtle one, less likely to arise but not so easy to dispel. It is seen in the following.

"How can you say that the equality of supply and demand determines a particular equilibrium price? For, after all, *the amount one person sells is precisely what another person buys.* The quantity bought must always equal the quantity sold, no matter what the price; for that matter, whether or not the market is in equilibrium, a statistician who records the Q bought and the Q sold will always find these necessarily identical, each being a different aspect of exactly the same transaction."

The answer to this must be phrased something like this:

You are quite right that measured Q bought and measured Q sold must be identical as recorded by a statistician. But the important question is this: At which P will the amount that consumers are *willing to go on buying* be just matched by the amount that producers are *willing to go on selling?* At such a price, where there is equality between the *scheduled* amounts that suppliers and demanders want to go on buying and selling, and only at such an equilibrium P, will there be no tendency for price to rise or for price to fall.

At any other price, such as the case where P is above the intersection of supply and demand, it is a trivial fact that whatever goods change hands will show a statistical identity of measured amount bought and sold. But this measured identity does not in the least deny that suppliers are eager at so high a price to sell more than demanders will continue to buy; and that this excess of *scheduled supply* over *scheduled demand* will put downward pressure on price until it has finally reached that equilibrium level where the two curves intersect.

At that equilibrium intersection, and there alone, will everybody be happy: the auctioneer, the suppliers, the demanders—as well as the patient statisti-

cian, who always reports an identity between the measured amounts bought and sold.[2]

What Supply and Demand Accomplished: General Equilibrium

Having seen how supply and demand work, let us take stock of what has been accomplished. The scarce goods of society have been rationed out among the possible users of them. Who was it who did the rationing? A board? A committee? No. The auctioneering mechanism of competitive market price did the rationing. It was a case of "rationing by the purse."

FOR WHOM goods are destined was *partially* determined by who was willing to pay for them. If you had the money votes, you got the wheat. If you did not, you went without. Or if you had the money votes, but preferred not to spend them on wheat, you did without. The most important needs or desires—if backed by cash!—got fulfilled.

The WHAT question was being *partially* answered at the same time. The rise in market price was the signal to coax out a higher supply of wheat—the signal for other scarce resources to move into the wheat-production industry from alternative uses.

Even the How question was being *partially* decided in the background. For with wheat prices now high, farmers could afford expensive tractors and fertilizers and could thus bring poorer soils into use.

Why the word "partially" in this description of how the competitive market helped solve the three problems? Because this wheat market is but one market of many.

What is happening in the corn and rye markets also counts; and what is happening in the market for fertilizer, workers, and tractors obviously matters much.

We must note that the pricing problem is one that involves *interdependent markets*, not just the "partial equilibrium" of a single market.[3]

---

[2] A similar question of "measured identity" versus "scheduled intersection" can rise in the saving-investment discussion of income determination in Chapter 12.

[3] The alert reader will not have to be reminded that the competitive market gives goods to those with money votes and does so efficiently. But the distribution of the money votes

There are, so to speak, auctioneers operating simultaneously in the many different markets—wheat, rye, corn, fertilizer, and land; labor, wool, cotton, mutton, and rayon; bonds, stocks, personal loans, and foreign exchange in the form of English pounds or German marks. Each ends up at the equilibrium intersection point of the supply and demand schedules—wheat, rye, corn, fertilizer prices, and land rent; labor wage, wool, cotton, mutton, and rayon prices; bond price and its interest yield, stock prices and dividend yield, interest charges on personal loans, an exchange rate of $2.20 per pound or 1.8 marks to the dollar.

No market is an island unto itself. When wool P rises (because, say, of sheep disease abroad), it pulls up the Ps of domestic labor, fertilizer, and land needed for expanded domestic wool output. It raises the Ps of rival goods like cotton that some demanders will now turn to. And it might well lower the wage of wool spinners and the price of suit-company stock shares, since the latter must now pay more for its raw materials and must bid less eagerly for spinning labor.

The new "general-equilibrium set of interdependent prices" adjusts to the new situation. The price system meets the problem posed in the basic definition of economics: the study of (1) how *scarce means with alternative uses*—limited land and labor that can be switched from one industry to another—are allocated, and of (2) how to *achieve ends or goals*—as prescribed by the tastes for wool, nylon, food, and housing of those sovereign consumers who possess factors of production that give them money-income votes for the marketplace.

Each separate market, with its supply and demand curves, is doing its bit toward creating the general-equilibrium set of prices, which in a mixed economy largely resolves the basic economic problems of WHAT, HOW, and FOR WHOM.

Perfection and Imperfections of Competition

Our curves of supply and demand strictly apply only to a *perfectly competitive* market where some kind of *standardized* good such as wheat is being auctioned by an organized exchange that registers transactions of *numerous* buyers and sellers.

The Board of Trade in Chicago is one such example, and the cotton exchanges in New York or Liverpool are others. The New York Stock Exchange, while it does not auction goods and commodities or productive services rendered by factors of production, does provide a market where shares of common stocks such as those of General Motors and Royal Dutch Petroleum are auctioned at each moment of the working day. Many corporate bonds are also bought and sold on the Exchange's bond division.

The economists' curves of supply and demand are important ways of *idealizing* the behavior of such markets. The curves do not pretend to give an accurate microscopic description of what is going on *during each changing moment* in such a marketplace—as various brokers mill around on the trading floor while frantically giving hand and voice signals to the specialist who serves as auctioneer for each grain or company stock. Nonetheless, the tools of supply and demand do summarize the *important average relationships resulting over a period of time* from such organized trading.

As far as these fundamental tools of supply and demand are concerned, it matters little what kind of exchange the goods are traded on: whether hand

---

depends on how much you can sell your labor and property for in competitive and imperfectly competitive factor markets, and it is affected in an important way by (1) how lucky you are, (2) how lucky your parents and in-laws were, and (3) the advantages and disadvantages of your genetic and acquired skills and aptitudes. The student who writes on a final exam, "FOR WHOM is decided (in part) by how people decide to use their money votes," is not wrong. Indeed, this answer gets

possibly 50 per cent credit. However, the other 50 per cent will be lost unless the student adds, "The basic problem of FOR WHOM is the process by which the money votes *themselves* get determined, which is primarily not by supply and demand in a single good's market, but by supply and demand in the labor, land, and other interdependent factor markets of Part Four; and factor supplies depend much on distribution of ownership."

signals or slips of paper or modern computers are used; whether the auction is of the familiar kind, where the auctioneer calls out a *minimum* starting price and accepts higher and higher bids until only one high bidder is left to get the Renoir painting in question; or, alternatively, whether there is a "Dutch auction," where the price *starts high* instead of low and moves downward at stated time intervals until an eager buyer, fearing that someone else will get in the bid first, finally gives the first bid and gets the merchandise; or, as a third alternative, whether the auctioneer asks for written bids and offers in order to be able to make up a table or chart like those of Fig. 4-3 and then proceeds to find the equilibrium intersection at one fell swoop, in effect by solving two simultaneous equations.

Indeed, the market need not have a single auctioneer: all the bidding may well take place by telephone calls, as in the case of the market for United States government bonds, which is a much more nearly perfect one than the corporate bond market on the floor of the New York Stock Exchange. The same can be true of stocks listed on the so-called "over-the-counter market," a market which is conducted throughout the country completely by telephone and by computer listing of price-quotation lists of different brokers.

Perfection of Competition as a Limiting Pole
Needless to say, the requirements for absolutely perfect competition are as hard to meet as the requirements for a perfectly frictionless pendulum in physics. We can approach closer and closer to perfection, but can never quite reach it. Yet this fact need not do serious damage to the usefulness of our employing the idealized concept. Actually, it matters little to the economic scientist that different grades of wheat will call for slight variations from the quoted market prices. Nor does it matter in the case of standardized cotton goods that they are sold and bought in an informal way by many competing firms.

So long as there are *numerous* buyers and sellers on each side, *well informed* about quality and about each other's prices and having no reason to discriminate in favor of one merchant rather than another and no reason to expect that variations in their *own* bids and offers will have an *appreciable effect* upon the prevailing market price—so long as all this is true, the behavior of price and quantity can be expected to be much like that predicted by our supply and demand curves.

The various diagrams in Fig. 4-5 illustrate how the tools of supply and demand might be used to give a good approximate description of various economic situations other than that of a staple commodity such as wheat. There is pictured a competitive market for standard cotton goods. Also shown is the market for a capital asset such as a corner lot of land. The second diagram shows an elevated price at which OPEC will now supply any amount of oil. Can you see why oil can now be sold only in reduced amount as consumers are moved up the *dd* curve? Finally, as will be explained later in the discussion of international trade in Part Five, there is shown a foreign exchange market in which the price of a French franc, a German mark, or a single unit of any other foreign currency is determined by the bids of those who need foreign currency and by the offers of those who want to sell such currencies to get American dollars.[4]

To be sure, not all today's markets are anywhere near to being perfectly competitive in the economist's sense. We shall see later, in Part Three, that elements of monopoly power or of market imperfection may enter in, and these imperfections will require us to modify the competitive model. After we have learned how to handle such cases, we shall recognize that the world is a blend of competition and imperfections—which means that the competitive analysis, properly qualified, is still an indispensable tool for interpreting reality.

---

[4]Question 11 on page 65 reproduces from a newspaper its financial reports for a single day, showing what might have been the market price quotations for grains, bonds, common stocks, and foreign exchange. After studying economics, one is in a better position to understand the basic forces underlying these price quotations; but only experience and study can make one reasonably expert at the hazardous game of forecasting. The stock market is met in this Appendix which starts on page 66; Chapter 21's Appendix treats the economics of speculation in organized commodity markets.

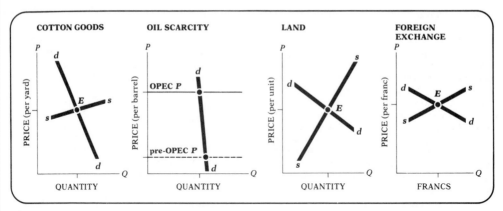

FIG. 4-5
Supply-and-demand tools have many applications: to goods, oil, acres of land, exchange rates
Economists often use straight-lined *dd* or *ss* schedules purely for simplicity. Can you interpret the four cases?

SUMMARY

1 A basic problem of economics is how the mechanism of market pricing grapples with the triad of problems: WHAT, HOW, and FOR WHOM.

2 By the *demand schedule* we mean a table showing the different quantities of a good that people will—at any time and with other things held equal—want to buy at each different price. This relationship, when plotted on a *P*-and-*Q* diagram, is the *demand curve, dd.*

3 With negligible exceptions, the higher the price the lower will be the quantity demanded, and vice versa. Almost all commodities obey this "law of *downward*-sloping demand," *Q* falling when *P* rises.

4 The *supply curve* or *schedule* gives the relations between the prices and the quantities of a good that producers will—other things equal—be willing to sell. Generally, supply curves rise *upward* and to the right: diminishing returns implies that, usually, higher *P* is needed to coax out higher-cost extra *Q* along *ss.*

5 Market equilibrium can take place only at a price where the quantities supplied and demanded are *equal.* At any price higher than the equilibrium intersection of the supply and demand curves, the quantity that producers will want to go on supplying will exceed the quantity that consumers will want to go on demanding: downward pressure on price will then result as some of the excess sellers undermine the going price. Similarly, the reader can show why a price lower than the equilibrium price will tend to generate shortages and to meet upward pressure from bids of excess buyers.

6 Competitive pricing *rations out* the limited supply of goods to those with desire or need backed by money votes. Along with helping to decide FOR WHOM, pricing signals changes in WHAT shall be produced and in HOW goods shall be produced. But any one market only "partially" helps solve

the WHAT, HOW, and FOR WHOM. This is so because of its interdependence with other commodity and factor markets in the setting of "the general-equilibrium system of prices."

7   Organized trading markets exist for a number of staple commodities such as wheat. They may also exist for some common stocks, bonds, and other financial items. There are still other markets that behave much like an auction market. Even if there is no formal auctioneering procedure, so long as there are numerous well-informed suppliers and demanders, each *too unimportant, if acting alone, to have an appreciable effect upon the price* of the standardized good in question—so long as such conditions prevail, the tools of supply and demand often give an adequate approximation of the behavior of such markets. Yet, as will be seen later, a good deal of modern economic reality departs from the strict competitive model, and economics must find tools applicable to monopoly and imperfect competition.

CONCEPTS FOR REVIEW

demand schedule or curve, *dd*
law of downward-sloping demand
supply schedule or curve, *ss*
diminishing returns and rising *ss*
equilibrium intersection
shifts of curves versus movements along a curve

shortages and excesses
how supply and demand in one market "partially" solves WHAT, HOW, and FOR WHOM
rationing by prices
general-equilibrium prices
imperfectly competitive situations

QUESTIONS FOR DISCUSSION

1   Although we'd all like to escape the hardship implied by higher price, show that rising market prices do perform some useful functions in time of scarcity. Discuss how scarcity hardships work themselves out in a different kind of economy. (Illustrate with the case of energy.)

2   Define carefully what is meant by a demand schedule or curve. State the law of downward-sloping demand—that there is some kind of *inverse* relation between *P* and *Q*, the latter going down when the former goes up. (Illustrate with the case of energy.)

3   Define the concept of a supply schedule or curve. Show that an increase in supply means a rightward and downward *shift* of the supply curve. Contrast this with the rightward and *upward* shift implied by an increase in demand. Why the difference? Treat cases of decrease.

4   What factors might increase the demand for wheat? The supply? What would cheap oil do to gasoline prices? To coal miners' wages?

5   Spell out arguments to show that competitive price settles down at the equilibrium intersection of supply and demand. Use too high or too low *P*.

6 "An increase (or decrease) in supply will lower (or raise) price." Verify. Puzzle out this use of parentheses, common in economics, for alternative cases. Now interpret: "An increase (decrease) in demand will generally raise (lower) price."

7 "A simultaneous increase of demand and decrease of supply is statistically and logically impossible. Demand and supply are identically the same thing." Comment in terms of the section "Two Stumbling Blocks."

8 Give the pros and cons, in peace and war, of gasoline rationing by coupons. Contrast sale of blood with voluntary donations.

9 "Suppose there is only one seller or only a few very large sellers. Then monopoly and imperfect competition theory will need to be considered rather than the tools of competitive supply and demand. If products are far from being standardized, then each brand-name seller may well have *a degree of control over sales price* not enjoyed by the perfect competitor as defined by the economist." Verify.

10 Explain why the following true-or-false questions have for correct answers the following: F, F, F, F.

____Failure of Brazil's coffee crop will lower *P*s of coffee, tea, lemon, and cream.
____Fad for long skirts will lower wool *P* and raise salt *P*.
____A new yen for meat will lower *P*s of grain and raise *P* of hide and horn.
____Development of the sugar beet raised rents on tropical cane lands.

11 Try to puzzle out what the following hypothetical newspaper reports would mean.

WHEAT

	Open	High	Low	Close	Change	Season's High	Season's Low
July . . .	332	335	330	331½–332	+1 to 1½	509	324½
Sept. . . .	340	341½	336½	338	+1¾	513	331½
Dec. . . .	349	352	347	348½–349	+1½ to 2	523	340
Mar. '81 .	356	358½	353½	356	+3	392½	349

CORN

	Open	High	Low	Close	Change	Season's High	Season's Low
July . . .	283	287½	283	285½–286	+3¾ to 4¼	411	254¾
Sept. . . .	275	278¾	274½	277¼–½	+4¾ to 5	388½	246¼
Dec. . . .	260	261¾	259	260½–261	+4 to 4½	355	234
Mar. '81 .	266	266¾	264¾	206	+3¾	358	239
May . . .	268¾	269¼	268¾	269¼	+3¾	283	262½

TREASURY BONDS

Rates	Maturities		Bid	Asked	Yield
7⅝s,	1980	Feb	98	98.4	9.83
7½s,	1980	Mar	97.24	97.28	9.80
7¾s,	1980	Apr	97.27	97.31	9.78
6⅞s,	1980	May	96.30	97.2	9.71
8s,	1980	May	97.31	98.3	9.78
7⅝s,	1980	Jun	97.13	97.17	9.78
8¼s,	1980	Jun	98.5	98.9	9.75
8½s,	1980	Jul	98.10	98.14	9.78
6¾s,	1980	Aug	96.2	96.6	9.79
9s,	1980	Aug	99.7	99.15	9.42
8⅜s,	1980	Aug	98.3	98.7	9.76
6⅞s,	1980	Sep	96	96.4	9.73
8⅝s,	1980	Sep	98.11	98.15	9.75

1980 HIGH	1980 LOW	STOCKS AND DIV. IN DOLLARS	HIGH	LOW	LAST	NET CHANGE
64¾	58½	Am Tel & Tel 5	61⅜	61	61	−⅛
29⅞	22	Bank of Am 1.10	25¼	25	25⅛	. . .
64½	45	CBS 2.60	46⅜	46	46¼	+¼
19⅜	12	Zenith 1	15⅛	14⅞	15	−⅛

	FRIDAY	THURSDAY	WEEK AGO	YEAR AGO
STERLING				
Spot	$2.0520	$2.0595	$2.0660	$1.9801
90 days	2.0190	2.0235	2.0480	1.9738
GERMANY				
Spot	$0.52218	$0.5245	$0.5227	$0.4595
90 days	0.5193	0.5220	0.5197	0.4565
JAPAN (# to $1)				
Spot	209.46	207.91	206.22	212.01
90 days	204.49	202.87	201.73	210.93

12 *Extra-credit problem* (only for those who know some mathematics): The demand curve is a functional relation between Q and P, namely; $Q = f(P)$. Downward-sloping demand means Q falls as P rises, or in terms of calculus that $df(P)/dP < 0$. Other variables, such as income (X_1) or price of rye (X_2), are being held constant, etc.; hence $f(P)$ is short for $f(P; X_1, X_2, \ldots)$, and a change in any X_i shifts the demand curve. Similarly, denote the supply functional relationship between Q and P by $Q = s(P)$, with $ds(P)/dp > 0$. Then, equilibrium intersection price, P^*, is the root of the equation $f(P) = s(P)$. [For $f(P) = 9 - P$ and $s(P) = 2P$, verify that $P^* = 3$ and $Q^* = 6$. Graph these intersecting straight-line schedules.]

APPENDIX: Stock-Market Fluctuations

To the public the most dramatic example of a competitive market is in Wall Street. Here, supply and demand bid up and bid down the prices of *common stocks* each day. One year, you make a fortune; another, you are ruined.

The New York Stock Exchange lists more than a thousand securities. It started as a private club with rules on its members, but these days it will cost you a quarter of a million dollars to buy a seat. The American Stock Exchange began as the Curb: it was literally a case where brokers met on *the street* to buy and sell, giving hand signals to the clerks hanging out the windows to record the transactions; and only in the twentieth century did the American Stock Exchange move indoors.

Every large financial center has its stock exchange. Important ones are in London, Paris, Tokyo, Frankfurt, Hong Kong, Toronto, and Zurich. Within the United States there are such regional markets as the Pacific Coast, Midwest, Boston, and PBW (Philadelphia-Baltimore-Washington) exchanges. They deal in stocks of local and smaller companies, and much of their function will disappear as the New York Exchange loses its monopoly privileges and a unified composite market comes into being.[1]

PEOPLE'S CAPITALISM

The New York Stock Exchange for many years tried to sell the notion of "people's capitalism"—in which everyone owns stock and therefore will vote to take account of the interests of property. Few would oppose the notion of a wider and more equal distribution of wealth. But it is a bit of a confidence trick to entice union workers into owning a few shares of a mutual fund so that at the polls they will go easy on corporation tax rates—when, in fact, their own well-being is trivially affected by what happens to the few shares they own in comparison with even a 1 per cent change in wage rates or pension benefits.

In any case, only about 25 million out of 225 million Americans directly own any appreciable amount of stocks, and that is a generous estimate. Indirectly, private and public pension funds are beginning to invest in equities (i.e., in common stocks) on the behalf of low-income and high-income families.

---

[1] Pressure by the Antitrust Division and SEC caused the Exchange to eliminate its minimum commission rates, and to outlaw "give-ups" (i.e., rebates or fee-splitting).

Questions and Exercises

1. As you read the chapter, write a brief summary of each of the ten sections. Then read the summary at the end of the chapter. Compare your ten summary points with those of Samuelson. How are they different? Do your summary sentences contain the eleven concepts Samuelson lists for review under Concepts for Review on p. 47? If not, go back to the chapter to find what you omitted and why.

2. Figure 4-4, on p. 41, includes a summary of previous information. Study it, close your book, and reproduce it. Now compare yours with the one in the text. If they are different, reread the explanation of the figure in the text.

3. Using key words rather than whole sentences, list the examples Samuelson uses. Then beside each key word, write a full sentence to explain the example.

4. Study Figure 4-1 and write out in words the information it contains. When you have finished, ask yourself whether there is a question that can be answered by the table but not by your paragraph.

5. Make two lists, one with those items that have increased dramatically in price during your lifetime, and the other with items that have decreased dramatically in price. Jot down what you know about the changes in supply or demand for each item.

6. Refer to your ten-point summary. Work with a small group of classmates to develop a mnemonic device for remembering three of these ideas. (A mnemonic device is a memory trick. For example, you may need to remember the classification system in biology: Kingdom, Phylum, Class, Order, Family, Genus, Species. Try this system: <u>K</u>ing <u>P</u>hilip <u>C</u>ame <u>O</u>ver <u>F</u>or <u>G</u>reater <u>S</u>ex. A classic mnemonic device is the jingle we learned as children to remember the irregularities of the calendar: "Thirty days has September, April, June, and November. All the rest have thirty-one except February alone . . ."

7. Turn to Samuelson's discussion questions. Work with a small group of classmates to answer or solve each one.

8. Read Samuelson's footnote 3. Here he discusses "the distribution of money votes." Why does Samuelson put this material in a footnote? What questions does this footnote pose about the scientific nature of economic study or about the value of economics as a discipline? Draft a letter to prospective economics majors in which you alert them to the possibilities and the limitations of economics as a field of study.

Hormonal Regulation in Females
HELENA CURTIS

from *Biology*

Textbooks in the natural sciences, as in the other disciplines, help you learn about a topic by providing an organizational framework for the basic concepts of the field. They also introduce you to the essential vocabulary required to understand the concepts. These functions are, perhaps, more critical in the natural sciences than in other fields because the concepts and vocabularies are not a part of most people's common knowledge. A natural science textbook is also a reference book, a book that you should keep after your introductory science courses are completed. Later, if you read more specialized scientific literature (for example, see pp. 321–377), you can use your introductory science textbook to remind yourself of basic definitions and explanations.

This particular textbook, *Biology*, by Helena Curtis, is now in its fourth edition. The relatively short time between the third and fourth editions (only four years) indicates how quickly new information must be incorporated if a natural science textbook is to be even reasonably up-to-date. We selected Curtis, not only because of the author's clean and lively style, but because she is writing for students who will probably not become science majors. She tries to make the natural sciences accessible to all by drawing relationships between the facts of biology and the everyday experiences of a reader.

This selection includes only portions of two chapters. For that reason you will not find the types of beginning or concluding aids to reading that we illustrated in the previous selection. But these fragments do demonstrate the major features of textbooks in the natural sciences: the generous use of illustrations, chemical structures, diagrams, tables; detailed explanation of graphic material, since most are not readily understandable; cross-referencing within the text, because scientific knowledge is cumulative; and headings and subheadings. When reading a natural science textbook, you must move constantly between reference points, that is, between earlier chapters and later ones, between sections within chapters, between glossaries and text, and between prose and graphic material.

The selection begins with references to spermatogenesis and oogenesis, two terms explained in earlier chapters. Always look for a glossary in a science textbook and refer to it frequently. Also look for tables. In paragraph one of this selection, five unfamiliar hormones are mentioned. In another section of the book Helena Curtis provides a table of the principal hormones of vertebrates. We have reproduced this table on pp. 58–59. But in your own study of a science textbook, you would have to use the index to find potential aids in other parts of the book. When you read the section on the menstrual cycle, you must refer to the diagrams on p. 55 and to the glossary for working vocabulary.

As you can see, you must be alert and active when you read a textbook. If you allow yourself to go numb, you will miss the helpful hints. Sometimes even the best textbook authors will provide insufficient directional cues, in which case you should develop your own. Look at the second paragraph of this selection (p. 54). This paragraph presents a number of complex relationships: ovarian follicles and estradiol; FSH and estrogen; estrogen and endometrium preparation. If these relationships are still unclear to you after you have read about them, try to visualize them on paper. One of our students developed the representation shown in Figure 1 to help remember the salient facts about estrogens.

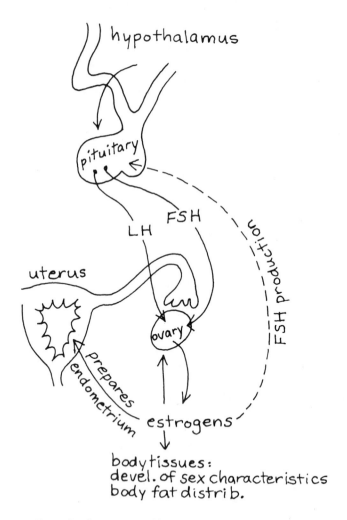

Figure 1. Example of a memory aid

Sample Glossary

endometrium [Gk. *endon,* within + *metrios,* of the womb]: The glandular lining of the uterus in mammals; thickens in response to progesterone secretion during ovulation and is sloughed off in menstruation.

hypothalamus [Gk. *hypo,* under + *thalamos,* inner room]: The floor and sides of the vertebrate brain just below the cerebral hemispheres; controls the autonomic nervous system and the pituitary gland and contains centers that regulate body temperature and appetite.

oogenesis [Gk. *oo,* egg + *genesis,* birth]: the process by which the ovum is formed in preparation for its fertilization and development.

pheromone (fair-o-moan) [Gk. *phero,* to bear, carry]: Substance secreted by an animal that influences the behavior or morphological development of other animals of the same species, such as the sex attractants of moths, the odor trail of ants.

spermatogenesis [Gk. *sperma,* seed + *genesis,* origin]: The process by which spermatogonia develop into sperm.

spermatogonia [Gk. *sperma,* seed + *gonos,* a child, the young]: The unspecialized diploid (2*n*) germ cells on the walls of the testes, which, by meiotic division, become spermatocytes, then spermatids, then spermatozoa, or sperm cells.

32-17

Implantation. The tiny embryo invades the lining of the uterus within a week after fertilization. Subsequently, the placenta begins to form; this organ is the source of hormones that help to maintain pregnancy. Implantation usually occurs three to four days after the young embryo reaches the uterus.

EMBRYO IN ITS SAC

UTERINE GLANDS

1 mm

32-18

The chemical structures of testosterone, estradiol, and progesterone. Note that the hormones differ only very slightly chemically, in contrast to the great differences in their physiological effects—another example of the extreme specificity of biochemical actions. All of these belong to a group of chemicals known as steroids, characterized by the four-ring structure shown here.

Hormonal Regulation in Females

Like spermatogenesis, oogenesis is under hormonal control. Unlike spermatogenesis in the human male, however, oogenesis in all vertebrate females is cyclic. It involves an interplay of hormones, including estrogens, progesterone, and the two gonadotropic (gonad-stimulating) hormones, follicle-stimulating hormone (FSH) and luteinizing hormone (LH). The timing and control of the cycle rest in the hypothalamus.

Estrogens are the female sex hormones. A variety of them, of which estradiol is probably the most important, are produced by the ovarian follicles under the stimulation of FSH. The production of estrogens inhibits the secretion of FSH in a feedback system similar to that which controls the production of sex hormones in males. Estrogens stimulate the development of the breasts and the external genitalia, and the distribution of body fat. Both estrogens and progesterone are required to prepare the endometrium for the implantation of the embryo; neither can do the job alone. This cooperation, or synergism, in which two or more agents act together to produce an effect that is greater in magnitude than the sum of the effects produced separately, is characteristic of many hormonal responses.

Synthetic estrogens have been prepared and are usually more potent than the natural product. For example, DES, diethylstilbestrol, which is used in the "morning-after pill," is a potent synthetic estrogen. It is believed to prevent implantation of the embryo in the endometrium. When administered late in pregnancy, however, it helps prevent spontaneous abortion. Recently this use has been discontinued because of the increased incidence of cervical cancer in women whose mothers were treated with DES late in pregnancy. For a time DES was used commercially to fatten cattle, but this use is now forbidden by government regulation since the hormone was found to cause cancer in experimental animals when administered in high doses.

The Menstrual Cycle

The beginning of the first menstrual cycle (menarche) marks the onset of puberty in human females. The average age of onset is $13\frac{1}{2}$, but the normal range is very wide. Puberty in the female begins on the average about a year and a half before puberty in the male. Puberty in the female is usually preceded by the appearance of the secondary sex characteristics, such as pubic and axillary hair and enlargement of the breasts.

Although the menstrual cycle does not require an environmental cue, as do reproductive cycles in many other vertebrates, it is clearly under the influence of external factors, to some extent. For example, some women find that emotional

TESTOSTERONE   ESTRADIOL   PROGESTERONE

From Helena Curtis, *Biology*, 3rd edition, Worth Publishers, New York, 1979, pages 75, 595, 596, 597, 657, 659. Reprinted by permission of the publisher. Photomicrograph (Figure 32-17) reprinted by permission of Ronan O'Rahilly, M.D., Carnegie Laboratories of Embryology.

upset delays a menstrual period or eliminates it completely. A similar mechanism may be responsible for the sterility that occurs among rodents, for example, when living in very crowded conditions or under other forms of stress. Human females living in groups—as in college dormitories—are familiar with the tendency of the menstrual cycles of the group to become synchronized. The mechanism for this is unknown, but it has been suggested that it may be a result of the exchange of a pheromone* among the individuals involved.

The menstrual cycle (Figure 32–19) begins with the casting off of the outer layer of endometrium (menstruation). After the menstrual flow ceases and under the influence of FSH and LH, another egg cell and its follicle begin to mature, and the follicle secretes increased amounts of estrogens. (Usually a number of follicles begin to enlarge simultaneously, but only one becomes mature enough to release its ovum, and the others regress.) The estrogens stimulate the regrowth of the endometrium. The rapid rise in estrogens near the midpoint of the cycle triggers a sharply increased production of LH by the pituitary gland (an example of positive feedback). Paradoxically, toward the end of the cycle, LH and FSH production decline as a result of the increased concentration of progesterone and estrogens (negative feedback).

---

* For another discussion of pheromones, see page 470.

32-19

Diagram of events taking place during the menstrual cycle. The cycle begins with the first day of menstrual flow, which is caused by the shedding of the endometrium, the lining of the uterine wall. The increase of FSH and LH during the first week promotes the growth of the ovarian follicle and its secretion of estrogens. Under the influence of estrogens, the endometrium regrows. A sharp increase of LH from the pituitary about midcycle stimulates the release of the egg cell (ovulation). (It is not known what role, if any, is played by the simultaneous increase in FSH.) Following ovulation, LH and FSH levels drop. The follicle is converted to the corpus luteum, which secretes estrogens and also progesterone. Progesterone further stimulates the endometrium, preparing it for implantation. If pregnancy does not occur, the corpus luteum degenerates, the production of progesterone and estrogens falls, the endometrium begins to slough off, FSH and LH concentrations increase once more, and the cycle begins anew.

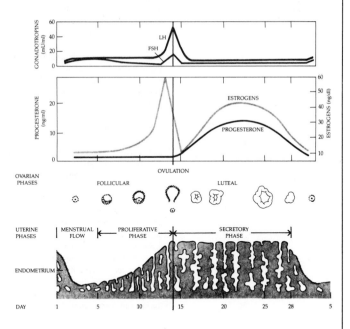

Table 32–2 *Major Mammalian Gonadotropic and Sex Hormones in Females*

HORMONE	PRINCIPAL SOURCE	PRINCIPAL EFFECTS	CONTROL
FSH	Pituitary	Stimulates growth of ovarian follicle, stimulates estrogen production	Hypothalamus
LH	Pituitary	Stimulates release of egg cell, stimulates progesterone production	Hypothalamus
Estrogens	Ovary, placenta	Produce and maintain female sex characteristics, thicken lining of uterus	FSH
Progesterone	Ovary, placenta	Further prepares uterine lining for pregnancy, inhibits uterine movements, promotes development of milk ducts	LH

All these events take place as a result of a shifting balance of hormones. The spurt of high LH stimulates the follicle to release the egg cell, which begins its passage to the uterus. Under the continued stimulus of LH, the cells of the emptied follicle grow larger and fill the cavity, producing the corpus luteum ("yellow body"). The cells of the corpus luteum, as they increase in size, begin to synthesize progesterone as well as estrogens. As the estrogen and progesterone levels increase, they inhibit the production of the gonadotropic hormones from the pituitary. Production of ovarian hormones then drops. The lining of the uterus can no longer sustain itself without hormonal support, and a portion of it is sloughed off in the menstrual fluid. Then, in response to the low level of ovarian hormones, the level of pituitary gonadotropic hormones begins to rise again, followed by development of a new follicle and a rise in estrogens as the next monthly cycle begins.

The cycle usually lasts about 28 days, but individual variation is common. Moreover, even in women with cycles of average length, ovulation does not always occur at the same time in the cycle.

Fertility pills for women contain either gonadotropins or a synthetic compound that decreases estrogen concentrations in the blood, stimulating the production of FSH by the pituitary. Multiple births may occur when several ova are released simultaneously as the result of such treatments.

Uterus, Vagina, and Vulva

The uterus is a hollow, muscular, pear-shaped organ about 7.5 centimeters long and 5 centimeters wide. It is lined by the endometrium, which has two principal layers, one of which is shed at menstruation and another from which the shed layer is regenerated. The smooth muscles in the walls of the uterus move in continuous waves that are more frequent at the broad fundus, or base, and less active at the narrower cervical end of the uterus. This motion possibly increases the motility of both the sperm on its journey to the oviduct and the oocyte as it passes from the oviduct to the uterus. The contractions increase when the endometrium is shed during a menstrual period and reach greatest strength when a woman is in labor.

597   CHAPTER 32 *The Continuity of Life: Reproduction*

prostaglandins have antagonistic effects; for example, one causes smooth muscle to relax, and another causes the same muscle to contract.

Prostaglandins differ from hormones in a number of ways. (1) They are fatty acids. (2) Their target tissues are those of another individual (if their role in fertilization has been correctly interpreted). (3) They are among the most potent of all known biological materials, producing marked effects in very small doses. A concomitant of their extraordinary potency is the fact that they are produced in very small amounts and are rapidly broken down by enzyme systems in the body. If it were not for their presence in unusually large amounts in semen, they might never have been discovered. (4) They appear to be produced by cell membranes. (5) They often exert their effect in the tissue that produces them.

MECHANISM OF ACTION OF HORMONES

Virtually all cells of the body are equally exposed to the hormones released into the bloodstream, yet not all respond. Recent research has indicated the mechanisms underlying specificity of action of two major groups of hormones, the steroids and the protein hormones.

Steroid hormones are relatively small molecules. These molecules, it has been found, pass easily through cell membranes and so freely enter all the cells of the body. However, in their target cells, and only in their target cells, the hormones encounter a specific receptor molecule in the cytoplasm that combines with them. The receptor, a protein, and the steroid together act directly on the DNA of the cell to promote the synthesis of messenger RNA and so of specific enzymes and other proteins. (Note that this is similar to the operation of the operon, described on page 291. However, it differs in that hormone and receptor apparently serve to stimulate RNA synthesis in these cells, rather than to remove a repressor molecule, as occurs in the operon.) These findings explain how the very slight differences in configuration among steroid molecules can be correlated with such drastically different effects: The protein receptors, like enzymes, are highly specific in their combining properties.

By contrast, it is more likely that protein hormones, which are much larger molecules, do not enter cells but rather combine with receptor molecules on the membrane surface, setting in motion a "second messenger" that is responsible for the sequence of events inside the cell. These findings may have important medical implications. For example, it has long been known that juvenile diabetes—diabetes in young persons—is caused by a deficiency of the hormone insulin, which as we noted, promotes the uptake of glucose by cells. It was assumed by analogy that the diabetes found commonly in older persons and associated with obesity had the same cause. It has now been found, however, that adult diabetes results from a decrease in the number of insulin binding sites on receptor cells. Such patients are treated most effectively by diet.

Another group of studies, for which Earl W. Sutherland was awarded the Nobel Prize in 1971, has shown that a chemical known as cyclic AMP (Figure 34-29) is the second messenger in a number of target cells. Hormones that trigger the action of cyclic AMP include ACTH, TSH, LH, ADH, epinephrine, and glucagon. The differences in their effects are due to the presence of different enzyme systems within the cells that respond to cyclic AMP.

At almost the same time that cyclic AMP was identified by these research

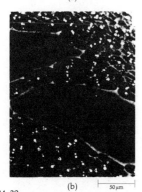

CYCLIC AMP

(a)

(b)   50 μm

34-29
(a) Cyclic AMP (adenosine monophosphate) acts as a "second messenger" within the cells of vertebrates. Following stimulation by various hormones—the "first messengers"—cyclic AMP is formed from ATP. "Cyclic" refers to the fact that the atoms of the phosphate group form a ring. (b) Cyclic AMP is also the chemical that attracts the amoebas of the cellular slime molds, causing them to aggregate into a sluglike body, which then behaves like a multicellular organism. The arrow shows the direction in which the cells are moving.

657   CHAPTER 34 Integration and Control

Figure 34-29b reprinted by permission of Professor K. B. Raper, Department of Bacteriology, University of Wisconsin.

Table 34-2 *Some of the Principal Endocrine Glands of Vertebrates and the Hormones They Produce*

GLAND	HORMONE	PRINCIPAL ACTION	MECHANISM CONTROLLING SECRETION	CHEMICAL COMPOSITION
Pituitary, anterior lobe	Thyroid-stimulating hormone (TSH)	Stimulates thyroid	Thyroxine in blood; hypothalamic-releasing hormone	Glycoprotein
	Follicle-stimulating hormone (FSH)	Stimulates ovarian follicle, spermatogenesis	Estrogen in blood; hypothalamic-releasing hormone	Glycoprotein
	Luteinizing hormone (LH)	Stimulates interstitial cells in male, corpus luteum and ovulation in female	Testosterone or progesterone in blood; hypothalamic-releasing hormone	Glycoprotein
	Adrenocorticotropic hormone (ACTH)	Stimulates adrenal cortex	Adrenal cortical hormone in blood; hypothalamic-releasing hormone	Protein
	Growth hormone (somatotropin)	Stimulates bone and muscle growth, inhibits oxidation of glucose, promotes breakdown of fatty acids	Hypothalamic-inhibiting hormone (somatostatin)	Protein
	Prolactin	Stimulates milk production and secretion in "prepared" gland	Hypothalamic-inhibiting hormone	Protein
Thyroid	Thyroxine, other thyroxinelike hormones	Stimulate and maintain metabolic activities	TSH	Iodinated amino acids
	Calcitonin	Inhibits release of calcium from bone	Concentration of calcium in blood	Peptide (32 amino acids)
Parathyroid	Parathyroid hormone (parathormone)	Stimulates release of calcium from bone, promotes calcium uptake from gastrointestinal tract, inhibits calcium excretion	Concentration of calcium in blood	Protein
Ovary, follicle	Estrogens	Develop and maintain sex characteristics in females, initiate buildup of endometrium	FSH	Steroids

Source	Hormone	Effect	Regulated by	Chemical class
Ovary, corpus luteum	Progesterone and estrogens	Promote continued growth of endometrium	LH	Steroids
Testis	Testosterone	Supports spermatogenesis, develops and maintains sex characteristics of males	LH	Steroid
Hypothalamus (via posterior pituitary)	Oxytocin	Stimulates uterine contractions, milk ejection	Nervous system	Peptide (9 amino acids)
	Antidiuretic hormone (vasopressin)	Controls water excretion	Osmotic concentration of blood; nervous system	Peptide (9 amino acids)
Adrenal cortex	Cortisol, other cortisol-like hormones	Affect carbohydrate, protein, and lipid metabolism	ACTH	Steroids
	Aldosterone	Affects salt and water balance	Renin from kidney, K^+ ions in blood	Steroid
Adrenal medulla	Epinephrine and norepinephrine	Increase blood sugar, dilate some blood vessels, increase rate of heartbeat	Nervous system	Catecholamines
Pancreas	Insulin	Lowers blood sugar, increases storage of glycogen	Concentration of glucose in blood	Protein
	Glucagon	Stimulates breakdown of glycogen to glucose in the liver	Concentration of glucose and amino acids in blood	Protein

Questions and Exercises

1. The first paragraph of "Hormonal Regulation in Females" would be incomprehensible to most lay readers without reference to the glossary (p. 53) and possibly to a dictionary. Using those reference tools, write a paraphrase of that paragraph. (A paraphrase is a translation of the material into more accessible terms. It is usually the same length as the original.)

2. Like most textbooks, Curtis's *Biology* provides a definite framework for the facts and concepts. By outlining, diagramming, or making a tree, show how the information in the section "Mechanism of Action of Hormones" is organized. (A topic tree uses words and connecting lines to show dominant and subordinate relationships.)

3. After carefully reading and taking notes on the section on "Hormonal Regulation in Females," put aside both the book and notes. Now write a summary of the information in the section. Compare your summary with the original text for both organization and informational content. What changes did you make?

4. After carefully reading and taking notes on "Mechanism of Action of Hormones," close the book and in your own words write a summary of the information in the section.

5. Write a description of the information displayed in the first two graphs of Figure 32-19. Using the graphs as a source of information, specify the timing of events and the blood concentrations of the various hormones. Compare hormone levels at different times in the cycle. For example, on day 14, do estrogen levels increase to twice, to five times, or to 100 times their day 5 level? Why do you think FSH and LH are shown on one graph, while progesterone and estrogen are shown on the other?

6. Write a paragraph addressed to your classmates, explaining the relationship between "Mechanism of Action of Hormones" and "Hormonal Regulation in Females."

7. Although most of the information in these excerpts is basic biology, several items are mentioned that might be considered newsworthy. Identify two of these newsworthy items. Look in *Reader's Guide to Periodic Literature* to see if either of your newsworthy items has been the subject of magazine articles in the last ten years. If so, list several of the articles, and locate one of them.

8. Develop mnemonic devices for remembering the information on Table 34-2. For instance, which hormones are made up of protein? Which hormones are steroids? What is the principal action of each hormone?

What Is Buddhism?

RICHARD PAUL JANARO and THELMA C. ALTSHULER

from *The Art of Being Human*

Textbooks in the humanities often differ markedly in structure and tone from science textbooks. While Samuelson's work has many subheadings, there are very few divisions in the following selection from a textbook in comparative religion. The prose is liberally spiced with quotations, verse, and extended discussions of individual points, features not often found in textbooks in the natural and social sciences. The following selection contains no graphs, tables, charts, formulas, or equations. The only visual representations are two highly symbolic drawings.

Humanities textbooks look different because scholars writing about history, art and music criticism, literature, language, philosophy, and religion approach the world from a different perspective. These fields centrally involve questions of human values and interpretation rather than objective descriptions of the physical world or of human behavior. Social and natural scientists present measurements and classifications. If you disagree, you can perform their tests and look at their statistics. Writers in the humanities present interpretations that are less easily tested. Textbook writers in the humanities are in effect presenting explanations of interpretations. When you read a humanities text, you are openly invited to question everything you read. In science and social science texts, this invitation is much less obvious.

The following selection is from a humanities textbook entitled *The Art of Being Human*. The title sums up the essence of study in the humanities. Critical thinking, the habit of challenging assumptions, defines one important feature of the characteristically human art. As you read humanities textbooks, you should seek more questions than answers.

The chapter subsection presented here is itself phrased as a question, "What is Buddhism?" Everything that follows the heading is intended to address that question. The passage is really the authors' extended definition of Buddhism. However, definitions in the humanities are open-ended; if you disagree, you cannot perform an experiment or check the authors' statistics. Janaro and Altshuler, the textbook authors, draw on years of studying religious documents, histories, and biographies to provide you with a map of the terrain, to make your own exploration easier. But you need to question your guides about the terrain itself and even about their mapmaking.

Janaro and Altshuler begin by identifying Buddhism as a religion that reflects several schools of Eastern thought that share a common basis. They contrast Buddhism with familiar Western religions, and then they summarize the basic principles of Buddhist beliefs. The only subheading, "Hinduism and Buddhism: An Historical Perspective," signals a discussion

	Buddhism	*Western Religions*
Presence of Godhead		
Ritual		
Definition of Self		
Morality		

Table 1. A sample table used to compare Buddhism with Western religions

that will place Buddhism in the unfolding history of Eastern thought, particularly in its relationship to Hinduism. Since Buddhism is an outgrowth of Hinduism, the principles of Hinduism should be introduced before Buddhism can be grasped; therefore, the authors devote a great deal of space to concepts in the earlier religion: existence, atman, nirvana, cycles of rebirth. Then the authors explain the origin of Buddhism in the enlightenment of Siddhartha Gautama. Here, too, specialized terms are introduced: samsara, karma, middle way, Dharma. These terms are all defined in the selection, and it is a good idea to keep a list of these definitions. Any good conversation depends on a shared vocabulary.

Most of these specialized terms appear in italics, but this humanities textbook, like many others in the field, offers fewer aids to reading than science textbooks do. The marginal notes in bold type do not provide a simple summary of the material opposite; instead they offer thought-provoking observations. The textbook authors invite you to talk with them, to add your own comments, questions, and summaries in the remaining marginal space. This dialogue is the essence of study in the humanities.

In fact, you may wish to go beyond marginal notes to a more organized interaction. Table 1 might be used to compare Buddhism with other religions. When you join a conversation about something new, you should try to connect the novel experiences under discussion with your own related memories. Western religions are probably more familiar to you. Look at the differences and similarities between the familiar and the unfamiliar.

profound understanding of the Eastern mind is now available to the Westerner who seeks to broaden his perspective.

The impact has been greatest from two particular Eastern schools of thought: Tibetan Buddhism and Zen Buddhism. For a number of reasons, which shall presently be investigated, these traditions offer many Americans *genuine alternatives* to a way of life and a value system they no longer find entirely satisfactory.

What Is Buddhism?

There is not one school of Eastern thought or religion to which the label *Buddhism* is applied. There are different *kinds* of Buddhism. But there is a common basis, a foundation shared by the various kinds.

In its most pervasive use, the term Buddhism connotes a religion practiced by millions of people, principally in Asia, including Japan and the Republic of Formosa but not those countries currently under communist rule. It is a religion in the sense that it involves certain rituals practiced in places appropriately designated and held sacred and has an ancient tradition of belief which unifies those people born into it or choosing to follow its teachings.

It differs from both Islamic and Judeo-Christian religions in that it does not have a principle of godhead. Its dominant ritual—the act of sitting quietly without any particular project—appears to resemble prayer, but it is not prayer. Buddhist meditation is a technique for tuning in to the subtleties of the present moment, for understanding the patterns of sensations, thoughts, and emotions that make up human experience, and for cultivating a wakeful state of mind.

Buddists believe all unethical behavior is motivated by self-interest.

Buddhists make no attempt to communicate with a transcendent god figure because they believe that before wondering about the godhead they must first come to understand themselves and the operation of their own perceptions.

According to Buddhist belief, the sense that people have of themselves as solid, separate, independent beings in a world of indifferent objects is an illusion—an illusion which is not imposed from outside but rather grows out of faulty perception and overhasty interpretations. Buddhism says this illusion is the source of most of our suffering and the source of all our immoral actions toward others.

Thus while Buddhists do not talk about a god figure, Buddhism is nonetheless profoundly ethical. All unethical behavior is motivated by self-interest. Whether acts of violence are physical or more subtle and psychological, they always spring from intense desire or intense fear, and underlying is always a sense of the self as isolated, vulnerable, and needy. Buddhists claim that as people see more clearly, and realize that the sense of separation is illusory, they uncover a tremendous warmth and resourcefulness within themselves which allows actions to be spontaneously appropriate to situations as they arise. Buddhist morality is not dependent on a transcendent god who lays down rules and punishes people for breaking them. It is instead dependent on freeing oneself from the idea of existing as a separate being, on discovering one's own *egolessness.* The recognition of egolessness as the natural state and of ego as an illusion is often in dramatic conflict with Western value systems which take the reality of the self for granted.

> **The recognition of the ego as an illusion is in dramatic conflict with Western value systems.**

Hinduism and Buddhism: An Historical Perspective

Hinduism came before Buddhism, and both religions share certain views. Buddhism is founded on the teachings of the Buddha, who, according to belief, was an actual person, an Indian prince named Siddhartha Gautama.[1] Siddhartha lived around 500 B.C., roughly a hundred years before the death of Socrates, and over a century before the great period of Greek philosophy dominated by Plato and Aristotle. His historic life span preceded that of Jesus by half a millenium.

The Buddha (a Sanskrit term meaning "He who is awake") was no doubt raised on Hindu scripture and must surely have been aware of the Hindu world view. What the Buddha was seeking is clearly implicit in Hindu belief. Hence it is impossible to understand Buddhism without some reference to the earlier religion of Hinduism.

In Hinduism there are deities with specific names like Brahman, the Creator; Shiva, the Destroyer; and Vishnu, the Preserver. Buddhism dispenses with deities, though many devout Buddhists have regarded and no doubt continue to regard the Buddha with as much awe as Jews and Christians regard God or Moslems regard Allah. The Buddha was very much flesh and blood, however; he was not the incarnation of godhead in any sense. To be a practicing Buddhist one need believe only that the Buddha was a perfectly actualized human being and that the enlightenment he attained represents a model, a *goal,* to which all may aspire.

The gods of Hinduism are really personifications of cosmic forces, much as the Egyptian Ra was the personification of the sun. These forces are said to have existed from the beginning and to be imperishable. They represent the workings of the universe. Brahman is the principle by which the endless variety of things comes into being. It is the inexhaustible creativity of existence. Shiva—familiar to Westerners in the famous guise of the multi-handed dancer—is the principle by which created forms pass out of existence and disappear. If Brahman is viewed as birth, then Shiva is assuredly death. If Brahman is youth, Shiva is age. If Brahman is the excitement of a new society in development, Shiva is the excitement of revolution and the shattering of old orders. Between the rising and falling actions of the universe, a balance is somehow achieved. For every birth, there must be a death. Hence the third member of the Hindu trinity: Vishnu, or the principle of balance.

In actuality, the three gods are all different facets of the same force: *existence itself.* They represent its modes of being. Underlying the diversity of things we experience there is fundamentally only *one* thing. For example, a person who is being born and a person who is dying share the common fact of being alive. Existence either is, or is not. In Western terms, we would say that the baby coming into the world and the person leaving it both have existence. But if we change the wording and say that they both *are* existence, then the *oneness* of everything according to Hindu belief becomes clearer. Differences—in age, sex, degree of intelligence, even species—are regarded as the *properties* of existence. Absolute separateness is an illusion, and is called *maya* in Sanskrit, the ancient language of India. It is not a negative term. The Hindu is not asked to believe differences are not real, only that they are ultimately not important.

The American poet Walt Whitman, who was very much influenced by Hindu thought, has captured the principle of unity-in-diversity in these lines:

> *I believe a leaf of grass is no less perfect*
> *than the journeywork of the stars,*

And the pismire is equally perfect, and a grain of sand,
 and the egg of the wren,
And the tree-toad is a chef-d'oeuvre for the highest,
And the running blackberry would adorn the parlors of heaven,
And the narrowest hinge in my hand puts to scorn all machinery,
And the cow crunching with depress'd head surpasses any statue,
And a mouse is miracle enough to stagger sextillions of infidels.

The continual equation Whitman makes between the gigantic and the tiny is characteristically Hindu. He refers to himself, in the humblest of terms, as a "kosmos."

Consider also the very title of Whitman's major work *Leaves of Grass.* Why this title? Why single out grass unless one mode of nature's being is just as important as any other?

"So long as one drop of water exists, there is water."

And is not one *leaf* of grass—one spear—just as important as all the grass there is? So long as one leaf of grass exists, there is grass. So long as one drop of water exists, there is water. Who needs oceans? Similarly, if the humblest human being that ever walked the earth survives a devastating nuclear blast, has not humanity itself survived?

In Hinduism Brahman is also identified as the world soul —the ongoing *isness* behind everything. It is without beginning or end. It manifests itself, however, not in its pure wholeness, but rather in its individual forms. Hence the term *atman,* which means the individual soul. Atman is to Brahman what the leaf of grass is to grass as a whole, what the drop of water is to all the water on earth. (Hence Whitman's line "I believe a leaf of grass is no less perfect than the journeywork of the stars. . . .")

When human beings regard themselves as separate entities, unrelated to the whole, they perpetuate an ancient human mistake—the source of all human misery. Separateness creates desire, for the individual self seeks to possess all that is not itself. It acts out of self-interest. But needs born of such a misunderstanding of existence can never be satisfied. If one sets out with the idea that the purpose of living is the gratification of desire, how can there *ever* be fulfillment? What, in the long run, is "enough"? Thus life, from the perspective of the individual, amounts to continual frustration.

Not only that, but life from the perspective of the individual is limited, while existence itself in reality is limitless. But the individual knows only that, having been born at a particular time, he or she is stranded—"stuck"—in one tiny historical moment, which will never recur and which will soon be gone. Hence, having been born, one may anticipate, in addition to the frustration of all desire, only the pains of aging and the agonies of death.

Hinduism thus views the human lot as one of suffering. Like many other religions, Hinduism has a vision of how such suffering is to be overcome—or more precisely, what it is that constitutes *relief* from suffering. In Hinduism this relief is *nirvana.*

Nirvana is not a place—not heaven, not the abode of the blessed—but a state of being free from all desire, frustration, and pain. It is the total *absence* of all the things that generally plague human life. It is therefore obliviousness, much closer to unending sleep than it is to heaven, though through the ages in *popular* Hinduism nirvana has probably been conceived in poetic terms—conceived as an active experience of bliss, if not indeed a place in which bliss happens.

In the strictest sense of the word, however, nirvana represents the reunion of atman and Brahman. It is the end of separateness. One's awareness of being a personal, discreet entity disappears. One is free of desire, confusion, and the frustration borne of continual striving for achievements and possessions.

Nirvana is unbroken sleep—deathlike, but in a special way. Central to the Hindu view of life is the doctrine of *rebirth.* Unlike the religions which believe the soul lives on after death in a realm far different from earth's, Hinduism believes that the soul keeps returning in a new body, beginning once more the cycle of striving and suffering until, at some distant point in time, it attains nirvana and is liberated from the pain of rebirth. Nirvana is the end of the road. It terminates the cycle.

What keeps the cycle going? That is: why is nirvana unattainable in one lifetime? The answer should not be illogical to those who practice any of the other major world religions (such as Judaism, Christianity, or Islam). All of these maintain that the knowledge of how to achieve the final goal is given to each person; that the requirement is purity of soul. The requirement is not, however, easily satisfied. There are too many temptations. The apparent pleasures of this world deceive us and lure us away from the practices that will keep the soul pure. In Hindu scripture these practices are clearly stated:

> *The requirements of duty are three. The first is sacrifice, study, almsgiving; the second is austerity; the third is life as a student in the home of a teacher and the practice of continence. Together, these three lead one to the realm of the blest.* [2]

Hinduism puts rebirth into an economic and sociological context. The idea is that in each lifetime the soul is supposed to have attained a somewhat more elevated state, and if this comes to pass, rebirth will take place in more comfortable surroundings than in the previous incarnation.

India has been for centuries dominated by a system of castes, social ranks or plateaus which once permitted absolutely no social mobility. Those born into the lowest caste—the so-called untouchables—could expect to remain there a lifetime. The highest caste, that of the Brahmins, was not only the wealthiest and most aristocratic, but traditionally was assumed inhabited by the purest and most virtuous. The Hindu caste system is somewhat similar to the class system of the European Middle Ages, in which the nobility were supposed to be quite literally nobler in virtue than the lower classes, who were supposed weaker and more readily ensnared by Satan's temptations.

The apparent pleasures of this world deceive us.

But even for a Brahmin the path of life was never simple. It could take eons of time for one soul to pass through all of the cycles before attaining nirvana. Also, *downward* mobility in reincarnation was always a strong possibility: that is, you might be reborn into a lower caste. Even the virtuous Brahmin might require many lifetimes before experiencing reunion with Brahman, before release from suffering could be attained.

Buddhism is founded, as has been stated, on the teachings of Siddhartha Gautama, who, according to legend, achieved nirvana after his coming had been prepared for some 25,000 years earlier. Buddhist scripture records that in all of his rebirths the eventual Buddha had intuitive knowledge that he was destined to find enlightenment and to lead others in the true path. His own "terminal" lifetime, however, was filled with doubt and suffering, and after his enlightenment, he was to alter the Hindu world view to such an extent that a new religion arose, as pervasive and powerful as the one it sought to replace.

John A. Hutchison

Misery is rooted in ignorant craving, or the delusory, itching will to exist, to get, and to possess.

on Buddha's teaching

What distinguished the Buddha from the many sages who had attained nirvana was that he renounced the privilege of remaining in nirvana and instead elected to dedicate his life to sharing his wisdom with others. In fact, the Buddha claimed that the attainment of nirvana is only a partial experience of enlightenment. He said clinging to nonexistence, cessation, and detachment as goals meant still being caught up in the delusion of a separate self. Although a major cause of suffering may be the belief in the self's separateness, thinking of the self as totally nonexistent is also a delusion and still a cause of suffering. It is not, the Buddha said, a matter of ending everything but rather a matter of waking up completely to see things as they are.

In his teachings, the Buddha came forth with a radical

reinterpretation of the old Hindu scriptures and put matters in a far less mystical, far more psychological perspective. In fact, the story of Siddhartha Gautama's enlightenment reads a good deal like a contemporary novel of an alienated human being's struggle to save himself from being dashed to pieces on the rocks of despair.

Chuang Tzu

To pursue infinite knowledge in this finite life is indeed hopeless!

According to legend, Siddhartha was born into the highest, or Brahmin, caste of India, had every possible advantage, every luxury, the opportunity to indulge himself in every imaginable sensory delight. And indeed he did indulge himself as a young man. He met and married a beautiful, sensual woman, showered her with jewels and other magnificence, had children by her and surrounded them also with the trappings of wealth. Gradually, however, his hedonistic, materialistic life style began to grow stale. The more Siddhartha possessed, the more he wanted and the less satisfied he felt. His life was somehow empty; his spirit seemed dead. At length he communicated his misery to his wife and family and told them that he must now leave them and undertake the long quest of purification. Somewhere an answer had to found—the way to live a holy and spiritual life.

In Buddhist terminology the prince was, like everyone else, caught up in *samsara,* a Sanskrit term Buddhists use to define the general futility of a life lived for the satisfaction of momentary desires, a life guaranteed to be hollow and frustrating. He was also trapped in *karma,* another Sanskrit term taken over by the Buddhists from Hinduism. In Hinduism karma is the debts accrued over a given lifetime—the unfinished business which prevents a person from attaining purity of soul, thus necessitating yet another rebirth. In Buddhism, karma is defined as the "law of sowing and reaping"—that is, the endless round of cause and effect, of one thing leading to another, that perpetuates the confused idea of a separate self which underlies samsara.

Siddhartha spent many years wandering, questioning people, going to holy places. At one point he decided that his problem had been too much wealth, too much self-indulgence; to make up for it, he began to live as an ascetic and hermit. Some stories say that in this period of his life he lived on as little as one sesame seed each day. He grew thin, emaciated and weak, but he seemed as far away from purity of soul as he was when he was self-indulgent. He began to realize that trying to purify his 'self' reinforced his separateness just as much as his earlier attempts to gratify it.

At length he resolved to seek a *middle way* between the two extremes of total asceticism and total materialism. After restoring himself to health, he continued his wanderings, still sick at heart, still confused, still seeking a fulfillment for which he had no name.

Hee-Jin Kim

Man is still to live with his native frailty, ambiguity, and sinfulness, i.e., his karma-boundness—but no longer bound by them.

Stories of the enlightenment—of Siddhartha's elevation to the status of the Buddha—are varied, but all agree that the transformation took place underneath a tree. Supposedly the former prince—weary in body after walking for days and sick at heart because of the confusion inside him—decided to rest for a bit, selecting a large tree with enormous shade. Many reports say that it was a rose-apple tree, but it has become known ever after in Buddhist legend as the Bodhi-tree, or Tree of Enlightenment. From some accounts one can imagine the coming of a great light, or the opening of the heavens and the revelation of all truth. Here is one such account:

> *The earth swayed like a woman drunken with wine, the sky shone bright with the Siddhas who appeared in crowds in all directions, and the mighty drums of thunder resounded through the air. Pleasant breezes blew softly, rain fell from a cloudless sky, flowers and fruits dropped from the trees out of season. . . . Mandarava flowers and lotus blossoms, and also water lilies made of gold and beryl, fell from the sky on to the ground near the Shakya sage, so that it looked like a place in the world of the gods. At that moment no one anywhere was angry, ill, or sad; no one did evil, none was proud; the world became quite quiet, as though it had reached full perfection.* [3]

Other stories indicate that evil demons attempted to distract the Buddha during his long trance, to prevent the enlightenment from taking place. But in any event, it *did* happen: the prince saw that all notions of self were beside the point. He opened completely to things as they are, and discovered boundless wisdom and compassion.

By the miraculous signs in the atmosphere it became known that the Enlightened One had indeed arrived. The Bodhisattva (he who is destined through all his previous lifetimes for enlightenment) had indeed been Prince Siddhartha (whose own given name had meant "he who reaches his goal").

When at length the Buddha again rose, it was not to

remain in nirvana, but to teach his followers the Dharma, or the Way, the Path of Enlightenment.

Buddha-Dharma Updated

Buddhism broke radically with Hinduism on the crucial matter of the identity of Brahman and atman. In doing so, it established itself as a completely different philosophical road with far different implications for the individual traveling on it.

The basis of the Hindu religion is the longing of atman for reunion with Brahman—a goal that is reached only after innumerable cycles of birth and rebirth. This belief presup-

Questions and Exercises

1. Fill in the table in the introduction to this selection.

2. Make a table showing the relationship between Shiva and Brahman.

3. Identify the key words that are italicized. Then make a list of other words that you would have liked defined for you. Look up these words in a dictionary. How does a better understanding of these words clarify the selection for you?

4. Write some notes to yourself about what attracts you to (or repels you from) Buddhism.

5. Read John Hutchison's marginal quotation on p. 69: "Misery is rooted in ignorant craving, or the delusory, itching will to exist, to get, and to possess." Prepare for small group discussion by writing brief responses to the following questions: What does it mean to say that the will to exist is delusory and itching? Think of the times you have been miserable. Can you trace the root of your misery to "an ignorant craving"? What might be the consequences of denying these cravings in ourselves?

6. In small groups, discuss the role of Whitman's poem in this chapter. Does it add to your understanding of Buddhism? Why or why not? Why did the authors decide to include the poem?

7. In small groups, define what we mean in the West by "free will" and "progress." Do these concepts have any place in Buddhism? Why or why not?

8. Write a one-sentence definition of Buddhism for someone to whom you want to introduce the subject. Ask that person what else he or she would need to know to understand it. Then draft a two-page essay to define the term.

3

Reading to Understand Liberal Learning

Just as any single conversation within a community depends on many other conversations, an individual lecture or an individual textbook chapter may seem built on a thousand unheard voices, a thousand unread books. The selections that follow give you a sampling of important names and ideas in Western culture. Instructors and textbooks in all disciplines refer to these writers, all of whom articulate great ideas that collectively determine the way we think about the world.

Membership in the educated community does not expire when one dies. Since writing gives voice to an individual's ideas, there are voices that speak vigorously from all historical periods, often in language that presents special difficulties for modern readers. Plato spoke and wrote in Greek; Descartes in French, making it necessary for us to use English translations. No translation ever exactly conveys the style and content of the original. Hobbes, Wollstonecraft, Mill, and Darwin wrote originally in English but in a style and vocabulary that were more easily accessible to the people of their own day. Just as you may have to strain to hear your grandmother tell a story about her girlhood, you may need to exert special patience and energy to listen to voices from other centuries. (Figure 2 will help you to place the writers in their appropriate times in history.)

In the introduction to each selection we present historical background on the authors and also some information on how and why the writers wrote each piece. Even the great ideas of Western culture began with a human being confronting a situation and then finding an occasion and audience for expression. These selections are from monographs, that is, literary works intended to discuss at length a single topic or problem. Whereas textbooks explain and synthesize the ideas of many people, monographs present and argue a distinct point of view.

The purpose of each writer is to convince you of the truth or validity of an idea. These selections include many different points of view, each one persuasive in its own way. Hobbes, for example, may totally convince you of his concept of human nature — until you read Mill. As you read,

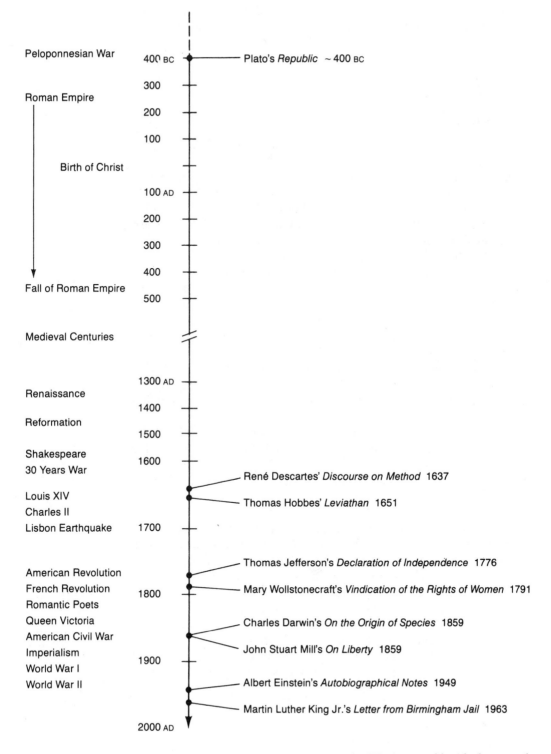

Figure 2. A time line comparing important historical events in the Western world with the year of publication of certain of the major works excerpted in this volume

try to hear clearly what is being said, but do not be shy about asking questions. Attentive, critical reading allows you to enter into conversation with great writers living and dead.

The Cave

PLATO

from *The Republic*

Plato's contribution to Western thought is immense. Indeed, Alfred North Whitehead once remarked that all of Western philosophy was nothing but a series of footnotes to Plato. Born in Athens in 428/7 B.C., his eighty-year life coincided with a turbulent period of Athenian history. Plato's aristocratic family wanted him to become a political leader, but he was disillusioned during his youth by a corrosive civil war that led to Athens' defeat and subsequent instability. Philosophy, rather than political action, became his chosen field.

The *Republic*, Plato's greatest work, is an indictment of the Athenian form of democratic government. In his view, democracy is rule by the mob, chaotic and arbitrary. Plato argues for a different way of organizing a state. His central conviction is asserted in his *Seventh Letter:* "I finally saw clearly in regard to all states now existing that without exception their government is bad . . . and that accordingly the human race will not see better days until either the stock of those who rightly and genuinely follow philosophy acquire political authority, or else the class who have political control be led by some dispensation of providence to become real philosophers."[1] In short, philosophers should rule.

Like most of Plato's works, the *Republic* is written in the form of a dialogue; as usual, Socrates, Plato's teacher, is the main character. He has been invited to dinner by some young men who ask him why they should live just lives since the unjust seem to profit from wrongdoing. Socrates answers by constructing a model of a state in which the just would prosper; that state would be ruled by philosophers — that is, people who are educated in "dialectic" method, through which they are led to see and understand "the Good." The dialectic method depends on dialogue, conversation, the respectful exchange of views. Since the young men did not study dialectic, they are unable to understand what Socrates means by "the Good." He therefore resorts to three analogies to try to explain the concept. The Allegory of the Cave, reprinted here, is the third of these parables. The person who frees himself from the cave is for Plato like the philosopher who comes to understand "the Good."

From our vantage point twenty-five hundred years later, we cannot know how Plato composed the *Republic* nor who his audience was. One

1. *Seventh Letter*, L. A. Post, trans., *Plato: The Collected Dialogues*, ed. Edith Hamilton, Huntington Cairns, Bollingen Series LXXI (N.J.: Princeton University Press, 1961).

scholar has suggested that the *Republic* was written to be read aloud at private meetings of conservative opponents of the regime then in power in Athens.[2] The immediate audience within the dialogue is Glaucon, who was, in fact, Plato's brother, but that is probably a literary device. We can, however, assume that Plato had a select, educated audience in mind. In Plato's time, centuries before the invention of the printing press, only an elite group would have access to written texts, which would be read aloud to a somewhat wider group. Plato presumably visualized his readers and auditors as members of this elite. In his *Seventh Letter* he provides some insight to his thinking: " . . . no serious man will ever think of writing about serious realities for the general public so as to make them a prey to envy and perplexity."[3] Lacking a date for the *Republic* and for the *Seventh Letter*, we cannot tell whether Plato means that he had learned from his writing of the *Republic* that a mass audience was not receptive or that the *Republic* was not intended for a popular audience. Normally we know the audience for a piece of writing and ask whether the writing is appropriate for that audience; in Plato's case we are forced to infer who the audience might have been from the writing itself. The problem has been the subject of extensive scholarly research.

Whatever Athenian audience Plato particularly addressed, we know for certain that he has spoken to serious questioners in all subsequent ages. Plato's audience includes everyone who has ever wondered about illusion and reality, about deception and truth, about superficiality and wisdom.

The Cave
PLATO

BOOK VII

— And now, I said, let me show in a figure how far our nature is enlightened or unenlightened: — Behold! human beings living in an underground den, which has a mouth open towards the light and reaching all along the den; here they have been from their childhood, and have their legs and necks chained so that they can not move, and can only see before them, being prevented by the chains from turning round their heads. Above and behind them a fire is blazing at a distance, and between the fire and the prisoners there is a raised way; and you will see, if you look, a low wall built along the way, like the screen which marionette players have in front of them, over which they show the puppets.

— I see.

2. Gilbert Ryle, *Plato's Progress* (Cambridge: University Press, 1966), pp. 49–52.
3. *Seventh Letter*, 344c.

— And do you see, I said, men passing along the wall carrying all sorts of vessels, and statues and figures of animals made of wood and stone and various materials, which appear over the wall? Some of them are talking, others silent.

— You have shown me a strange image, and they are strange prisoners.

— Like ourselves, I replied; and they see only their own shadows, or the shadows of one another, which the fire throws on the opposite wall of the cave?

— True, he said; how could they see anything but the shadows if they were never allowed to move their heads?

— And of the objects which are being carried in like manner they would only see the shadows?

— Yes, he said.

— And if they were able to converse with one another, would they not suppose that they were naming what was actually before them?

— Very true.

— And suppose further that the prison had an echo which came from the other side, would they not be sure to fancy when one of the passers-by spoke that the voice which they heard came from the passing shadow?

— No question, he replied.

— To them, I said, the truth would be literally nothing but the shadows of the images.

— That is certain.

— And now look again, and see what will naturally follow if the prisoners are released and disabused of their error. At first, when any of them is liberated and compelled suddenly to stand up and turn his neck round and walk and look towards the light, he will suffer sharp pains; the glare will distress him, and he will be unable to see the realities of which in his former state he had seen the shadows; and then conceive some one saying to him, that what he saw before was an illusion, but that now, when he is approaching nearer to being and his eye is turned towards more real existence, he has a clearer vision, — what will be his reply? And you may further imagine that his instructor is pointing to the objects as they pass and requiring him to name them, — will he not be perplexed? Will he not fancy that the shadows which he formerly saw are truer than the objects which are now shown to him?

— Far truer.

— And if he is compelled to look straight at the light, will he not have a pain in his eyes which will make him turn away to take refuge in the objects of vision which he can see, and which he will conceive to be in reality clearer than the things which are now being shown to him?

— True, he said.

— And suppose once more, that he is reluctantly dragged up a steep and rugged ascent, and held fast until he is forced into the presence of the sun himself, is he not likely to be pained and irritated? When he approaches the light his eyes will be dazzled, and he will not be able to see anything at all of what are now called realities.

— Not all in a moment, he said.

— He will require to grow accustomed to the sight of the upper world. And first he will see the shadows best, next the reflections of men and other objects in the water, and then the objects themselves; then he will gaze upon the light of the moon and the stars and the spangled heaven; and he will see the sky and the stars by night better than the sun or the light of the sun by day?

— Certainly.

— Last of all he will be able to see the sun, and not mere reflections of him in the water, but he will see him in his own proper place, and not in another; and he will contemplate him as he is.

— Certainly.

— He will then proceed to argue that this is he who gives the season and the years, and is the guardian of all that is in the visible world, and in a certain way the cause of all things which he and his fellows have been accustomed to behold?

— Clearly, he said, he would first see the sun and then reason about him.

— And when he remembered his old habitation, and the wisdom of the den and his fellow-prisoners, do you not suppose that he would felicitate himself on the change, and pity them?

— Certainly, he would.

— And if they were in the habit of conferring honors among themselves on those who were quickest to observe the passing shadows and to remark which of them went before, and which followed after, and which were together; and who were therefore best able to draw conclusions as to the future, do you think that he would care for such honors and glories, or envy the possessors of them? Would he not say with Homer,

"Better to be the poor servant of a poor master,"

and to endure anything, rather than think as they do and live after their manner?

— Yes, he said, I think that he would rather suffer anything than entertain these false notions and live in this miserable manner.

— Imagine once more, I said, such an one coming suddenly out of the sun to be replaced in his old situation; would he not be certain to have his eyes full of darkness?

— To be sure, he said.

— And if there were a contest, and he had to compete in measuring the shadows with the prisoners who had never moved out of the den, while his sight was still weak, and before his eyes had become steady (and the time which would be needed to acquire this new habit of sight might be very considerable), would he not be ridiculous? Men would say of him that up he went and down he came without his eyes; and that it was better not even to think of ascending; and if any one tried to loose another and lead him up to the light, let them only catch the offender, and they would put him to death.

— No question, he said.

— This entire allegory, I said, you may now append, dear Glaucon, to the previous argument; the prison-house is the world of sight, the light of the fire is the sun, and you will not misapprehend me if you interpret the journey upwards to be the ascent of the soul into the intellectual world according to my poor belief, which, at your desire, I have expressed — whether rightly or wrongly God knows. But, whether true or false, my opinion is that in the world of knowledge the idea of good appears last of all, and is seen only with an effort; and, when seen, is also inferred to be the universal author of all things beautiful and right, parent of light and of the lord of light in this visible world, and the immediate source of reason and truth in the intellectual; and that this is the power upon which he who would act rationally either in public or private life must have his eye fixed.

Questions and Exercises

1. Draw a diagram of the cave. List the steps taken in order to be free of the cave.

2. What do the images flickering on the wall represent? the fire in the cave? the prisoners chained down? the sun outside?

3. Suppose an avant-garde producer commissioned you to direct a film presenting Plato's allegory of the cave. Create a story board for this film. (A story board is a series of pictures, each one with a caption of a sentence or two.)

4. Draft answers to the following questions: Why should someone who leaves the cave want to return to it? If the person who leaves is supposed to stand for the philosopher, why then does Plato think a philosopher would care to rule? Why does Plato think a philosopher-ruler would not turn into a tyrant? In class, discuss these questions in small study groups.

5. If the philosopher is in contact with a world different from that of a nonphilosopher — that is, the philosopher sees things as they really are, while nonphilosophers see things as they appear to be — then is a present-day atomic physicist who sees the world in terms of atoms and subatomic particles a philosopher in Plato's sense? Draft a paper that

speculates on these questions for an audience including your classmates and instructor.

Leviathan

THOMAS HOBBES

Thomas Hobbes (1588–1679) was born in the year that England defeated the Spanish Armada. That event marked one of the few times during Hobbes's lifetime that the British nation would fight an outside enemy. British political conflict from then until after Hobbes's death would be mainly at home.

Hobbes lived through the English civil wars, the struggle to determine whether England would be governed by a despotism or a parliamentary democracy. King Charles I, who reigned from 1625 to 1649, believed in the Divine Right of Kings, and, therefore, claimed that he was appointed by God to rule England. Charles thereby reflected the attitude of European royalty, but he did not sufficiently recognize the power of English common law, those practices based on custom and on the decisions and opinions of law courts. In answer, Parliament articulated the concept of civil liberties as the basis for English society and promoted rule by common law against the King's claim that government sprang from royal will. The conflict between King and Parliament led King Charles to try to rule without a Parliament for eleven years (1629–1640). As a result, a long and complex war erupted in 1642, leading to ten years of political instability and insecurity. In 1649, Charles I was beheaded, and Parliament itself was soon dominated by the military leader, Oliver Cromwell.

During these years of conflict, Hobbes searched for a philosophy that would justify political security and order. He feared the chaos that resulted from a lack of leadership. His first published work was an English translation of Thucydides, whose history is an account of the Greek civil war that destroyed Athens. Hobbes believed that this historical account of how easily a civilized society can be dissolved might bring his fellow countrymen to their senses. His overriding concern thereafter remained the problem of political authority, that is, the nature of the bond which holds societies together and enables citizens to act together for the common good.

Hobbes wrote the *Leviathan* in 1651, in the middle of the four-year interval between the execution of King Charles I and the establishment of another stable government, the Protectorate of Oliver Cromwell. Hobbes wrote in English, not Latin (the language of scholarship and theology), because he wanted English politicians to read and understand what he had to say.

Hobbes introduced two fundamental concepts into Western thought — the state of nature and the social contract. The essence of political authority can be discovered, Hobbes thought, if one considers what life would be like if social structures were removed and humans reverted to a presocial state. Hobbes's psychological analysis was that in the state of nature people would be selfish and competitive, and everyone's life would be, in his most famous phrase, "solitary, poor, nasty, brutish, and short." No one would feel secure. The need for security and for the benefits of peace impels humans in the state of nature to erect an authority powerful enough to guarantee peace and order through a social contract. People come together in the state of nature and transfer some of the rights they possess to one person who will subsequently act on behalf of all of them. Since trust is impossible in the state of nature, it is impossible to enter into a contract, since that requires trust in the promise of another person to fulfill some commitment in the future. Contracts become possible through the authority of a sovereign, a "common power," who will enforce contracts by punishing those who fail to fulfill them.

We know only a little about how Hobbes composed the *Leviathan*, but we do know that he wrote it from some type of outline. Aubrey, his biographer, has this to say about the composition of the book:

> He said that he sometimes would set his thoughts upon researching and contemplating, always with this Rule that he very much and deeply considered one thing at a time (*scilicet*, a week or sometimes a fortnight). He walked much and contemplated, and he had in the head of his staff a pen and ink-horn, carried always a notebook in his pocket, and as soon as a notion darted, he presently entered it into his book, or else he should perhaps have lost it. He had drawn the design of the book into chapters, etc., so he knew whereabouts it would come in. Thus that book was made.[1]

The selection reprinted here is an example of deductive organization: Hobbes states his theory about the human condition if the state did not exist and then infers why people are motivated to live under a central authority. He deduces the state of nature from some basic characteristics of human beings — that they are equal and quarrelsome. He confirms his account of the state of nature by some actual behavior of human beings. In Chapter XIV, he tries to prove that if we existed in a state of nature, we would be motivated to eliminate it by setting up a "common power" to maintain order. In Chapter XVII, he describes the social contract — what rational people would do to leave the state of nature.

1. R. S. Peters, as cited in *Hobbes* (Baltimore: Penguin, 1956), p. 31.

Leviathan
THOMAS HOBBES

CHAPTER XIII

Of the Natural Condition of Mankind as Concerning Their Felicity and Misery

Nature hath made men so equal in the faculties of body and mind as that, though there be found one man sometimes manifestly stronger in body or of quicker mind than another, yet when all is reckoned together the difference between man and man is not so considerable as that one man can thereupon claim to himself any benefit to which another may not pretend as well as he. For as to the strength of body, the weakest has strength enough to kill the strongest, either by secret machination or by confederacy with others that are in the same danger with himself.

And as to the faculties of the mind, setting aside the arts grounded upon words, and especially that skill of proceeding upon general and infallible rules, called *science*, which very few have and but in few things, as being not a native faculty born with us, nor attained, as prudence, while we look after somewhat else, I find yet a greater equality amongst men than that of strength. For prudence is but experience, which equal time equally bestows on all men in those things they equally apply themselves unto. That which may perhaps make such equality incredible is but a vain conceit of one's own wisdom, which almost all men think they have in a greater degree than the vulgar; that is, than all men but themselves, and a few others, whom by fame, or for concurring with themselves, they approve. For such is the nature of men that howsoever they may acknowledge many others to be more witty, or more eloquent, or more learned, yet they will hardly believe there be many so wise as themselves; for they see their own wit at hand, and other men's at a distance. But this proveth rather that men are in that point equal, than unequal. For there is not ordinarily a greater sign of the equal distribution of anything than that every man is contented with his share.

From this equality of ability ariseth equality of hope in the attaining of our ends. And therefore if any two men desire the same thing, which nevertheless they cannot both enjoy, they become enemies; and in the way to their end (which is principally their own conservation, and sometimes their delectation only) endeavour to destroy or subdue one another. And from hence it comes to pass that where an invader hath no more to fear than another man's single power, if one plant, sow, build, or possess a convenient seat, others may probably be expected to come prepared with forces united to dispossess and deprive him, not only of the fruit of his labour, but also of his life or liberty. And the invader again is in the like danger of another.

And from this diffidence of one another, there is no way for any man to secure himself so reasonable as anticipation; that is, by force, or wiles, to master the persons of all men he can so long till he see no other power great enough to endanger him: and this is no more than his own conservation requireth, and is generally allowed. Also because there be some that, taking pleasure in contemplating their own power in the acts of conquest, which they pursue farther than their security requires, if others, that otherwise would be glad to be at ease within modest bounds, should not by invasion increase their power, they would not be able, long time, by standing only on their defence, to subsist. And by consequence, such augmentation of dominion over men being necessary to a man's conservation, it ought to be allowed him.

Again, men have no pleasure (but on the contrary a great deal of grief) in keeping company where there is no power able to overawe them all. For every man looketh that his companion should value him at the same rate he sets upon himself, and upon all signs of contempt or undervaluing naturally endeavours, as far as he dares (which amongst them that have no common power to keep them in quiet is far enough to make them destroy each other), to extort a greater value from his contemners, by damage; and from others, by the example.

So that in the nature of man, we find three principal causes of quarrel. First, competition; secondly, diffidence; thirdly, glory.

The first maketh men invade for gain; the second, for safety; and the third, for reputation. The first use violence, to make themselves masters of other men's persons, wives, children, and cattle; the second, to defend them; the third, for trifles, as a word, a smile, a different opinion, and any other sign of undervalue, either direct in their persons or by reflection in their kindred, their friends, their nation, their profession, or their name.

Hereby it is manifest that during the time men live without a common power to keep them all in awe, they are in that condition which is called *war*; and such a war as is of every man against every man. For war consisteth not in battle only, or the act of fighting, but in a tract of time, wherein the will to contend by battle is sufficiently known: and therefore the notion of *time* is to be considered in the nature of war, as it is in the nature of weather. For as the nature of foul weather lieth not in a shower or two of rain, but in an inclination thereto of many days together: so the nature of war consisteth not in actual fighting, but in the known disposition thereto during all the time there is no assurance to the contrary. All other time is *peace*.

Whatsoever therefore is consequent to a time of war, where every man is enemy to every man, the same is consequent to the time wherein men live without other security than what their own strength and their own invention shall furnish them withal. In such condition there is no place for industry, because the fruit thereof is uncertain: and consequently no culture of the earth; no navigation, nor use of the commodities that may be imported by sea; no commodious building; no instruments of moving and removing such things as require much force; no knowledge of the face of the earth; no account of time; no arts; no letters; no society; and which is worst of all, continual fear, and danger of violent death; and the life of man, solitary, poor, nasty, brutish, and short.

It may seem strange to some man that has not well weighed these things that Nature should thus dissociate and render men apt to invade and destroy one another: and he may therefore, not trusting to this inference, made from the passions, desire perhaps to have the same confirmed by experience. Let him therefore consider with himself: when taking a journey, he arms himself and seeks to go well accompanied; when going to sleep, he locks his doors; when even in his house he locks his chests; and this when he knows there be laws and public officers, armed, to revenge all injuries shall be done him; what opinion he has of his fellow subjects, when he rides armed; of his fellow citizens, when he locks his doors; and of his children, and servants, when he locks his chests. Does he not there as much accuse mankind by his actions as I do by my words? But neither of us accuse man's nature in it. The desires, and other passions of man, are in themselves no sin. No more are the actions that proceed from those passions till they know a law that forbids them; which till laws be made they cannot know, nor can any law be made till they have agreed upon the person that shall make it.

It may peradventure be thought there was never such a time nor condition of war as this; and I believe it was never generally so, over all the world: but there are many places where they live so now. For the savage people in many places of America, except the government of small families, the concord whereof dependeth on natural lust, have no government at all, and live at this day in that brutish manner, as I said before. Howsoever, it may be perceived what manner of life there would be, where there were no common power to fear, by the manner of life which men that have formerly lived under a peaceful government use to degenerate into a civil war.

But though there had never been any time wherein particular men were in a condition of war one against another, yet in all times kings and persons of sovereign authority, because of their independency, are in continual jealousies, and in the state and posture of gladiators, having their weapons pointing, and their eyes fixed on one another; that is, their forts, garrisons, and guns upon the frontiers of their kingdoms, and continual spies upon their neighbours, which is a posture of war. But because they uphold thereby the industry of their subjects, there does not follow from it that misery which accompanies the liberty of particular men.

To this war of every man against every man, this also is consequent; that nothing can be unjust. The notions of right and wrong, justice and injustice, have there no place. Where there is no common power, there is no law; where no law, no injustice. Force and fraud are in war the two cardinal virtues. Justice and injustice are none of the faculties neither of the body nor mind. If they were, they might be in a man that were alone in the world, as well as his senses and passions. They are qualities that relate to men in society, not in solitude. It is consequent also to the same condition that there be no propriety, no dominion, no *mine* and *thine* distinct; but only that to be every man's that he can get, and for so long as he can keep it. And thus much for the ill condition which man by mere nature is actually placed in; though with a possibility to come out of it, consisting partly in the passions, partly in his reason.

The passions that incline men to peace are: fear of death; desire of such things as are necessary to commodious living; and a hope by their industry to obtain them. And reason suggesteth convenient articles of peace upon which men may be drawn to agreement. These articles are they which otherwise are called the *laws of nature*, whereof I shall speak more particularly in the two following chapters.

CHAPTER XIV

Of the First and Second Natural Laws, and of Contracts

The *right of nature*, which writers commonly call *jus naturale*, is the liberty each man hath to use his own power as he will himself for the preservation of his own nature; that is to say, of his own life; and consequently, of doing anything which, in his own judgement and reason, he shall conceive to be the aptest means thereunto. . . .

A *law of nature, lex naturalis*, is a precept, or general rule, found out by reason, by which a man is forbidden to do that which is destructive of his life, or taketh away the means of preserving the same, and to omit that by which he thinketh it may be best preserved. . . .

And because the condition of man . . . is a condition of war of every one against every one, in which case every one is governed by his own reason, and there is nothing he can make use of that may not be a help unto him in preserving his life against his enemies; it followeth that in such a condition every man has a right to every thing, even to one another's body. And therefore, as long as this natural right of every man to every thing endureth, there can be no security to any man, how strong or wise soever he be, of living out the time which nature ordinarily alloweth men to live. And consequently it is a precept, or general rule of reason: *that* every man ought to endeavour peace, as far as he has hope of obtaining it; and when he cannot obtain it, that he may seek and use all helps and advantages of war. The first branch of which rule containeth the first and fundamental law of nature, which is: *to seek peace and follow it.* The second, the sum of the right of nature, which is: *by all means we can to defend ourselves.*

From this fundamental law of nature, by which men are commanded to endeavour peace, is derived this second law: *that a man be willing, when others are so too, as far forth as for peace and defence of himself he shall think it necessary, to lay down this right to all things; and be contented with so much liberty against other men as he would allow other men against himself.* For as long as every man holdeth this right, of doing anything he liketh; so long are all men in the condition of war. But if other men will not lay down their right, as well as he, then there is no reason for anyone to divest himself of his: for that were to expose himself to prey, which no man is bound to, rather than to dispose himself to peace. This is that law of the gospel: *Whatsoever you require that others should do to you, that do ye to them.* . . .

Right is laid aside, either by simply renouncing it, or by transferring it to another. By simply *renouncing,* when he cares not to whom the benefit thereof redoundeth. By *transferring,* when he intendeth the benefit thereof to some certain person or persons. And when a man hath in either manner abandoned or granted away his right, then is he said to be *obliged,* or *bound,* not to hinder those to whom such right is granted, or abandoned, from the benefit of it: and that he *ought,* and it is his *duty,* not to make void that voluntary act of his own: and that such hindrance is *injustice,* and *injury.* . . .

The mutual transferring of right is that which men call *contract.* . . .

If a covenant be made wherein neither of the parties perform presently, but trust one another, in the condition of mere nature (which is a condition of war of every man against every man) upon any reasonable suspicion, it is void: but if there be a common power set over them both, with right and force sufficient to compel performance, it is not void. For he that performeth first has no assurance the other will perform after, because the bounds of words are too weak to bridle men's ambition, avarice, anger, and other passions, without the fear of some coercive power; which in the condition of mere nature, where all men are equal, and judges of the justness of their own fears, cannot possibly be supposed. And therefore he which performeth first does but betray himself to his enemy, contrary to the right he can never abandon of defending his life and means of living.

But in a civil estate, where there is a power set up to constrain those that would otherwise violate their faith, that fear is no more reasonable; and for that cause, he which by the covenant is to perform first is obliged so to do.

CHAPTER XVII

Of the Causes, Generation, and Definition of a Commonwealth

... The only way to erect such a common power, as may be able to defend them from the invasion of foreigners, and the injuries of one another, and thereby to secure them in such sort as that by their own industry and by the fruits of the earth they may nourish themselves and live contentedly, is to confer all their power and strength upon one man, or upon one assembly of men, that may reduce all their wills, by plurality of voices, unto one will: which is as much as to say, to appoint one man, or assembly of men, to bear their person; and every one to own and acknowledge himself to be author of whatsoever he that so beareth their person shall act, or cause to be acted, in those things which concern the common peace and safety; and therein to submit their wills, every one to his will, and their judgements to his judgement. This is more than consent, or concord; it is a real unity of them all in one and the same person, made by covenant of every man with every man, in such manner as if every man should say to every man: *I authorise and give up my right of governing myself to this man, or to this assembly of men, on this condition; that thou give up thy right to him, and authorise all his actions in like manner.* This done, the multitude so united in one person is called a COMMONWEALTH; in Latin, CIVITAS. This is the generation of that great LEVIATHAN, or rather, to speak more reverently, of that mortal god to which we owe, under the immortal God, our peace and defence. For by this authority, given him by every particular man in the Commonwealth, he hath the use of so much power and strength conferred on him that, by terror thereof, he is enabled to form the wills of them all, to peace at home, and mutual aid against their enemies abroad. And in him consisteth the essence of the Commonwealth; which, to define it, is: *one person, of whose acts a great multitude, by mutual covenants one with another, have made themselves every one the author, to the end he may use the strength and means of them all as he shall think expedient, for their peace and common defence.*

And he that carrieth this person is called SOVEREIGN, and said to have *sovereign power*; and every one besides, his SUBJECT. ...

Questions and Exercises

1. Hobbes gives three reasons why people in the state of nature would fight with one another, the third being the desire for glory. What are the first two?

2. What three facts does Hobbes appeal to in confirming his account of the state of nature?

3. How does Hobbes define: war, right of nature, law of nature, contract, sovereign?

4. Hobbes's defense of state authority depends on its advantages over its absence in the state of nature. Draw up two lists, one headed "State of Nature" and the other headed, "State." Under "State of Nature" enter a list of characteristics Hobbes attributes to it. Then under "State" enter the opposite characteristic, for example:

State of Nature	State
brutish	humane
insecure	safe
no private property	private property

Select five items from the "State of Nature" list and write a paragraph using all five words. Do the same for the "State" list.

5. Reread the selection to find words and phrases that serve as pointers to the logical structure of Hobbes's argument. (Note, for example, Hobbes's tendency to present three reasons or three characteristics.) After you have made some notes on Hobbes's organization, meet in small groups to compare what you have recorded. As a group, formulate an outline showing the logical structure of the selection.

6. In what sense would people in the state of nature be equal? Hobbes admits that they are not all equal in physical strength or in intelligence. In what ways are they all equal in Hobbes's view?

7. a) Does Hobbes believe that the state of nature existed as a historical reality and that states were historically created by a social contract?
b) If Hobbes does not claim that the state of nature is historical, then his writing is an example of speculative writing, addressing the question, "what would happen if . . . ?" In Hobbes's view, how would we behave if there were no central authority? Draft a paper explaining why Hobbes's speculation is different from fiction. Assume that your readers are your classmates.

8. The selection printed here comes from a book that Hobbes called the *Leviathan*. Look up the word "leviathan" in a dictionary and identify its primary and secondary meanings. Then, speculate on what Hobbes might have had in mind by this title. Draft a paper on this subject. Assume that your readers are classmates who have read the anthologized selection but not the whole work.

The Search for Certainty

RENÉ DESCARTES

from *Discourse on Method*

If Plato is considered the father of all Western philosophy, then René Descartes (1596–1650) deserves to be considered the father of modern philosophy. His writing, much of which is devoted to explaining the scientific method, represents the main turning point between medieval and modern thought and was instrumental in creating the age of science.

The selection that follows is taken from Decartes's *Discourse on Method,* his first published work. Its historical significance is that it advocated the independence of science at a time when science was seen as a dangerous challenger to the established authority, religion. He had not intended the *Discourse* to be his first work, but he withdrew his original writing, entitled *The World,* in 1632, when he learned that Galileo Galilei, a Florentine astronomer, had been condemned by the Church for advocating opinions that were similar to those Descartes himself was about to set forth.

After decades of careful observations with a then-recent invention, the telescope, Galileo reported evidence to confirm the theory of Copernicus (1473–1543) that the earth orbited around the sun, which was in opposition to the Church's teaching that the earth was the center of the universe. In the seventeenth century, the Roman Catholic Church had the authority throughout much of Europe to enforce its interpretations of the nature of the universe. Human observations, even systematic efforts aided by advanced equipment like the telescope, were considered inaccurate and deluded when compared with the eye of God, as interpreted by the hierarchy of the Church. Galileo was brought to trial in Rome, forced to recant his views, and made to promise that he would never again publish opinions which the Church thought erroneous.

Descartes understood the message. In the *Discourse* he puts forth ideas about human capacities for seeking the truth, but he does so more obliquely. Descartes had a clear, sometimes terrifying image of his potential readers, and worked to express his revolutionary doctrine without incurring retaliation from the authorities. Intellectual freedom was literally a matter of life and death for writers in the seventeenth century.

We have a good record of the way the *Discourse* was composed, since Descartes wrote many letters to his friend, Mersenne, who continually encouraged the project. In one letter Descartes wrote:

> My work on it is going very slowly, because I take much more
> pleasure in acquiring knowledge than in putting into writing the little
> that I know. . . . Altogether, I pass the time so contentedly in the
> acquisition of knowledge that I never settle down to write any of my
> treatise except under duress, in order to carry out my resolution,

which is, if I am still living, to have it ready for posting to you by the beginning of the year 1633. I am telling you a definite time so as to put myself under a greater obligation, so that you can reproach me if I fail to keep to the date.[1]

Descartes enjoyed reading and writing for himself. He found writing for others difficult because he was acutely aware of the demands of an audience. In the *Discourse* he writes that, whereas eloquence and poetry are "gifts of nature," "those who reason most cogently and work over their thoughts to make them clear and intelligible, are always the most persuasive." He certainly succeeded, for his writing has become the model of clarity in French. Still, he did not write swiftly. The manuscript which he promised Mersenne at the beginning of 1633 was not delivered until 1637.

Like Thomas Hobbes, Descartes decided not to write in Latin. Descartes wrote in French for an influential lay audience. He went over the heads of the theologians in the hope of reaching the political powers. He distributed just two hundred copies of the work, sending them to, among others, King Louis XIII and Cardinal Richelieu. Because this printing was so limited, it can be assumed that Descartes thought seriously about the specific characteristics of his readers.

The "method" that Descartes is concerned with is a method for discovering what is true. His ultimate purpose is to seek certainty in what he believes, that is, to believe only what is certainly true. To do this, he proposes to go back to the very foundation of knowledge and build only upon what he knows to be true, leaving aside all those opinions picked up from others. He hopes to achieve certainty by applying four rules for thinking. In setting up these rules, he dismisses others' opinions as well as evidence that comes to us through our senses, relying on philosophy as the only way to understand truth. He wants to build a system of knowledge that is like the system of geometry, and to discover a few simple axioms from which many theorems could be derived with certainty.

In Part Four of the *Discourse* he asserts that one belief alone is immune to all doubt and provides the secure foundation for building an understanding of truth. His belief is: "I think, therefore I am." Nobody, he said, could doubt his own existence and be correct. To think that you exist implies that you exist, but the you that exists is not your body because knowledge of your body comes only from sense perception. Descartes does not doubt that he has a body, but he believes that the body is not the first dimension of the self that one can know exists. He reasons toward the existence of the body as he reasons to the existence of all truthful things, by using his method.

1. Descartes, *Philosophical Letters*, translated and edited by Anthony Kenny (Oxford: Clarendon Press, 1970), p. 9.

Descartes raises questions that philosophers are still debating: How can we know anything? Is sense perception reliable at all? Descartes understands in his own way that we all live in Plato's cave and that only those who think about the shadows and the light can live an examined life.

The Search for Certainty
RENÉ DESCARTES

PART ONE

Some Thoughts on the Sciences

Good sense is mankind's most equitably divided endowment, for everyone thinks that he is so abundantly provided with it that even those most difficult to please in other ways do not usually want more than they have of this. As it is not likely that everyone is mistaken, this evidence shows that the ability to judge correctly, and to distinguish the true from the false — which is really what is meant by good sense or reason — is the same by nature in all men; and that differences of opinion are not due to differences in intelligence, but merely to the fact that we use different approaches and consider different things. For it is not enough to have a good mind: one must use it well. The greatest souls are capable of the greatest vices as well as of the greatest virtues; and those who walk slowly can, if they follow the right path, go much farther than those who run rapidly in the wrong direction.

As for myself, I have never supposed that my mind was above the ordinary. On the contrary, I have often wished to have as quick a wit or as clear and distinct an imagination, or as ready and retentive a memory, as another person. And I know of no other qualities which make for a good mind, because as far as reason is concerned, it is the only thing which makes us men and distinguishes us from the animals, and I am therefore satisfied that it is fully present in each one of us. In this I follow the general opinion of philosophers, who say that there are differences in degree only in the *accidental* qualities, and not in the *essential* qualities or natures of individuals of the same species.

But I do not hesitate to claim the good fortune of having stumbled, in my youth, upon certain paths which led me to certain considerations and maxims from which I formed a method of gradually increasing my knowledge and of improving my abilities as much as the mediocrity of my talents and the shortness of my life will permit. For I have already had such results that although in self-judgment I try to lean rather toward undervaluation than to presumption, I cannot escape a feeling of extreme satisfaction with

Excerpts from *The Discourse on Method*, pp. 1–21, Rene Descartes, translated by Laurence J. LaFleur. Bobbs-Merrill Company, Inc. (The Library of Liberal Arts) Reprinted by permission of the publisher.

the progress I believe I have already made in the search for truth. And although from the philosophers' viewpoint almost all the activities of men appear to me as vain and useless, yet I conceive such hopes for the future that if some single one of the occupations of men, as men, should be truly good and important, I dare to believe that it is the one I have chosen.

It is always possible that I am wrong, and that I am mistaking a bit of copper and glass for gold and diamonds. I know how subject we are to making false judgments in things that concern ourselves, and how much we ought to mistrust the judgments of our friends when they are in our own favor. But I should be glad to show in this *Discourse* what are the paths I have taken, and to present a sketch of my life, so that each one can form his own judgment of it. In this way I may learn from the opinions of those who read it, and thus add another to the methods of progress which I am accustomed to use.

So it is not my intention to present a method which everyone ought to follow in order to think well, but only to show how I have made the attempt myself. Those who counsel others must consider themselves superior to those whom they counsel, and if they fall short in the least detail they are to blame. I only propose this writing as an autobiography, or, if you prefer, as a story in which you may possibly find some examples of conduct which you might see fit to imitate, as well as several others which you would have no reason to follow. I hope that it will prove useful to some without being harmful to any, and that all will take my frankness kindly.

From my childhood I lived in a world of books, and since I was taught that by their help I could gain a clear and assured knowledge of everything useful in life, I was eager to learn from them. But as soon as I had finished the course of studies which usually admits one to the ranks of the learned, I changed my opinion completely. For I found myself saddled with so many doubts and errors that I seemed to have gained nothing in trying to educate myself unless it was to discover more and more fully how ignorant I was.

Nevertheless I had been in one of the most celebrated schools in Europe, where I thought there should be wise men if wise men existed anywhere on earth. I had learned there everything that others learned, and, not satisfied with merely the knowledge that was taught, I had perused as many books as I could find which contained more unusual and recondite knowledge. I also knew the opinions of others about myself, and that I was in no way judged inferior to my fellow students, even though several of them were preparing to become professors. And finally, it did not seem to me that our own times were less flourishing and fertile than were any of the earlier periods. All this led me to conclude that I could judge others by myself, and to decide that there was no such wisdom in the world as I had previously hoped to find.

I did not, however, cease to value the disciplines of the schools. I knew that the languages which one learns there are necessary to understand the works of the ancients; and that the delicacy of fiction enlivens the mind; that famous deeds of history ennoble it and, if read with understanding, aid in maturing one's judgment; that the reading of all the great books is like conversing with the best people of earlier times: it is even a studied conversation in which the authors show us only the best of their thoughts; that eloquence has incomparable powers and beauties; that poetry has enchanting delicacy and sweetness; that mathematics has very subtle processes which can serve as much to satisfy the inquiring mind as to aid all the arts and to diminish man's labor; that treatises on morals contain very useful teachings and exhortations to virtue; that theology teaches us how to go to heaven; that philosophy teaches us to talk with an appearance of truth about all things, and to make ourselves admired by the less learned; that law, medicine, and the other sciences bring honors and wealth to those who pursue them; and finally, that it is desirable to have examined all of them, even to the most superstitious and false, in order to recognize their real worth and avoid being deceived thereby.

But I thought that I had already spent enough time on languages, and even on reading the works of the ancients, and their histories and fiction. For conversing with the ancients is much like traveling. It is good to know something of the customs of various peoples, in order to judge our own more objectively, and so that we do not make the mistake of the untraveled in supposing that everything contrary to our customs is ridiculous and irrational. But when one spends too much time traveling, one becomes at last a stranger at home; and those who are too interested in things which occurred in past centuries are often remarkably ignorant of what is going on today. In addition, fiction makes us imagine a number of events as possible which are really impossible, and even the most faithful histories, if they do not alter or embroider episodes to make them more worth reading, almost always omit the meanest and least illustrious circumstances so that the remainder is distorted. Thus it happens that those who regulate their behavior by the examples they find in books are apt to fall into the extravagances of the knights of romances, and undertake projects which it is beyond their ability to complete.

I esteemed eloquence highly, and loved poetry, but I felt that both were gifts of nature rather than fruits of study. Those who reason most cogently, and work over their thoughts to make them clear and intelligible, are always the most persuasive, even if they speak only a provincial dialect and have never studied rhetoric. Those who have the most agreeable imaginations and can express their thoughts with the most grace and color cannot fail to be the best poets, even if the poetic art is unknown to them.

I was especially pleased with mathematics, because of the certainty and self-evidence of its proofs; but I did not yet see its true usefulness and, thinking that it was good only for the mechanical arts, I was astonished that nothing more noble had been built on so firm and solid a foundation. On the other hand, I compared the ethical writings of the ancient pagans to very superb and magnificent palaces built only on mud and sand: they laud the virtues and make them appear more desirable than anything else in the world; but they give no adequate criterion of virtue, and often what they call by such a name is nothing but apathy, parricide, pride or despair.

I revered our theology, and hoped as much as anyone else to get to heaven, but having learned on great authority that the road was just as open to the most ignorant as to the most learned, and that the truths of revelation which lead thereto are beyond our understanding, I would not have dared to submit them to the weakness of my reasonings. I thought that to succeed in their examination it would be necessary to have some extraordinary assistance from heaven, and to be more than a man.

I will say nothing of philosophy except that it has been studied for many centuries by the most outstanding minds without having produced anything which is not in dispute and consequently doubtful. I did not have enough presumption to hope to succeed better than the others; and when I noticed how many different opinions learned men may hold on the same subject, despite the fact that no more than one of them can ever be right, I resolved to consider almost as false any opinion which was merely plausible.

Finally, when it came to the other branches of learning, since they took their cardinal principles from philosophy, I judged that nothing solid could have been built on so insecure a foundation. Neither the honor nor the profit to be gained thereby sufficed to make me study them, for I was fortunately not in such a financial condition as to make it necessary to trade upon my learning; and though I was not enough of a cynic to despise fame, I was little concerned with that which I could only obtain on false pretenses. And finally, I thought I knew enough of the disreputable doctrines not to be taken in by the promises of an alchemist, the predictions of an astrologer, the impostures of a magician, or by the tricks and boasts of any of those who profess to know that which they do not know.

This is why I gave up my studies entirely as soon as I reached the age when I was no longer under the control of my teachers. I resolved to seek no other knowledge than that which I might find within myself, or perhaps in the great book of nature. I spent a few years of my adolescence traveling, seeing courts and armies, living with people of diverse types and stations of life, acquiring varied experience, testing myself in the episodes which fortune sent me, and, above all, thinking about the things around me so that I could derive some profit from them. For it seemed to me that I might find much more of the truth in the cogitations which each man made on things which were important to him, and where he would be the loser if he judged badly, than in the cogitations of a man of letters in his study, concerned with speculations which produce no effect, and which have no consequences to him except perhaps that the farther they are removed from common sense, the more they titillate his vanity, since then he needs so much more wit and skill to make them seem plausible. Besides, I was always eager to learn to distinguish truth from falsehood, so that I could make intelligent decisions about the affairs of this life.

It is true that while I did nothing but observe the customs of other men, I found nothing there to satisfy me, and I noted just about as much difference of opinion as I had previously remarked among philosophers. The greatest profit to me was, therefore, that I became acquainted with customs generally approved and accepted by other great peoples that would appear extravagant and ridiculous among ourselves, and so I learned not to believe too firmly what I learned only from example and custom. Also I gradually freed myself from many errors which could obscure the light of nature and make us less capable of correct reasoning. But after spending several years in thus studying the book of nature and acquiring experience, I eventually reached the decision to study my own self, and to employ all my abilities to try to choose the right path. This produced much better results in my case, I think, than would have been produced if I had never left my books and my country.

PART TWO

The Principal Rules of the Method

I was then in Germany, where I had gone because of the wars which are still not ended; and while I was returning to the army from the coronation of the Emperor, I was caught by the onset of winter. There was no conversation to occupy me, and being untroubled by any cares or passions, I remained all day alone in a warm room. There I had plenty of leisure to examine my ideas. One of the first that occurred to me was that frequently there is less perfection in a work produced by several persons than in one produced by a single hand. Thus we notice that buildings conceived and completed by a single architect are usually more beautiful and better planned than those remodeled by several persons using ancient walls that had originally been built for quite other purposes. Similarly, those ancient towns which were originally nothing but hamlets, and in the course of time have become great cities, are ordinarily very badly arranged compared to one of the symmetrical metropolitan districts which a city planner has laid out on an open plain according to his own designs. It is true that when we consider their buildings one by one, there is often as much beauty in the first city as in the second, or even more; nevertheless, when we observe how they are arranged, here a large unit, there a small; and how the streets are crooked and uneven, one would rather suppose that chance and not the decisions of rational men had so arranged them. . . .

It is true that we never tear down all the houses in a city just to rebuild them in a different way and to make the streets more beautiful; but we do see that individual owners often have theirs torn down and rebuilt, and even that they may be forced to do so when the foundation is not firm and it is in danger of collapsing. By this example I was convinced that a private individual should not seek to reform a nation by changing all its customs and destroying it to construct it anew, nor to reform the body of knowledge or the system of education. Nevertheless, as far as the opinions which I had been receiving since my birth were concerned, I could not do better than to reject them completely for once in my lifetime, and to resume them afterwards, or perhaps accept better ones in their place, when I had determined how they fitted into a rational scheme. And I firmly believed that by this means I would succeed in conducting my life much better than if I built only upon the old foundations and gave credence to the principles which I had acquired in my childhood without ever having examined them to see whether they were true or not. . . .

Nevertheless, like a man who walks alone in the darkness, I resolved to go so slowly and circumspectly that if I did not get ahead very rapidly I was at least safe from falling. Also, I did not want to reject all the opinions which had slipped irrationally into my consciousness since birth, until I had first spent enough time planning how to accomplish the task which I was then undertaking, and seeking the true method of obtaining knowledge of everything which my mind was capable of understanding. . . .

. . . [J]ust as the multitude of laws frequently furnishes an excuse for vice, and a state is much better governed with a few laws which are strictly adhered to, so I thought that instead of the great number of precepts of which logic is composed, I would have enough with the four following ones, provided that I made a firm and unalterable resolution not to violate them even in a single instance.

The first rule was never to accept anything as true unless I recognized it to be evidently such: that is, carefully to avoid precipitation and prejudgment, and to include nothing in my conclusions unless it presented itself so clearly and distinctly to my mind that there was no occasion to doubt it.

The second was to divide each of the difficulties which I encountered into as many parts as possible, and as might be required for an easier solution.

The third was to think in an orderly fashion, beginning with the things which were simplest and easiest to understand, and gradually and by degrees reaching toward more complex knowledge, even treating as though ordered materials which were not necessarily so.

The last was always to make enumerations so complete, and reviews so general, that I would be certain that nothing was omitted.

Those long chains of reasoning, so simple and easy, which enabled the geometricians to reach the most difficult demonstrations, had made me wonder whether all things knowable to men might not fall into a similar logical sequence. If so, we need only refrain from accepting as true that which is not true, and carefully follow the order necessary to deduce each one from the others, and there cannot be any propositions so abstruse that we cannot prove them, or so recondite that we cannot discover them. It was not very difficult, either, to decide where we should look for a beginning, for I knew already that one begins with the simplest and easiest to know. Considering that among all those who have previously sought truth in the sciences, mathematicians alone have been able to find some demonstrations, some certain and evident reasons, I had no doubt that I should begin where they did, although I expected no advantage except to accustom my mind to work with truths and not to be satisfied with bad reasoning. I do not mean that I intended to learn all the particular branches of mathematics; for I saw that although the objects they discuss are different, all these branches are in agreement in limiting their consideration to the relationships or proportions between their various objects. I judged therefore that it would be better to examine these proportions in general, and use particular objects as illustrations only in order to make their principles easier to comprehend, and to be able the more easily to apply them afterwards, without any forcing, to anything for which they would be suitable. I realized that in order to understand the principles of relationships I would sometimes have to consider them singly, and sometimes in groups. I thought I could consider them better singly as relationships between lines, because I could find nothing more simple or more easily pictured to my imagination and my senses. But in order to remember and understand them better when taken in groups, I had to express them in numbers, and in the smallest numbers possible. Thus I took the best traits of geometrical analysis and algebra, and corrected the faults of one by the other.

The exact observation of the few precepts which I had chosen gave me such facility in clarifying all the issues in these two sciences that it took only two or three months to examine them. I began with the most simple and general, and each truth that I found was a rule which helped me to find others, so that I not only solved many problems which I had previously judged very difficult, but also it seemed to me that toward the end I could determine to what extent a still-unsolved problem could be solved, and what procedures should be used in solving it. In this I trust that I shall not appear too vain, considering that there is only one true solution to a given problem, and whoever finds it knows all that anyone can know about it. Thus, for example, a child who has learned arithmetic and had performed an addition according to the rules may feel certain that as far as that particular sum is concerned, he has found everything that a human mind can discover. For, after all, the method of following the correct order and stating precisely all the circumstances of what we are investigating is the whole of what gives certainty to the rules of arithmetic.

What pleased me most about this method was that it enabled me to reason in all things, if not perfectly, at least as well as was in my power. In addition, I felt that in practicing it my mind was gradually becoming accustomed to conceive its objects more clearly and distinctly, and since I had not directed this method to any particular subject matter, I was in hopes of applying it just as usefully to the difficulties of other sciences as I had already to those of algebra. Not that I would dare to undertake to examine at once all the difficulties that presented themselves, for that would have been contrary to the principle of order. But I had observed that all the basic principles of the sciences were taken from philosophy, which itself had no certain ones. It therefore seemed that I should first attempt to establish philosophic principles, and that since this was the most important thing in the world and the place where precipitation and prejudgment were most to be feared, I should not attempt to reach conclusions until I had attained a much more mature age than my then twenty-three years, and had spent much time in preparing for it. This preparation would consist partly in freeing my mind from the false opinions which I had previously acquired, partly in building up a fund of experiences which should serve afterwards as the raw material of my reasoning, and partly in training myself in the method which I had determined upon, so that I should become more and more adept in its use.

PART THREE

Some Moral Rules Derived from the Method

In planning to rebuild one's house it is not enough to draw up the plans for the new dwelling, tear down the old one, and provide materials and obtain workmen for the task. We must see that we are provided with a comfortable place to stay while the work of rebuilding is going on. Similarly in my own case; while reason obliged me to be irresolute in my beliefs, there was no reason why I should be so in my actions. In order to live as happily as possible during the interval I prepared a provisional code of morality for myself, consisting of three or four maxims which I here set forth.

The first was to obey the laws and customs of my country, constantly retaining the religion in which, by God's grace, I had been brought up since childhood, and in all other matters to follow the most moderate and least excessive opinions to be found in the practices of the more judicious part of the community in which I would live. For I was then about to discard my own opinions in order to re-examine them, and meanwhile could do no better than to follow those of the most reliable judges. While there may be, no doubt, just as reliable persons among the Persians or the Chinese as among ourselves, it seemed more practical to pattern my conduct on that of the society in which I would have to live. Furthermore, it seemed to me that to learn people's true opinions, I should pay attention to their conduct rather than to their words, not only because in our corrupt times there are few who are ready to say all that they believe, but also because many are not aware of their own beliefs, since the mental process of knowing a thing is distinct from, and can occur without, the mental process of knowing that we know it. Among a number of opinions equally widely accepted, I chose only the most moderate, partly because these are always the most convenient in practice and, since excess is usually bad, presumably the best; but also so that I should stray a shorter distance from the true road in case I should make a mistake, than I would in choosing one extreme when it was the other that should have been followed. . . .

My second maxim was to be as firm and determined in my actions as I could be, and not to act on the most doubtful decisions, once I had made them, any less resolutely than on the most certain. In this matter I patterned my behavior on that of travelers, who, finding themselves lost in a forest, must not wander about, now turning this way, now that, and still less should remain in one place, but should go as straight as they can in the direction they first select and not change the direction except for the strongest reasons. By this method, even if the direction was chosen at random, they will presumably arrive at some destination, not perhaps where they would like to be, but at least where they will be better off than in the middle of the forest. Similarly, situations in life often permit no delay; and when we cannot determine the course which is certainly best, we must follow the one which is probably the best; and when we cannot determine even that, we must nevertheless select one and follow it thereafter as though it were certainly best. If the course selected is not indeed a good one, at least the reasons for selecting it are excellent. This frame of mind freed me also from the repentance and remorse commonly felt by those vacillating individuals who are always seeking as worth while things which they later judge to be bad.

My third maxim was always to seek to conquer myself rather than fortune, to change my desires rather than the established order, and generally to believe that nothing except our thoughts is wholly under our control, so that after we have done our best in external matters, what remains to be done is absolutely impossible, at least as far as we are concerned. This maxim in itself should suffice to prevent me from desiring in the future anything which I could not acquire, and thus to make me happy. For it is our nature to desire only that which we imagine to be somehow attainable, and if we consider all external benefits equally beyond our reach we will no more regret being unjustly deprived of our birthright than we regret not possessing the kingdoms of China or Mexico. Thus, making a virtue of necessity, we no more desire to be well when we are sick, or to be free when we are in prison, than we now desire bodies as incorruptible as diamonds, or wings to fly like the birds. But I must admit that it takes much practice and frequently repeated meditations to become accustomed to view things in this manner, and I think that this must have been the principal secret of those philosophers of ancient times who were able to rise above fortune, and, despite pains and poverty, to vie with the gods in happiness. Being constantly occupied in considering the limits imposed upon them by nature, they were so perfectly convinced that nothing was really theirs but their thoughts that that alone was sufficient to keep them from any concern in other things. Their control of their thoughts, on the other hand, was so absolute that they had some justification for considering themselves richer and more powerful, more free and happier, than any other man who did not have this philosophy, and who, however much he might be favored by nature and fortune, had no such control over his desires.

Finally, I planned to make a review of the various occupations possible in this life, in order to choose the best. Without intending to disparage other occupations, I thought I could do no better than to continue in the one I was engaged in, employing my life in improving my mind and increasing as far as I could my knowledge of the truth by following the method that I had outlined for myself. I had experienced such periods of great happiness after I had begun to use this method, that I could hope for no greater or more innocent joys in this life. In discovering day after day truths which seemed fairly important and generally unknown to other men, I was filled with such satisfaction that other considerations did not affect me. . . .

After thus assuring myself of these maxims, and having put them aside with the truths of the Faith, which have always been most certain to me, I judged that I could proceed freely to reject all my other beliefs. And inasmuch as I hoped to obtain my end more readily by conversing with men than by remaining any longer in my warm retreat, where I had had all these thoughts, I proceeded on my way before winter was wholly passed. In the nine years that followed I wandered here and there throughout the world, trying everywhere to be spectator rather than actor in all the comedies that go on. I took particular pains in judging each thing to seek out whatever elements of uncertainty it contained, which might cause us to conceive false opinions about it. Meanwhile I tried to clear my mind of all the errors that had previously accumulated. In this I did not wish to imitate the sceptics, who doubted only for the sake of doubting and intended to remain always irresolute; on the contrary, my whole purpose was to achieve greater certainty and to reject the loose earth and sand in favor of rock and clay.

In all these things I seemed to succeed well enough, for, as I was trying to discover the falsity or uncertainty of the propositions I was examining, not by feeble conjectures but by clear and assured reasonings, I encountered nothing that did not lead me to some certain conclusions, even if it were only that the matter was wholly uncertain. And just as in tearing down a building we usually retain the debris to help build a new one, so in destroying all of my opinions which seemed to me ill-founded, I made many observations and acquired much experience which has since aided me in establishing more certain knowledge. In addition, I continued to practice the method which I had decided upon; and besides conducting all my thoughts according to its rules, I set aside a few hours now and then for practice upon mathematical difficulties. In some cases I even practiced upon some other difficulties which could be made to parallel mathematical ones by rejecting those principles of the sciences in question which I did not find sufficiently well established, as I have explained in some of my other writings. Thus I lived, in appearance, just like those who have nothing to do but to live a pleasant and innocent life and attempt to obtain the pleasures without the vices, to enjoy their leisure without ennui, and to occupy their time with all the respectable amusements available. But in reality I never desisted from my design and continued to achieve greater acquaintance with truth, perhaps more than I would have if I had only read books or sought the society of men of letters.

In any case, nine years passed before I reached my decision about the difficulties ordinarily in dispute among the learned, and before I sought to lay the groundwork of a philosophy more certain than popular belief. The example of several men of excellent abilities who had previously attempted my task and who, in my opinion, had failed, made me fear so many difficulties that I should perhaps not have dared to start so soon if I had not learned of a rumor that I had already completed my philosophy. I did not know on what such an opinion was based; if I contributed somewhat to it by my conversation, it must have been by confessing my ignorance more freely than is usually the case among those who have studied a little, and possibly also by presenting my reasons for doubting many things that others deemed certain. I am sure that I did not boast of any doctrines. But I did not want to be taken for more than I was, and so I thought that I should try by all means to make myself worthy of my reputation. Just eight years ago, therefore, I decided to abandon those places where I would be among acquaintances, and retired to Holland, where the long duration of the war produced such conditions that the armies billeted there seemed but to guarantee the fruits of peace. There, in the midst of a great and busy people, more interested in their own affairs than curious about those of others, I was able to enjoy all the comforts of life to be found in the most populous cities while living in as solitary and retired a fashion as though in the most remote of deserts.

PART FOUR

Proofs of the Existence of God and of the Human Soul

I do not know whether I ought to touch upon my first meditations here, for they are so metaphysical and out of the ordinary that they might not be interesting to most people. Nevertheless, in order to show whether my fundamental notions are sufficiently sound, I find myself more or less constrained to speak of them. I had noticed for a long time that in practice it is sometimes necessary to follow opinions which we know to be very uncertain, just as though they were indubitable, as I stated before; but inasmuch as I desired to devote myself wholly to the search for truth, I thought that I should take a course precisely contrary, and reject as absolutely false anything of which I could have the least doubt, in order to see whether anything would be left after this procedure which could be called wholly certain. Thus, as our senses deceive us at times, I was ready to suppose that nothing was at all the way our senses represented them to be. As there are men who make mistakes in reasoning even on the simplest topics in geometry, I judged that I was as liable to error as any other, and rejected as false all the reasoning which I had previously accepted as valid demonstration. Finally, as the same precepts which we have when awake may come to us when asleep without their being true, I decided to suppose that nothing that had ever entered my mind was more real than the illusions of my dreams. But I soon noticed that while I thus wished to think everything false, it was necessarily true that I who thought so was something. Since this truth, *I think, therefore I am,* was so firm and assured that all the most extravagant suppositions of the sceptics were unable to shake it, I judged that I could safely accept it as the first principle of the philosophy I was seeking.

I then examined closely what I was, and saw that I could imagine that I had no body, and that there was no world nor any place that I occupied, but that I could not imagine for a moment that I did not exist. On the contrary, from the very fact that I doubted the truth of other things, it followed very evidently and very certainly that I existed. On the other hand, if I had ceased to think while all the rest of what I had ever imagined remained true, I would have had no reason to believe that I existed; therefore I concluded that I was a substance whose whole essence or nature was only to think, and which, to exist, has no need of space nor of any material thing. Thus it follows that this ego, this soul, by which I am what I am, is entirely distinct from the body and is easier to know than the latter, and that even if the body were not, the soul would not cease to be all that it now is.

Questions and Exercises

1. As a second rule, Descartes proposes that questions should be broken up into simpler parts. Take a paragraph from this selection and see if it conforms to this rule — does it proceed from the simple to the complex?

2. Apply Descartes's second rule to the problem of writing an essay. What are the simpler parts of the project that can be done separately?

3. In view of the political situation at the time that Descartes wrote the *Discourse,* what tone would you expect him to adopt? Find sentences in the selection to illustrate that tone.

4. Compare the tone of the *Discourse* with the tone of Einstein's "Autobiographical Notes," reprinted on pp. 143–150.

5. Descartes uses the expression on p. 100, "making a virtue of necessity." Write in your journals about the meaning of that phrase. Drawing on your own experience, describe a time when you made a virtue of necessity.

6. Explain how Descartes uses building a house as a metaphor for his project of reconstructing knowledge. In what ways are the two activities similar and dissimilar?

7. Descartes begins by claiming that all people are equal in good sense. What does he mean by "good sense"? Is it the same as intelligence? Compare Descartes's view on good sense with what Hobbes says about wisdom at the beginning of the selection from Hobbes on p. 83.

8. We know that Descartes feared persecution by church authorities. Find passages in the selection which may have been written to protect himself from inquisition.

9. Descartes writes on p. 99 that although there may be "just as reliable persons among the Persians or the Chinese as among ourselves, it seemed more practical to pattern my conduct on that of the society in which I would have to live." Since you have read a little about Eastern religions, on pp. 63–72 of this book, you may see some similarities between Descartes's intellectual autobiography and the paths of thought recommended by Buddhism. In your journal comment on this comparison. How does Descartes's way of knowing differ from religious ways of knowing?

10. Make a chronological chart by age and fill in what Descartes tells us about himself at each age — as an infant, as a child, as an adolescent, and so on.

11. The translation reprinted here presents Descartes's famous phrase as, "I think, therefore I am." Other translations say, "I think, therefore I exist." Discuss the differences between the two translations.

12. Based on this selection, write a rough character sketch of Descartes. Meet in small groups to read your sketches to each other. Appoint one group member to report to the class on your consensus or lack of it.

13. Descartes writes analytically, but he does so in the first person. In a small group discuss whether the use of "I" is effective or ineffective in clarifying his ideas.

14. Although Descartes is considered to be the founder of the scientific method of discovery, he says here that he doubts information that we perceive through our senses. Drawing on work in your science courses, write a tentative definition of the scientific method. Meet in small groups to read your definitions and reach consensus on a definition of

the method. Then discuss why Descartes is thought to be a pioneer in articulating the scientific method.

15. Descartes's first rule was not to believe anything until he could see for himself that it was true. Draft an essay addressed to your classmates to discuss whether this is a practical rule for living your life. What beliefs would you have to eliminate on this standard?

16. What led Descartes to try to build his knowledge from the bottom up? How do the wide disagreements among academic authorities that he complains of also apply to the experience of a twentieth-century college student? Draft an essay addressed to your classmates to discuss this comparison.

17. List instances in your own life when you found that some beliefs you had always thought were true were in fact false. When that happened, was your situation like that of a homeowner who needed to repair the house? Does it make a difference whether what needed to be repaired was a sinking foundation or a leaky roof? Or is it like a person in a boat at sea who discovers a leak in the bottom of the boat? In an essay addressed to your classmates discuss your own autobiographical experience in this regard. You may, if you wish, create your own metaphor for your situation.

Vindication of the Rights of Woman
MARY WOLLSTONECRAFT

Mary Wollstonecraft (1759–1797) endured family rejection, poverty, and a life of suffering as the price for believing in human freedom and equality. A true pioneer, she tried to maintain her independence by writing in an age when such a career was not acceptable for a woman. She was thirty years old and a struggling writer at the start of the French Revolution. She completely accepted the revolutionary ideals of liberty and equality, and emigrated to France to live in a "society of equals," where all people were supposed to be free. When the promise of the revolution collapsed in the Reign of Terror and her personal life fell apart, she tried to commit suicide. Returning to England reluctantly in 1795, she lived with and later married the radical thinker William Godwin. Her untimely death in 1797 resulted from complications that attended the birth of her second child, Mary, who was to become the author of *Frankenstein* and the wife of the English poet, Percy Bysshe Shelley.

Vindication of the Rights of Woman (1792) is one of the most forceful defenses of women's equality in Western history, and the first feminist tract in the modern era. Two years before, in 1790, Mary Wollstonecraft had published her *Vindication of the Rights of Man*, to refute Edmund Burke's conservative essay, *Reflections on the Revolution in France*. Her

Rights of Woman extended to women the basic rights that she had claimed for humankind in her first tract. Arguing that the right of liberty must exist "without regard for difference of sex," she saw women's rights as part of the larger context of human rights.

Mary Wollstonecraft wrote *Vindication* with a very clear audience in mind. Dismissing upper class "ladies" as creatures of "false refinement, immorality and vanity," she prefaced her essay this way:

> I wish also to steer clear of an error which many respectable writers
> have fallen into; for the instruction which has hitherto been
> addressed to women, has rather been applicable to *ladies* . . . but
> addressing my sex in a firmer tone, I pay particular attention to those
> in the middle class, because they appear to be in the most natural
> state. . . . My own sex, I hope will excuse me, if I treat them like
> rational creatures, instead of flattering their *fascinating* graces, and
> viewing them as if they were in a state of perpetual childhood.[1]

She wrote for women of her own social station, the middle class, but her book, unlike other works addressed to "ladies," was no book of etiquette. Because of the seriousness of her topic, she wanted "rather to persuade by the force of my arguments, than dazzle by the elegances of my language."[2] Therefore, in her preface, she warned her readers that she was not going to write as a woman was expected to. She adamantly refused to descend into "flowery diction" and "pretty superlatives" that "create a kind of sickly delicacy that turns away from simple, unadorned truth."[3] As a purposeful writer, she composed with a clear sense of audience at every stage of the writing process.

As you read these excerpts from her conclusion, keep in mind that the tract was written about two hundred years ago. Its language is complex by today's standards, and the sentences complicated by clauses and phrases in the manner of that neoclassical age. But the writing should not be totally unfamiliar, for the ideas expressed, and the words used, are drawn from many of the same sources as the *Declaration of Independence*. Like Thomas Jefferson, Mary Wollstonecraft bases her arguments on the existence of "immutable principles," which are the same as Jefferson's "self-evident" truths. Her argument also is for revolution against tyranny and for the human rights which Jefferson termed "unalienable." Jefferson blamed the tyranny of King George III for the problems of the colonies. Who is the tyrant to Wollstonecraft? In comparing these two pieces, consider the importance of "reason" to the arguments of the two authors.

1. Mary Wollstonecraft, "Introduction to the First Edition" in *Vindication of the Rights of Woman*, Charles W. Hazelman, ed. (W. W. Norton, New York, 1967), pp. 33–34.

2. *Ibid.*, p. 34.

3. *Ibid.*, p. 35.

Mary Wollstonecraft argues that society as a whole will benefit if women assume public rights and responsibilities. In the third paragraph she presents this argument most directly. The rest of the selection examines women's disenfranchised, uneducated status and its negative consequences for the community.

Vindication of the Rights of Woman
MARY WOLLSTONECRAFT

SECT. VI.

It is not necessary to inform the sagacious reader, now I enter on my concluding reflections, that the discussion of this subject merely consists in opening a few simple principles and clearing away the rubbish which obscured them. But as all readers are not sagacious, I must be allowed to add some explanatory remarks to bring the subject home to reason — to that sluggish reason which supinely takes opinions on trust, and obstinately supports them to spare itself the labour of thinking.

Moralists have unanimously agreed, that unless virtue be nursed by liberty, it will never attain due strength — and what they say of man I extend to mankind, insisting that in all cases morals must be fixed on immutable principles; and that the being cannot be termed rational or virtuous who obeys any authority but that of reason.

To render women truly useful members of society, I argue that they should be led, by having their understandings cultivated on a large scale, to acquire a rational affection for their country, founded on knowledge, because it is obvious that we are little interested about what we do not understand. And to render this general knowledge of due importance, I have endeavoured to show that private duties are never properly fulfilled unless the understanding enlarges the heart; and that public virtue is only an aggregate of private. But the distinctions established in society undermine both, by beating out the solid gold of virtue, till it becomes only the tinsel-covering of vice; for whilst wealth renders a man more respectable than virtue, wealth will be sought before virtue; and whilst women's persons are caressed when a childish simper shows an absence of mind — the mind will lie fallow. Yet, true voluptuousness must proceed from the mind — for what can equal the sensations produced by mutual affection supported by mutual respect? What are the cold or feverish caresses of appetite, but sin embracing death, compared with the modest overflowings of a pure heart and exalted imagination? Yes, let me tell the libertine of fancy when he despises understanding in woman — that the mind, which he disregards, gives life to the enthusiastic affection from which rapture, shortlived as it is, alone can flow! And that without virtue a sexual attachment must expire, like a tallow candle in the socket, creating intolerable disgust. To prove this, I need only observe that men who have wasted great part of their lives with women, and with whom they have sought for pleasure with eager thirst, entertain the meanest opinion of the sex. — Virtue, true refiner of joy! — if foolish men were to fright thee from earth in order to give loose to all their appetites without a check — some sensual wight of taste would scale the heavens to invite thee back, to give a zest to pleasure!

That women at present are by ignorance rendered foolish or vicious, is, I think, not to be disputed; and that the most salutary effects tending to improve mankind might be expected from a REVOLUTION in female manners, appears, at least with a face of probability, to rise out of the observation. For as marriage has been termed the parent of those endearing charities which draw man from the brutal herd, the corrupting intercourse that wealth, idleness, and folly produce between the sexes, is more universally injurious to morality than all the other vices of mankind collectively considered. To adulterous lust the most sacred duties are sacrificed, because before marriage, men, by a promiscuous intimacy with women, learned to consider love as a selfish gratification — learned to separate it not only from esteem, but from the affection merely built on habit, which mixes a little humanity with it. Justice and friendship are also set at defiance, and that purity of taste is vitiated which would naturally lead a man to relish an artless display of affection rather than affected airs. But that noble simplicity of affection which dares to appear unadorned, has few attractions for the libertine, though it be the charm which, by cementing the matrimonial tie, secures to the pledges of a warmer passion the necessary parental attention; for children will never be properly educated till friendship subsists between parents. Virtue flies from a house divided against itself — and a whole legion of devils take up their residence there.

The affection of husbands and wives cannot be pure when they have so few sentiments in common, and when so little confidence is established at home, as must be the case when their pursuits are so different. That intimacy from which tenderness should flow, will not, cannot subsist between the vicious.

Contending, therefore, that the sexual distinction which men have so warmly insisted upon is arbitrary, I have dwelt on an observation that several sensible men, with whom I have conversed on the subject, allowed to be well founded; and it is simply this, that the little chastity to be found amongst men, and consequent disregard of modesty, tend to degrade both sexes; and further, that the modesty of women, characterized as such, will often be only the artful veil of wantonness instead of being the natural reflection of purity, till modesty be universally respected.

From the tyranny of man, I firmly believe, the greater number of female follies proceed; and the cunning, which I allow makes at present a part of their character, I likewise have repeatedly endeavoured to prove, is produced by oppression.

Were not dissenters, for instance, a class of people with strict truth characterized as cunning? And may I not lay some stress on this fact to prove, that when any power but reason curbs the free spirit of man, dissimulation is practised, and the various shifts of art are naturally called forth? Great attention to decorum which was carried to a degree of scrupulosity, and all that puerile bustle about trifles and consequential solemnity which Butler's caricature of a dissenter brings before the imagination, shaped their persons as well as their minds in the mould of prim littleness. I speak collectively, for I know how many ornaments to human nature have been enrolled amongst sectaries; yet, I assert that the same narrow prejudice for their sect which women have for their families, prevailed in the dissenting part of the community, however worthy in other respects; and also that the same timid prudence, or headstrong efforts, often disgraced the exertions of both. Oppression thus formed many of the features of their character perfectly to coincide with that of the oppressed half of mankind; for is it not notorious that dissenters were, like women, fond of deliberating together, and asking advice of each other, till by a complication of little contrivances some little end was brought about? A similar attention to preserve their reputation was conspicuous in the dissenting and female world, and was produced by a similar cause.

Asserting the rights which women in common with men ought to contend for, I have not attempted to extenuate their faults; but to prove them to be the natural consequence of their education and station in society. If so, it is reasonable to suppose that they will change their character, and correct their vices and follies, when they are allowed to be free in a physical, moral, and civil sense.[1]

Let women share the rights and she will emulate the virtues of man; for she must grow more perfect when emancipated, or justify the authority that chains such a weak being to her duty. — If the latter, it will be expedient to open a fresh trade with Russia for whips: a present which a father should always make to his son-in-law on his wedding day, that a husband may keep his whole family in order by the same means; and without any violation of justice reign, wielding this sceptre, sole master of his house, because he is the only being in it who has reason: — the divine, indefeasible earthly sovereignty breathed into man by the Master of the universe. Allowing this position, women have not any inherent rights to claim; and by the same rule their duties vanish, for rights and duties are inseparable.

---

1. I had further enlarged on the advantages which might reasonably be expected to result from an improvement in female manners, towards the general reformation of society; but it appeared to me that such reflections would more properly close the last volume.

Be just then, O ye men of understanding! and mark not more severely what women do amiss, than the vicious tricks of the horse or the ass for whom ye provide provender — and allow her the privileges of ignorance, to whom ye deny the rights of reason, or ye will be worse than Egyptian task-masters, expecting virtue where nature has not given understanding!

Questions and Exercises

1. List the metaphors and analogies Wollstonecraft uses. Are they effective: Why or why not?

2. Divide this selection into sections and give each an appropriate subheading.

3. Does Wollstonecraft imagine men or women to be her primary audience? Explain your answer.

4. Refer to the selection from Peter Singer on pp. 214–224. Consider how he treats Taylor's attempted ridicule of Wollstonecraft. What does Singer's treatment show of a change in the climate of opinion in the two centuries since Wollstonecraft wrote?

5. Identify and copy those words, phrases, and sentences that are unusual to your ear or eye. In small groups discuss how these language segments could be modernized.

6. If this selection were written today as an essay in a social science book on women and marriage, what changes would be necessary? Discuss this problem in small groups and produce the new form.

7. What purpose is served in this essay by the paragraph on dissenters? (Dissenters were Protestants who refused to accept the doctrines and forms of the Established Church of England.) Is it an effective paragraph? What analogy would you use to describe the condition of women today? In a paragraph, explain your analogy to an audience of classmates and instructor.

8. List the words Wollstonecraft uses to characterize women in her day (for example, cunning, modest, and so on). Use your list to generate a paragraph in which you present her explanation of these characteristics. Your audience includes classmates and instructor.

9. Identify the parts of the selection in which Wollstonecraft gives reasons for believing that equality for women would:
   a) make them more virtuous,
   b) make them more useful members of society,
   c) make sexual relationships more enjoyable.
Write three paragraphs in which you state Wollstonecraft's argument for each thesis.

10. What can you infer from this selection about the author's view of men? List the words Wollstonecraft uses to characterize men. Use your list to generate a paragraph in which you present her explanation of these characteristics.

11. Identify what you consider to be Wollstonecraft's strongest arguments in support of equality for women. Write a short essay in which you present to your classmates and instructor the extent to which these arguments are valid today.

On Liberty
JOHN STUART MILL

1859 was a seminal year in intellectual history: it witnessed the publication of three works of enduring impact — Charles Darwin's *On the Origin of Species*, Karl Marx's *Critique of Political Economy*, and John Stuart Mill's *On Liberty*. Even in such company, *On Liberty* is not overshadowed: it stands as the finest defense of individual liberty and freedom of thought in Western literature and as one of the fundamental classics of liberal political thought.

John Stuart Mill (1806–1873), philosopher, social reformer, economist, and political theorist, is associated primarily with the social theory of utilitarianism. The founder of utilitarianism — Jeremy Bentham (1748–1832) — conceived it as a critique of the legal institutions of his time. Bentham believed that English law had become a confused collection of arbitrary rights and privileges which had lost touch with the new realities of the gathering industrial revolution. The law, he thought, needed reform, and he sought a rational principle to guide the reform. The result was the principle of utility, commonly stated as "the greatest happiness of the greatest number." The point of the principle was that when assessing a law or a social policy one should look, not back to traditional rights or practice, but rather forward to the consequences of implementing the law: who will be affected by it, and how? Does it advance human interests more than other choices might? We now take this idea for granted, but it was a revolutionary concept to Bentham's contemporaries.

Utilitarianism was revolutionary in several respects. It attended to the future rather than to customary practice; it was egalitarian in its effect (since everyone's interests were to be considered equal when working out consequences), and it opened the door to social science as the arbiter of major social questions. To make it possible to apply quantitative scientific methods to social questions, Bentham proposed that the only consequences that mattered were the pleasures and pains flowing from the various proposals (and not even specifically *human* pleasures and pains, as elaborated later by Peter Singer in the selection on animal rights on pp. 214–224). Thus, one would calculate how much pleasure was associated with each action — how intense it was, how long it lasted, how soon it would occur, and so on — and then one adopted that action that produced the most pleasure and the least pain.

Because Bentham placed all value on pleasure and pain (what philosophers call "hedonism"), some believed that his views threatened deep human values. Should, for example, football and poetry be compared simply on the *amount* of pleasure they provide? What room was there for the finer feelings amid cold calculation? Thomas Carlyle (1795–1881), British essayist and historian, charged that utilitarianism was "pig philosophy."

John Stuart Mill thoroughly appreciated the force of this criticism. His major contribution to utilitarianism was to enlarge the view of human nature on which the theory was grounded. He insisted that one must evaluate the quality of pleasures as well as quantity. Thus, his efforts were devoted to making the essential insights of utilitarians congenial to his Victorian contemporaries at a time when Romanticism was the major trend in literature, and many of the most advanced thinkers valued the imagination over cold philosophy.

Mill was uniquely situated to understand the Romantic attack on reason. His father, James Mill (1773–1836), was a close friend and supporter of Bentham, and the elder Mill had given John Stuart an exacting early education along utilitarian lines. John was a child prodigy: by the age of eight he had read *Aesop's Fables* in Greek. The amount and sophistication of his early reading is astonishing, not just in literature, but also in economics, law, and mathematics. He seemed to thrive on the intellectual give and take he was exposed to through his father's friends. But in 1826 he suffered what he called a "mental crisis," evoked by a feeling that he had become some kind of intellectual machine, a "mechanical man" formed by his father, with a highly trained intellect but lacking a developed emotional life. "The habit of analysis," he tells us in his *Autobiography*, "has a tendency to wear away the feelings."[1] One day as he was reading, however, he was moved to tears by an account of a son's loss of his father. Mill was consoled to discover he still had the capacity to feel emotion, and so his crisis led to a better integrated intellectual and emotional life.

Dickens's *Hard Times* (pp. 182–187) attacks the utilitarian view of education. Dickens's portrayal of Gradgrind is probably unfair to utilitarians; it is certainly unfair as a description of the kind of education John Stuart Mill had. However, Mill does agree with Dickens that "Fancy" is essential to a balanced life.

Intellectually, Mill still remained a utilitarian to the end. It is in this spirit that he approached the question of how much freedom is compatible with an organized society. As a utilitarian he could not appeal to any doc-

---

1. Excerpts from *The Autobiography of John Stuart Mill*. Foreword by Asa Briggs. New York: New American Library. Signet Classics. 1964. Reprinted by permission.

trine of a "natural right" to freedom; his argument had to be that the consequences of permitting freedom were more fruitful for human interests overall than restrictions would be.

On Liberty asks whether any rational principle can be formulated to decide when society may interfere with individual freedom. Mill explains that in the past this problem was conceived primarily as a matter of the government restricting the freedom of citizens. With the rise of democracies, however, the problem has become the tyranny of majority opinion over the right to individual dissent. He complains that most people support freedom only when they agree with what the dissenter is doing or saying; such fair-weather support does not represent true support for individual liberty.

In Mill's day, atheists were persecuted for not accepting majority religious beliefs, because, simply, the majority did not like atheism. Consider other kinds of cases where the problem comes up today: Should access to recreational drugs be regulated? Should certain forms of sexual activity among consenting adults be forbidden? Should the government ban pornography? Abortion? Racist literature? Public nudity? Burning the flag? Advocacy of the overthrow of government?

Mill proposes one principle to resolve these questions: only those actions that cause harm directly to other people are subject to social regulation; all other actions are protected. Consider two alternative positions opposed to Mill's: One is legal moralism, which asserts that a society has the right to defend its values by forbidding actions which violate those values, even if they do no direct harm. Laws against "victimless crimes" are usually defended on this ground. Another position is paternalism, which holds that we have the right to interfere with people for their own good: it was partially on these grounds that alcohol was banned in the United States during Prohibition (1920–1933). When the Federal Drug Administration prevents access to an untested drug, even to fully rational people who freely choose to accept the risk, it is acting on paternalistic grounds. Mill insists that we should be permitted to forbid an action only when we can show that it causes direct harm to other people. You may not agree with Mill, but his position is one from which all others begin and against which you can test and temper your own views.

When it comes to freedom of speech Mill takes an almost absolute position against censorship. The structure of his argument for it is notable. The consequences of censoring speech, he claims, are detrimental even when what is banned is false. The evil consequences of censorship affect not just those whose dissenting opinions are banned (the "heretics") but also the majority whose confidence in their true opinion is undermined when that opinion is not tested in free debate. He links the right to free speech and thought to the growth of fully developed individuals who can think for themselves. It is therefore in your interest to permit others to challenge and test your opinions.

Mill's audience was a difficult one. Intellectuals, embued with Romantic hostility to reason, were suspicious of a utilitarian appeal. The opposition from the wider English public was even greater. By mid-century they
had become smugly confident that they had worked out the best of all
possible civilizations. Victorian values emphasized "duty" and "collective
responsibility," and so they were unlikely to be receptive to criticism,
especially from radicals who believed one's first responsibility was to oneself. But Mill had long experience with writing for a judgmental audience.
When he was a child, he wrote for his demanding father. At seventeen he
joined the East India Company, where his job was to write drafts of letters
which, he remarks, "required, for some time, much revision from my
immediate superiors."[2] Later he was charged with writing delicate political
correspondence of such a nature that

> ... I could not issue an order or express an opinion, without
> satisfying various persons very unlike myself that the thing was fit to
> be done. I was thus in a good position for finding out by practice the
> mode of putting a thought which gives it easiest admittance into
> minds not prepared for it by habit. ...[3]

From these experiences he developed a method for composing:

> ... It is in this way that all my books have been composed. They
> were always written at least twice over; a first draft of the entire work
> was completed to the very end of the subject, then the whole begun
> again de novo; but incorporating, in the second writing, all sentences
> and parts of sentences of the old draft which appeared as suitable to
> my purpose as anything which I could write in lieu of them. I have
> found great advantages in this system of double redaction. It
> combines, better than any other mode of composition, the freshness
> and vigour of the first conception with the superior precision and
> completeness resulting from prolonged thought. In my own case,
> moreover, I have found that the patience necessary for a careful
> elaboration of the details of composition and expression costs much
> less effort after the entire subject has been once gone through, and
> the substance of all that I find to say has in some manner, however
> imperfect, been got upon paper. The only thing which I am careful,
> in the first draft, to make as perfect as I am able, is the arrangement.
> If that is bad, the whole thread on which the ideas string themselves
> becomes twisted: thoughts placed in a wrong connexion are not
> expounded in a manner that suits the right, and a first draft with this
> original vice is next to useless as a foundation for the final treatment.[4]

2. Ibid., p. 75
3. Ibid., p. 77.
4. Ibid., p. 162.

Because Mill freely chose to devote a great deal of time and energy to his writing, we must assume that the activity finally yielded him more pleasure than pain. Invoking the same utilitarian theory, we predict that your reading of Mill will fully repay your intellectual efforts.

On Liberty
JOHN STUART MILL

CHAPTER I

Introductory

Like other tyrannies, the tyranny of the majority was at first, and is still vulgarly, held in dread, chiefly as operating through the acts of the public authorities. But reflecting persons perceived that when society is itself the tyrant — society collectively over the separate individuals who compose it — its means of tyrannising are not restricted to the acts which it may do by the hands of its political functionaries. Society can and does execute its own mandates: and if it issues wrong mandates instead of right, or any mandates at all in things with which it ought not to meddle, it practises a social tyranny more formidable than many kinds of political oppression, since, though not usually upheld by such extreme penalties, it leaves fewer means of escape, penetrating much more deeply into the details of life, and enslaving the soul itself. Protection, therefore, against the tyranny of the magistrate is not enough: there needs protection also against the tyranny of the prevailing opinion and feeling; against the tendency of society to impose, by other means than civil penalties, its own ideas and practices as rules of conduct on those who dissent from them; to fetter the development, and, if possible, prevent the formation, of any individuality not in harmony with its ways, and compels all characters to fashion themselves upon the model of its own. There is a limit to the legitimate interference of collective opinion with individual independence: and to find that limit, and maintain it against encroachment, is as indispensable to a good condition of human affairs, as protection against political despotism.

But though this proposition is not likely to be contested in general terms, the practical question, where to place the limit — how to make the fitting adjustment between individual independence and social control — is a subject on which nearly everything remains to be done. All that makes existence valuable to any one, depends on the enforcement of restraints upon the actions of other people. Some rules of conduct, therefore, must be imposed, by law in the first place, and by opinion on many things which

From *Utilitarianism: John Stuart Mill*, ed. Mary Warnock. Fount Paperbacks, Collins, London, 1962. Reprinted by permission of Fount Paperbacks and the New American Library, Inc.

are not fit subjects for the operation of law. What these rules should be is the principal question in human affairs; but if we except a few of the most obvious cases, it is one of those which least progress has been made in resolving. No two ages, and scarcely any two countries, have decided it alike; and the decision of one age or country is a wonder to another. Yet the people of any given age and country no more suspect any difficulty in it, than if it were a subject on which mankind had always been agreed. The rules which obtain among themselves appear to them self-evident and self-justifying. This all but universal illusion is one of the examples of the magical influence of custom, which is not only, as the proverb says, a second nature, but is continually mistaken for the first. The effect of custom, in preventing any misgivings respecting the rules of conduct which mankind impose on one another, is all the more complete because the subject is one on which it is not generally considered necessary that reasons should be given, either by one person to others or by each to himself. People are accustomed to believe, and have been encouraged in the belief by some who aspire to the character of philosophers, that their feelings, on subjects of this nature, are better than reasons, and render reasons unnecessary. The practical principle which guides them to their opinions on the regulation of human conduct, is the feeling in each person's mind that everybody should be required to act as he, and those with whom he sympathises, would like them to act. No one, indeed, acknowledges to himself that his standard of judgment is his own liking; but an opinion on a point of conduct, not supported by reasons, can only count as one person's preference; and if the reasons, when given, are a mere appeal to a similar preference felt by other people, it is still only many people's liking instead of one. To an ordinary man, however, his own preference, thus supported, is not only a perfectly satisfactory reason, but the only one he generally has for any of his notions of morality, taste, or propriety, which are not expressly written in his religious creed; and his chief guide in the interpretation even of that. Men's opinions, accordingly, on what is laudable or blamable, are affected by all the multifarious causes which influence their wishes in regard to the conduct of others, and which are as numerous as those which determine their wishes on any other subject. Sometimes their reason — at other times their prejudices or superstitions: often their social affections, not seldom their antisocial ones, their envy or jealousy, their arrogance or contemptuousness: but most commonly their desires or fears for themselves — their legitimate or illegitimate self-interest. . . .

The likings and dislikings of society, or of some powerful portion of it, are thus the main thing which has practically determined the rules laid down for general observance, under the penalties of law or opinion. And in general, those who have been in advance of society in thought and feeling, have left this condition of things unassailed in principle, however they may have come into conflict with it in some of its details. They have occupied themselves rather in inquiring what things society ought to like or dislike, than in questioning whether its likings or dislikings should be a law to individuals. . . .

In England, from the peculiar circumstances of our political history, though the yoke of opinion is perhaps heavier, that of law is lighter, than in most other countries of Europe; and there is considerable jealousy of direct interference, by the legislative or the executive power, with private conduct; not so much from any just regard for the independence of the individual, as from the still subsisting habit of looking on the government as representing an opposite interest to the public. The majority have not yet learnt to feel the power of the government their power, or its opinions their opinions. When they do so, individual liberty will probably be as much exposed to invasion from the government, as it already is from public opinion. But, as yet, there is a considerable amount of feeling ready to be called forth against any attempt of the law to control individuals in things in which they have not hitherto been accustomed to be controlled by it; and this with very little discrimination as to whether the matter is, or is not, within the legitimate sphere of legal control; insomuch that the feeling, highly salutary on the whole, is perhaps quite as often misplaced as well grounded in the particular instances of its application. There is, in fact, no recognised principle by which the propriety or impropriety of government interference is customarily tested. People decide according to their personal preferences. Some, whenever they see any good to be done, or evil to be remedied, would willingly instigate the government to undertake the business; while others prefer to bear almost any amount of social evil, rather than add one to the departments of human interests amenable to governmental control. And men range themselves on one or the other side in any particular case, according to this general direction of their sentiments; or according to the degree of interest which they feel in the particular thing which it is proposed that the government should do, or according to the belief they entertain that the government would, or would not, do it in the manner they prefer; but very rarely on account of any opinion to which they consistently adhere, as to what things are fit to be done by a government. And it seems to me that in consequence of this absence of rule or principle, one side is at present as often wrong as the other; the interference of government is, with about equal frequency, improperly invoked and improperly condemned.

The object of this Essay is to assert one very simple principle, as entitled to govern absolutely the dealings of society with the individual in the way of compulsion and control, whether the means used be physical force in the form of legal penalties, or the moral coercion of public opinion. That principle is, that the sole end for which mankind are warranted, individually or collectively, in interfering with the liberty of action of any of their number, is self-protection. That the only purpose for which power can be rightfully exercised over any member of a civilised community, against his will, is to prevent harm to others. His own good, either physical or moral, is not a sufficient warrant. He cannot rightfully be compelled to do or forbear because it will be better for him to do so, because it will make him happier, because, in the opinions of others, to do so would be wise, or even right. These are good reasons for remonstrating with him, or reasoning with him, or persuading him, or entreating him, but not for compelling him, or visiting him with any evil in case he do otherwise. To justify that, the conduct from which it is desired to deter him must be calculated to produce evil to some one else. The only part of the conduct of any one, for which he is amenable to society, is that which concerns others. In the part which merely concerns himself, his independence is, of right, absolute. Over himself, over his own body and mind, the individual is sovereign.

It is, perhaps, hardly necessary to say that this doctrine is meant to apply only to human beings in the maturity of their faculties. We are not speaking of children, or of young persons below the age which the law may fix as that of manhood or womanhood. Those who are still in a state to require being taken care of by others, must be protected against their own actions as well as against external injury. For the same reason, we may leave out of consideration those backward states of society in which the race itself may be considered as in its nonage. The early difficulties in the way of spontaneous progress are so great, that there is seldom any choice of means for overcoming them; and a ruler full of the spirit of improvement is warranted in the use of any expedients that will attain an end, perhaps otherwise unattainable. Despotism is a legitimate mode of government in dealing with barbarians, provided the end be their improvement, and the means justified by actually effecting that end. Liberty, as a principle, has no application to any state of things anterior to the time when mankind have become capable of being improved by free and equal discussion. Until then, there is nothing for them but implicit obedience to an Akbar or a Charlemagne, if they are so fortunate as to find one. But as soon as mankind have attained the capacity of being guided to their own improvement by conviction or persuasion (a period long since reached in all nations with whom we need here concern ourselves), compulsion, either in the direct form or in that of pains and penalties for non-compliance, is no longer admissible as a means to their own good, and justifiable only for the security of others.

It is proper to state that I forego any advantage which could be derived to my argument from the idea of abstract right, as a thing independent of utility. I regard utility as the ultimate appeal on all ethical questions; but it must be utility in the largest sense, grounded on the permanent interests of a man as a progressive being. Those interests, I contend, authorise the subjection of individual spontaneity to external control, only in respect to those actions of each, which concern the interest of other people. If any one does an act hurtful to others, there is a *prima facie* case for punishing him, by law, or, where legal penalties are not safely applicable, by general disapprobation. There are also many positive acts for the benefit of others, which he may rightfully be compelled to perform; such as to give evidence in a court of justice; to bear his fair share in the common defence, or in any other joint work necessary to the interest of the society of which he enjoys the protection; and to perform certain acts of individual beneficence, such as saving a fellow-creature's life, or interposing to protect the defenceless against ill-usage, things which whenever it is obviously a man's duty to do, he may rightfully be made responsible to society for not doing. A person may cause evil to others not only by his actions but by his inaction, and in either case he is justly accountable to them for the injury. The latter case, it is true, requires a much more cautious exercise of compulsion than the former. To make any one answerable for doing evil to others is the rule; to make him answerable for not preventing evil is, comparatively speaking, the exception. Yet there are many cases clear enough and grave enough to justify that exception. In all things which regard the external relations of the individual, he is *de jure* amenable to those whose interests are concerned, and, if need be, to society as their protector. There are often good reasons for not holding him to the responsibility; but these reasons must arise from the special expediencies of the case: either because it is a kind of case in which he is on the whole likely to act better, when left to his own discretion, than when controlled in any way in which society have it in their power to control him; or because the attempt to exercise control would produce other evils, greater than those which it would prevent. When such reasons as these preclude the enforcement of responsibility, the conscience of the agent himself should step into the vacant judgment seat, and protect those interests of others which have no external protection; judging himself all the more rigidly, because the case does not admit of his being made accountable to the judgment of his fellow-creatures.

But there is a sphere of action in which society, as distinguished from the individual, has, if any, only an indirect interest; comprehending all that portion of a person's life and conduct which affects only himself, or if it also affects others, only with their free, voluntary, and undeceived consent and participation. When I say only himself, I mean directly, and in the first instance; for whatever affects himself, may affect others through himself; and the objection which may be grounded on this contingency, will receive consideration in the sequel. This, then, is the appropriate region of human liberty. It comprises, first, the inward domain of consciousness; demanding liberty of conscience in the most comprehensive sense; liberty of thought and feeling; absolute freedom of opinion and sentiment on all subjects, practical or speculative, scientific, moral, or theological. The liberty of expressing and publishing opinions may seem to fall under a different principle, since it belongs to that part of the conduct of an individual which concerns other people; but, being almost of as much importance as the liberty of thought itself, and resting in great part on the same reasons, is practically inseparable from it. Secondly, the principle requires liberty of tastes and pursuits; of framing the plan of our life to suit our own character;

of doing as we like, subject to such consequences as may follow: without impediment from our fellow-creatures, so long as what we do does not harm them, even though they should think our conduct foolish, perverse, or wrong. Thirdly, from this liberty of each individual, follows the liberty, within the same limits, of combination among individuals; freedom to unite, for any purpose not involving harm to others: the persons combining being supposed to be of full age, and not forced or deceived.

No society in which these liberties are not, on the whole, respected, is free, whatever may be its form of government; and none is completely free in which they do not exist absolute and unqualified. The only freedom which deserves the name, is that of pursuing our own good in our own way, so long as we do not attempt to deprive others of theirs, or impede their efforts to obtain it. Each is the proper guardian of his own health, whether bodily, or mental and spiritual. Mankind are greater gainers by suffering each other to live as seems good to themselves, than by compelling each to live as seems good to the rest.

Though this doctrine is anything but new, and, to some persons, may have the air of a truism, there is no doctrine which stands more directly opposed to the general tendency of existing opinion and practice. Society has expended fully as much effort in the attempt (according to its lights) to compel people to conform to its notions of personal as of social excellence. The ancient commonwealths thought themselves entitled to practise, and the ancient philosophers countenanced, the regulation of every part of private conduct by public authority, on the ground that the State had a deep interest in the whole bodily and mental discipline of every one of its citizens; a mode of thinking which may have been admissible in small republics surrounded by powerful enemies, in constant peril of being subverted by foreign attack or internal commotion, and to which even a short interval of relaxed energy and self-command might so easily be fatal that they could not afford to wait for the salutary permanent effects of freedom. In the modern world, the greater size of political communities, and, above all, the separation between spiritual and temporal authority (which placed the direction of men's consciences in other hands than those which controlled their worldly affairs), prevented so great an interference by law in the details of private life; but the engines of moral repression have been wielded more strenuously against divergence from the reigning opinion in self-regarding, than even in social matters; religion, the most powerful of the elements which have entered into the formation of moral feeling, having almost always been governed either by the ambition of a hierarchy, seeking control over every department of human conduct, or by the spirit of Puritanism. . . .

It will be convenient for the argument, if, instead of at once entering upon the general thesis, we confine ourselves in the first instance to a single branch of it, on which the principle here stated is, if not fully, yet to a certain point, recognised by the current opinions. This one branch is the

Liberty of Thought: from which it is impossible to separate the cognate liberty of speaking and of writing. Although these liberties, to some considerable amount, form part of the political morality of all countries which profess religious toleration and free institutions, the grounds, both philosophical and practical, on which they rest, are perhaps not so familiar to the general mind, nor so thoroughly appreciated by many even of the leaders of opinion, as might have been expected. Those grounds, when rightly understood, are of much wider application than to only one division of the subject, and a thorough consideration of this part of the question will be found the best introduction to the remainder. Those to whom nothing which I am about to say will be new, may therefore, I hope, excuse me, if on a subject which for now three centuries has been so often discussed, I venture on one discussion more.

CHAPTER II

Of the Liberty of Thought and Discussion

The time, it is to be hoped, is gone by, when any defence would be necessary of the "liberty of the press" as one of the securities against corrupt or tyrannical government. No argument, we may suppose, can now be needed, against permitting a legislature or any executive, not identified in interest with the people, to prescribe opinions to them, and determine what doctrines or what arguments they shall be allowed to hear. This aspect of the question, besides, has been so often and so triumphantly enforced by preceding writers, that it needs not be specially insisted on in this place. Though the law of England, on the subject of the press, is as servile to this day as it was in the time of the Tudors, there is little danger of its being actually put in force against political discussion, except during some temporary panic, when fear of insurrection drives ministers and judges from their propriety; and, speaking generally, it is not, in constitutional countries, to be apprehended, that the government, whether completely responsible to the people or not, will often attempt to control the expression of opinion, except when in doing so it makes itself the organ of the general intolerance of the public. Let us suppose, therefore, that the government is entirely at one with the people, and never thinks of exerting any power of coercion unless in agreement with what it conceives to be their voice. But I deny the right of the people to exercise such coercion, either by themselves or by their government. The power itself is illegitimate. The best government has no more title to it than the worst. It is as noxious, or more noxious, when exerted in accordance with public opinion, then when in opposition to it. If all mankind minus one were of one opinion, and only one person were of the contrary opinion, mankind would be no more justified in silencing that one person, than he, if he had the power, would be justified in silencing mankind. Were an opinion a personal possession of no value except to the owner; if to be obstructed in the enjoyment of it were simply a private injury, it would make some difference whether the injury was inflicted only on a few persons or on many. But the peculiar evil of silencing the expression of an opinion is, that it is robbing the human race; posterity as well as the existing generation; those who dissent from the opinion, still more than those who hold it. If the opinion is right, they are deprived of the opportunity of exchanging error for truth: if wrong, they lose, what is almost as great a benefit, the clearer perception and livelier impression of truth, produced by its collision with error.

It is necessary to consider separately these two hypotheses, each of which has a distinct branch of the argument corresponding to it. We can never be sure that the opinion we are endeavouring to stifle is a false opinion; and if we were sure, stifling it would be an evil still.

First: the opinion which it is attempted to suppress by authority may possibly be true. Those who desire to suppress it, of course deny its truth; but they are not infallible. They have no authority to decide the question for all mankind, and exclude every other person from the means of judging. To refuse a hearing to an opinion, because they are sure that it is false, is to assume that *their* certainty is the same thing as *absolute* certainty. All silencing of discussion is an assumption of infallibility. Its condemnation may be allowed to rest on this common argument, not the worse for being common.

Unfortunately for the good sense of mankind, the fact of their fallibility is far from carrying the weight in their practical judgment which is always allowed to it in theory; for while every one well knows himself to be fallible, few think it necessary to take any precaution against their own fallibility, or admit the supposition that any opinion, of which they feel very certain, may be one of the examples of the error to which they acknowledge themselves to be liable. Absolute princes, or others who are accustomed to unlimited deference, usually feel this complete confidence in their own opinions on nearly all subjects. People more happily situated, who sometimes hear their opinions disputed, and are not wholly unused to be set right when they are wrong, place the same unbounded reliance only on such of their opinions as are shared by all who surround them, or to whom they habitually defer; for in proportion to a man's want of confidence in his own solitary judgment, does he usually repose, with implicit trust, on the infallibility of "the world" in general. And the world, to each individual, means the part of it with which he comes in contact; his party, his sect, his church, his class of society; the man may be called, by comparison, almost liberal and large-minded to whom it means anything so comprehensive as his own country or his own age. Nor is his faith in this collective authority at all shaken by his being aware that other ages, countries, sects, churches, classes, and parties have thought, and even now think, the exact reverse. He devolves upon his own world the responsibility of being in the right against the dissentient worlds of other people; and it never troubles him that mere accident has decided which of these numerous worlds is the object of his reliance, and that the same causes which make him a Churchman in London, would have made him a Buddhist or a Confucian in Pekin. Yet it is as evident in itself, as any amount of argument can make it, that ages are no more infallible than individuals; every age having held many opinions which subsequent ages have deemed not only false but absurd; and it is as certain that many opinions now general will be rejected by future ages, as it is that many, once general, are rejected by the present. . . .

. . . But it is not the minds of heretics that are deteriorated most by the ban placed on all inquiry which does not end in the orthodox conclusions. The greatest harm done is to those who are not heretics, and whose whole mental development is cramped, and their reason cowed, by the fear of heresy. Who can compute what the world loses in the multitude of promising intellects combined with timid characters, who dare not follow out any bold, vigorous, independent train of thought, lest it should land them in something which would admit of being considered irreligious or immoral? Among them we may occasionally see some man of deep conscientiousness, and subtle and refined understanding, who spends a life in sophisticating with an intellect which he cannot silence and exhausts the resources of ingenuity in attempting to reconcile the promptings of his conscience and reason with orthodoxy, which yet he does not, perhaps, to the end succeed in doing. No one can be a great thinker who does not recognise that as a thinker it is his first duty to follow his intellect to whatever conclusions it may lead. Truth gains more even by the errors of one who, with due study and preparation, thinks for himself, then by the true opinions of those who only hold them because they do not suffer themselves to think. Not that it is solely, or chiefly, to form great thinkers, that freedom of thinking is required. On the contrary, it is as much and even more indispensable to enable average human beings to attain the mental stature which they are capable of. There have been, and may again be, great individual thinkers in a general atmosphere of mental slavery. But there never has been, nor ever will be, in that atmosphere an intellectually active people. Where any people has made a temporary approach to such a character, it has been because the dread of heterodox speculation was for a time suspended. Where there is a tacit convention that principles are not to be disputed; where the discussion of the greatest questions which can occupy humanity is considered to be closed, we cannot hope to find that generally high scale of mental activity which has made some periods of history so remarkable. Never when controversy avoided the subjects which are large and important enough to kindle enthusiasm was the mind of a people stirred up from its foundations, and the impulse given which raised even persons of the most ordinary intellect to something of the dignity of thinking beings. . . .

Let us now pass to the second division of the argument, and dismissing the supposition that any of the received opinions may be false, let us assume them to be true, and examine into the worth of the manner in which they are likely to be held, when their truth is not freely and openly canvassed. However unwillingly a person who has a strong opinion may admit the possibility that his opinion may be false, he ought to be moved by the consideration that, however true it may be if it is not fully, frequently, and fearlessly discussed, it will be held as a dead dogma, not a living truth. . . .

If the intellect and judgment of mankind ought to be cultivated, a thing which Protestants at least do not deny, on what can these faculties be more appropriately exercised by any one, than on the things which concern him so much that it is considered necessary for him to hold opinions on them? If the cultivation of the understanding consists in one thing more than in another, it is surely in learning the grounds of one's own opinions. Whatever people believe, on subjects on which it is of the first importance to believe rightly, they ought to be able to defend against at least the common objections. But, some one may say, "Let them be *taught* the grounds of their opinions. It does not follow that opinions must be merely parroted because they are never heard controverted. Persons who learn geometry do not simply commit the theorems to memory, but understand and learn likewise the demonstrations; and it would be absurd to say that they remain ignorant of the grounds of geometrical truths, because they never hear any one deny, and attempt to disprove them." Undoubtedly: and such teaching suffices on a subject like mathematics, where there is nothing at all to be said on the wrong side of the question. The peculiarity of the evidence of mathematical truths is that all the argument is on one side. There are no objections, and no answers to objections. But on every subject on which difference of opinion is possible, the truth depends on a balance to be struck between two sets of conflicting reasons. Even in natural philosophy, there is always some other explanation possible of the same facts; some geocentric theory instead of heliocentric, some phlogiston instead of oxygen; and it has to be shown why that other theory cannot be the true one: and until this is shown, and until we know how it is shown, we do not understand the grounds of our opinion. But when we turn to subjects infinitely more complicated, to morals, religion, politics, social relations, and the business of life, three-fourths of the arguments for every disputed opinion consists in dispelling the appearances which favour some opinion different from it. The greatest orator, save one, of antiquity, has left it on record that he always studied his adversary's case with as great, if not still greater, intensity than even his own. What Cicero practised as the means of forensic success requires to be imitated by all who study any subject in order to arrive at the truth. He who knows only his own side of the case knows little of that. His reasons may be good, and no one may have been able to refute them. But if he is equally unable to refute the reasons on the opposite side; if he does not so much as know what they are, he has no ground for preferring either opinion. The rational position for him would be suspension of judgment, and unless he contents himself with that, he is either led by authority, or adopts, like the generality of the world, the side to which he feels most inclination. Nor is it enough that he should hear the arguments of adversaries from his own teachers, presented as they state them, and accompanied by what they offer as refutations. That is not the way to do justice to the arguments, or bring them into real contact with his own mind. He must be able to hear them from persons who actually believe them; who defend them in earnest, and do their very utmost for them. He must know them in their most plausible and persuasive form; he must feel the whole force of the difficulty which the true view of the subject has to encounter and dispose of; else he will never really possess himself of the portion of truth which meets and removes that difficulty. Ninety-nine in a hundred of what are called educated men are in this condition; even of those who can argue fluently for their opinions. Their conclusion may be true, but it might be false for anything they know: they have never thrown themselves into the mental position of those who think differently from them, and considered what such persons may have to say; and consequently they do not, in any proper sense of the word, know the doctrine which they themselves profess. They do not know those parts of it which explain and justify the remainder; the considerations which show that a fact which seemingly conflicts with another is reconcilable with it, or that, of two apparently strong reasons, one and not the other ought to be preferred. All that part of the truth which turns the scale, and decides the judgment of a completely informed mind, they are strangers to; nor is it ever really known, but to those who have attended equally and impartially to both sides, and endeavoured to see the reasons of both in the strongest light. So essential is this discipline to a real understanding of moral and human subjects, that if opponents of all important truths do not exist, it is indispensable to imagine them, and supply them with the strongest arguments which the most skilful devil's advocate can conjure up. . . .

It still remains to speak of one of the principal causes which make diversity of opinion advantageous, and will continue to do so until mankind shall have entered a stage of intellectual advancement which at present seems at an incalculable distance. We have hitherto considered only two possibilities: that the received opinion may be false, and some other opinion, consequently, true; or that, the received opinion being true, a conflict with the opposite error is essential to a clear apprehension and deep feeling of its truth. But there is a commoner case than either of these; when the conflicting doctrines, instead of being one true and the other false, share the truth between them; and the nonconforming opinion is needed to supply the remainder of the truth, of which the received doctrine embodies only a part. Popular opinions, on subjects not palpable to sense, are often true, but seldom or never the whole truth. They are a part of the truth; sometimes a greater, sometimes a smaller part, but exaggerated, distorted, and disjointed from the truths by which they ought to be accompanied and limited. Heretical opinions, on the other hand, are generally some of these suppressed and neglected truths, bursting the bonds which kept them down, and either seeking reconciliation with the truth contained in the common opinion, or fronting it as enemies, and setting themselves up, with similar exclusiveness, as the whole truth. The latter case is hitherto the most frequent, as, in the human mind, one-sidedness has always been the rule, and many-sidedness the exception. Hence, even in revolutions of opinion, one part of the truth usually sets while another rises. Even progress, which ought to superadd, for the most part only substitutes, one partial and incomplete truth for another; improvement consisting chiefly in this, that the new fragment of truth is more wanted, more adapted to the needs of the time, than that which it displaces. Such being the partial character of prevailing opinions, even when resting on a true foundation, every opinion which embodies somewhat of the portion of truth which the common opinion omits, ought to be considered precious, with whatever amount of error and confusion that truth may be blended. No sober judge of human affairs will feel bound to be indignant because those who force on our notice truths which we should otherwise have overlooked, overlook some of those which we see. Rather, he will think that so long as popular truth is one-sided, it is more desirable than otherwise that unpopular truth should have one-sided assertors too; such being usually the most energetic, and the most likely to compel reluctant attention to the fragment of wisdom which they proclaim as if it were the whole. . . .

We have now recognised the necessity to the mental well-being of mankind (on which all their other well-being depends) of freedom of opinion, and freedom of the expression of opinion, on four distinct grounds; which we will now briefly recapitulate.

First, if any opinion is compelled to silence, that opinion may, for aught we can certainly know, be true. To deny this is to assume our own infallibility.

Secondly, though the silenced opinion be an error, it may, and very commonly does, contain a portion of truth; and since the general or prevailing opinion on any subject is rarely or never the whole truth, it is only by the collision of adverse opinions that the remainder of the truth has any chance of being supplied.

Thirdly, even if the received opinion be not only true, but the whole truth, unless it is suffered to be, and actually is, vigorously and earnestly contested, it will, by most of those who receive it, be held in the manner of a prejudice, with little comprehension or feeling of its rational grounds.

And not only this, but, fourthly, the meaning of the doctrine itself will be in danger of being lost, or enfeebled, and deprived of its vital effect on the character and conduct: the dogma becoming a mere formal profession, inefficacious for good, but cumbering the ground, and preventing the growth of any real and heartfelt conviction, from reason or personal experience. . . .

CHAPTER III

Of Individuality, As One of the Elements of Well-Being

Such being the reasons which make it imperative that human beings should be free to form opinions, and to express their opinions without reserve; and such the baneful consequences to the intellectual, and through that to the moral nature of man, unless this liberty is either conceded, or asserted in spite of prohibition; let us next examine whether the same reasons do not require that men should be free to act upon their opinions — to carry these out in their lives, without hindrance, either physical or moral, from their fellow-men, so long as it is at their own risk and peril. This last proviso is of course indispensable. No one pretends that actions should be as free as opinions. On the contrary, even opinions lose their immunity when the circumstances in which they are expressed are such as to constitute their expression a positive instigation to some mischievous act. An opinion that corn-dealers are starvers of the poor, or that private property is robbery, ought to be unmolested when simply circulated through the press, but may justly incur punishment when delivered orally to an excited mob assembled before the house of a corn-dealer, or when handed about among the same mob in the form of a placard. Acts, of whatever kind, which, without justifiable cause, do harm to others, may be, and in the more important cases absolutely require to be, controlled by the unfavourable sentiments, and, when needful, by the active interference of mankind. The liberty of the individual must be thus far limited; he must not make himself a nuisance to other people. But if he refrains from molesting others in what concerns them, and merely acts according to his own inclination and judgment in things which concern himself, the same reasons which show that opinion should be free, prove also that he should be allowed without molestation to carry his opinions into practice at his own cost. That mankind are not infallible; that their truths, for the most part, are only half-truths; that unity of opinion, unless resulting from the fullest and freest comparison of opposite opinions, is not desirable, and diversity not an evil, but a good, until mankind are much more capable than at present of recognising all sides of the truth, are principles applicable to men's modes of action, not less than to their opinions. As it is useful that while mankind are imperfect there should be different opinions, so it is that there should be different experiments of living; that free scope should be given to varieties of character, short of injury to others; and that the worth of different modes of life should be proved practically, when any one thinks fit to try them. It is desirable, in short, that in things which do not primarily concern others, individuality should assert itself. Where, not the person's own character, but the traditions or customs of other people are the rule of conduct, there is wanting one of the principal ingredients of human happiness, and quite the chief ingredient of individual and social progress. . . .

CHAPTER IV

Of the Limits to the Authority of Society Over the Individual

What, then, is the rightful limit to the sovereignty of the individual over himself? Where does the authority of society begin? How much of human life should be assigned to individuality, and how much to society?

Each will receive its proper share, if each has that which more particularly concerns it. To individuality should belong the part of life in which it is chiefly the individual that is interested; to society, the part which chiefly interests society.

Though society is not founded on a contract, and though no good purpose is answered by inventing a contract in order to deduce social obligations from it, every one who receives the protection of society owes a return for the benefit, and the fact of living in society renders it indispensable that each should be bound to observe a certain line of conduct towards the rest. This conduct consists, first, in not injuring the interests of one another; or rather certain interests, which, either by express legal provision or by tacit understanding, ought to be considered as rights; and secondly, in each person's bearing his share (to be fixed on some equitable principle) of the labours and sacrifices incurred for defending the society or its members from injury and molestation. These conditions society is justified in enforcing, at all costs to those who endeavour to withhold fulfilment. Nor is this all that society may do. The acts of an individual may be hurtful to others, or wanting in due consideration for their welfare, without going to the length of violating any of their constituted rights. The offender may then be justly punished by opinion, though not by law. As soon as any part of a person's conduct affects prejudicially the interests of others, society has jurisdiction over it, and the question whether the general welfare will or will not be promoted by interfering with it, becomes open to discussion. But there is no room for entertaining any such question when a person's conduct affects the interests of no person besides himself, or needs not affect them unless they like (all the persons concerned being of full age, and the ordinary amount of understanding). In all such cases, there should be perfect freedom, legal and social, to do the action and stand the consequences. . . .

Questions and Exercises

1. Identify and locate Mill's statement of his thesis in this work. As a class, try to reach consensus.

2. Do you agree with Mill that there are actions which affect only the agent? List actions you can take that will affect only yourself and will not have consequences for your family or your friends.

3. Identify the three spheres of action that Mill believes affect only the agent and should therefore be protected from social control?

4. At the end of Chapter II, his defense of liberty of thought and discussion, Mill summarizes his argument as having four distinct grounds. What are these? Earlier in the chapter he says he will argue from two separate hypotheses ("First: the opinion which it is attempted to suppress may possibly be true. . . . Let us now pass to the second division of the argument . . ."). But in fact he considers *three* hypotheses. Find the words that indicate a third step to the argument.

5. What is the relationship between the three steps of the argument given early in Chapter II and the later summary in four steps?

6. Ever since Oliver Wendell Holmes's Supreme Court opinion, the standard for free speech in the United States has been that it must not "create a clear and present danger." How do you think Mill would respond to that as a standard?

7. Mill believes "the engines of moral repression have been wielded more strenuously against divergence from reigning opinion in self-regarding, than even in social matters." Do you think that contemporary American society is more repressive about private than about public matters? Consider the state of public opinion and attitudes toward cults, the Moral Majority, the teaching of scientific creationism in public schools, and censoring of books in school libraries.

8. Mill writes of England in his time that while the "yoke of the law" is light, the "yoke of opinion" is heavy. Consider two social groups to which you belong and compare how heavy the "yoke of opinion" is in each. What conclusions can you draw from the rigor with which the group enforces its expectations?

9. Mill argues that the "principal question in human affairs" is now to "make the fitting adjustment between individual independence and social control." Draft an essay addressed to your classmates about your solutions to the problem of "victimless crimes," that is, crimes such as gambling, prostitution, and the selling of pornography.

10. Are there any circumstances in which you would be willing to intervene in the actions of relatives or friends to stop them from doing

something that would harm them? Would you prevent a friend from committing suicide? from taking a harmful drug? Would you try to stop a friend from entering into a marriage you thought would be disastrous? Would you take the car keys from a friend who was intoxicated? Draft an essay explaining your position to your classmates.

11. Mill thinks that the domain which should be protected from social control includes: "absolute freedom of opinion and sentiment on all subjects, practical or speculative, scientific, moral, or theological." What of plagiarism? If we censure a person for plagiarism, have we violated that person's right to freedom of opinion? Draft an essay explaining your position to your classmates.

Struggle for Existence

CHARLES DARWIN

from *On the Origin of Species*

Charles Darwin (1809–1881) thought that his book, *On the Origin of Species*, was going to stir up great controversy, and his awareness of this probability caused him to do two things that are quite characteristic of apprehensive writers: he kept delaying publication, and he wrote and rewrote until he was at least fairly confident that he had anticipated the objections of a hostile audience. What he did not anticipate was that he would preside over a revolution in thought as far-reaching as Copernicus's speculation that the earth was not the center of the universe.

Just as Copernicus was born into a world that believed the earth was the center of the universe, so Darwin grew up being taught that the species of organic life were fixed and unchangeable. Against this view, Darwin claimed that species have evolved, that they have gradually been modified over centuries, and that the multiplicity of species we now observe originated in a few very simple forms. The concept of evolution was not an invention of Darwin; it had been a matter of speculation since ancient times. Through reading and through his ongoing scientific work, Darwin joined the conversation carried on by those interested in the possibility of evolution as a way to explain phenomena. Darwin's contribution was to collect a massive body of evidence which could best be explained by the hypothesis that species have evolved, thereby making the theory a respectable scientific opinion.

The possibility of evolution became clear to him from biological observations made between 1831 and 1836, during a voyage aboard the *H.M.S. Beagle* to explore the Southern Hemisphere of the Americas. By 1838, Darwin had amassed the evidence that seemed to confirm the theory of evolution, and he began trying to explain how evolution occurs. In that year he read a book that Thomas Malthus had written forty years earlier,

An Essay on the Principle of Population as it Affects the Future Improvement of Society. Malthus, an English economist, argues that human populations, unless checked, necessarily produce more people than can survive. The picture of human beings in continual competition for scarce resources struck Darwin's imagination and led him to conceive the theory of natural selection as the missing mechanism for evolution. If modifications occur among species, some of those modifications will give an advantage to their possessor; the individuals that are best modified to adapt to a given environment are more likely to survive and to pass the modification on to their offspring.

Darwin had developed these ideas by 1842, when he wrote a short abstract of his theory, one that remained basically unaltered. But his public pronouncement of his theory in *On the Origin of Species* was not published until 1859. What was Darwin doing for those intervening years? His concern about his audience led him to write and rewrite, do further research, and rewrite again, until he produced a book that was so thorough and so carefully and clearly written that it would persuade all but the harshest critics. By 1858 the manuscript was still only half finished when Darwin received a paper from Alfred Russell Wallace, who had arrived at many of Darwin's conclusions independently. Darwin resolved the dilemma of who should be first to announce the theory by submitting a jointly written paper to the Linnaean Society, one of the major nineteenth-century scientific organizations. But the incident forced him to hurry the completion of his own work, which he finally published on November 24, 1859.

The first printing sold out the first day and the book went on to become one of the most important books of the century. Wallace also published, but his initial work was largely ignored. Darwin created a best-seller by combining massive evidence, the power of his principle of natural selection, and a clear, lucid style. Hence, it is Darwin who is credited with ushering in "a new era in our thinking about the nature of man."[1]

On the Origin of Species is almost 500 pages long. Darwin's explanation of natural selection takes up one page of the third chapter. The first two chapters lead the audience carefully through familiar cases of variations within plant and animal species in England, to remind readers of the very ordinariness of the facts upon which he is to build the theory. The third chapter explains his theory. Over the years he added ten additional chapters of examples to buttress, illustrate, and explain his theory.

Excerpts from the third chapter, "Struggle for Existence," are reproduced here. As you read, note the careful counterpoint of theory and examples.

1. Ernest Mayer, "Introduction" to the Harvard edition of *On the Origin of Species* (Cambridge, Mass., 1964), vii.

Struggle for Existence

CHARLES DARWIN

Before entering on the subject of this chapter, I must make a few preliminary remarks, to show how the struggle for existence bears on Natural Selection. It has been seen in the last chapter that amongst organic beings in a state of nature there is some individual variability; indeed I am not aware that this has ever been disputed. It is immaterial for us whether a multitude of doubtful forms be called species or sub-species or varieties; what rank, for instance, the two or three hundred doubtful forms of British plants are entitled to hold, if the existence of any well-marked varieties be admitted. But the mere existence of individual variability and of some few well-marked varieties, though necessary as the foundation for the work, helps us but little in understanding how species arise in nature. How have all those exquisite adaptations of one part of the organisation to another part, and to the conditions of life, and of one distinct organic being to another being, been perfected? We see these beautiful co-adaptations most plainly in the woodpecker and missletoe; and only a little less plainly in the humblest parasite which clings to the hairs of a quadruped or feathers of a bird; in the structure of the beetle which dives through the water; in the plumed seed which is wafted by the gentlest breeze; in short, we see beautiful adaptations everywhere and in every part of the organic world.

Again, it may be asked, how is it that varieties, which I have called incipient species, become ultimately converted into good and distinct species, which in most cases obviously differ from each other far more than do the varieties of the same species? How do those groups of species, which constitute what are called distinct genera, and which differ from each other more than do the species of the same genus, arise? All these results, as we shall more fully see in the next chapter, follow inevitably from the struggle for life. Owing to this struggle for life, any variation, however slight and from whatever cause proceeding, if it be in any degree profitable to an individual of any species, in its infinitely complex relations to other organic beings and to external nature, will tend to the preservation of that individual, and will generally be inherited by its offspring. The offspring, also, will thus have a better chance of surviving, for, of the many individuals of any species which are periodically born, but a small number can survive. I have called this principle, by which each slight variation, if useful, is preserved by the term of Natural Selection, in order to mark its relation to man's power of selection. We have seen that man by selection can certainly produce great results, and can adapt organic beings to his own uses, through the accumulation of slight but useful variations, given to him by the hand of Nature. But Natural Selection, as we shall hereafter see, is a power incessantly ready for action, and is as immeasurably superior to man's feeble efforts, as the works of Nature are to those of Art.

We will now discuss in a little more detail the struggle for existence. In my future work this subject shall be treated, as it well deserves, at much greater length. The elder De Candolle and Lyell have largely and philosophically shown that all organic beings are exposed to severe competition. In regard to plants, no one has treated this subject with more spirit and ability than W. Herbert, Dean of Manchester, evidently the result of his great horticultural knowledge. Nothing is easier than to admit in words the truth of the universal struggle for life, or more difficult — at least I have found it so — than constantly to bear this conclusion in mind. Yet unless it be thoroughly engrained in the mind, I am convinced that the whole economy of nature, with every fact on distribution, rarity, abundance, extinction, and variation, will be dimly seen or quite misunderstood. We behold the face of nature bright with gladness, we often see superabundance of food; we do not see, or we forget, that the birds which are idly singing round us mostly live on insects or seeds, and are thus constantly destroying life; or we forget how largely these songsters, or their eggs, or their nestlings, are destroyed by birds and beasts of prey; we do not always bear in mind, that though food may be now superabundant, it is not so at all seasons of each recurring year.

I should premise that I use the term Struggle for Existence in a large and metaphorical sense, including dependence of one being on another, and including (which is more important) not only the life of the individual, but success in leaving progeny. Two canine animals in a time of dearth, may be truly said to struggle with each other which shall get food and live. But a plant on the edge of a desert is said to struggle for life against the drought, though more properly it should be said to be dependent on the moisture. A plant which annually produces a thousand seeds, of which on an average only one comes to maturity, may be more truly said to struggle with the plants of the same and other kinds which already clothe the ground. The missletoe is dependent on the apple and a few other trees, but can only in a far-fetched sense be said to struggle with these trees, for if too many of these parasites grow on the same tree, it will languish and die. But several seedling missletoes, growing close together on the same branch, may more truly be said to struggle with each other. As the missletoe is disseminated by birds, its existence depends on birds; and it may metaphorically be said to struggle with other fruit-bearing plants, in order to tempt birds to devour and thus disseminate its seeds rather than those of other plants. In these several senses, which pass into each other, I use for convenience sake the general term of struggle for existence.

A struggle for existence inevitably follows from the high rate at which all organic beings tend to increase. Every being, which during its natural lifetime produces several eggs or seeds, must suffer destruction during some period of its life, and during some season or occasional year, otherwise, on the principle of geometrical increase, its numbers would quickly become so inordinately great that no country could support the product. Hence, as more individuals are produced than can possibly survive, there must in every case be a struggle for existence, either one individual with another of the same species, or with the individuals of distinct species, or with the physical conditions of life. It is the doctrine of Malthus applied with manifold force to the whole animal and vegetable kingdoms; for in this case there can be no artificial increase of food, and no prudential restraint from marriage. Although some species may be now increasing, more or less rapidly, in numbers, all cannot do so, for the world would not hold them.

There is no exception to the rule that every organic being naturally increases at so high a rate, that if not destroyed, the earth would soon be covered by the progeny of a single pair. Even slow-breeding man has doubled in twenty-five years, and at this rate, in a few thousand years, there would literally not be standing room for his progeny. Linnaeus has calculated that if an annual plant produced only two seeds — and there is no plant so unproductive as this — and their seedlings next year produced two, and so on, then in twenty years there would be a million plants. The elephant is reckoned to be the slowest breeder of all known animals, and I have taken some pains to estimate its probable minimum rate of natural increase: it will be under the mark to assume that it breeds when thirty years old, and goes on breeding till ninety years old, bringing forth three pair of young in this interval; if this be so, at the end of the fifth century there would be alive fifteen million elephants, descended from the first pair.

But we have better evidence on this subject than mere theoretical calculations, namely, the numerous recorded cases of the astonishingly rapid increase of various animals in a state of nature, when circumstances have been favourable to them during two or three following seasons. Still more striking is the evidence from our domestic animals of many kinds which have run wild in several parts of the world: if the statements of the rate of increase of slow-breeding cattle and horses in South-America, and latterly in Australia, had not been well authenticated, they would have been quite incredible. So it is with plants: cases could be given of introduced plants which have become common throughout whole islands in a period of less than ten years. Several of the plants now most numerous over the wide plains of La Plata, clothing square leagues of surface almost to the exclusion of all other plants, have been introduced from Europe; and there are plants which now range in India, as I hear from Dr. Falconer, from Cape Comorin to the Himalaya, which have been imported from America since its discovery. In such cases, and endless instances could be given, no one supposes that the fertility of these animals or plants has been suddenly and temporarily increased in any sensible degree. The obvious explanation is that the conditions of life have been very favourable, and that there has consequently been less destruction of the old and young, and that nearly all the young have been enabled to breed. In such cases the geometrical ratio of increase, the result of which never fails to be surprising, simply explains the extraordinarily rapid increase and wide diffusion of naturalised productions in their new homes.

In a state of nature almost every plant produces seed, and amongst animals there are very few which do not annually pair. Hence we may confidently assert, that all plants and animals are tending to increase at a geometrical ratio, that all would most rapidly stock every station in which they could any how exist, and that the geometrical tendency to increase must be checked by destruction at some period of life. Our familiarity with the larger domestic animals tends, I think, to mislead us: we see no great destruction falling on them, and we forget that thousands are annually slaughtered for food, and that in a state of nature an equal number would have somehow to be disposed of.

The only difference between organisms which annually produce eggs or seeds by the thousand, and those which produce extremely few, is, that the slow-breeders would require a few more years to people, under favourable conditions, a whole district, let it be ever so large. The condor lays a couple of eggs and the ostrich a score, and yet in the same country the condor may be the more numerous of the two: the Fulmar petrel lays but one egg, yet it is believed to be the most numerous bird in the world. One fly deposits hundreds of eggs, and another, like the hippobosca, a single one; but this difference does not determine how many individuals of the two species can be supported in a district. A large number of eggs is of some importance to those species, which depend on a rapidly fluctuating amount of food, for it allows them rapidly to increase in number. But the real importance of a large number of eggs or seeds is to make up for much destruction at some period of life; and this period in the great majority of cases is an early one. If an animal can in any way protect its own eggs or young, a small number may be produced, and yet the average stock be fully kept up; but if many eggs or young are destroyed, many must be produced, or the species will become extinct. It would suffice to keep up the full number of a tree, which lived on an average for a thousand years, if a single seed were produced once in a thousand years, supposing that this seed were never destroyed, and could be ensured to germinate in a fitting place. So that in all cases, the average number of any animal or plant depends only indirectly on the number of its eggs or seeds.

In looking at Nature, it is most necessary to keep the foregoing considerations always in mind — never to forget that every single organic being around us may be said to be striving to the utmost to increase in numbers; that each lives by a struggle at some period of its life; that heavy destruction inevitably falls either on the young or old, during each generation or at recurrent intervals. Lighten any check, mitigate the destruction ever so little, and the number of the species will almost instantaneously increase to any amount. The face of Nature may be compared to a yielding surface, with ten thousand sharp wedges packed close together and driven inwards by incessant blows, sometimes one wedge being struck, and then another with greater force.

What checks the natural tendency of each species to increase in number is most obscure. Look at the most vigorous species; by as much as it swarms in numbers, by so much will its tendency to increase be still further increased. We know not exactly what the checks are in even one single instance. Nor will this surprise any one who reflects how ignorant we are on this head, even in regard to mankind, so incomparably better known than any other animal. This subject has been ably treated by several authors, and I shall, in my future work, discuss some of the checks at considerable length, more especially in regard to the feral animals of South America. Here I will make only a few remarks, just to recall to the reader's mind some of the chief points. Eggs or very young animals seem generally to suffer most, but this is not invariably the case. With plants there is a vast destruction of seeds, but, from some observations which I have made, I believe that it is the seedlings which suffer most from germinating in ground already thickly stocked with other plants. Seedlings, also, are destroyed in vast numbers by various enemies; for instance, on a piece of ground three feet long and two wide, dug and cleared, and where there could be no choking from other plants, I marked all the seedlings of our native weeds as they came up, and out of the 357 no less than 295 were destroyed, chiefly by slugs and insects. If turf which has long been mown, and the case would be the same with turf closely browsed by quadrupeds, be let to grow, the more vigorous plants gradually kill the less vigorous, though fully grown, plants: thus out of twenty species growing on a little plot of turf (three feet by four) nine species perished from the other species being allowed to grow up freely.

The amount of food for each species of course gives the extreme limit to which each can increase; but very frequently it is not the obtaining food, but the serving as prey to other animals, which determines the average numbers of a species. Thus, there seems to be little doubt that the stock of partridges, grouse, and hares on any large estate depends chiefly on the destruction of vermin. If not one head of game were shot during the next twenty years in England, and, at the same time, if no vermin were destroyed, there would, in all probability, be less game than at present, although hundreds of thousands of game animals are now annually killed. On the other hand, in some cases, as with the elephant and rhinoceros, none are destroyed by beasts of prey: even the tiger in India most rarely dares to attack a young elephant protected by its dam.

Climate plays an important part in determining the average numbers of a species, and periodical seasons of extreme cold or drought, I believe to be the most effective of all checks. I estimated that the winter of

1854–55 destroyed four-fifths of the birds in my own grounds; and this is a tremendous destruction, when we remember that ten percent is an extraordinarily severe mortality from epidemics with man. The action of climate seems at first sight to be quite independent of the struggle for existence; but in so far as climate chiefly acts in reducing food, it brings on the most severe struggle between the individuals, whether of the same or of distinct species, which subsist on the same kind of food. Even when climate, for instance extreme cold, acts directly, it will be the least vigorous, or those which have got least food through the advancing winter, which will suffer most. When we travel from south to north, or from a damp region to a dry, we invariably see some species gradually getting rarer and rarer, and finally disappearing; and the change of climate being conspicuous we are tempted to attribute the whole effect to its direct action. But this is a very false view: we forget that each species, even where it most abounds, is constantly suffering enormous destruction at some period of its life, from enemies or from competitors for the same place and food; and if these enemies or competitors be in the least degree favoured by any slight change of climate, they will increase in numbers, and, as each area is already fully stocked with inhabitants, the other species will decrease. When we travel southward and see a species decreasing in numbers, we may feel sure that the cause lies quite as much in other species being favoured, as in this one being hurt. So it is when we travel northward, but in a somewhat lesser degree, for the number of species of all kinds, and therefore of competitors, decreases northwards; hence in going northward, or in ascending a mountain, we far oftener meet with stunted forms, due to the *directly* injurious action of climate, than we do in proceeding southwards or in descending a mountain. When we reach the Arctic regions, or snow-capped summits, or absolute deserts, the struggle for life is almost exclusively with the elements.

That climate acts in main part indirectly by favouring other species, we may clearly see in the prodigious number of plants in our gardens which can perfectly well endure our climate, but which never become naturalised, for they cannot compete with our native plants, nor resist destruction by our native animals.

When a species, owing to highly favourable circumstances, increases inordinately in numbers in a small tract, epidemics — at least, this seems generally to occur with our game animals — often ensue: and here we have a limiting check independent of the struggle for life. But even some of these so-called epidemics appear to be due to parasitic worms, which have from some cause, possibly in part through facility of diffusion amongst the crowded animals, been disproportionably favoured: and here comes in a sort of struggle between the parasite and its prey.

On the other hand, in many cases, a large stock of individuals of the same species, relatively to the numbers of its enemies, is absolutely necessary for its preservation. Thus we can easily raise plenty of corn and rape-seed, &c., in our fields, because the seeds are in great excess compared with the number of birds which feed on them; nor can the birds, though having a superabundance of food at this one season, increase in number proportionally to the supply of seed, as their numbers are checked during winter: but any one who has tried, knows how troublesome it is to get seed from a few wheat or other such plants in a garden; I have in this case lost every single seed. This view of the necessity of a large stock of the same species for its preservation, explains, I believe, some singular facts in nature, such as that of very rare plants being sometimes extremely abundant in the few spots where they do occur; and that of some social plants being social, that is, abounding in individuals, even on the extreme confines of their range. For in such cases, we may believe, that a plant could exist only where the conditions of its life were so favourable that many could exist together, and thus save each other from utter destruction. I should add that the good effects of frequent intercrossing, and the ill effects of close interbreeding, probably come into play in some of these cases; but on this intricate subject I will not here enlarge. . . .

As species of the same genus have usually, though by no means invariably, some similarity in habits and constitution, and always in structure, the struggle will generally be more severe between species of the same genus, when they come into competition with each other, than between species of distinct genera. We see this in the recent extension over parts of the United States of one species of swallow having caused the decrease of another species. The recent increase of the missel-thrush in parts of Scotland has caused the decrease of the song-thrush. How frequently we hear of one species of rat taking the place of another species under the most different climates! In Russia the small Asiatic cockroach has everywhere driven before it its great congener. One species of charlock will supplant another, and so in other cases. We can dimly see why the competition should be most severe between allied forms, which fill nearly the same place in the economy of nature; but probably in no one case could we precisely say why one species has been victorious over another in the great battle of life.

A corollary of the highest importance may be deduced from the foregoing remarks, namely, that the structure of every organic being is related, in the most essential yet often hidden manner, to that of all other organic beings, with which it comes into competition for food or residence, or from which it has to escape, or on which it preys. This is obvious in the structure of the teeth and talons of the tiger; and in that of the legs and claws of the parasite which clings to the hair on the tiger's body. But in the beautifully plumed seed of the dandelion, and in the flattened and fringed legs of the water-beetle, the relation seems at first confined to the elements of air and water. Yet the advantage of plumed seeds no doubt stands in the closest relation to the land being already thickly clothed by other plants; so that the seeds may be widely distributed and fall on unoccupied ground. In the water-beetle, the structure of its legs, so well adapted for diving, allows it to compete with other aquatic insects, to hunt for its own prey, and to escape serving as prey to other animals.

The store of nutriment laid up within the seeds of many plants seems at first sight to have no sort of relation to other plants. But from the strong growth of young plants produced from such seeds (as peas and beans), when sown in the midst of long grass, I suspect that the chief use of the nutriment in the seed is to favour the growth of the young seedling, whilst struggling with other plants growing vigorously all around.

Look at a plant in the midst of its range, why does it not double or quadruple its numbers? We know that it can perfectly well withstand a little more heat or cold, dampness or dryness, for elsewhere it ranges into slightly hotter or colder, damper or drier districts. In this case we can clearly see that if we wished in imagination to give the plant the power of increasing in number, we should have to give it some advantage over its competitors, or over the animals which preyed on it. On the confines of its geographical range, a change of constitution with respect to climate would clearly be an advantage to our plant; but we have reason to believe that only a few plants or animals range so far, that they are destroyed by the rigour of the climate alone. Not until we reach the extreme confines of life, in the arctic regions or on the borders of an utter desert, will competition cease. The land may be extremely cold or dry, yet there will be competition between some few species, or between the individuals of the same species, for the warmest or dampest spots.

Hence, also, we can see that when a plant or animal is placed in a new country amongst new competitors, though the climate may be exactly the same as in its former home, yet the conditions of its life will generally be changed in an essential manner. If we wished to increase its average numbers in its new home, we should have to modify it in a different way to what we should have done in its native country; for we should have to give it some advantage over a different set of competitors or enemies.

It is good thus to try in our imagination to give any form some advantage over another. Probably in no single instance should we know what to do, so as to succeed. It will convince us of our ignorance on the mutual relations of all organic beings; a conviction as necessary, as it seems to be difficult to acquire. All that we can do, is to keep steadily in mind that each organic being is striving to increase at a geometrical ratio; that each at some period of its life, during some season of the year, during each generation or at intervals, has to struggle for life, and to suffer great destruction. When we reflect on this struggle, we may console ourselves with the full belief, that the war of nature is not incessant, that no fear is felt, that death is generally prompt, and that the vigorous, the healthy, and the happy survive and multiply.

Questions and Exercises

1. State the principle of natural selection.

2. What four factors check the unrestricted increase of species?

3. Copy the passage you consider to be the most difficult paragraph to understand. Does writing it out help you to understand?

4. Darwin says he used the phrase "struggle for existence" metaphorically (see paragraph 4). Why is it not literal?

5. On p. 136, Darwin compares the "face of Nature" to a "yielding surface." What is the point of the comparison?

6. Make a list of five to ten words you do not understand. What can you tell about their possible meaning from the context? Look them up in a dictionary.

7. By checking a biology textbook or by asking a biology instructor, find out how biologists use the words: species, variety, genus, variation. Check an economics textbook and ask an economics instructor to find out how the same words are used by economists.

8. Paraphrase the fourth sentence of paragraph 2, "Owing to this . . . ."

9. Identify what you think is the thesis of the chapter and rewrite it in one sentence using your own words. Meet in a small group to read and compare your sentences. Write a thesis sentence on which the group can agree.

10. Darwin got his idea of "struggle for existence" from an economist. Apply the idea to other situations, selecting a mate, electing a President, surviving on the battlefield. After making your own list, meet in a small group to exchange ideas.

11. In small groups discuss the last paragraph. Come to a consensus on why Darwin might have included it.

12. Check reference books — encyclopedias, the Dictionary of National Biography — to find out who Thomas Malthus was and what he contributed to economics. Make notes for an oral report to the class.

13. On p. 135, Darwin speaks of how animal populations behave in the "state of nature." Compare Darwin's use of the concept with Hobbes's earlier use of it in political theory. Draft an essay on this subject. Your readers are your classmates who have read the selections from Darwin and Hobbes in this text.

14. Draft an essay addressed to your classmates on Darwin's practice of the scientific method as first articulated by Descartes.

15. Draft a letter to a young-man still in high school who is worried about classmates stealing the ideas he articulates in class discussion. Draw on what you have learned about Darwin and Wallace and on what you can discover from consulting biographers and reference books.

16. Pretend that you are a British intellectual living in 1859. Draft a letter to a friend in which you comment on two works that you have just read, Charles Darwin's *On the Origin of Species* and John Stuart Mill's *On Liberty*. Explain to your friend why you think 1859 is an *annus mirabilis* (year of wonders).

Autobiographical Notes

ALBERT EINSTEIN

from *Albert Einstein: Philosopher-Scientist*

Albert Einstein, who was born in Ulm, Germany, in 1879, died in Princeton in 1955 as the most celebrated scientist of his age. Ranked by other scientists with Isaac Newton, Einstein has become a name to symbolize genius.

With all his fame, Einstein was also characterized by modest, unassuming personal behavior. Einstein was embarrassed by the attention he received. His discomfort was not the resentment celebrities feel at the intrusions of the public into their private lives. What embarrassed Einstein was to be thought a genius, although he acknowledged legitimate interest in why he was so creative in science. In a statement quoted by a biographer, he said:

> I sometimes ask myself how did it come that I was the one to develop the theory of relativity. The reason, I think, is a normal adult never stops to think about problems of space and time. These are things which he has thought of as a child. But my intellectual development was retarded, as a result of which I began to wonder about space and time only when I had already grown up. Naturally, I could go deeper into the problem than a child with normal abilities.[1]

Einstein is saying here that he was successful because he was slow, not because he was bright. Few have accepted this self-analysis.

Einstein was baffled by any interest in him as a person. Once he was asked to write a foreword to a biography of another scientist. The focus of

1. Ronald W. Clark, *Einstein: The Life and Times* (New York: World, 1971), pp. 27–28.

it, he said, should be on the person's scientific contributions. About other information, he had this to say:

> Of course, in such a book, the personal side must be taken account of; but it should not be made the main thing especially when no book exists dealing with the actual achievement. Otherwise, the result is a banal hero-worship, based on emotion and not on insight. I have learned by my own experience how hateful and ridiculous it is, when a serious man, absorbed in important endeavors, is ignorantly lionized.[2]

It is not surprising, then, that when he agreed to write an autobiography — what he referred to as his "obituary" — he spent little time on "the personal side." He says nothing about where or when he was born, who his parents were or whether he married and had children (he did). His purpose was to produce an *intellectual* autobiography to which such facts, he thought, were irrelevant. As he wrote, "the being of a man of my type lies precisely in *what* he thinks and *how* he thinks, not in what he does or suffers."[3]

In fact, fame came to Einstein with extraordinary suddenness. He had an undistinguished scholastic career, dropping out of school and soon settling into a sedate and unremarkable career as an examiner of patent applications for the Patent Office in Bern, Switzerland. He thought about fundamental problems in physics in his spare time. Then in 1905, this obscure twenty-six-year-old with mediocre academic credentials had four papers published in one of the most prestigious of physics journals, *Annalen der Physik*. One of the papers contained his work on the photoelectric effect, for which he later won the Nobel Prize. Another contained his statement of the Special Theory of Relativity, the theory with which Einstein is associated in the popular mind. Within two years, at the age of twenty-eight, he was widely acknowledged as one of the greatest physicists of all time. He later published a paper on the General Theory of Relativity. Using this abstract theory, he predicted that light from the sun to earth would curve as a result of gravitational forces. That prediction was confirmed in a spectacular way in 1919 by an expedition to West Africa which measured light from the sun during an eclipse. Einstein's elevation to the stature of Newton was assured.

Despite the fact that Einstein thought only his intellectual contributions were important, he wrote his autobiography in an intimate, first-person style. The beginning of the piece, reproduced here, opens with the

2. Quoted in Banesh Hoffman, *Albert Einstein: Creator and Rebel* (New York: Viking Press, 1973), p. 10.

3. Albert Einstein, "Autobiographical Notes," in *Albert Einstein: Philosopher-Scientist*, ed. Paul Schilpp (Evanston, Illinois: The Library of Living Philosophers, 1949), p. 33.

words, "Here I sit...." In fact, even in his scientific writings, he was famous for being informal. For example, he began an important paper on the theory of gravitation with the words, "In a memoir published four years ago I tried to answer the question whether the propagation of light is influenced by gravitation. I return to this theme, because my previous presentation of the subject does not satisfy me."[4] Unlike many scientists, Einstein did not artificially distance himself from the material which he studied.

The selection below appeared in the Library of Living Philosophers, a series of volumes designed to let significant philosophers write about the development of their thought. In this passage Einstein recounts some events from his early life, but only for the purpose of illuminating his intellectual development. Since he continually jumps back and forth from his past opinions to present ones, it may help to consider this brief outline of the selection: He begins by stating his purpose for writing an autobiography. Then he discusses his loss of traditional religious faith and his growing belief in the powers of intellectual contemplation. He narrates two incidents from his childhood that influenced his intellectual development. After commenting on the kind of education he received, he turns to what he believes is required for good scientific thinking. The excerpts conclude with Einstein's account of the enormous impact that the classical theory of thermodynamics had on his intellectual development; every science student has studied that theory, but it inspired Einstein with universe-changing questions.

Autobiographical Notes*
ALBERT EINSTEIN

Here I sit in order to write, at the age of 67, something like my own obituary. I am doing this not merely because Dr. Schilpp has persuaded me to do it; but because I do, in fact, believe that it is a good thing to show those who are striving alongside of us, how one's own striving and searching appears to one in retrospect. After some reflection, I felt how insufficient any such attempt is bound to be. For, however brief and limited one's working life may be, and however predominant may be the ways of error, the exposition of that which is worthy of communication does nonetheless not come easy — today's person of 67 is by no means the same as was the one of 50, of 30, or of 20. Every reminiscence is colored by today's being

4. Quoted in Jeremy Bernstein, *Einstein* (New York: Viking, Modern Masters Series, 1973), p. 171.

Reprinted from *Albert Einstein: Philosopher-Scientist* edited by Paul Arthur Schilpp, vol. 7, Library of Living Philosophers, Evanston, IL, Reprinted by permission of The Open Court Publishing Company, LaSalle, Illinois. Copyright © 1970.
* Translated from the original German manuscript by Paul Arthur Schilpp.

what it is, and therefore by a deceptive point of view. This consideration could very well deter. Nevertheless much can be lifted out of one's own experience which is not open to another consciousness.

Even when I was a fairly precocious young man the nothingness of the hopes and strivings which chases most men restlessly through life came to my consciousness with considerable vitality. Moreover, I soon discovered the cruelty of that chase, which in those years was much more carefully covered up by hypocrisy and glittering words than is the case today. By the mere existence of his stomach everyone was condemned to participate in that chase. Moreover, it was possible to satisfy the stomach by such participation, but not man in so far as he is a thinking and feeling being. As the first way out there was religion, which is implanted into every child by way of the traditional education-machine. Thus I came — despite the fact that I was the son of entirely irreligious (Jewish) parents — to a deep religiosity, which, however, found an abrupt ending at the age of 12. Through the reading of popular scientific books I soon reached the conviction that much in the stories of the Bible could not be true. The consequence was a positively fanatic [orgy of] freethinking coupled with the impression that youth is intentionally being deceived by the state through lies; it was a crushing impression. Suspicion against every kind of authority grew out of this experience, a skeptical attitude towards the convictions which were alive in any specific social environment — an attitude which has never again left me, even though later on, because of a better insight into the causal connections, it lost some of its original poignancy.

It is quite clear to me that the religious paradise of youth, which was thus lost, was a first attempt to free myself from the chains of the "merely-personal," from an existence which is dominated by wishes, hopes and primitive feelings. Out yonder there was this huge world, which exists independently of us human beings and which stands before us like a great, eternal riddle, at least partially accessible to our inspection and thinking. The contemplation of this world beckoned like a liberation, and I soon noticed that many a man whom I had learned to esteem and to admire had found inner freedom and security in devoted occupation with it. The mental grasp of this extrapersonal world within the frame of the given possibilities swam as highest aim half consciously and half unconsciously before my mind's eye. Similarly motivated men of the present and of the past, as well as the insights which they had achieved, were the friends which could not be lost. The road to this paradise was not as comfortable and alluring as the road to the religious paradise; but it has proved itself as trustworthy, and I have never regretted having chosen it.

What I have here said is true only within a certain sense, just as a drawing consisting of a few strokes can do justice to a complicated object, full of perplexing details, only in a very limited sense. If an individual enjoys well-ordered thoughts, it is quite possible that this side of his nature may grow more pronounced at the cost of other sides and thus may determine his mentality in increasing degree. In this case it is well posible that such an individual in retrospect sees a uniformly systematic development, whereas the actual experience takes place in kaleidoscopic particular situations. The manifoldness of the external situations and the narrowness of the momentary content of consciousness bring about a sort of atomizing of the life of every human being. In a man of my type the turning-point of the development lies in the fact that gradually the major interest disengages itself to a far-reaching degree from the momentary and the merely personal and turns towards the striving for a mental grasp of things. Looked at from this point of view the above schematic remarks contain as much truth as can be uttered in such brevity.

What, precisely, is "thinking"? When, at the reception of sense-impressions, memory-pictures emerge, this is not yet "thinking." And when such pictures form series, each member of which calls forth another, this too is not yet "thinking." When, however, a certain picture turns up in many such series, then — precisely through such return — it becomes an ordering element for such series, in that it connects series which in themselves are unconnected. Such an element becomes an instrument, a concept. I think that the transition from free association or "dreaming" to thinking is characterized by the more or less dominating rôle which the "concept" plays in it. It is by no means necessary that a concept must be connected with a sensorily cognizable and reproducible sign (word); but when this is the case thinking becomes by means of that fact communicable.

With what right — the reader will ask — does this man operate so carelessly and primitively with ideas in such a problematic realm without making even the least effort to prove anything? My defense: all our thinking is of this nature of a free play with concepts; the justification for this play lies in the measure of survey over the experience of the senses which we are able to achieve with its aid. The concept of "truth" can not yet be applied to such a structure; to my thinking this concept can come in question only when a far-reaching agreement (*convention*) concerning the elements and rules of the game is already at hand.

For me it is not dubious that our thinking goes on for the most part without use of signs (words) and beyond that to a considerable degree unconsciously. For how, otherwise, should it happen that sometimes we "wonder" quite spontaneously about some experience? This "wondering" seems to occur when an experience comes into conflict with a world of concepts which is already sufficiently fixed in us. Whenever such a conflict is experienced hard and intensively it reacts back upon our thought world in a decisive way. The development of this thought world is in a certain sense a continuous flight from "wonder."

A wonder of such nature I experienced as a child of 4 or 5 years, when my father showed me a compass. That this needle behaved in such a determined way did not at all fit into the nature of events, which could find a place in the unconscious world of concepts (effect connected with direct "touch"). I can still remember — or at least believe I can remember — that this experience made a deep and lasting impression upon me. Something deeply hidden had to be behind things. What man sees before him from infancy causes no reaction of this kind; he is not surprised over the falling of bodies, concerning wind and rain, nor concerning the moon or about the fact that the moon does not fall down, nor concerning the differences between living and non-living matter.

At the age of 12 I experienced a second wonder of a totally different nature: in a little book dealing with Euclidian plane geometry, which came into my hands at the beginning of a schoolyear. Here were assertions, as for example the intersection of the three altitudes of a triangle in one point, which — though by no means evident — could nevertheless be proved with such certainty that any doubt appeared to be out of the question. This lucidity and certainty made an indescribable impression upon me. That the axiom had to be accepted unproved did not disturb me. In any case it was quite sufficient for me if I could peg proofs upon propositions the validity of which did not seem to me to be dubious. For example I remember that an uncle told me the Pythagorean theorem before the holy geometry booklet had come into my hands. After much effort I succeeded in "proving" this theorem on the basis of the similarity of triangles; in doing so it seemed to me "evident" that the relations of the sides of the right-angled triangles would have to be completely determined by one of the acute angles. Only something which did not in similar fashion seem to be "evident" appeared to me to be in need of any proof at all. Also, the objects with which geometry deals seemed to be of no different type than the objects of sensory perception, "which can be seen and touched." . . .

If thus it appeared that it was possible to get certain knowledge of the objects of experience by means of pure thinking, this "wonder" rested upon an error. Nevertheless, for anyone who experiences it for the first time, it is marvellous enough that man is capable at all to reach such a degree of certainty and purity in pure thinking as the Greeks showed us for the first time to be possible in geometry. . . .

And now back to the obituary. At the age of 12–16 I familiarized myself with the elements of mathematics together with the principles of differential and integral calculus. In doing so I had the good fortune of hitting upon books which were not too particular in their logical rigour, but which made up for this by permitting the main thoughts to stand out clearly and synoptically. This occupation was, on the whole, truly fascinating; climaxes were reached whose impression could easily compete with that of elementary geometry — the basic idea of analytical geometry, the infinite series, the concepts of differential and integral. I also had the good fortune of getting to know the essential results and methods of the entire field of the natural sciences in an excellent popular exposition, which limited itself almost throughout to qualitative aspects (Bernstein's

People's Books on Natural Science, a work of 5 or 6 volumes), a work which I read with breathless attention. I had also already studied some theoretical physics when, at the age of 17, I entered the Polytechnic Institute of Zürich as a student of mathematics and physics.

There I had excellent teachers (for example, Hurwitz, Minkowski), so that I really could have gotten a sound mathematical education. However, I worked most of the time in the physical laboratory, fascinated by the direct contact with experience. The balance of the time I used in the main in order to study at home the works of Kirchhoff, Helmholtz, Hertz, etc. The fact that I neglected mathematics to a certain extent had its cause not merely in my stronger interest in the natural sciences than in mathematics but also in the following strange experience. I saw that mathematics was split up into numerous specialities, each of which could easily absorb the short lifetime granted to us. Consequently I saw myself in the position of Buridan's ass which was unable to decide upon any specific bundle of hay. This was obviously due to the fact that my intuition was not strong enough in the field of mathematics in order to differentiate clearly the fundamentally important, that which is really basic, from the rest of the more or less dispensable erudition. Beyond this, however, my interest in the knowledge of nature was also unqualifiedly stronger; and it was not clear to me as a student that the approach to a more profound knowledge of the basic principles of physics is tied up with the most intricate mathematical methods. This dawned upon me only gradually after years of independent scientific work. True enough, physics also was divided into separate fields, each of which was capable of devouring a short lifetime of work without having satisfied the hunger for deeper knowledge. The mass of insufficiently connected experimental data was overwhelming here also. In this field, however, I soon learned to scent out that which was able to lead to fundamentals and to turn aside from everything else, from the multitude of things which clutter up the mind and divert it from the essential. The hitch in this was, of course, the fact that one had to cram all this stuff into one's mind for the examinations, whether one liked it or not. This coercion had such a deterring effect [upon me] that, after I had passed the final examination, I found the consideration of any scientific problems distasteful to me for an entire year. In justice I must add, moreover, that in Switzerland we had to suffer far less under such coercion, which smothers every truly scientific impulse, than is the case in many another locality. There were altogether only two examinations; aside from these, one could just about do as one pleased. This was especially the case if one had a friend, as did I, who attended the lectures regularly and who worked over their content conscientiously. This gave one freedom in the choice of pursuits until a few months before the examination, a freedom which I enjoyed to a great extent and have gladly taken into the bargain the bad conscience connected with it as by far the lesser evil. It is, in fact, nothing short of a miracle that the modern methods of instruction have not yet entirely strangled the holy curiosity of inquiry; for this delicate little plant, aside from stimulation, stands mainly in need of freedom; without this it goes to wreck and ruin without fail. It is a very grave mistake to think that the enjoyment of seeing and searching can be promoted by means of coercion and a sense of duty. To the contrary, I believe that it would be possible to rob even a healthy beast of prey of its voraciousness, if it were possible, with the aid of a whip, to force the beast to devour continuously, even when not hungry, especially if the food, handed out under such coercion, were to be selected accordingly. . . .

Before I enter upon a critique of mechanics as the foundation of physics, something of a broadly general nature will first have to be said concerning the points of view according to which it is possible to criticize physical theories at all. The first point of view is obvious: the theory must not contradict empirical facts. However evident this demand may in the first place appear, its application turns out to be quite delicate. For it is often, perhaps even always, possible to adhere to a general theoretical foundation by securing the adaptation of the theory to the facts by means of artificial additional assumptions. In any case, however, this first point of view is concerned with the confirmation of the theoretical foundation by the available empirical facts.

The second point of view is not concerned with the relation to the material of observation but with the premises of the theory itself, with what may briefly but vaguely be characterized as the "naturalness" or "logical simplicity" of the premises (of the basic concepts and of the relations between these which are taken as a basis). This point of view, an exact formulation of which meets with great difficulties, has played an important rôle in the selection and evaluation of theories since time immemorial. The problem here is not simply one of a kind of enumeration of the logically independent premises (if anything like this were at all unequivocally possible), but that of a kind of reciprocal weighing of incommensurable qualities. Furthermore, among theories of equally "simple" foundation that one is to be taken as superior which most sharply delimits the qualities of systems in the abstract (i.e., contains the most definite claims). Of the "realm" of theories I need not speak here, inasmuch as we are confining ourselves to such theories whose object is the *totality* of all physical appearances. The second point of view may briefly be characterized as concerning itself with the "inner perfection" of the theory, whereas the first point of view refers to the "external confirmation." The following I reckon as also belonging to the "inner perfection" of a theory: We prize a theory more highly if, from the logical standpoint, it is not the result of an arbitrary choice among theories which among themselves, are of equal value and analogously constructed.

The meager precision of the assertions contained in the last two paragraphs I shall not attempt to excuse by lack of sufficient printing space at my disposal, but confess herewith that I am not, without more ado [immediately], and perhaps not at all, capable to replace these hints by more precise definitions. . . .

Enough of this. Newton, forgive me; you found the only way which, in your age, was just about possible for a man of highest thought-and creative power. The concepts, which you created, are even today still guiding our thinking in physics, although we now know that they will have to be replaced by others farther removed from the sphere of immediate experience, if we aim at a profounder understanding of relationships.

"Is this supposed to be an obituary?" the astonished reader will likely ask. I would like to reply: essentially yes. For the essential in the being of a man of my type lies precisely in *what* he thinks and *how* he thinks, not in what he does or suffers. Consequently, the obituary can limit itself in the main to the communicating of thoughts which have played a considerable rôle in my endeavors. — A theory is the more impressive the greater the simplicity of its premises is, the more different kinds of things it relates, and the more extended is its area of applicability. Therefore the deep impression which classical thermodynamics made upon me. It is the only physical theory of universal content concerning which I am convinced that, within the framework of the applicability of its basic concepts, it will never be overthrown (for the special attention of those who are skeptical on principle). . . .

. . . By and by I despaired of the possibility of discovering the true laws by means of constructive efforts based on known facts. The longer and the more despairingly I tried, the more I came to the conviction that only the discovery of a universal formal principle could lead us to assured results. The example I saw before me was thermodynamics. The general principle was there given in the theorem: the laws of nature are such that it is impossible to construct a *perpetuum mobile* (of the first and second kind). How, then, could such a universal principle be found? After ten years of reflection such a principle resulted from a paradox upon which I had already hit at the age of sixteen: If I pursue a beam of light with the velocity c (velocity of light in a vacuum), I should observe such a beam of light as a spatially oscillatory electromagnetic field at rest. However, there seems to be no such thing, whether on the basis of experience or according to Maxwell's equations. From the very beginning it appeared to me intuitively clear that, judged from the standpoint of such an observer, everything would have to happen according to the same laws as for an observer who, relative to the earth, was at rest. For how, otherwise, should the first observer know, i.e., be able to determine, that he is in a state of fast uniform motion?

One sees that in this paradox the germ of the special relativity theory is already contained. Today everyone knows, of course, that all attempts to clarify this paradox satisfactorily were condemned to failure as long as the axiom of the absolute character of time, viz., of simultaneity, unrecognizedly was anchored in the unconscious. Clearly to recognize this axiom and its arbitrary character really implies already the solution of the problem. The type of critical reasoning which was required for the discovery of this central point was decisively furthered, in my case, especially by the reading of David Hume's and Ernst Mach's philosophical writings.

Questions and Exercises

1. What were the two experiences Einstein reports from his childhood which incited him to wonder? Write a paragraph on each incident, describing it and explaining why it was significant.

2. Einstein makes some brief comments on his own formal education. What inferences can you draw from these comments about Einstein's views on the most effective forms of education?

3. Einstein moves back and forth between relating what he thought at certain times in the past and what he thinks now. Draw a diagram of what he has to say about each period of his past, from ages four to twenty; that is, what does he tell us about himself up to age five, then up to age twelve, and so on?

4. Einstein states two criteria that any legitimate physical theory must satisfy. What are they? Look back at Darwin's theory of evolution and try to decide whether his theory satisfies Einstein's two criteria?

5. Einstein refers to "Buridan's ass." Identify the reference.

6. Einstein's early questioning of traditional religious faith began to free him, he says, from the "merely-personal." What does he mean by that? After recording your own response, meet in small groups to exchange notes.

7. Consider what Einstein has to say about what thinking is. What is the relationship between this view and the way the autobiography is written? After recording your own response, meet in small groups to exchange notes.

8. Einstein found a paradox at the age of sixteen, which he says contained the "germ of the special relativity theory." What is the paradox? What makes it paradoxical? Relate his account of the paradox to what he says about wonder on p. 145. After recording your own response, meet in small groups to exchange notes.

9. What does Einstein say motivated him to science? Draft an essay comparing Einstein's sense that science liberates with Plato's account of the Cave. Assume that your readers are undergraduates who have read the selections in this text.

10. Compare the selection from Einstein and the one from Descartes as examples of intellectual autobiography. Again, assume that your read-

ers are undergraduates who have read the selections in this text. You might want instead to compare and contrast Descartes's and Einstein's views of the scientific method.

11. Since Einstein believed that only his intellectual contributions were important and that he must free himself from the "merely-personal," why did he choose to write personally and informally? In an essay addressed to your classmates, present your views on this issue.

Letter from Birmingham Jail

MARTIN LUTHER KING, JR.

When writers have something important to say, a strong compelling reason to write, they write, whatever their circumstances. John Milton wrote *Paradise Lost* when he was blind; Condorcet (1743–94) composed his great optimistic treatise, "On the Progress of the Human Spirit," while languishing in a French prison in 1794. Martin Luther King, Jr. (1929–1968) wrote this letter in 1963, from a jail in Birmingham, Alabama. So urgent was his need to explain why he invited arrest, he began to write the letter on the margins of the newspaper which had printed the letter to which he was responding. He continued on scraps of paper supplied to him by a friendly jailer and finished on a legal pad.

King's arrest in 1963 was not the first or last time that the civil rights leader had sought imprisonment to dramatize the injustice of the legal system as it applied to blacks. In 1955, when King was the pastor of the Dexter Avenue Baptist Church in Montgomery, Alabama, a black woman, Rosa Parks, was arrested for refusing to give up her seat on a Montgomery bus to a white person. In response, King led a successful 382-day boycott of the city's bus system. In 1957, King founded the Southern Christian Leadership Conference (S.C.L.C.), which was to become one of the leading civil rights organizations. In 1960, King became the pastor of his father's church, the Ebenezer Baptist Church in Atlanta.

In addition to the massive civil rights campaign documented in the "Letter from Birmingham Jail," King led efforts for black voter registration in the South, for desegregation of the schools, and for better education and housing. While organizing a march of striking sanitation workers in Memphis, Tennessee, Martin Luther King was assassinated by James Earl Ray on April 4, 1968.

The situation in Birmingham in 1963 was fraught with the same degree of danger as the later circumstances in Memphis. King knew that his nonviolent actions and his measured words, like those of Henry David Thoreau and Mohandas Gandhi, inspired civil unrest and angry responses. But, as King said in one of his most famous speeches, he had a dream that people of all races would one day "be able to sit down together at the table of brotherhood."[1] Through peaceful exchange, whites and blacks could build a community.

In Birmingham, King had been arrested for leading a march of one thousand people to protest racial segregation. The Birmingham Project, aimed at ridding the city of its segregationist laws, had begun on April 3, 1963, with sit-ins and picketing at stores with segregated lunch counters. Eight local clergymen, in an open letter, acknowledged the demonstrators' "natural impatience," but called their protests "unwise and untimely" and urged blacks to "withdraw support from those demonstrations." As confrontations between protestors and civil authorities grew, King announced that he would break the unfair law and invite arrest on Good Friday by leading a march that had been prohibited by a state court. He was thrown in jail, where he answered the clergymen's letter.

The "Letter from Birmingham Jail" has become a classic statement in defense of civil disobedience. In July, 1964, just a little over a year after King wrote the letter, Congress passed the first Civil Rights Act and followed it in August 1965 with the Voting Rights Act. King's assassination in 1968 was followed by the Second Civil Rights Act. These pieces of legislation were all designed to extend legal and political equality to blacks.

Although after King's death the civil rights movement seemed to fragment and diminish, in fact, its leaders began to change its focus away from marches and into the courts and voting booths. King had given the movement visibility and had helped to make it part of the national consciousness. His followers worked to consolidate the gains made in the turbulent 1960s. Although the tactics changed, the movement has maintained the inspiration and nonviolent character given to it by Dr. King.

Letter from Birmingham Jail*
MARTIN LUTHER KING, JR.

April 16, 1963

My Dear Fellow Clergymen:

While confined here in the Birmingham city jail, I came across your recent statement calling my present activities "unwise and untimely." Seldom do I pause to answer criticism of my work and

---

1. "I Have a Dream," August 28, 1963, Washington D.C., quoted in Coretta Scott King, *My Life with Martin Luther King, Jr.* (N.Y.: Holt, Rinehart, Winston, 1969), p. 239.

"Letter from Birmingham Jail—April 16, 1963" from *Why We Can't Wait* by Martin Luther King, Jr. Copyright © 1963 by Martin Luther King, Jr. Reprinted by permission of Harper & Row, Publishers, Inc.

* Author's Note: This response to a published statement by eight fellow clergymen from Alabama (Bishop C. C. J. Carpenter, Bishop Joseph A. Durick, Rabbi Hilton L. Grafman, Bishop Paul Hardin, Bishop Holan B. Harmon, The Reverend George M. Murray, the Rev-

ideas. If I sought to answer all the criticisms that cross my desk, my secretaries would have little time for anything other than such correspondence in the course of the day, and I would have no time for constructive work. But since I feel that you are men of genuine good will and that your criticisms are sincerely set forth, I want to try to answer your statement in what I hope will be patient and reasonable terms.

I think I should indicate why I am here in Birmingham, since you have been influenced by the view which argues against "outsiders coming in." I have the honor of serving as president of the Southern Christian Leadership Conference, an organization operating in every southern state, with headquarters in Atlanta, Georgia. We have some eighty-five affiliated organizations across the South, and one of them is the Alabama Christian Movement for Human Rights. Frequently we share staff, educational and financial resources with our affiliates. Several months ago the affiliate here in Birmingham asked us to be on call to engage in a nonviolent direct-action program if such were deemed necessary. We readily consented, and when the hour came we lived up to our promise. So I, along with several members of my staff, am here because I was invited here. I am here because I have organizational ties here.

But more basically, I am in Birmingham because injustice is here. Just as the prophets of the eighth century B.C. left their villages and carried their "thus saith the Lord" far beyond the boundaries of their home towns, and just as the Apostle Paul left his village of Tarsus and carried the gospel of Jesus Christ to the far corners of the Greco-Roman world, so am I compelled to carry the gospel of freedom beyond my own home town. Like Paul, I must constantly respond to the Macedonian call for aid.

Moreover, I am cognizant of the interrelatedness of all communities and states. I cannot sit idly by in Atlanta and not be concerned about what happens in Birmingham. Injustice anywhere is a threat to justice everywhere. We are caught in an inescapable network of mutuality, tied in a single garment of destiny. Whatever affects one directly, affects all indirectly. Never again can we afford to live with the narrow, provincial "outside agitator" idea. Anyone who lives inside the United States can never be considered an outsider anywhere within its bounds.

---

erend Edward V. Ramage and the Reverend Earl Stallings) was composed under somewhat constricting circumstances. Begun on the margins of the newspaper in which the statement appeared while I was in jail, the letter was continued on scraps of writing paper supplied by a friendly Negro trusty, and concluded on a pad my attorneys were eventually permitted to leave me. Although the text remains in substance unaltered, I have indulged in the author's prerogative of polishing it for publication.

You deplore the demonstrations taking place in Birmingham. But your statement, I am sorry to say, fails to express a similar concern for the conditions that brought about the demonstrations. I am sure that none of you would want to rest content with the superficial kind of social analysis that deals merely with effects and does not grapple with underlying causes. It is unfortunate that demonstrations are taking place in Birmingham, but it is even more unfortunate that the city's white power structure left the Negro community with no alternative.

In any nonviolent campaign there are four basic steps: collection of the facts to determine whether injustices exist; negotiation; self-purification; and direct action. We have gone through all these steps in Birmingham. There can be no gainsaying the fact that racial injustice engulfs this community. Birmingham is probably the most thoroughly segregated city in the United States. Its ugly record of brutality is widely known. Negroes have experienced grossly unjust treatment in the courts. There have been more unsolved bombings of Negro homes and churches in Birmingham than in any other city in the nation. These are the hard, brutal facts of the case. On the basis of these conditions, Negro leaders sought to negotiate with the city fathers. But the latter consistently refused to engage in good-faith negotiations.

Then, last September, came the opportunity to talk with leaders of Birmingham's economic community. In the course of the negotiations, certain promises were made by the merchants — for example, to remove the stores' humiliating racial signs. On the basis of these promises, The Reverend Fred Shuttlesworth and the leaders of the Alabama Christian Movement for Human Rights agreed to a moratorium on all demonstrations. As the weeks and months went by, we realized that we were the victims of a broken promise. A few signs, briefly removed, returned; the others remained.

As in so many past experiences, our hopes had been blasted, and the shadow of deep disappointment settled upon us. We had no alternative except to prepare for direct action, whereby we would present our very bodies as a means of laying our case before the conscience of the local and the national community. Mindful of the difficulties involved, we decided to undertake a process of self-purification. We began a series of workshops on nonviolence, and we repeatedly asked ourselves: "Are you able to accept blows without retaliating?" "Are you able to endure the ordeal of jail?" We decided to schedule our direct-action program for the Easter season, realizing that except for Christmas, this is the main shopping period of the year. Knowing that a strong economic-withdrawal program would be the by-product of direct action, we felt that this would be the best time to bring pressure to bear on the merchants for the needed change.

Then it occurred to us that Birmingham's mayoral election was coming up in March, and we speedily decided to postpone action until after election day. When we discovered that the Commissioner of Public Safety, Eugene "Bull" Connor, had piled up enough votes to be in the run-off, we decided again to postpone action until the day after the run-off so that the demonstrations could not be used to cloud the issues. Like many others, we waited to see Mr. Connor defeated, and to this end we endured postponement after postponement. Having aided in this community need, we felt that our direct-action program could be delayed no longer.

You may well ask: "Why direct action? Why sit-ins, marches and so forth? Isn't negotiation a better path?" You are quite right in calling for negotiation. Indeed, this is the very purpose of direct action. Nonviolent direct action seeks to create such a crisis and foster such a tension that a community which has constantly refused to negotiate is forced to confront the issue. It seeks so to dramatize the issue that it can no longer be ignored. My citing the creation of tension as part of the work of the nonviolent-resister may sound rather shocking. But I must confess that I am not afraid of the word "tension." I have earnestly opposed violent tension, but there is a type of constructive, nonviolent tension which is necessary for growth. Just as Socrates felt that it was necessary to create a tension in the mind so that individuals could rise from the bondage of myths and half-truths to the unfettered realm of creative analysis and objective appraisal, so must we see the need for nonviolent gadflies to create the kind of tension in society that will help men rise from the dark depths of prejudice and racism to the majestic heights of understanding and brotherhood.

The purpose of our direct-action program is to create a situation so crisis-packed that it will inevitably open the door to negotiation. I therefore concur with you in your call for negotiation. Too long has our beloved Southland been bogged down in a tragic effort to live in monologue rather than dialogue.

One of the basic points in your statement is that the action that I and my associates have taken in Birmingham is untimely. Some have asked: "Why didn't you give the new city administration time to act?" The only answer that I can give to this query is that the new Birmingham administration must be prodded about as much as the outgoing one, before it will act. We are sadly mistaken if we feel that the election of Albert Boutwell as mayor will bring the millennium to Birmingham. While Mr. Boutwell is a much more gentle person than Mr. Connor, they are both segregationists, dedicated to maintenance of the status quo. I have hope that Mr. Boutwell will be reasonable enough to see the futility of massive resistance to desegregation. But he will not see this without pressure from devotees of civil rights. My friends, I must say to you that we have not made a single gain in civil rights without determined legal and nonviolent pressure. Lamentably, it is an historical fact that privileged groups seldom give up their privileges voluntarily. Individuals may see the moral light and voluntarily give up their unjust posture; but, as Reinhold Niebuhr has reminded us, groups tend to be more immoral than individuals.

We know through painful experience that freedom is never voluntarily given by the oppressor; it must be demanded by the oppressed. Frankly, I have yet to engage in a direct-action campaign that was "well-timed" in the view of those who have not suffered unduly from the disease of segregation. For years now I have heard the word "Wait!" It rings in the ear of every Negro with piercing familiarity. This "Wait" has almost always meant "Never." We must come to see, with one of our distinguished jurists, that "justice too long delayed is justice denied."

We have waited for more than 340 years for our constitutional and God-given rights. The nations of Asia and Africa are moving with jetlike speed toward gaining political independence, but we still creep at horse-and-buggy pace toward gaining a cup of coffee at a lunch counter. Perhaps it is easy for those who have never felt the stinging darts of segregation to say, "Wait." But when you have seen vicious mobs lynch your mothers and fathers at will and drown your sisters and brothers at whim; when you have seen hate-filled policemen curse, kick and even kill your black brothers and sisters; when you see the vast majority of your twenty million Negro brothers smothering in an airtight cage of poverty in the midst of an affluent society; when you suddenly find your tongue twisted and your speech stammering as you seek to explain to your six-year-old daughter why she can't go to the public amusement park that has just been advertised on television, and see tears welling up in her eyes when she is told that Funtown is closed to colored children, and see ominous clouds of inferiority beginning to form in her little mental sky, and see her beginning to distort her personality by developing an unconscious bitterness toward white people; when you have to concoct an answer for a five-year-old son who is asking: "Daddy, why do white people treat colored people so mean?"; when you take a cross-country drive and find it necessary to sleep night after night in the uncomfortable corners of your automobile because no motel will accept you; when you are humiliated day in and day out by nagging signs reading "white" and "colored"; when your first name becomes "nigger," your middle name becomes "boy" (however old you are) and your last name becomes "John," and your wife and mother are never given the respected title "Mrs."; when you are harried by day and haunted by night by the fact that you are a Negro, living constantly at tiptoe stance, never quite knowing what to expect next, and are plagued with inner fears and outer resentments; when you are forever fighting a degenerating sense of "nobodiness" — then you will understand why we find it difficult to wait. There comes a time when the cup of endurance runs over, and men are no longer willing to be plunged into the abyss of despair. I hope, sirs, you can understand our legitimate and unavoidable impatience.

You express a great deal of anxiety over our willingness to break laws. This is certainly a legitimate concern. Since we so diligently urge people to obey the Supreme Court's decision of 1954 outlawing segregation in the public schools, at first glance it may seem rather paradoxical for us consciously to break laws. One may well ask: "How can you advocate breaking some laws and obeying others?" The answer lies in the fact that there are two types of laws: just and unjust. I would be the first to advocate obeying just laws. One has not only a legal but a moral responsibility to obey just laws. Conversely, one has a moral responsibility to disobey unjust laws. I would agree with St. Augustine that "an unjust law is no law at all."

Now, what is the difference between the two? How does one determine whether a law is just or unjust? A just law is a man-made code that squares with the moral law or the law of God. An unjust law is a code that is out of harmony with the moral law. To put it in the terms of St. Thomas Aquinas: An unjust law is a human law that is not rooted in eternal law and natural law. Any law that uplifts human personality is just. Any law that degrades human personality is unjust. All segregation statutes are unjust because segregation distorts the soul and damages the personality. It gives the segregator a false sense of superiority and the segregated a false sense of inferiority. Segregation, to use the terminology of the Jewish philosopher Martin Buber, substitutes an "I-it" relationship for an "I-thou" relationship and ends up relegating persons to the status of things. Hence segregation is not only politically, economically and sociologically unsound, it is morally wrong and sinful. Paul Tillich has said that sin is separation. Is not segregation an existential expression of man's tragic separation, his awful estrangement, his terrible sinfulness? Thus it is that I can urge men to obey the 1954 decision of the Supreme Court, for it is morally right; and I can urge them to disobey segregation ordinances, for they are morally wrong.

Let us consider a more concrete example of just and unjust laws. An unjust law is a code that a numerical or power majority group compels a minority group to obey but does not make binding on itself. This is *difference* made legal. By the same token, a just law is a code that a majority compels a minority to follow and that it is willing to follow itself. This is *sameness* made legal.

Let me give another explanation. A law is unjust if it is inflicted on a minority that, as a result of being denied the right to vote, had no part in enacting or devising the law. Who can say that the legislature of Alabama which set up that state's segregation laws was democratically elected? Throughout Alabama all sorts of devious methods are used to prevent Negroes from becoming registered voters, and there are some counties in which, even though Negroes constitute a majority of the population, not a single Negro is registered. Can any law enacted under such circumstances be considered democratically structured?

Sometimes a law is just on its face and unjust in its application. For instance, I have been arrested on a charge of parading without a permit. Now, there is nothing wrong in having an ordinance which requires a permit for a parade. But such an ordinance becomes unjust when it is used to maintain segregation and to deny citizens the First-Amendment privilege of peaceful assembly and protest.

I hope you are able to see the distinction I am trying to point out. In no sense do I advocate evading or defying the law, as would the rabid segregationist. That would lead to anarchy. One who breaks an unjust law must do so openly, lovingly, and with a willingness to accept the penalty. I submit that an individual who breaks a law that conscience tells him is unjust, and who willingly accepts the penalty of imprisonment in order to arouse the conscience of the community over its injustice, is in reality expressing the highest respect for law.

Of course, there is nothing new about this kind of civil disobedience. It was evidenced sublimely in the refusal of Shadrach, Meshach and Abednego to obey the laws of Nebuchadnezzar, on the ground that a higher moral law was at stake. It was practiced superbly by the early Christians, who were willing to face hungry lions and the excruciating pain of chopping blocks rather than submit to certain unjust laws of the Roman Empire. To a degree, academic freedom is a reality today because Socrates practiced civil disobedience. In our own nation, the Boston Tea Party represented a massive act of civil disobedience.

We should never forget that everything Adolf Hitler did in Germany was "legal" and everything the Hungarian freedom fighters did in Hungary was "illegal." It was "illegal" to aid and comfort a Jew in Hitler's Germany. Even so, I am sure that, had I lived in Germany at the time, I would have aided and comforted my Jewish brothers. If today I lived in a Communist country where certain principles dear to the Christian faith are suppressed, I would openly advocate disobeying that country's antireligious laws.

I must make two honest confessions to you, my Christian and Jewish brothers. First, I must confess that over the past few years I have been gravely disappointed with the white moderate. I have almost reached the regrettable conclusion that the Negro's great stumbling block in his stride toward freedom is not the White

Citizen's Counciler or the Ku Klux Klanner, but the white moderate, who is more devoted to "order" than to justice; who prefers a negative peace which is the absence of tension to a positive peace which is the presence of justice; who constantly says: "I agree with you in the goal you seek, but I cannot agree with your methods of direct action"; who paternalistically believes he can set the timetable for another man's freedom; who lives by a mythical concept of time and who constantly advises the Negro to wait for a "more convenient season." Shallow understanding from people of good will is more frustrating than absolute misunderstanding from people of ill will. Lukewarm acceptance is much more bewildering than outright rejection.

I had hoped that the white moderate would understand that law and order exist for the purpose of establishing justice and that when they fail in this purpose they become the dangerously structured dams that block the flow of social progress. I had hoped that the white moderate would understand that the present tension in the South is a necessary phase of the transition from an obnoxious negative peace, in which the Negro passively accepted his unjust plight, to a substantive and positive peace, in which all men will respect the dignity and worth of human personality. Actually, we who engage in nonviolent direct action are not the creators of tension. We merely bring to the surface the hidden tension that is already alive. We bring it out in the open, where it can be seen and dealt with. Like a boil that can never be cured so long as it is covered up but must be opened with all its ugliness to the natural medicines of air and light, injustice must be exposed, with all the tension its exposure creates, to the light of human conscience and the air of national opinion before it can be cured.

In your statement you assert that our actions, even though peaceful, must be condemned because they precipitate violence. But is this a logical assertion? Isn't this like condemning a robbed man because his possession of money precipitated the evil act of robbery? Isn't this like condemning Socrates because his unswerving commitment to truth and his philosophical inquiries precipitated the act by the misguided populace in which they made him drink hemlock? Isn't this like condemning Jesus because his unique God-consciousness and never-ceasing devotion to God's will precipitated the evil act of crucifixion? We must come to see that, as the federal courts have consistently affirmed, it is wrong to urge an individual to cease his efforts to gain his basic constitutional rights because the quest may precipitate violence. Society must protect the robbed and punish the robber.

I had also hoped that the white moderate would reject the myth concerning time in relation to the struggle for freedom. I have just received a letter from a white brother in Texas. He writes: "All Christians know that the colored people will receive equal rights eventually, but it is possible that you are in too great a religious hurry. It has taken Christianity almost two thousand years to accomplish what it has. The teachings of Christ take time to come to earth." Such an attitude stems from a tragic misconception of time, from the strangely irrational notion that there is something in the very flow of time that will inevitably cure all ills. Actually, time itself is neutral; it can be used either destructively or constructively. More and more I feel that the people of ill will have used time much more effectively than have the people of good will. We will have to repent in this generation not merely for the hateful words and actions of the bad people but for the appalling silence of the good people. Human progress never rolls in on wheels of inevitability; it comes through the tireless efforts of men willing to be co-workers with God, and without this hard work, time itself becomes an ally of the forces of social stagnation. We must use time creatively, in the knowledge that the time is always ripe to do right. Now is the time to make real the promise of democracy and transform our pending national elegy into a creative psalm of brotherhood. Now is the time to lift our national policy from the quicksand of racial injustice to the solid rock of human dignity.

You speak of our activity in Birmingham as extreme. At first I was rather disappointed that fellow clergymen would see my nonviolent efforts as those of an extremist. I began thinking about the fact that I stand in the middle of two opposing forces in the Negro community. One is a force of complacency, made up in part of Negroes who, as a result of long years of oppression, are so drained of self-respect and a sense of "somebodiness" that they have adjusted to segregation; and in part of a few middle-class Negroes who because of a degree of academic and economic security and because in some ways they profit by segregation, have become insensitive to the problems of the masses. The other force is one of bitterness and hatred, and it comes perilously close to advocating violence. It is expressed in the various black nationalist groups that are springing up across the nation, the largest and best-known being Elija Muhammad's Muslim movement. Nourished by the Negro's frustration over the continued existence of racial discrimination, this movement is made up of people who have lost faith in America, who have absolutely repudiated Christianity, and who have concluded that the white man is an incorrigible "devil."

I have tried to stand between these two forces, saying that we need emulate neither the "do-nothingism" of the complacent nor the hatred and despair of the black nationalist. For there is the more excellent way of love and nonviolent protest. I am grateful to God that, through the influence of the Negro church, the way of nonviolence became an integral part of our struggle.

If this philosophy had not emerged, by now many streets of the South would, I am convinced, be flowing with blood. And I am further convinced that if our white brothers dismiss as "rabble-rousers" and "outside agitators" those of us who employ nonviolent direct action, and if they refuse to support our nonviolent efforts, millions of Negroes will, out of frustration and despair, seek solace and security in black-nationalist ideologies — a development that would inevitably lead to a frightening racial nightmare.

Oppressed people cannot remain oppressed forever. The yearning for freedom eventually manifests itself, and that is what has happened to the American Negro. Something within has reminded him of his birthright of freedom, and something without has reminded him that it can be gained. Consciously or unconsciously, he has been caught up by the *Zeitgeist*, and with his black brothers of Africa and his brown and yellow brothers of Asia, South America and the Caribbean, the United States Negro is moving with a sense of great urgency toward the promised land of racial justice. If one recognizes this vital urge that has engulfed the Negro community, one should readily understand why public demonstrations are taking place. The Negro has many pent-up resentments and latent frustrations, and he must release them. So let him march; let him make prayer pilgrimages to the city hall; let him go on freedom rides — and try to understand why he must do so. If his repressed emotions are not released in nonviolent ways, they will seek expression through violence; this is not a threat but a fact of history. So I have not said to my people: "Get rid of your discontent." Rather, I have tried to say that this normal and healthy discontent can be channeled into the creative outlet of nonviolent direct action. And now this approach is being termed extremist.

But though I was initially disappointed at being categorized as an extremist, as I continued to think about the matter I gradually gained a measure of satisfaction from the label. Was not Jesus an extremist for love: "Love your enemies, bless them that curse you, do good to them that hate you, and pray for them which despitefully use you, and persecute you." Was not Amos an extremist for justice: "Let justice roll down like waters and righteousness like an ever-flowing stream." Was not Paul an extremist for the Christian gospel: "I bear in my body the marks of the Lord Jesus." Was not Martin Luther an extremist: "Here I stand; I cannot do otherwise, so help me God." And John Bunyan: "I will stay in jail to the end of my days before I make a butchery of my conscience." And Abraham Lincoln: "This nation cannot survive half slave and half free." And Thomas Jefferson: "We hold these truths to be self-evident, that all men are created equal. . ." So the question is not whether we will be extremists, but what kind of extremists we will be. Will we be extremists for hate or for love? Will we be extremists for the preservation of injustice or for the extension of justice? In that dramatic scene on Calvary's hill three men were crucified. We must never forget that all three were crucified for the same crime — the crime of extremism. Two were extremists for immorality, and thus fell below their environment. The other, Jesus Christ, was an extremist for love, truth and goodness, and thereby rose above his environment. Perhaps the South, the nation and the world are in dire need of creative extremists.

I had hoped that the white moderate would see this need. Perhaps I was too optimistic; perhaps I expected too much. I suppose I should have realized that few members of the oppressor race can understand the deep groans and passionate yearnings of the oppressed race, and still fewer have the vision to see that injustice must be rooted out by strong, persistent and determined action. I am thankful, however, that some of our white brothers in the South have grasped the meaning of this social revolution and committed themselves to it. They are still all too few in quantity, but they are big in quality. Some — such as Ralph McGill, Lillian Smith, Harry Golden, James McBride Dabbs, Ann Braden and Sarah Patton Boyle — have written about our struggle in eloquent and prophetic terms. Others have marched with us down nameless streets of the South. They have languished in filthy, roach-infested jails, suffering the abuse and brutality of policemen who view them as "dirty nigger-lovers." Unlike so many of their moderate brothers and sisters, they have recognized the urgency of the moment and sensed the need for powerful "action" antidotes to combat the disease of segregation.

Let me take note of my other major disappointment. I have been so greatly disappointed with the white church and its leadership. Of course, there are some notable exceptions. I am not unmindful of the fact that each of you has taken some significant stands on this issue. I commend you, Reverend Stallings, for your Christian stand on this past Sunday, in welcoming Negroes to your workship service on a nonsegregated basis. I commend the Catholic leaders of this state for integrating Spring Hill College several years ago.

But despite these notable exceptions, I must honestly reiterate that I have been disappointed with the church. I do not say this as one of those negative critics who can always find something wrong with the church. I say this as a minister of the gospel, who loves the church; who was nurtured in its bosom; who has been sustained by its spiritual blessings and who will remain true to it as long as the cord of life shall lengthen.

When I was suddenly catapulated into the leadership of the bus protest in Montgomery, Alabama, a few years ago, I felt we would be supported by the white church. I felt that the white ministers, priests and rabbis of the South would be among our strongest allies. Instead, some have been outright opponents, refusing to understand the freedom movement and misrepresenting its leaders; all too many others have been more cautious than courageous and have remained silent behind the anesthetizing security of stained-glass windows.

In spite of my shattered dreams, I came to Birmingham with the hope that the white religious leadership of this community would see the justice of our cause and, with deep moral concern, would serve as the channel through which our just grievances could reach the power structure. I had hoped that each of you would understand. But again I have been disappointed.

I have heard numerous southern religious leaders admonish their worshipers to comply with a desegregation decision because it is the law, but I have longed to hear white ministers declare: "Follow this decree because integration is morally right and because the Negro is your brother." In the midst of blatant injustices inflicted upon the Negro, I have watched white churchmen stand on the sideline and mouth pious irrelevancies and sanctimonious trivialities. In the midst of a mighty struggle to rid our nation of racial and economic injustice, I have heard many ministers say: "Those are social issues, with which the gospel has no real concern." And I have watched many churches commit themselves to a completely otherworldly religion which makes a strange, un-Biblical distinction between body and soul, between the sacred and the secular.

I have traveled the length and breadth of Alabama, Mississippi and all the other southern states. On sweltering summer days and crisp autumn mornings I have looked at the South's beautiful churches with their lofty spires pointing heavenward. I have beheld the impressive outlines of her massive religious-education buildings. Over and over I have found myself asking: "What kind of people worship here? Who is their God? Where were their voices when the lips of Governor Barnett dripped with words of interposition and nullification? Where were they when Governor Wallace gave a clarion call for defiance and hatred? Where were their voices of support when bruised and weary Negro men and women decided to rise from the dark dungeons of complacency to the bright hills of creative protest?"

Yes, these questions are still in my mind. In deep disappointment I have wept over the laxity of the church. But be assured that my tears have been tears of love. There can be no deep disappointment where there is not deep love. Yes, I love the church. How could I do otherwise? I am in the rather unique position of being the son, the grandson and the great-grandson of preachers. Yes, I see the church as the body of Christ. But, oh! How we have blemished and scarred that body through social neglect and through fear of being nonconformists.

There was a time when the church was very powerful — in the time when early Christians rejoiced at being deemed worthy to suffer for what they believed. In those days the church was not merely a thermometer that recorded the ideas and principles of popular opinion; it was a thermostat that transformed the mores of society. Whenever the early Christians entered a town, the people in power become disturbed and immediately sought to convict the Christians for being "disturbers of the peace" and "outside agitators." But the Christians pressed on, in the conviction that they were "a colony of heaven," called to obey God rather than man. Small in number, they were big in commitment. They were too God-intoxicated to be "astronomically intimidated." By their effort and example they brought an end to such ancient evils as infanticide and gladiatorial contests.

Things are different now. So often the contemporary church is a weak, ineffectual voice with an uncertain sound. So often it is an archdefender of the status quo. Far from being disturbed by the presence of the church, the power structure of the average community is consoled by the church's silent — and often even vocal — sanction of things as they are.

But the judgment of God is upon the church as never before. If today's church does not recapture the sacrificial spirit of the early church, it will lose its authenticity, forfeit the loyalty of millions, and be dismissed as an irrelevant social club with no meaning for the twentieth century. Every day I meet young people whose disappointment with the church has turned into outright disgust.

Perhaps I have once again been too optimistic. Is organized religion too inextricably bound to the status quo to save our nation and the world? Perhaps I must turn my faith to the inner spiritual church, the church within the church, as the true *ekklesia* and the hope of the world. But again I am thankful to God that some noble souls from the ranks of organized religion have broken loose from the paralyzing chains of conformity and joined us as active partners in the struggle for freedom. They have left their secure congregations and walked the streets of Albany, Georgia, with us. They have gone down the highways of the South on tortuous rides for freedom. Yes, they have gone to jail with us. Some have been dismissed from their churches, have lost the support of their bishops and fellow ministers. But they have acted in the faith that right defeated is stronger than evil triumphant. Their witness has been the spiritual salt that has preserved the true meaning of the gospel in these troubled times. They have carved a tunnel of hope through the dark mountain of disappointment.

I hope the church as a whole will meet the challenge of this decisive hour. But even if the church does not come to the aid of justice, I have no despair about the future. I have no fear about the outcome of our struggle in Birmingham, even if our motives are at present misunderstood. We will reach the goal of freedom in Birmingham and all over the nation, because the goal of America is freedom. Abused and scorned though we may be, our destiny is tied up with America's destiny. Before the pilgrims landed at Plymouth, we were here. Before the pen of Jefferson etched the majestic words of the Declaration of Independence across the pages of history, we were here. For more than two centuries our forebears labored in this country without wages; they made cotton king; they built the homes of their masters while suffering gross injustice and shameful humiliation — and yet out of a bottomless vitality they continued to thrive and develop. If the inexpressible cruelties of slavery could not stop us, the opposition we now face will surely fail. We will win our freedom because the sacred heritage of our nation and the eternal will of God are embodied in our echoing demands.

Before closing I feel impelled to mention one other point in your statement that has troubled me profoundly. You warmly commended the Birmingham police force for keeping "order" and "preventing violence." I doubt that you would have so warmly commended the police force if you had seen its dogs sinking their teeth into unarmed, nonviolent Negroes. I doubt that you would so quickly commend the policemen if you were to observe their ugly and inhumane treatment of Negroes here in the city jail; if you were to watch them push and curse old Negro women and young Negro girls; if you were to see them slap and kick old Negro men and young boys; if you were to observe them, as they did on two occasions, refuse to give us food because we wanted to sing our grace together. I cannot join you in your praise of the Birmingham police department.

It is true that the police have exercised a degree of discipline in handling the demonstrators. In this sense they have conducted themselves rather "nonviolently" in public. But for what purpose? To preserve the evil system of segregation. Over the past few years I have consistently preached that nonviolence demands that the means we use must be as pure as the ends we seek. I have tried to make clear that it is wrong to use immoral means to attain moral ends. But now I must affirm that it is just as wrong, or perhaps even more so, to use moral means to preserve immoral ends. Perhaps Mr. Connor and his policemen have been rather nonviolent in public, as was Chief Pritchett in Albany, Georgia, but they have used the moral means of nonviolence to maintain the immoral end of racial injustice. As T.S. Eliot has said: "The last temptation is the greatest treason: To do the right deed for the wrong reason."

I wish you had commended the Negro sit-inners and demonstrators of Birmingham for their sublime courage, their willingness to suffer and their amazing discipline in the midst of great provocation. One day the South will recognize its real heroes. They will be the James Merediths, with the noble sense of purpose that enables them to face jeering and hostile mobs, and with the agonizing loneliness that characterizes the life of the pioneer. They will be old, oppressed, battered Negro women, symbolized in a seventy-two-year-old woman in Montgomery, Alabama, who rose up with a sense of dignity and with her people decided not to ride segregated buses, and who responded with ungrammatical profundity to one who inquired about her weariness: "My feets is tired, but my soul is at rest." They will be the young high school and college students, the young ministers of the gospel and a host of their elders, courageously and nonviolently sitting in at lunch counters and willingly going to jail for conscience' sake. One day the South will know that when these disinherited children of God sat down at lunch counters, they were in reality standing up for what is best in the American dream and for the most sacred values in our Judaeo-Christian heritage, thereby bringing our nation back to those great wells of democracy which were dug deep by the founding fathers in their formulation of the Constitution and the Declaration of Independence.

Never before have I written so long a letter. I'm afraid it is much too long to take your precious time. I can assure you that it would have been much shorter if I had been writing from a comfortable desk, but what else can one do when he is alone in a narrow jail cell, other than write long letters, think long thoughts and pray long prayers?

If I have said anything in this letter that overstates the truth and indicates an unreasonable impatience, I beg you to forgive me. If I have said anything that understates the truth and indicates my having a patience that allows me to settle for anything less than brotherhood, I beg God to forgive me.

I hope this letter finds you strong in the faith. I also hope that circumstances will soon make it possible for me to meet each of you, not as an integrationist or a civil-rights leader but as a fellow clergyman and a Christian brother. Let us all hope that the dark clouds of racial prejudice will soon pass away and the deep fog of misunderstanding will be lifted from our fear-drenched communities, and in some not too distant tomorrow the radiant stars of love and brotherhood will shine over our great nation with all their scintillating beauty.

Yours for the cause of Peace and Br_
Martin Luther King, Jr.

Questions and Exercises

1. List all the analogies King uses in his letter — other cases of disobedience, other cases of supposed extremism. Do you see a pattern among them? Write a paragraph explaining why he relies so heavily on analogies.

2. We can infer from the letter that four objections were made against what King was doing:

    a) His protest was untimely.

    b) He is from Atlanta: what business did he have interfering in Birmingham?

    c) It is never right to disobey a law.

    d) He is being an extremist.

   Separate the strands of his response to each of these criticisms. Write a paragraph summarizing each response. Which of the four criticisms do you think he regarded as most serious? How can you tell?

3. King insists that four conditions must be fulfilled if an act of breaking the law is to be justified. What are these conditions?

4. What does "Zeitgeist" mean?

5. King says that Socrates practiced civil disobedience. Consult the Oxford Classical Dictionary to find information about Socrates' situation.

6. Find the story of Shadrach, Meshach, and Abednego in the Anchor Annotated Bible. How does their situation compare to King's?

7. Record King's examples of comparable acts of civil disobedience. For each case, write a description of the kind of person who might find that case persuasive. What authority is the person likely to accept? After answering these questions on your own, meet to compare notes with a small group of classmates. Then reach consensus on King's actual audience. Was it larger than the group of clergymen to whom the letter was addressed?

8. By King's account, how can you tell if a law is unjust? Are there laws which in your opinion are unjust? If so, does King's description apply to them? After writing your own notes on the subject, compare notes with a small group of classmates.

9. Based on your reading of Hobbes (pp. 83–88), compose the kind of response Hobbes might have written to King's letter. How might Mill have responded?

10. Read Henry David Thoreau's "Civil Disobedience" (1849). Draft a comparison of Thoreau's essay and King's letter. Assume that your readers have not read either document.

11. Consult reference books on the history of modern India for information on Mohandas Gandhi. Draft an essay explaining what King might have learned from Gandhi's example. Assume that your readers have read the "Letter from Birmingham Jail" but that they know very little about Gandhi's influence on King.

12. Consult the *New York Times Index* and the *Times* itself for the first week in April, 1963. Draft a report on the national response to King's imprisonment. Address these reports to your classmates.

13. Consult the *New York Times Index* and the *Times* itself for April, 1968. Draft a report to your classmates on the events surrounding King's assassination.

Cancer (
G. Scat
1949).
V. L. W
J. Gilbe
48, 119 (
W. L. M
docrinol
A. B. Ol
1975).
A. B. O
1977).
J. Solom
b. 875.
R. H. Sh
Fed. Am

drocannabinol wi

trogen Receptor

periments with Δ^9-tetr

th rat uterine cytosol

rtheless significant, co

se data support, at the

estrogenic activity (at

trogen-like binding su

causes a primary estro

Reading in the Academic Disciplines

Med. 28
Found. (
R. C. K
Engl. J.
M. A. A
. Solom
uck, A.
. Solom
Med. 29
R. C. K
rds, J.
New Yo
R. M. V
Rawitch,
1976).
. Jakub

Competition of Δ⁹-

Estrogen in Rat U

Abstract. Direct com
nd estradiol in bindin
hat Δ⁹-THC was a wea
oplasmic estrogen rec
ations that Δ⁹-THC h
strogen receptors). M
t the level of estrogen

The Arts and Humanities

Whenever we read, we become partners with the writer in constructing a text. Whenever we write, we imagine a reader who will enter into the world which we create on the page. All reading and writing are thus, to some extent, exercises in the humanities because the discovery, formulation, and expression of meaning through a system of verbal symbols are essentially humanistic processes in that they involve human creativity and judgment. The selections in this section, however, are humanistic in a more specific sense, since they are drawn from the traditional humanities disciplines: literature, criticism, history, and philosophy.

We begin this section with two works of the artistic imagination — James Joyce's short story, "Araby," and an excerpt from Charles Dickens's novel, *Hard Times*. Both Joyce and Dickens were quite consciously creating fictional worlds for the reader to enter and, once there, to observe, judge, and enjoy. You may wonder what there is to enjoy in the rather bleak scenes created by Joyce and Dickens. Certainly, the characters within these scenes are not having a very good time. Our enjoyment, however, comes from appreciation of the writers' artistry. The contemplation of such artistry leads to an aesthetic awareness, which is a keynote of humanistic study. David Lodge's essay on *Hard Times* exemplifies the process of aesthetic interpretation.

When writers in the humanities contemplate and interpret works of art, they function as critics — people who are discerning about aesthetic experience, not necessarily in a fault-finding way. When writers in the humanities make systematic judgments about the past, they function as historians. The essays by Antonia Fraser and Carl Becker exemplify the humanistic process of recalling the past and explaining why that past developed as it did.

Fraser and Becker, like other historians, make every attempt to be fair-minded, but they do not pretend to be neutral. They are intelligent human beings contemplating the past, not mechanical cataloguers promising total objectivity. When you read each of their articles, you will hear a human voice. No one, not even the most practiced historian, knows the whole truth about the past. Historians devote themselves to gathering evidence from documents and interviews, reconstructing the story of what occurred, and then sharing versions with one another. This kind of conversation defines the community of historians, just as a shared aesthetic conversation defines the communities of literary, art, and music critics.

The conversation of philosophers reflects yet another approach. They may, for example, examine and explain the principles underlying a particular way of looking at experience. Elizabeth Janeway contemplates the division of the world into males and females; Thomas Szasz questions the division into the sane and insane. Such inquiry is philosophical because the writers are systematically searching for wisdom about the way we live our lives.

Philosophical inquiry focuses on questions of right and wrong (ethics); of knowledge (epistemology); of beauty (aesthetics); and of cause and purpose (metaphysics). Although philosophers cannot prove their theories once and for all, they work to refine the consistency of their logical arguments. In this section, Peter Singer makes an ethical argument for the rights of animals, while several other writers engage in an exchange about justice and discrimination.

This exchange about justice and discrimination exemplifies the ongoing conversation of philosophy and indeed of the humanities in general. You can enter this conversation, which transcends time and geography, by writing about the questions which humanists contemplate. These questions may never be answered finally, but through writing and reading in the humanities, you will join a worthy group of seekers.

4
Readings in the Arts and Humanities

Fiction

Araby
JAMES JOYCE
from *Dubliners*

James Joyce (1882–1941) wrote "Araby" as the third in a collection of fifteen connected stories called *Dubliners*. A native of Dublin himself, Joyce saw this city as representative of the frustration and spiritual paralysis of the modern world. Joyce completed *Dubliners* in 1907, but the collection was not published until 1914. During the intervening years, Joyce experienced the frustration and encountered the spiritual paralysis that he had described in his fiction. Publishers thought that sections of the stories were improper because of their sexual or blasphemous references and tried to convince Joyce to make a number of changes to avoid offending the public. Joyce refused, explaining his position in a letter as follows:

> I cannot alter what I have written. All these objections of which
> the printer is now the mouthpiece arose in my mind when I was
> writing the book, both as to the themes of the stories and their
> manner of treatment. Had I listened to them I would not have
> written the book.[1]

Joyce carefully revised his stories to find precisely the right words and sentences to communicate his vision. He makes every word, sound, and

---

1. Letter to Grant Richards, 5 May 1906, in *Letters of James Joyce*, ed. Richard Ellmann, Vol. II (N.Y.: Viking Press, 1966), p. 134.

image count. "Araby" is written with the meticulous care of a poem. Skimming, as you would skim a magazine in a doctor's office, might leave you with the idea that the story is about a preadolescent boy who has a crush on a friend's older sister, for whom he wants to buy a gift at a fair called "Araby." Only through close attention will you understand and fully enjoy the story. Close, critical reading does not tear the story apart. Such analysis helps you to participate in the story and to formulate for yourself the significance of events.

Since Joyce loves to explore the possibilities of language, he often uses words that may be unfamiliar: imperturbable, litanies, chalice, florin. Joyce also uses everyday words in unfamiliar ways. North Richmond Street is *blind*, that is, it leads to a dead end. Mangan's sister cannot attend Araby because she must go on a retreat at her *convent*. She is not a nun; she simply attends a convent school that has arranged for all the students to commit a week to communal living and prayer. Staying alert to special meanings of ordinary words will help you to enter the action of the story.

Looking closely even at the words you understand will open up new ways of looking at the story. In the second paragraph, the air in the back drawing room is described as *musty*. Musty derives from the word *moist* and suggests stagnant water, water that does not have the freedom to flow. Looking inside words may be interesting in itself, and in reading a literary work you will find that the suggestions conveyed by several words form a pattern. Look in the story for other words and phrases that suggest water imagery: muddy, dripping gardens, tears, flood, rainy. Ask yourself why Joyce has chosen these specific words and then arranged them as he has done.

Because literary works are not simply about life but also about other works of literature, Joyce makes several references to the works of other authors. *The Abbot* by Walter Scott is a romantic novel about Mary Queen of Scots. The *Devout Communicant* is a book of pious meditations. *The Memoirs of Vidocq* is a sexually suggestive tale of a criminal who becomes a chief of detectives. Why do you think that Joyce chose to mention these particular books on the first page of the story?

Although Joyce has made decisions about such details, we do not hear the story told in the author's voice. The young boy himself is the narrator, and he cannot give us an objective view of people and events. In fact, he sees himself and other people in different ways as the story progresses.

Sight and insight are important concepts to Joyce. "Araby" builds toward a moment of insight which Joyce calls *epiphany*. (The Feast of Epiphany celebrates the revelation of Christ's divinity to the Magi.) The young narrator of "Araby" has a sudden insight as he listens to the saleswoman's trivial flirtation with the two gentlemen. What does the boy see? What do you see?

Araby

JAMES JOYCE

North Richmond Street, being blind, was a quiet street except at the hour when the Christian Brothers' School set the boys free. An uninhabited house of two storeys stood at the blind end, detached from its neighbours in a square ground. The other houses of the street, conscious of decent lives within them, gazed at one another with brown imperturbable faces.

The former tenant of our house, a priest, had died in the back drawing-room. Air, musty from having been long enclosed, hung in all the rooms, and the waste room behind the kitchen was littered with old useless papers. Among these I found a few paper-covered books, the pages of which were curled and damp: *The Abbot*, by Walter Scott, *The Devout Communicant* and *The Memoirs of Vidocq*. I liked the last best because its leaves were yellow. The wild garden behind the house contained a central apple-tree and a few straggling bushes under one of which I found the late tenant's rusty bicycle-pump. He had been a very charitable priest; in his will he had left all his money to institutions and the furniture of his house to his sister.

When the short days of winter came dusk fell before we had well eaten our dinners. When we met in the street the houses had grown sombre. The space of sky above us was the colour of ever-changing violet and towards it the lamps of the street lifted their feeble lanterns. The cold air stung us and we played till our bodies glowed. Our shouts echoed in the silent street. The career of our play brought us through the dark muddy lanes behind the houses where we ran the gantlet of the rough tribes from the cottages, to the back doors of the dark dripping gardens where odours arose from the ashpits, to the dark odorous stables where a coachman smoothed and combed the horse or shook music from the buckled harness. When we returned to the street light from the kitchen windows had filled the areas. If my uncle was seen turning the corner we hid in the shadow until we had seen him safely housed. Or if Mangan's sister came out on the doorstep to call her brother in to his tea we watched her from our shadow peer up and down the street. We waited to see whether she would remain or go in and, if she remained, we left our shadow and walked up to Mangan's steps resignedly. She was waiting for us, her figure defined by the light from the half-opened door. Her brother always teased her before he obeyed and I stood by the railings looking at her. Her dress swung as she moved her body and the soft rope of her hair tossed from side to side.

Every morning I lay on the floor in the front parlour watching her door. The blind was pulled down to within an inch of the sash so that I could not be seen. When she came out on the doorstep my heart leaped. I ran to the hall, seized my books and followed her. I kept her brown figure always in my eye and, when we came near the point at which our ways diverged, I quickened my pace and passed her. This happened morning after morning. I had never spoken to her, except for a few casual words, and yet her name was like a summons to all my foolish blood.

Her image accompanied me even in places the most hostile to romance. On Saturday evenings when my aunt went marketing I had to go to carry some of the parcels. We walked through the flaring streets, jostled by drunken men and bargaining women, amid the curses of labourers, the shrill litanies of shop-boys who stood on guard by the barrels of pigs' cheeks, the nasal chanting of street-singers, who sang a come-all-you about O'Donovan Rossa, or a ballad about the troubles in our native land. These noises converged in a single sensation of life for me: I imagined that I bore my chalice safely through a throng of foes. Her name sprang to my lips at moments in strange prayers and praises which I myself did not understand. My eyes were often full of tears (I could not tell why) and at times a flood from my heart seemed to pour itself out into my bosom. I thought little of the future. I did not know whether I would ever speak to her or not or, if I spoke to her, how I could tell her of my confused adoration. But my body was like a harp and her words and gestures were like fingers running upon the wires.

One evening I went into the back drawing-room in which the priest had died. It was a dark rainy evening and there was no sound in the house. Through one of the broken panes I heard the rain impinge upon the earth, the fine incessant needles of water playing the sodden beds. Some distant lamp or lighted window gleamed below me. I was thankful that I could see so little. All my senses seemed to desire to veil themselves and, feeling that I was about to slip from them, I pressed the palms of my hands together until they trembled, murmuring: *O love! O love!* many times.

At last she spoke to me. When she addressed the first words to me I was so confused that I did not know what to answer. She asked me was I going to *Araby*. I forget whether I answered yes or no. It would be a splendid bazaar, she said; she would love to go.

— And why can't you? I asked.

While she spoke she turned a silver bracelet round and round her wrist. She could not go, she said, because there would be a retreat that week in her convent. Her brother and two other boys were fighting for their caps and I was alone at the railings. She held one of the spikes, bowing her head towards me. The light from the lamp opposite our door caught the white curve of her neck, lit up her hair that rested there and, falling, lit up the hand upon the railing. It fell over one side of her dress and caught the white border of a petticoat, just visible as she stood at ease.

— It's well for you, she said.

— If I go, I said, I will bring you something.

What innumerable follies laid waste my waking and sleeping thoughts after that evening? I wished to annihilate the tedious intervening days. I chafed against the work of school. At night in my bedroom and by day in the classroom her image came between me and the page I strove to read. The syllables of the word *Araby* were called to me through the silence in which my soul luxuriated and cast an Eastern enchantment over me. I asked for leave to go to the bazaar on Saturday night. My aunt was surprised and hoped it was not some Freemason affair. I answered few questions in class. I watched my master's face pass from amiability to sternness; he hoped I was not beginning to idle. I could not call my wandering thoughts together. I had hardly any patience with the serious work of life which, now that it stood between me and my desire, seemed to me child's play, ugly monotonous child's play.

On Saturday morning I reminded my uncle that I wished to go to the bazaar in the evening. He was fussing at the hall-stand, looking for the hat-brush, and answered me curtly:

— Yes, boy, I know.

As he was in the hall I could not go into the front parlour and lie at the window. I left the house in bad humour and walked slowly towards the school. The air was pitilessly raw and already my heart misgave me.

When I came home to dinner my uncle had not yet been home. Still it was early. I sat staring at the clock for some time and, when its ticking began to irritate me, I left the room. I mounted the staircase and gained the upper part of the house. The high cold empty gloomy rooms liberated me and I went from room to room singing. From the front window I saw my companions playing below in the street. Their cries reached me weakened and indistinct and, leaning my forehead against the cool glass, I looked over at the dark house where she lived. I may have stood there for an hour, seeing nothing but the brown-clad figure cast by my imagination, touched discreetly by the lamplight at the curved neck, at the hand upon the railings and at the border below the dress.

When I came downstairs again I found Mrs. Mercer sitting at the fire. She was an old garrulous woman, a pawnbroker's widow, who collected used stamps for some pious purpose. I had to endure the gossip of the tea-table. The meal was prolonged beyond an hour and still my uncle did not come. Mrs. Mercer stood up to go: she was sorry she couldn't wait any longer, but it was after eight o'clock and she did not like to be out late, as the night air was bad for her. When she had gone I began to walk up and down the room, clenching my fists. My aunt said:

— I'm afraid you may put off your bazaar for this night of Our Lord.

At nine o'clock I heard my uncle's latchkey in the halldoor. I heard him talking to himself and heard the hallstand rocking when it had received the weight of his overcoat. I could interpret these signs. When he was midway through his dinner I asked him to give me the money to go to the bazaar. He had forgotten.

— The people are in bed and after their first sleep now, he said.

I did not smile. My aunt said to him energetically:

— Can't you give him the money and let him go? You've kept him late enough as it is.

My uncle said he was very sorry he had forgotten. He said he believed in the old saying: *All work and no play makes Jack a dull boy.* He asked me where I was going and, when I had told him a second time he asked me did I know *The Arab's Farewell to his Steed.* When I left the kitchen he was about to recite the opening lines of the piece to my aunt.

I held a florin tightly in my hand as I strode down Buckingham Street towards the station. The sight of the streets thronged with buyers and glaring with gas recalled to me the purpose of my journey. I took my seat in a third-class carriage of a deserted train. After an intolerable delay the train moved out of the station slowly. It crept onward among ruinous houses and over the twinkling river. At Westland Row Station a crowd of people pressed to the carriage doors; but the porters moved them back, saying that it was a special train for the bazaar. I remained alone in the bare carriage. In a few minutes the train drew up beside an improvised wooden platform. I passed out on to the road and saw by the lighted dial of a clock that it was ten minutes to ten. In front of me was a large building which displayed the magical name.

I could not find any sixpenny entrance and, fearing that the bazaar would be closed, I passed in quickly through a turnstile, handing a shilling to a weary-looking man. I found myself in a big hall girdled at half its height by a gallery. Nearly all the stalls were closed and the greater part of the hall was in darkness. I recognised a silence like that which pervades a church after a service. I walked into the centre of the bazaar timidly. A few people were gathered about the stalls which were still open. Before a curtain, over which the words *Café Chantant* were written in coloured lamps, two men were counting money on a salver. I listened to the fall of the coins.

Remembering with difficulty why I had come I went over to one of the stalls and examined porcelain vases and flowered tea-sets. At the door of the stall a young lady was talking and laughing with two young gentlemen. I remarked their English accents and listened vaguely to their conversation.

— O, I never said such a thing!

— O, but you did!

— O, but I didn't!

— Didn't she say that?

— Yes, I heard her.

— O, there's a ... fib!

Observing me the young lady came over and asked me did I wish to buy anything. The tone of her voice was not encouraging; she seemed to have spoken to me out of a sense of duty. I looked humbly at the great jars that stood like eastern guards at either side of the dark entrance to the stall and murmured:

— No, thank you.

The young lady changed the position of one of the vases and went back to the two young men. They began to talk of the same subject. Once or twice the young lady glanced at me over her shoulder.

I lingered before her stall, though I knew my stay was useless, to make my interest in her wares seem the more real. Then I turned away slowly and walked down the middle of the bazaar. I allowed the two pennies to fall against the sixpence in my pocket. I heard a voice call from one end of the gallery that the light was out. The upper part of the hall was now completely dark.

Gazing up into the darkness I saw myself as a creature driven and derided by vanity; and my eyes burned with anguish and anger.

Questions and Exercises

1. Write in your private journal about your own first crush. How old were you? How did you feel? How were your actions and reactions similar or dissimilar to those of the narrator of "Araby"?

2. As you read the story, stop to copy down at least five sentences. Simply select sentences that you like or that sound important to understanding the story. After you finish the story, study your recorded sentences to see if they connect to each other in any interesting way. Jot down some ideas about their connections.

3. Choose one word from your recorded sentences. Look up that word in the Oxford English Dictionary (O.E.D.). What parts of the word's history does Joyce expect his readers to know?

4. Write your own sentence built on the model of Joyce's concluding one:

participial phrase	(noun)	(verb)	
_____ as a _____	_____ and		
(noun or pronoun)	(noun)	(past participle)	
_____ by _____; and _____			
(past participle)	(noun)	(possessive pronoun)	
_____	_____	_____	_____
(noun)	(verb)	(preposition)	(noun)
and _____.			
(noun)			

5. In small groups, discuss the boy's sudden insight or epiphany. What does he see? How is epiphany a useful term? Apply the term to your own experience.

6. Why does Joyce use so many words and phrases with religious connotations: "the house where the priest died," "chalice," "litanies,"

"strange prayers," "convent retreat," "confused adoration"? Discuss in small groups.

7. "Araby" builds to a concluding sentence: "Gazing up into the darkness I saw myself as a creature driven and derided by vanity; and my eyes burned with anguish and anger." Draft a thorough analysis of that sentence and its significance to the story as a whole. Before you begin your draft, check the meanings and histories of key words in a good desk dictionary or in the O.E.D. Assume that your readers are your classmates who have read "Araby" but who would appreciate a clarifying discussion of the story's last sentence.

8. Draft a paper on Joyce's use of water imagery in the story. How does this pattern help us to understand the story's main ideas? Assume that your audience is your classmates, who have read the story but have not thought through the significance of the water imagery.

9. Draft a paper on the significance of the title, "Araby." You are writing for your classmates, who have read the story but need clarification of the meaning of the title.

Hard Times
CHARLES DICKENS

Charles Dickens (1812–1870) first published *Hard Times* in weekly installments from April 1 through August 12, 1854, in his own magazine, *Household Words*. In August 1853, when Dickens completed *Bleak House,* a lengthy novel of 350,000 words, he wanted a long vacation, perhaps a year. The printers of *Household Words* had other ideas, however. They convinced Dickens to curtail his vacation and to work on a weekly serial for the magazine, since a weekly serial by Dickens himself might boost the slumping sales of *Household Words*. The printers were right. Five months of *Hard Times* in weekly installments more than doubled the sales of *Household Words*. Later in 1854, *Hard Times* was published in a single volume.

Of course, even before the printers' suggestions, Dickens's active mind had been working, vacation or not. He never let his thinking wait for a specific demand for a novel. First of all, he was annoyed at George Cruikshank for publishing a retelling of many old fairy tales with inserted warnings about drinking and betting. Dickens wrote an article entitled "Frauds on the Fairies" for *Household Words*, October 1, 1853: "In a utilitarian age ... it is a matter of grave importance that Fairy tales should be respected. ... A nation without fancy, without some romance, never did, never can, never will, hold a great place under the sun."

During his brief vacation in Italy in November 1853, Dickens read about the industrial strikes that had led to some rioting, especially against the manufacturers of a town called Preston. Certainly the general situation of class conflict in an industrial society weighed on Dickens's mind, and these concerns found their way into his new book. Dickens vehemently denied, however, that the Preston strike was the sudden inspiration for the work.

Dickens did not want his readers to believe in the myth that novels were created by a sudden, magic act of inspiration. He also did not want readers to reduce the novel to one local recognizable place and to only one theme. To Dickens, writing and reading were complex activities that required concentration and commitment as much as inspiration.

After you read the first two chapters excerpted here, we hope that you will read all of *Hard Times*. The novel is primarily about education: What and how should children learn in modern society? What will be the result of an education that deals only with hard facts and that mistrusts anything fanciful or poetic?

To some extent, Dickens may have been thinking of James Mill (1773–1836), the father of John Stuart Mill, in his satirical presentation of Mr. Gradgrind's school of facts. (See the introduction to "On Liberty," pp. 111–15.) In addition Dickens was almost certainly asking himself how modern society had developed so many hard edges. Look in the following pages for Dickens's use of words expressing hardness and linearity, "square forefinger," "square forehead," "line," "vault," all in a book subtitled, "Sowing," with its reference to the softer edges of nature, the earth yielding to and nurturing the seeds.

The children themselves are not seen as part of nature but as things, "little vessels then and there arranged in order, ready to have imperial gallons of facts poured into them until they were full to the brim." Vessels, mechanical objects, do not grow, but children must. From this conflict Dickens works out his novel.

Hard Times
CHARLES DICKENS

BOOK THE FIRST. SOWING

CHAPTER I

The One Thing Needful

"Now, what I want is, Facts. Teach these boys and girls nothing but Facts. Facts alone are wanted in life. Plant nothing else, and root out everything else. You can only form the minds of reasoning animals upon Facts: noth-

Reprinted from Charles Dickens' *Hard Times*. Norton Critical Edition edited by George Ford and Sylvere Monod. By permission of W. W. Norton & Company, Inc. Copyright ©1966 by W. W. Norton & Company, Inc.

ing else will ever be of any service to them. This is the principle on which I bring up my own children, and this is the principle on which I bring up these children. Stick to Facts, Sir!"

The scene was a plain, bare, monotonous vault of a school-room, and the speaker's square forefinger emphasized his observations by underscoring every sentence with a line on the schoolmaster's sleeve. The emphasis was helped by the speaker's square wall of a forehead, which had his eyebrows for its base, while his eyes found commodious cellarage in two dark caves, overshadowed by the wall. The emphasis was helped by the speaker's mouth, which was wide, thin, and hard set. The emphasis was helped by the speaker's voice, which was inflexible, dry, and dictatorial. The emphasis was helped by the speaker's hair, which bristled on the skirts of his bald head, a plantation of firs to keep the wind from its shining surface, all covered with knobs, like the crust of a plum pie, as if the head had scarcely warehouse-room for the hard facts stored inside. The speaker's obstinate carriage, square coat, square legs, square shoulders — nay, his very neckcloth, trained to take him by the throat with an unaccommodating grasp, like a stubborn fact, as it was, — all helped the emphasis.

"In this life, we want nothing but Facts, Sir; nothing but Facts!"

The speaker, and the schoolmaster, and the third grown person present, all backed a little, and swept with their eyes the inclined plane of little vessels then and there arranged in order, ready to have imperial gallons of facts poured into them until they were full to the brim.

CHAPTER II

Murdering the Innocents

Thomas Gradgrind, Sir. A man of realities. A man of facts and calculations. A man who proceeds upon the principle that two and two are four, and nothing over, and who is not to be talked into allowing for anything over. Thomas Gradgrind, Sir — peremptorily Thomas — Thomas Gradgrind. With a rule and a pair of scales, and the multiplication table always in his pocket, Sir, ready to weigh and measure any parcel of human nature, and tell you exactly what it comes to. It is a mere question of figures, a case of simple arithmetic. You might hope to get some other nonsensical belief into the head of George Gradgrind, or Augustus Gradgrind, or John Gradgrind, or Joseph Gradgrind (all supposititious, non-existent persons), but into the head of Thomas Gradgrind — no, Sir!

In such terms Mr. Gradgrind always mentally introduced himself, whether to his private circle of acquaintance, or to the public in general. In such terms, no doubt, substituting the words "boys and girls," for "Sir," Thomas Gradgrind now presented Thomas Gradgrind to the little pitchers before him, who were to be filled so full of facts.

Indeed, as he eagerly sparkled at them from the cellarage before mentioned, he seemed a kind of cannon loaded to the muzzle with facts, and prepared to blow them clean out of the regions of childhood at one discharge. He seemed a galvanizing apparatus, too, charged with a grim mechanical substitute for the tender young imaginations that were to be stormed away.

"Girl number twenty," said Mr. Gradgrind, squarely pointing with his square forefinger, "I don't know that girl. Who is that girl?"

"Sissy Jupe, Sir," explained number twenty, blushing, standing up, and curtseying.

"Sissy is not a name," said Mr. Gradgrind. "Don't call yourself Sissy. Call yourself Cecilia."

"It's father as calls me Sissy, Sir," returned the young girl in a trembling voice, and with another curtsey.

"Then he has no business to do it," said Mr. Gradgrind. "Tell him he mustn't. Cecilia Jupe. Let me see. What is your father?"

"He belongs to the horse-riding, if you please, Sir."

Mr. Gradgrand frowned, and waved off the objectionable calling with his hand.

"We don't want to know anything about that, here. You mustn't tell us about that, here. Your father breaks horses, don't he?"

"If you please, Sir, when they can get any to break, they do break horses in the ring, Sir."

"You mustn't tell us about the ring, here. Very well, then. Describe your father as a horsebreaker. He doctors sick horses, I dare say?"

"Oh yes, Sir."

"Very well, then. He is a veterinary surgeon, a farrier, and horsebreaker. Give me your definition of a horse."

(Sissy Jupe thrown into the greatest alarm by this demand.)

"Girl number twenty unable to define a horse!" said Mr. Gradgrind, for the general behoof of all the little pitchers. "Girl number twenty possessed of no facts, in reference to one of the commonest of animals! Some boy's definition of a horse. Bitzer, yours."

The square finger, moving here and there, lighted suddenly on Bitzer, perhaps because he chanced to sit in the same ray of sunlight which, darting in at one of the bare windows of the intensely whitewashed room, irradiated Sissy. For, the boys and girls sat on the face of the inclined plane in two compact bodies, divided up the centre by a narrow interval; and Sissy, being at the corner of a row on the sunny side, came in for the beginning of a sunbeam, of which Bitzer, being at the corner of a row on the other side, a few rows in advance, caught the end. But, whereas the girl was so dark-eyed and dark-haired, that she seemed to receive a deeper and more lustrous colour from the sun, when it shone upon her, the boy was so light-eyed and light-haired that the self-same rays appeared to draw out of him what little colour he ever possessed. His cold eyes would hardly have been eyes, but for the short ends of lashes which, by bringing them into immediate contrast with something paler than themselves, expressed their form.

His short-cropped hair might have been a mere continuation of the sandy freckles on his forehead and face. His skin was so unwholesomely deficient in the natural tinge, that he looked as though, if he were cut, he would bleed white.

"Bitzer," said Thomas Gradgrind. "Your definition of a horse."

"Quadruped. Graminivorous. Forty teeth, namely, twenty-four grinders, four eye-teeth, and twelve incisive. Sheds coat in the spring; in marshy countries, sheds hoofs, too. Hoofs hard, but requiring to be shod with iron. Age known by marks in mouth." Thus (and much more) Bitzer.

"Now girl number twenty," said Mr. Gradgrind. "You know what a horse is."

She curtseyed again, and would have blushed deeper, if she could have blushed deeper than she had blushed all this time. Bitzer, after rapidly blinking at Thomas Gradgrind with both eyes at once, and so catching the light upon his quivering ends of lashes that they looked like the antennae of busy insects, put his knuckles to his freckled forehead, and sat down again.

The third gentleman now stepped forth. A mighty man at cutting and drying, he was; a government officer; in his way (and in most other people's too), a professed pugilist; always in training, always with a system to force down the general throat like a bolus, always to be heard of at the bar of his little Public-office, ready to fight all England. To continue in fistic phraseology, he had a genius for coming up to the scratch, wherever and whatever it was, and proving himself an ugly customer. He would go in and damage any subject whatever with his right, follow up with his left, stop, exchange, counter, bore his opponent (he always fought All England) to the ropes, and fall upon him neatly. He was certain to knock the wind out of common sense, and render that unlucky adversary deaf to the call of time. And he had it in charge from high authority to bring about the great public-office Millennium, when Commissioners should reign upon earth.

"Very well," said this gentleman, briskly smiling, and folding his arms. "That's a horse. Now, let me ask you girls and boys, Would you paper a room with representations of horses?"

After a pause, one half of the children cried in chorus, "Yes, Sir!" Upon which the other half, seeing in the gentleman's face that Yes was wrong, cried out in chorus, "No, Sir!" — as the custom is, in these examinations.

"Of course, No. Why wouldn't you?"

A pause. One corpulent slow boy, with a wheezy manner of breathing, ventured the answer, Because he wouldn't paper a room at all, but would paint it.

"You *must* paper it," said the gentleman, rather warmly.

"You must paper it," said Thomas Gradgrind, "whether you like it or not. Don't tell *us* you wouldn't paper it. What do you mean, boy?"

"I'll explain to you, then," said the gentleman, after another and a dismal pause, "why you wouldn't paper a room with representations of horses. Do you ever see horses walking up and down the sides of rooms in reality — in fact? Do you?"

"Yes, Sir!" from one half. "No, Sir!" from the other.

"Of course, No," said the gentleman, with an indignant look at the wrong half. "Why, then, you are not to see anywhere, what you don't see in fact; you are not to have anywhere, what you don't have in fact. What is called Taste, is only another name for Fact."

Thomas Gradgrind nodded his approbation.

"This is a new principle, a discovery, a great discovery," said the gentleman. "Now, I'll try you again. Suppose you were going to carpet a room. Would you use a carpet having a representation of flowers upon it?"

There being a general conviction by this time that "No, Sir!" was always the right answer to this gentleman, the chorus of No was very strong. Only a few feeble stragglers said Yes: among them Sissy Jupe.

"Girl number twenty," said the gentleman, smiling in the calm strength of knowledge.

Sissy blushed, and stood up.

"So you would carpet your room — or your husband's room, if you were a grown woman, and had a husband — with representations of flowers, would you?" said the gentleman. "Why would you?"

"If you please, Sir, I am very fond of flowers," returned the girl.

"And is that why you would put tables and chairs upon them, and have people walking over them with heavy boots?"

"It wouldn't hurt them, Sir. They wouldn't crush and wither, if you please, Sir. They would be the pictures of what was very pretty and pleasant, and I would fancy——"

"Ay, ay, ay! But you mustn't fancy," cried the gentleman, quite elated by coming so happily to his point. "That's it! You are never to fancy."

"You are not, Cecilia Jupe," Thomas Gradgrind solemnly repeated, "to do anything of that kind."

"Fact, fact, fact!" said the gentleman. And "Fact, fact, fact!" repeated Thomas Gradgrind.

"You are to be in all things regulated and governed," said the gentleman, "by fact. We hope to have, before long, a board of fact, composed of commissioners of fact, who will force the people to be a people of fact, and of nothing but fact. You must discard the word Fancy altogether. You have nothing to do with it. You are not to have, in any object of use or ornament, what would be a contradiction in fact. You don't walk upon flowers in fact; you cannot be allowed to walk upon flowers in carpets. You don't find that foreign birds and butterflies come and perch upon your crockery; you cannot be permitted to paint foreign birds and butterflies upon your crockery. You never meet with quadrupeds going up and down walls; you must not have quadrupeds represented upon walls. You must use," said the gentleman, "for all these purposes, combinations and modifications (in primary colours) of mathematical figures which are susceptible of proof and demonstration. This is the new discovery. This is fact. This is taste."

The girl curtseyed, and sat down. She was very young, and she looked as if she were frightened by the matter-of-fact prospect the world afforded.

"Now, if Mr. M'Choakumchild," said the gentleman, "will proceed to give his first lesson here, Mr. Gradgrind, I shall be happy, at your request, to observe his mode of procedure."

Mr. Gradgrind was much obliged. "Mr. M'Choakumchild, we only wait for you."

So, Mr. M'Choakumchild began in his best manner. He and some one hundred and forty other schoolmasters, had been lately turned at the same time, in the same factory, on the same principles, like so many pianoforte legs. He had been put through an immense variety of paces, and had answered volumes of head-breaking questions. Orthography, etymology, syntax, and prosody, biography, astronomy, geography, and general cosmography, the sciences of compound proportion, algebra, land-surveying and levelling, vocal music, and drawing from models, were all at the ends of his ten chilled fingers. He had worked his stony way into Her Majesty's most Honourable Privy Council's Schedule B, and had taken the bloom off the higher branches of mathematics and physical science, French, German, Latin, and Greek. He knew all about all the Water Sheds of all the world (whatever they are), and all the histories of all the peoples, and all the names of all the rivers and mountains, and all the productions, manners, and customs of all the countries, and all their boundaries and bearings on the two-and-thirty points of the compass. Ah, rather overdone, M'Choakumchild. If he had only learnt a little less, how infinitely better he might have taught much more!

He went to work in this preparatory lesson, not unlike Morgiana in the Forty Thieves: looking into all the vessels ranged before him, one after another, to see what they contained. Say, good M'Choakumchild. When from thy boiling store, thou shalt fill each jar brim full by-and-by, dost thou think that thou wilt always kill outright the robber Fancy lurking within — or sometimes only maim him and distort him!

Questions and Exercises

1. Write one paragraph to explain Thomas Gradgrind's educational theory.

2. Analyze Dickens's description of Thomas Gradgrind. First list the descriptive words that Dickens uses. What words tell about Gradgrind's physical appearance? How do those words relate to the descriptive words about his attitudes and goals? Write a factual definition of Mr. Gradgrind. Is Dickens's definition factual?

3. Look up the story of Morgiana, Ali Baba's slave in the story of the Forty Thieves in *Arabian Nights' Entertainment*. What did Morgiana do to kill the thieves? Why does Dickens make reference to this circumstance in the last paragraph of Chapter II?

4. In small groups, discuss the significance of the title of Chapter II, "Murdering the Innocents."

5. Look up "fact" and "truth" in the *Oxford English Dictionary*. Discuss in small groups the difference between facts and truth.

6. Read all of *Hard Times*. Then pursue one of the following questions for library research:
   a) What was the contemporary reception of *Hard Times*?
   b) Is the Gradgrind School a fair representation of utilitarian educational theories?

7. Read David Lodge's essay, "The Rhetoric of *Hard Times*" (pp. 190–205). With reference to Lodge's essay, write your own analysis of the rhetoric of *Hard Times*. Assume that your audience has read *Hard Times*, but not David Lodge's essay. Your audience also needs some explanation of what it means to discuss the rhetoric of fiction.

Essays of Analysis and Contemplation

The Rhetoric of *Hard Times*

DAVID LODGE

from *Language of Fiction*

Much writing in the humanities involves the thoughtful inspection of a work of art: a painting, a musical composition, or, as in the case of the essay at hand, a work of literary imagination. The British literary critic, David Lodge, Professor of Modern English Literature at the University of Birmingham, selects Charles Dickens's *Hard Times* as the object of his study. Lodge's purpose is to illuminate the novel, not to tear it apart, to see the work steadily and see it whole.

Students of literature can learn a great deal from Lodge's working method. In a letter to the editors of this anthology he describes his mode of composition as follows:

> ... I start with an enigma or question, the answer to which constitutes the "point" of the essay. In the case of "The rhetoric of *Hard Times*" the initial question or enigma is the existence of radically opposed evaluations and interpretations of the text in question.[1]

Lodge writes to make a point; that is, he does not present to us a series of disconnected ideas all loosely organized into a single essay about *Hard Times*. Instead, he focuses his critical analysis to answer a central question. Your instructors have probably advised you to find a controlling question which will help you to organize your critical essays. Lodge's process of composition represents a good example of the movement from curiosity to puzzlement to controlling question.

Lodge's essay on *Hard Times* originally appeared in *Language of Fiction*, a book of connected critical essays published in 1966. In that broader context, "The Rhetoric of *Hard Times*" is, as Lodge says, "itself part of the answer to theoretical questions raised in the first section of the book."[2] Since language is the novelist's medium, how might a close study of linguistic and rhetorical forms aid in a more enlightened reading of the novel?

The essay on *Hard Times* is one of seven chapters in *Language of Fiction*, each chapter exploring the function of language in a different work of prose fiction. The situation and occasion for the essay on *Hard Times* differ significantly from the context for a student's paper of literary anal-

---

1. Reprinted by permission of Professor David Lodge, Department of English, The University of Birmingham, England.
2. Ibid.

ysis. As a work of professional literary criticism, "The Rhetoric of *Hard Times*" is a hybrid form of two typical student assignments: the critical paper and the term paper. Lodge's emphasis is on his own close reading of *Hard Times*, and in that sense the essay resembles the critical analyses that students are often asked to write. Lodge, however, also demonstrates complete command of the secondary sources available on the novel. He exhibits that control subtly, without the extensive explanation that student writers would be expected to provide in a term paper. Lodge is writing, after all, for an audience of other literary critics, who presumably know the writing of Leavis, Holloway, House, and the other critics whom Lodge mentions.

Undergraduates too often make the mistake of writing for the teacher and, as a consequence, omit important material. Although instructors will finally grade the essays, students must assume a wider group of readers. Undergraduates ought to be writing for their own peers, classmates who may need more detailed reminders of the ideas of cited authorities. By writing critical analyses of literary texts and term papers that demonstrate some secondary sources, students perform two apprentice exercises. These exercises can certainly enhance the reading of fiction and once in a while might even lead to the publication of professional literary criticism.

Lodge, in fact, refers to the work of one of his own undergraduates, Miss Margaret Thomas, who first pointed out to her professor the "fairy-tale" element in *Hard Times*. Thomas presumably came up with this idea after a close reading of the novel. She did not know, as her professor did, that no published literary critic had yet written about this motif in the novel. Lodge places Thomas's reading into the larger conversation of Dickens scholarship. He also connects the fairy-tale element to his own thesis about the language of *Hard Times*. He then develops this thesis in an essay that transcends the interpretation of a single novel to comment on the general possibilities of fictional language.

More than simply illuminating another piece of prose, Lodge's critical essay, like all good literary criticism, has its own aesthetic appeal. As we read it, we better appreciate the complexities of the language of fiction and the language of criticism.

The Rhetoric of Hard Times

DAVID LODGE

On every page *Hard Times* manifests its identity as a polemical work, a critique of mid-Victorian industrial society dominated by materialism, acquisitiveness, and ruthlessly competitive capitalist economics. To Dickens, at the time of writing *Hard Times*, these things were represented most articulately, persuasively, (and therefore dangerously) by the Utilitarians. It is easy to abstract the argument behind the novel, and to demonstrate its logical and practical weaknesses. The argument has two stages: (1) that the dominant philosophy of Utilitarianism, particularly as it expresses itself in education, results in a damaging impoverishment of the moral and emotional life of the individual; and (2) that this leads in turn to social and economic injustice, since individuals thus conditioned are incapable of dealing with the human problems created by industrialism. On the level of plot (1) is expounded in terms of the Nemesis which punishes Gradgrind through his children and (2) is expounded in terms of Stephen Blackpool's sufferings. That Dickens makes a connection between the two propositions and the two areas of the plot is made clear in the scene where Blackpool confronts Bounderby and Harthouse, and is challenged to offer a solution for the "muddle" he is always complaining about. Stephen expresses himself negatively. He repudiates the employers' exploitation of their power ("the strong hand will never do't"); their reliance on *laissez faire* ("lettin' alone will never do't"); their withdrawal from social contact with the working classes ("not drawin' nigh to fok, wi' kindness and patience an' cheery ways . . . will never do't"); and, "most o' aw," their mental habit of regarding the workers as soulless units in the economic machine while inconsistently accusing them of ingratitude if they protest:

> Most o' aw, rating 'em as so much Power, and reg'lating 'em as if they was figures in a soom, or machines; wi'out loves and likens, wi'out memories and inclinations, wi'out souls to weary and souls to hope — when aw goes quiet draggin' on wi' 'em as if they'd nowt o' th' kind, and when aw goes onquiet, reproachin' 'em for their want o' sitch humanly feelins in their dealins wi' yo — this will never do't, Sir, till God's work is onmade. (II,v)

It is clear that Dickens is speaking through Stephen here, and what the speech amounts to in positive terms is a plea for generosity, charity, imaginative understanding of the spiritual and emotional needs of humanity.

While these values have an obvious relevance to the field of personal relations (the Gradgrind-Bounderby circle) they are less viable as a basis for reform of the body politic, because there are no sanctions to ensure their application. They are not—apart from Louisa's abortive attempt to help Stephen — shown in action in the novel vertically through the class structure: Stephen's martyr-like death bears witness to this. Yet Dickens could only offer a disembodied and vaguely defined benevolence as a cure for the ills of Coketown because he had rejected all the alternatives. In his hostile portrait of Gradgrind, Dickens repudiated not only the narrowest kind of Utilitarian rationalism, but also, as House and others have pointed out, the processes by which most of the great Victorian reforms were carried out — statistical enquiry, commissions, reports, acted on by Parliamentary legislation. In his hostile portrait of Slackbridge, and his account of Stephen's ostracism because of his refusal to join the Trade Union, Dickens repudiated the workers' claim to secure justice by collective bargaining. Dickens is, then, opposed to any change in the political and economic structure of society, and places his hopes for amelioration in a change of heart, mind, and soul in those who possess power, who will then disseminate the fruits of this change over the lower echelons of society. Dickens's ideal State would be one of "benevolent and genial anarchy."

This is an insecure basis from which to launch a critique of society, and its insecurity becomes all the more obvious when we look outside *Hard Times* to Dickens's journalism of the same period, and find him enthusing over the wonders of Victorian manufacture and expressing surprised admiration for the Preston cotton-workers' conduct of their strike in 1854.

And yet, when all this has been said, and the contradictions, limitations, and flaws in Dickens's argument extrapolated, *Hard Times* remains a novel of considerable polemical effectiveness. The measure of this effectiveness, it seems to me, can only be accounted for in terms of Dickens's rhetoric. This approach should recommend itself to the author of *The Victorian Sage*, a study which shows how many key Victorian writers, disarmed of logic by their opponents, resorted to non-logical methods of persuasion in order to communicate their ideas. In the criticism of fiction we have learned, notably from Wayne Booth, to use "rhetoric" as a term for all the techniques by which a novelist seeks to persuade us of the validity of his vision of experience, a vision which cannot usually be formulated in abstract terms. But in a novel like *Hard Times*, which can be called a *roman à thèse*, rhetoric functions very nearly in its traditional rôle as the vehicle of an argument.

There is another reason why rhetoric seems a particularly useful term in discussing Dickens's work. Not only is the "author's voice" always insistent in his novels, but it is characteristically a public-speaking voice, an oratorical or histrionic voice; and it is not difficult to see a connection between this feature of his prose and his fondness for speech-making and public reading of his works.

I shall try to show that *Hard Times* succeeds where its rhetoric succeeds and fails where its rhetoric fails; and that success and failure correspond fairly closely to the negative and positive aspects, respectively, of the argument inherent in the novel.

The very first chapter of *Hard Times* affords an excellent illustration of Dickens's rhetoric. . . . [See pp. 182–83.]

This chapter communicates, in a remarkably compact way, both a description and a judgment of a concept of education. This concept is defined in a speech, and then evaluated — not in its own terms, but in terms of the speaker's appearance and the setting. Dickens, of course, always relies heavily on the popular, perhaps primitive, assumption that there is a correspondence between a person's appearance and his character; and as Gradgrind is a governor of the school, its design may legitimately function as a metaphor for his character. Dickens also had a fondness for fancifully appropriate names, but — perhaps in order to stress the representativeness of Gradgrind's views — he does not reveal the name in this first chapter.[1]

Because of the brevity of the chapter, we are all the more susceptible to the effect of its highly rhetorical patterning, particularly the manipulation of certain repeated words, notably *fact, square,* and *emphasis.* The kind of education depicted here is chiefly characterized by an obsession with facts. The word occurs five times in the opening speech of the first paragraph, and it is twice repeated towards the end of the second, descriptive paragraph to prepare for the reintroduction of Gradgrind speaking — "'we want nothing but Facts, sir — nothing but Facts'"; and it occurs for the tenth and last time towards the end of the last paragraph. In Gradgrind's speeches the word is capitalized, to signify his almost religious devotion to Facts.

Gradgrind's concept of education is further characterized in ways we can group into three categories, though of course they are closely connected:

(1) It is authoritarian, fanatical and bullying in its application.
(2) It is rigid, abstract and barren in quality.
(3) It is materialistic and commercial in its orientation.

The first category is conveyed by the structure of the second paragraph, which is dominated by "emphasis." This paragraph comprises six sentences. In the first sentence we are told how the "speaker's square forefinger emphasised his observations." The next four, central sentences are each introduced, with cumulative force, by the clause "The emphasis was helped," and this formula, translated from the passive to the active voice, makes a fittingly "emphatic" conclusion to the paragraph in the sixth sentence: "all helped the emphasis." This rhetorical pattern has a dual function. In one way it reflects or imitates Gradgrind's own bullying, overemphatic rhetoric, of which we have an example in the first paragraph; but in another way it helps to *condemn* Gradgrind, since it "emphasises" the narrator's own pejorative catalogue of details of the speaker's person and

1. Mary McCarthy has suggested that an anonymous "he" at the beginning of a novel usually moves the reader to sympathetic identification (Mary McCarthy, "Characters in Fiction," *The Partisan Review Anthology* [1962], pp. 260–61). That the effect is quite the reverse in this example shows that the effect of any narrative strategy is determined finally by the narrator's language.

immediate environment. The narrator's rhetoric is, as it must be, far more skillful and persuasive than Gradgrind's.

The qualities in category (2) are conveyed in a number of geometrical or quasi-geometrical terms, *wide, line, thin, base, surface, inclined plane* and, particularly, *square* which recurs five times; and in words suggestive of barren regularity, *plain, bare, monotonous, arranged in order, inflexible*. Such words are particularly forceful when applied to human beings — whether Gradgrind or the children. The metamorphosis of the human into the non-human is, as we shall find confirmed later, one of Dickens's main devices for conveying his alarm at the way Victorian society was moving.

Category (3), the orientation towards the world of commerce, is perhaps less obvious than the other categories, but it is unmistakably present in some of the boldest tropes of the chapter: *commodious cellarage, warehouse room, plantation, vessels, imperial gallons.*

The authoritarian ring of *"imperial"* leads us back from category (3) to category (1), just as *"under-scoring every sentence with a line"* leads us from (1) to (2). There is a web of connecting strands between the qualities I have tried to categorize: it is part of the rhetorical strategy of the chapter that all the qualities it evokes are equally applicable to Gradgrind's character, person, ideas, his school and the children (in so far as he has shaped them in his own image).

Metaphors of growth and cultivation are of course commonplace in discussion of education, and we should not overlook the ironic invocation of such metaphors, with a deliberately religious, prophetic implication (reinforced by the Biblical echo of the chapter heading, "The One Thing Needful") in the title of the Book, "SOWING," later to be followed by Book the Second, "REAPING," and Book the Third, "GARNERING." These metaphors are given a further twist in Gradgrind's recommendation to "Plant nothing else and root out everything else" (except facts).

If there is a flaw in this chapter it is the simile of the plum pie, which has pleasant, genial associations alien to the character of Gradgrind, to whose head it is, quite superfluously, applied. Taken as a whole, however, this is a remarkably effective and densely woven beginning of the novel.

The technique of the first chapter of *Hard Times* could not be described as "subtle." But subtle effects are often lost in a first chapter, where the reader is coping with the problem of "learning the author's language." Perhaps with some awareness of this fact, sharpened by his sense of addressing a vast, popular audience, Dickens begins many of his novels by nailing the reader's attention with a display of sheer rhetorical power, relying particularly on elaborate repetition. One thinks, for instance, of the fog at the beginning of *Bleak House* or the sun and shadow in the first chapter of *Little Dorrit*. In these novels the rhetoric works to establish a symbolic atmosphere; in *Hard Times*, to establish a thematic Idea — the despotism of Fact. But this abstraction — Fact — is invested with a remarkable solidity through the figurative dimension of the language.

The gross effect of the chapter is simply stated, but analysis reveals that it is achieved by means of a complex verbal activity that is far from simple. Whether it represents fairly any actual educational theory or practice in mid-nineteenth-century England is really beside the point. It aims to convince us of the *possibility* of children being taught in such a way, and to make us recoil from the imagined possibility. The chapter succeeds or fails as rhetoric; and I think it succeeds.

Dickens begins as he means to continue. Later in the novel we find Gradgrind's house, which, like the school-room, is a function of himself, described in precisely the same terms of fact and rigid measurement, partly geometrical and partly commercial.

> A very regular feature on the face of the country, Stone Lodge was. Not the least disguise toned down or shaded off that uncompromising fact in the landscape. A great square house, with a heavy portico darkening the principal windows, as its master's heavy brows over-shadowed his eyes. A calculated, cast up, balanced and proved house. Six windows on this side of the door, six on that side; a total of twelve in this wing, a total of twelve in the other wing; four and twenty carried over to the back wings. A lawn and garden and an infant avenue, all ruled straight like a botanical account book. (I, iii)

It has been observed that Dickens individualizes his characters by making them use peculiar locutions and constructions in their speech, a technique which was particularly appropriate to serial publication in which the reader's memory required to be frequently jogged. This technique extends beyond the idiosyncratic speech of characters, to the language in which they are described. A key-word, or group of key-words, is insistently used when the character is first introduced, not only to identify him but also to evaluate him, and is invoked at various strategic points in the subsequent action. Dickens's remarkable metaphorical inventiveness ensures that continuity and rhetorical emphasis are not obtained at the expense of monotony. The application of the key-words of the first chapter to Mr. Gradgrind's house gives the same delight as the development of a metaphysical conceit. The observation that Mrs. Gradgrind, "whenever she showed a symptom of coming to life, was invariably stunned by some weighty piece of fact tumbling on her" (I, iv), affords a kind of verbal equivalent of knockabout comedy, based on a combination of expectancy (we know the word will recur) and surprise (we are not prepared for the particular formulation).

Bounderby offers another illustration of Dickens's use of key-words in characterization. He is first introduced as "a big, loud man, with a stare, and a metallic laugh" (I, iv). The metallic quality is shortly afterwards defined as "that brassy speaking-trumpet of a voice of his" *(ibid.)*. His house has a front door with "BOUNDERBY (in letters very like himself) upon a brazen plate, and a round brazen door-handle underneath it, like a brazen full stop" (I, xi). Bounderby's bank "was another red brick house, with black outside shutters, green inside blinds, a black street door up two white steps, a brazen door-plate, and a brazen door-handle full-stop" (II, i). The buildings Bounderby inhabits take their character from him, as Gradgrind's do from him. But here the emphasis is on the brass embellishments which, by the use of the word *brazen* (rather than *brass* used adjectivally) epitomize several facets of his characters: his hardness, vanity, crude enjoyment of wealth, and, most important of all, the fact that he is a brazen liar. (We do not know for certain that he is a liar until the end of the novel; the "brazen" fittings reinforce other hints which prepare us for the revelation.)

The failures of characterization in *Hard Times* are generally failures in using rhetorical strategies which Dickens elsewhere employs very successfully. The portrait of Slackbridge, the trade union demagogue, for instance, seeks to exploit a relationship between character and appearance in a way which is familiar in Dickens and well exemplified in the first chapter; but it does so crudely and clumsily:

> Judging him by Nature's evidence, he was above the mass in very little but the stage on which he stood. In many respects he was essentially below them. He was not so honest, he was not so manly, he was not so good-humoured; he substituted cunning for their simplicity, and passion for their safe solid sense. An ill-made, high shouldered man, with lowering brows, and his features crushed into an habitually sour expression, he contrasted most unfavourably, even in his mongrel dress, with the great body of his hearers in their plain working clothes. (II, iv)

Apart from the vividness of "crushed," the description of Slackbridge is carelessly vague, and we miss the metaphorical inventiveness that characterizes Dickens's best descriptions of people. But the main error of the passage is the ordering of its material. The rhetorical strategy announced by the opening sentence is that Slackbridge's character is to be read in his appearance. But in fact the character is read *before* we are given the appearance. It is as if Dickens has so little confidence in his own imaginative evidence that he must inform us, over-explicitly, what conclusions we are to draw, before we come to the evidence. We know from external sources that Dickens was in a confused state of mind about the trade union movement at the time of writing *Hard Times*, and we can rarely expect to receive a balanced account of organized labour from any middle-class Victorian novelist. However, the failure of understanding here reveals itself in the first place as a failure of expression; the portrait of Gradgrind, on the other hand, though it probably derives from an equivalent misunderstanding of Utilitarianism, succeeds.

Another, more significant failure of Dickens's rhetoric is to be observed in the treatment of Tom Gradgrind. In this connection, I must register my disagreement with John Holloway's opinion that "the gradual degeneration of Tom . . . is barely (as in fact it is treated) related to Dickens's major problems in the book, though it is one of its best things." It is gradual (though not very extensively treated) up to the beginning of Book II, by which point we have gathered that Tom, so far from drawing strength of character from his repressive and rationalist upbringing, is turning into a selfish young man prepared to exploit others for his own advantage. He is still a long way, however, from the depravity that allows him to connive at the seduction of his own sister and to implicate an innocent man (Stephen Blackpool) in his own crime. This moral gap is rather clumsily bridged by Dickens in the second chapter of Book II, where he suddenly introduces a key-word for Tom: "whelp."

The Bounderbys are entertaining James Harthouse to dinner. Louisa does not respond to Harthouse's attempts to flirt, but when Tom comes in, late, "She changed . . . and broke into a beaming smile. . . ."

> "Ay, ay?" thought the visitor. "This whelp is the only creature she cares for. So, so!"
> The whelp was presented, and took his chair. The appellation was not flattering, but not unmerited. (II, ii)

The chapter ends very shortly afterwards, but Dickens contrives to use the word "whelp" three more times, and the title of the following chapter (II, iii), in which Tom betrays Louisa's situation to Harthouse, is entitled "The Whelp."

"Whelp" is a cliché, and it will be noticed that the word is first used by Harthouse, and then adopted by the novelist in his authorial capacity. When a novelist does this, it is usually with ironical intent, suggesting some inadequacy in the speaker's habits of thought.[2] Dickens plays on

---

2. Compare E. M. Forster, a master of this device, in *A Room with a View* (George Emerson has been indiscreet enough to mention in company that his father is taking a bath):

> "Oh dear!" breathed the little old lady, and shuddered as if all the winds of heaven had entered the apartment. "Gentlemen sometimes do not realise — " Her voice faded away. But Miss Bartlett seemed to understand, and a conversation developed in which gentlemen who did not realise played a principal part. (I, i)

Much later in the novel, Lucy, engaged to another, is desperately fighting off the advances of George. "What does a girl do when she comes across a cad?" she asks Miss Bartlett.

> "I always said he was a cad, dear. Give me credit for that at all events. From the very first moment — when he said his father was having a bath." . . . She moved feebly to the window, and tried to detect the cad's white flannels among the laurels. (II, 16)

Gradgrind's "facts" to this effect. But in the case of Harthouse's "whelp" he has taken a moral cliché from a character who is morally unreliable, and invested it with his own authority as narrator. This gives away the fact that Tom is being forced into a new rôle halfway through the book. For Tom's degeneration *should* be related to the major problems with which Dickens is concerned in *Hard Times*. According to the overall pattern of the novel, Tom and Louisa are to act as indices of the failure of Mr. Gradgrind's philosophy of education, and should thus never be allowed to stray outside the area of our pity, since they are both victims rather than free agents. But Tom's actions do take him beyond our pity, and diminish the interest of his character.

Perhaps Dickens was misled by feeling the need to inject a strong crime-interest into his story, of which Tom was a handy vehicle; or perhaps he lost his head over the preservation of Louisa's purity (the somewhat hysterical conclusion to Chapter iii, Book II, "The Whelp," seems to suggest this). Whatever the explanation, "the whelp," unlike those key-words which organize and concentrate the represented character of individuals and places, acts merely as a slogan designed to generate in the reader such a contempt for Tom that he will not enquire too closely into the pattern of his moral development — a pattern that will not, in fact, bear very close scrutiny.

In the conduct of his central argument, Dickens explicitly calls our attention to a "key-note." The first occasion on which he does so is when introducing the description of Coketown, in Chapter v of Book I, entitled "The Key-note."

> Coketown, to which Messrs. Bounderby and Gradgrind now walked, was a triumph of fact; it had no greater taint of fancy in it than Mrs. Gradgrind herself. Let us strike the keynote, Coketown before pursuing our tune.
>
> It was a town of red brick, or of brick that would have been red if the smoke and ashes had allowed it; but as matters stood it was a town of unnatural red and black like the painted face of a savage. It was a town of machinery and tall chimneys, out of which interminable serpents of smoke trailed themselves for ever and ever, and never got uncoiled. It had a black canal in it, and a river that ran purple with ill-smelling dye, and vast piles of building full of windows where there was a rattling and a trembling all day long, and where the piston of the steam engine worked monotonously up and down like the head of an elephant in a state of melancholy madness. It contained several large streets all very like one another, and many small streets still more like one another, inhabited by people equally like one another, who all went in and out at the same hours, with the same sound upon the same pavements, to do the same work, and to

whom every day was the same as yesterday and tomorrow, and every year the counterpart of the last and the next.

Dorothy Van Ghent has commented on the effects Dickens gains by investing the inanimate with animation and vice versa. "The animation of inanimate objects suggests both the quaint gaiety of a forbidden life, and an aggressiveness that has got out of control. . . . The animate is treated as if it is a thing. It is as if the life absorbed by things had been drained out of people who have become incapable of their humanity." The description of Coketown illustrates this process. The buildings and machinery of Coketown are invested with a sinister life of their own, the life of savages, serpents, and elephants (the serpent and elephant images are reiterated at least five times in the novel). The people of Coketown, on the other hand, take their character from the architecture of the town non-metaphorically conceived — "large streets all very like one another, and many small streets still more like one another." They are reduced to indistinguishable units caught up in a mindless, monotonous, mechanical process, superbly represented in the droning repetition of sound and syntax in the last sentence of the passage quoted.

In the rest of this chapter Dickens goes on to say that, despite the efficiency of the town, it was afflicted by *malaise*, social and moral: drunkenness, idleness, irreligion. "Is it possible," he asks, "that there was any analogy between the case of the Coketown populace and the little Gradgrinds?" He goes on to suggest that in both "there was fancy in them demanding to be brought into healthy existence instead of struggling on in convulsions."

The antithesis of "fact and fancy" introduces the chapter (see the quotation above). It has been previously introduced in the school-room chapters, where Sissy Jupe's words, "I would fancy——," are rudely interrupted by the government official:

> "Ay, ay, ay! But you mustn't fancy," cried the gentleman, quite elated coming so happily to his point. "That's it! You are never to fancy. . . . You are to be in all things regulated and governed . . . by fact. . . . You must discard the word Fancy altogether." (I. ii)

A very similar interruption establishes the same antithesis in slightly different terms in Chapter viii, Book I, "Never Wonder," where Dickens again proposes to strike the key-note:

> Let us strike the key-note again, before pursuing the tune.
> When she was half a dozen years younger, Louisa had been overheard to begin a conversation with her brother one day, by saying "Tom, I wonder" — upon which Mr. Gradgrind, who was the

person overhearing, stepped forth into the light, and said, "Louisa, never wonder!"

Herein lay the spring of the mechanical art and mystery of educating the reason without stooping to the cultivation of the sentiments and affections. Never wonder. By means of addition, subtraction, multiplication and division, settle everything somehow, and never wonder. Bring to me, says M'Choakumchild, yonder baby just able to walk, and I will engage that it shall never wonder.

The antithesis between fact and fancy (or wonder), is, then, the dominant key-note of *Hard Times*. It relates the public world of the novel to the private world, the *malaise* of the Gradgrind-Bounderby circle to the *malaise* of Coketown as a social community; and it draws together the two stages of the central argument of the book; the relationship between education in the broad sense and social health. In this respect Dickens is not so very far removed from the position of the Romantic critics of industrialist society. Compare Shelley:

> We have more moral, political and historical wisdom than we know how to reduce into practice; we have more scientific and economical knowledge than can be accommodated to the just distribution of the produce which it multiplies. The poetry, in these systems of thought, is concealed by the accumulations of facts and calculating processes. . . . We want the creative faculty to imagine that which we know. . . . To what but a cultivation of the mechanical arts in a degree disproportioned to the presence of the creative faculty, which is the basis of all knowledge, is to be attributed the abuses of all invention for abridging and combining labour, to the exasperation of the inequality of mankind? From what other cause has it arisen that the discoveries which should have lightened, have added a weight to the curse of Adam? Poetry, and the principle of Self, of which money is the visible incarnation, are the God and Mammon of the world.

There is a real community of feeling between Shelley and Dickens here: one might almost think that *Hard Times* takes its cue for the criticism of "the accumulation of facts," "calculating processes" and "the principle of Self" from the *Defence*. But whereas Shelley opposes to these things poetry, imagination, the creative faculty, Dickens can only offer Fancy, wonder, sentiments — though he does so with the same seriousness and the same intentions as Shelley, as a panacea for the ills of modern society. It is tempting to relate the inadequacy of Dickens's concept of Fancy to the discussion familiar in Romantic criticism of Fancy and Imagination. But it is on the rhetorical level that the inadequacy of Dickens's concept manifests itself. In the first "key-note" chapter, the authorial voice inquiries, with heavy irony, whether we are to be told "at this time of day"

> that one of the foremost elements in the existence of the Coketown working people had been for scores of years deliberately set at nought? That there was any Fancy in them demanding to be brought into healthy existence instead of struggling on in convulsions? That, exactly in the ratio as they worked long and monotonously, the craving grew within them for some physical relief — some relaxation, encouraging good humour and good spirits, and giving them a vent — some recognized holiday, though it were but for an honest dance to a stirring band of music — some occasional light pie in which even M'Choakumchild had no finger — which craving must and would be satisfied aright, or must and would inevitably go wrong, until the laws of the Creation were repealed? (I, v)

The rhetorical questions here impede and confuse the argument. The parallelism of "which craving must and would be satisfied aright, or must and would inevitably go wrong" is tired and mechanical. A mathematical image is enlisted in arguing *against* the mathematical, calculating faculty: it is precisely Dickens's case in the novel as a whole that the "laws of Creation" are not accountable in terms of "ratios." The vagueness of "*some* relaxation," "*some* recognized holiday" is by no means clarified by the unexciting offer of an "honest dance" or a "light pie" as specific palliatives for the people of Coketown.

Dickens is struggling to assert, here, the existence of a universal need in humanity, a need which arises from quite a different side of man's nature from that which is occupied with the mechanical processes of industrialism, a need which must be satisfied, a need distantly related to that need for poetry which Shelley asserts. But whereas Shelley's "poetry" is a faculty which involves and enhances and transforms the total activity of man — "We must imagine that which we know" — Dickens's Fancy is merely a temporary escape from what is accepted as inevitably unpleasant. It is "relief," "a vent," a "holiday." To be cruel, one might say that Dickens offers the oppressed workers of Coketown bread and circuses: bread in the metaphorical "light pie" and circuses in the "honest dance" — and, of course, in Mr. Sleary's circus.

The realm of Fancy is most vividly evoked by the rhetoric of *Hard Times* in what might be called the "fairy-tale" element of the novel.[3] Many

---

3. My attention was first directed to this (apart from the characterization of Mrs. Sparsit) by a Birmingham undergraduate, Miss Margaret Thomas. Possibly it has been observed before, but I have not been able to find it in Dickens criticism.

of the characters and events are derived from the staple ingredients of the fairy-tale, and this derivation is clearly revealed in the language.

Louisa and Tom first figure as the brother and sister who often appear in fairy-tales as waifs, exiles, victims of circumstance, hedged about with dangers (the Babes in the Woods, etc.). As they sit by the fire of their room, "Their shadows were defined upon the wall, but those of the high presses in the room were all blended together on the wall and on the ceiling, as if the brother and sister were overhung by a dark cavern" (I, viii). In their childhood their father wears the aspect of an "Ogre":

> Not that they knew, by name or nature, anything about an Ogre. Fact forbid! I only use the word to express a monster in a lecturing castle, with Heaven knows how many heads manipulated into one, taking childhood captive, and dragging it into gloomy statistical dens by the hair. (I, iii)

Later, Louisa becomes the enchanted princess with a heart of ice, while Tom takes on the rôle of the knave. Harthouse is the demon king, popping up suddenly in the action with mischievous intent, in a cloud of (cigar) smoke:

> James Harthouse continued to lounge in the same place and attitude, smoking his cigar in his own easy way, and looking pleasantly at the whelp, as if he knew himself to be a kind of agreeable demon who had only to hover over him, and he must give up his whole soul if required. (II, iii)

Sissy tells Mrs. Gradgrind that she used to read to her father "About the fairies, sir, and the dwarf, and the hunchback, and the genies" (I, vii); and the circus folk in *Hard Times* are comparable to the chorus of benevolent, comic, grotesque, half-supernatural creatures who inhabit the world of romance and fairy-tale. They are persistently associated with legend and myth — Pegasus (I, v), Cupid (*ibid.*), Jack the Giant Killer (III, vii), etc. Mr. Bounderby's mother, Mrs. Pegler, "the mysterious old woman" (III, v) is the crone who figures in many fairy tales and who brings about a surprising turn in the action. Mr. Bounderby refers to her as "an old woman who seems to have been flying into the town on a broomstick now and then" (II, viii). But the proper witch of the story, and Dickens's most effective adaptation of a stock-figure from fairy-tale, is Mrs. Sparsit. "Mrs. Sparsit considered herself, in some sort, the Bank Fairy," we are told, but the townspeople "regarded her as the Bank Dragon, keeping watch over the treasures of the mine." Her heavy eyebrows and hooked nose are exploited for vivid effects of cruelty:

> Mr. Bounderby sat looking at her, as, with the points of a stiff, sharp pair of scissors, she picked out holes for some inscrutable

purpose, in a piece of cambric. An operation which, taken in connexion with the bushy eyebrows and the Roman nose, suggested with some liveliness the idea of a hawk engaged upon the eyes of a tough little bird. (I, xvi)

She flatters Bounderby to his face, but secretly insults his portrait. She wills Louisa into Harthouse's clutches, figuring Louisa's progress as the descent of a "Giant's Staircase," on which she keeps anxious watch (II, x). The boldest treatment of Mrs. Sparsit as a witch occurs in the scene where she steals through the grounds of Mr. Gradgrind's country house, hoping to catch Louisa and Harthouse together.

> She thought of the wood and stole towards it, heedless of long grass and briers: of worms, snails and slugs, and all the creeping things that be. With her dark eyes and her hook nose warily in advance of her, Mrs. Sparsit softly crushed her way through the thick undergrowth, so intent upon her object that she would probably have done no less, if the wood had been a wood of adders.
> Hark!
> The smaller birds might have tumbled out of their nests, fascinated by the glittering of Mrs. Sparsit's eyes in the gloom. . . .
> (II, xi)

When a thunderstorm bursts immediately afterwards, Mrs. Sparsit's appearance becomes still more grotesque:

> It rained now, in a sheet of water. Mrs. Sparsit's white stockings were of many colours, green predominating; prickly things were in her shoes; caterpillars slung themselves, in hammocks of their own making, from various parts of her dress; rills ran from her bonnet, and her Roman nose. (II, xi)

Traditionally, witches are antipathetic to water. It is appropriate, therefore, that the frustration of Mrs. Sparsit's spite, when she loses track of Louisa, is associated with her ludicrous, rain-soaked appearance (see the conclusion to II, xi).

We may add to these examples of the invocation of fairy tale, the repeated description of the factories illuminated at night as "fairy palaces" (I, x; I, xi; II, i, et passim), and Mr. Bounderby's often espressed conviction that his men "expect to be set up in a coach and six, and to be fed on turtle soup and venison and fed with a gold spoon" (I, xi; I, vi; II, i, et passim). These phrases contrast ironically with the actual drab environment and existence of the Coketown people.

It is, indeed, as an ironic rhetorical device that the fairy-tale element operates most successfully. On one level it is possible to read the novel as an ironic fairy-tale, in which the enchanted princess is released from her spell but does not find a Prince Charming, in which the honest, persecuted servant (Stephen) is vindicated but not rewarded, and in which the traditional romantic belief in blood and breeding, confirmed by a discovery, is replaced by the exposure of Bounderby's inverted snobbery.

In other respects, however, the fairy-tale element sets up unresolved tensions in the novel. It encourages a morally-simplified, non-social, and non-historical view of human life and conduct, whereas Dickens's undertaking in *Hard Times* makes quite opposite demands. Mr. Sleary's ruse for releasing Tom from the custody of Bitzer, for instance (III, viii), is acceptable on the level of fairy-tale motivation: he returns Mr. Gradgrind's earlier good deed (the adoption of Sissy) and scores off an unsympathetic character (Bitzer). But the act is essentially lawless, and conflicts with Dickens's appeals elsewhere in the novel for justice and social responsibility. As long as the circus-folk represent a kind of life that is anarchic, seedy, socially disreputable, but cheerful and humane, they are acceptable and enjoyable. But when they are offered as agents or spokesmen of social and moral amelioration, we reject them. The art they practice is Fancy in its tawdriest form, solemnly defended by Mr. Sleary in terms we recognize as the justification of today's mass entertainers:

> People mutht be amuthed. They can't be alwayth a learning, nor yet they can't be alwayth a working, they an't made for it. You *mutht* have uth, Thquire. (III, viii)

Sissy is meant to represent a channel through which the values of the circus folk are conveyed to the social order. But her one positive act, the dismissal of Harthouse (III, ii), depends for its credibility on a simple faith in the superiority of a good fairy over a demon king.

In other words, where Dickens invokes the world of fairy-tale ironically, to dramatize the drabness, greed, spite, and injustice which characterize a society dominated by materialism, it is a highly effective rhetorical device; but where he relies on the simplifications of the fairy-tale to suggest means of redemption, we remain unconvinced.

If Dickens's notion of Fancy was attached mainly to fairy-tale and nursery rhyme (cf. the allusions to the cow with the crumpled horn and Peter Piper in I, iii), his own art is very much one of Fancy in the Coleridgean sense: "Fancy has no other counters to play with, but fixities and definites. The Fancy is indeed no other than a mode of Memory emancipated from the order of time and space. . . ." This seems an appropriate description of Dickens's method in, for instance, the first chapter of *Hard Times*, or in the description of Coketown, or in the treatment of Mrs. Sparsit as a witch. To appreciate this, is to feel that Coleridge was wrong to depreciate Fancy as a literary mode; but it is also to understand why Dickens's greatest achievement as a novelist was his depiction of a disordered universe in which the organic and the mechanical have exchanged places, rather than in his attempts to trace moral and emotional processes within the individual psyche.

In *Hard Times*, Dickens expounds a diagnosis of the ills of modern industrial society for which no institutions can supply a cure: society, represented by a group of characters, must therefore change itself, learning from a group outside the social order — the circus. But Dickens's characters are incapable of change: the language in which they are embodied fixes them in their "given" condition. They can only die (like Stephen Blackpool) or be broken (like Mr. Bounderby). Mr. Gradgrind may lose his "squareness," but he is left a shadow: he cannot become a Michelin Man, all circles and spheres. Louisa when her heart has been melted is a far less convincing character than Louisa with a heart of ice. (This can be quickly seen by comparing the scene of her interview with Gradgrind to discuss Bounderby's proposal (I, xv), rightly singled out for praise by Leavis, with the parallel scene at the end of the book where she returns to her father to reproach him for her upbringing, and where she is given the most embarrassing lines in the novel to speak (II, xii).) Dickens falters in his handling of the character of Tom Gradgrind precisely because he uses a device for fixing character *(whelp)* to express a process of change.

If *Hard Times* is a polemical novel that is only partially persuasive, it is because Dickens's rhetoric is only partially adequate to the tasks he set himself.

Questions and Exercises

1. Lodge writes several paragraphs of his essay before he states his thesis. What is his thesis? Where does it appear in the essay? What is the function of the paragraphs that precede the statement of the thesis?

2. Find the articles and books which Lodge cites. Record your reactions to Lodge's use of the secondary material. Does he accurately summarize the main ideas in the material?

3. What does Lodge mean by rhetoric? Read Wayne Booth's definition of rhetoric in Chapter 1 of *The Rhetoric of Fiction* (University of Chicago Press, 1961). Compare and contrast Lodge's and Booth's use of the term.

4. Bring to class a critical paper of your own composition. Write some notes comparing and contrasting the structure of this paper to the structure of Lodge's chapter. In small groups, reach some consensus on the differences between student papers and professional literary criticism.

5. Read Chapter II of Dickens's *Hard Times*, pp. 183–87 of this text. What key words are associated with Thomas Gradgrind? with Sissy

Jupe? In small groups, discuss the patterns that emerge from the use of these key words.

6. Draft an essay on the use of language to express character in Chapter Two of *Hard Times*. Your readers are your classmates; they have read *Hard Times* but need clarification on the issue at hand.

7. Check the *Humanities Citation Index* for books and articles that refer to Lodge's essay; that essay was published in 1966, and thus relevant books and articles would be dated later than that. Using that material, write a term paper on the rhetoric of *Hard Times*. Your readers are your classmates, who have read *Hard Times* and who are interested in current critical work on the rhetoric of the novel.

Restoring Charles II

ANTONIA FRASER

from *The New Republic*

Nobody took Lady Antonia Fraser seriously when she told her friends that she was going to write a history. Perhaps it was because she was in her thirties and had not been trained as a professional historian; perhaps it was because of her position in life as a member of a socially prominent British family, one that had not before produced serious historians. She remembers, when she began doing research for her massive biography of *Mary Queen of Scots*, that she tried to tell her friends what she was doing, but "nobody would listen. . . . They thought I was doing a novel."[1]

In fact, Lady Antonia's high opinion of history and biography went back to her childhood reading of Lytton Strachey's *Eminent Victorians*. "What I admired about Lytton Strachey — and still do admire, incidentally — was his immense readability."[2] This admiration, she wrote later, planted the idea that "biography could be exciting, that information could be communicated in a highly readable form."[3]

Her first biography, *Mary Queen of Scots*, was acclaimed by the academic community and read avidly by the general public. Seven years later, after long research, Antonia Fraser published *Royal Charles: Charles II and the Restoration*. In the following essay, entitled, "Restoring Charles II," she discusses the king whose life engaged her for seven years. And she poses for us the questions that keep her fascinated with biographical writing. Antonia Fraser demonstrates that historical scholarship can be as lively and vigorous as life itself.

1. Interview with Nan Robertson, *New York Times*, November 13, 1979.
2. Antonia Fraser, "Restoring Charles II," in *The New Republic*, 29 December 1978, p. 21.
3. *Ibid.*

Restoring Charles II

ANTONIA FRASER

I

In his book *On Historians*, Professor J. H. Hexter quotes Donald Kagan as
dividing historians into "lumpers and splitters." This division, Professor
Hexter believes, is far more effective than that, for example, between
quantifiers and non-quantifiers or that between Marxists and non-Marxists.
I quote Professor Hexter: "Historians who are splitters," that is those who
like "to point out divergences, to perceive differences . . . do not mind unti-
diness and accident in the past: they rather like them." Lumpers, that is
those who "want to put all the past into tidy boxes . . . do not like acci-
dents; they would prefer to have them vanish." Now if the analogy is carried through to biography, I think biographers can be divided into provers
and inquirers. Provers want to prove a thesis about a given person, and
will rake their material very thoroughly — that is not in question — in
order to establish it. Inquirers, on the other hand, will read the same material with an open mind and ask themselves not *how* can I prove X, but
what does this material prove? In short, one might sum up the two schools
of biographers even more simply as "Hows" and "Whats." Here are two
examples. How can I prove from her letters that Mary Queen of Scots was
a sexually passionate woman? As opposed to: what do her letters prove
about Mary Queen of Scots? I found her, incidentally, fascinating but not
passionate, more interested in power than in sex.

By temperament, I am a "whatter" — and my researches about Queen
Mary confirmed my view that I would never have discovered the facts I
did if I had approached her from the stereotyped point of view of so many
other books.

Coming on, then, to the subject of King Charles II (1630–85) it was
invaluable that I was a "whatter." Here the equivalent of Mary's alleged
passionate nature is the delusive catch phrase about Charles — the Merry
Monarch. So delusive is it — in England certainly — that my English publisher kept optimistically advertising the book in advance in their trailer
catalogues as "the coming biography of the Merry Monarch." But to me,
one of the important discoveries I made about King Charles II, which both
stole over me and astounded me, is that if anything he was a melancholy
monarch, although that isn't a quite accurate phrase either. But the conventional picture of this roisterous fellow — a girl at each elbow, chucking
Nell Gwynn under the chin and enjoying her oranges, a spaniel somewhere around — no, this simply did not emerge at all. Yet it would have

From Lady Antonia Fraser, "Restoring Charles II," *The New Republic*, December 29,
1979. Reprinted by permission of Lady Antonia Fraser.

been easy to have discovered that evidence had I been specifically looking for it.

After all here is a man who *did* love pleasure. King Charles himself said on the subject of sin to Bishop Burnet that he rated falsehood and cruelty the two greatest sins. But God, he was convinced, would never damn a man "for allowing himself a little pleasure." The pleasures he loved certainly included women. The roll call of his mistresses is an impressive one, from Lucy Walter, his first mistress, to Louise Duchess of Portsmouth, his last.

Then, he loved the theater, and it was thanks to his patronage that actors and actresses, hitherto a rather derided race, attained proper respectability. He loved horses, and the great English racing center of Newmarket owed everything to his patronage. He took part himself — it wasn't just a spectator sport — and he rode and won a race when he was 45, which the reports make clear was due to his horsemanship, not the sycophancy of courtiers giving way to their king.

Charles II also loved gardens and all aspects of what we would now call the environment — town and garden planning. The fire of London, appalling story as it was, did give the opportunity of replanning London; Windsor Castle and St. James Park both owe an enormous amount to his replanning, although the fact is sometimes ignored because King George IV came afterward and replanned it again. Charles made St. James Park into a wonderful place of popular recreation, introducing gondolas onto the new canals, rare birds, including a pair of pelicans from Astrakhan, a present from the Russian ambassador.

All this, and he loved swimming (five a.m. in the Thames — ugh — the courtiers didn't love that so much) and spaniels. His love of dogs was another thing the courtiers had reserved feelings about: I always imagine they felt as present day courtiers are alleged to do about Queen Elizabeth II's corgis. "God bless your Majesty, but God damn your dogs" cried one stalwart after being nipped, for the king's dogs were extremely spoiled.

Now this was obviously a man who was not indifferent to pleasure. I would go further and say that King Charles II was a genuine hedonist. Yet the more I examined his extraordinary and dramatic life, the more I realized that he could not possibly be described as "merry." A happy childhood — the boy in the Van Dyck pictures — yes, loved by his parents and loving them in return. But how was this a preparation for the traumatic events that followed? At the age of 10 he was sent by his father to the House of Lords, to plead for the life of his minister Strafford — a man Prince Charles knew and revered. Strafford was executed and, in a way, the Stuart family never recovered.

At the age of 12 the prince was involved in battle — the most bewildering form of battle to a boy, civil war. He left his father forever at the age of not quite 14, left England for Jersey and France when he was nearly 16. Finally when he was 18, his father was, as Charles viewed it, cruelly murdered by the English revolutionaries, and there was not a thing the Prince of Wales, demanding, pleading, but moneyless and troopless, could do about it. So at 18, Charles II was, as a contemporary put it, "King in nothing but the name."

From this point on, things got worse. For the next 11 years the new King Charles II was mainly in exile, always poor, always begging, always aware that he could not help those who depended on him, turning now to France, now to Spain, now to anyone who might assist him. His mother Henrietta Maria nagged at him. They quarreled about religion. The commonwealth officials from over the water insulted him. When Charles did embark on a campaign with the aid of the Scots, the Scottish Presbyterians insulted his parents and made him pray to atone for their "blood-guiltiness" — an appalling prospect. When the Scottish army was defeated at Worcester, thereafter the king wandered in perhaps the most famous escape story in history, a fugitive hunted by the very people he had been brought up to believe were his loyal subjects. And when it got worse — worse and worse, more poverty, more humiliation until the totally unexpected wonder of the Restoration in 1660 which occurred, as all contemporaries said, out of the blue. As a young civil servant named Samuel Pepys wrote in one of the first entries in his dary: "Indeed it was past imagination both the greatness and the suddenness of it."

As I studied this period, first when I wrote about Cromwell and then concentrating on King Charles II, I began to realize that no man could emerge unmarked by these experiences. It was then I understood or began to understand what a wary if affable creature was greeted by those crowds on Restoration Day, May 29, 1660. Here was a man who had been betrayed, and never knew when it might happen again. King Charles II, then, feared revolution because he had experienced it. What he couldn't know was that he would die in his bed 25 years after this Restoration, the last absolute king of Great Britain.

II

People argue about whether a biography can be written of a person to whom the writer is hostile. The answer is yes, of course it can. Otherwise there would be no dispassionate biographies of characters like Adolf Hitler. Nevertheless, for me personally it would not be possible. I must feel a kind of initial sympathy if I am to spend five years of my life on a given subject. Besides, in the kind of interpretative biography I aim to write, I think some kind of sympathy is positively important. After all, prejudice against people makes one a bad judge of them — worse than prejudice in favor of them. If you are basically not in favor of someone and do not try to get inside his or her skin, you may fail to create a coherent picture. Carlyle put this very well, I think, in his studies of *Heroes and Hero-Worship* when he reached the subject of Mohammed and wrote unabashedly:

"I mean to say all the good of him I justly can. It is a way to get at his secret." That's it: getting at the secret is not achieved by hostility.

Nevertheless I do not acquit Charles II of many moral failings both in my mind and, more important, in my book. I think his dreadful experiences dulled him, so that he was kind by nature, cynical by training. Yet a biography is not a series of moral judgments: it is essentially a recreation of one particular individual, set against the background of his age. Ah, there's the rub. This to me is the real problem of the biographer's art, the placing of the individual. How much background do you select, how typical is a man of his background, how much is he atypical? Above all, a biography is not a history of the 17th century. In many ways Charles II was not at all typical of his time.

Let us take three examples. I will begin with his tolerance. King Charles II was undeniably a very tolerant man. He wanted everyone to have his or her own religion. As the Declaration of Breda stated on the eve of the Restoration, he promised "a liberty to tender consciences." He was, at first, as good as his word, allowing the Jews officially to reenter Britain for the first time and attempting toleration for the Catholics, though in that he finally failed.

All very delightful: but we must realize that what seems delightful to us was frightening and highly suspect in the king's own time. People wondered: what was his game? Was he giving away England to the foreign papists? It can indeed be argued that this toleration was politically unwise, if morally agreeable. Thus we must be wary of bringing our own values into our judgments on the past: they become warped.

Take another example — acceptance of secret subsidies from the French king. Here the position is reversed. We find this perfectly dreadful, as if the president of the United States were discovered taking bribes from Russia. How underhand, how corrupt, how dangerous! Now here we have to realize that what the king did, reprehensible or not, was not in any way unusual. The Whig leaders were in fact being heavily bribed at the same time by Louis XIV, although all their public utterances were against monarchical absolutism. This discovery incidentally so upset the editor of their state papers in the 18th century, that he wrote: "I felt very near the same shock as if I had seen a son turn his back in the day of battle."

The third example is rather more beguiling. King Charles II had a sense of humor which we much appreciate today. You really could make up a book of the wit and wisdom of King Charles II, and it would not be a short book, I can assure you. Perhaps the most famous example of his quick-wittedness occurred when his crony Lord Rochester composed an impromtu rhyme about him. Rochester produced:

> We have a pritty witty King
> Whose word no man relies on
> He never said a foolish thing
> And never did a wise one.

To which the king replied urbanely that his words were his own but his deeds were his ministers!

Then at the moment of the Restoration itself, on the day of the triumphal processions into London, the King remarked that it was obviously his own fault that he had been away from England so long, for since he had arrived in England he had met no one who did not passionately wish for his return. Finally, when the courtiers twitted him because his mistress Barbara Castlemaine had become a Catholic, King Charles replied that he never interfered with the souls of ladies, but only with their bodies, in so far as they were gracious enough to allow him.

However, I must emphasize that this lovely kind of wit was not as popular then as it would be now: indeed one of his critics, Lord Halifax, described him as having wit rather more than became a prince; there was a suggestion of *lèse-majesté* about these wisecracks, not quite what was expected of a king.

Lastly let us take the question of Charles II's relations with women. He adored the company of women, their conversation, to have supper with them, chat with them; he was astonishingly faithful to his mistresses, even if he was faithful to several of them at once. It's typical of him, I always think, that on the last active night of his life King Charles had supper with three of his mistresses, transformed into duchesses: Barbara Duchess of Cleveland, Louise Duchess of Portsmouth, and Hortense Duchesse de Mazarin. None of them was even remotely young by the standards of the time: in fact I worked it out that among them they had been in his service, if I may so term it, nearly 50 years.

Yet once again this liking for women's company was not a good quality in the eyes of King Charles's contemporaries — smacking of petticoat government, quite apart from immorality. There was a popular anecdote to illustrate this. In the late 1670s, the Accession Day of Queen Elizabeth I was increasingly celebrated, actually as a piece of Protestant propaganda. Somebody asked why such a fuss was made about the Accession Day of a Queen. The reply was: because she, being a woman, chose *men* for her counselors, a heavy hint that the opposite was taking place with King Charles II.

I must end on a more personal note. While I was researching my book on King Charles, I asked myself which of all my subjects I would most like to have met: Mary, the fascinating queen, Cromwell, the great man, or King Charles. I decided without hesitation that for his humanity, his warmth, even for his inner melancholy, my choice would always be King Charles II.

Questions and Exercises

1. In one paragraph, sum up Antonia Fraser's opinion of Charles II.

2. In one paragraph, write the opinion that you have formed of Charles II. In what ways is your opinion similar to or different from hers?

3. What are "Hows" and "Whats"? Which of these does Fraser consider herself? How do these terms help you understand more about historians? How can we tell from Fraser's first paragraph that she will identify herself as a "whatter"?

4. In this essay Fraser recounts four examples of Charles II's behavior: tolerance, acceptance of secret subsidies, sense of humor, relations with women. In small groups, discuss the purpose of each example.

5. Does Fraser believe that a person can write a biography of someone toward whom the writer is hostile? In small groups, first come to consensus about what she says on the issue. Then discuss the following: Could each of you write a report about someone you disliked or about someone who bored you? How might your feelings affect your historical inquiry?

6. In small groups, discuss the purpose of this essay. In what sense is it about Charles II? In what sense is it not about Charles II?

7. Read a biography of an historical figure. Decide whether the biographer liked or disliked the individual. Cite key passages to support your point. Assume that your readers are classmates who have not read the biography.

8. Lady Antonia Fraser says that of all her biographical subjects she would most like to meet Charles II. Draft an essay identifying the historical figure you would most like to meet. Explain your reasons to an audience of classmates. In preparation for this assignment you should read at least two biographical accounts of your subject's life. You might also check to see if his or her letters have been collected and read some of these. Does this research change or confirm your desire to meet the individual?

9. Historians often write biographies of people who are still alive. Interview an older relative or friend about the events of his or her childhood. Read an historical account of the period (10–20 years) in which your subject grew up. Draft a biographical sketch connecting the events of his or her childhood to the period in question. Imagine an audience similar to the general readers for whom Lady Antonia Fraser wrote in her essay on Charles II.

All Animals Are Equal

PETER SINGER

from *Philosophic Exchange*

Humanists often pose ethical questions about racism and sexism, both forms of discrimination that diminish humankind. In this selection, the Australian philosopher, Peter Singer (1946–   ) presents a vigorous attack against the moral fault of "speciesism," that is, the tyranny of human over nonhuman animals. At the time he published this essay, in 1973, black liberation and women's liberation were already dynamic enough to give rise to an age of liberation movements. So, as a defender of animals' rights, Singer was confronted with two immediate problems of audience. How does one write about this issue without making it sound as if it is a parody, and how does one avoid sounding so absurd, in comparison with other liberation movements, that the issue is ignored?

Singer was very much aware of the lack of sympathy that his thesis would evoke. In his book on the subject he published in 1975, entitled *Animal Liberation* (New York: *New York Review of Books*), he addressed the problem directly. He wrote: "Most readers will take what they have just read to be wild exaggeration. Five years ago I myself would have laughed at some of the statements I have now written in complete seriousness" (p. vii). Therefore, his first strategy was a challenge for the reader to grow. What may appear absurd, may not, in fact, be absurd. Singer writes in a way that suggests very strongly that the topic is important. In addition to writing about it logically and analytically, he writes in the style of an impassioned social reformer.

Singer wants more than to be taken seriously, he wants to be convincing about the validity of his position. He begins with the observation that Mary Wollstonecraft's views on women, written in 1791, were ridiculed and regarded as absurd in her day, thereby implying that defenders of radically new ideas such as animals' rights may be, equally, prophets whose ideas should not be rejected simply because they are new and unusual. Similarly, Singer quotes from Jeremy Bentham, a nineteenth-century British utilitarian philosopher whose work is highly respected in the philosophical community, to show that his own opinions have respectable antecedents. (See pp. 111–12.)

Also as part of his defensive preparation, which, of course, is really a carefully orchestrated offensive, Singer constructs the logic of his argument with great care. His audience was composed of philosophers — that is, readers of the journal in which his article appeared, *Philosophic Exchange*. The uses of precedent and authority are merely preparatory for the argument itself. Like many philosophers, Singer develops his points slowly and thoughtfully. He does not state his thesis until the end of the third paragraph and does not assert the fundamental principle of his argument until the seventh paragraph; even then, he does so only after he has considered and rejected other ways of viewing equality. His strategy, then, is to place the burden of proof on his opponents; they must show that it is possible to argue, without contradiction, that racism is immoral, and that brutal treatment of animals is not.

The parallel of "speciesism" to racism is important to Singer's argument. He explains in the preface of his book that "the tyranny of human over nonhuman animals . . . has caused and today still is causing an amount of pain and suffering that can only be compared with that which resulted from the centuries of tyranny by white humans over black humans" (p. *vii*). Obviously, Singer is writing for readers who consider racism wrong; without this assumption, his arguments lose their force. On the other hand, Singer does not invoke racism as an emotional issue designed to force his readers to accept animal rights out of a sense of guilt. Racism is the analogy that presents a point of common reference for his argument, and, to Singer, logical argument is the key to the acceptance or rejection of his case for animal equality.

All Animals Are Equal

PETER SINGER

In recent years a number of oppressed groups have campaigned vigorously for equality. The classic instance is the Black Liberation movement, which demands an end to the prejudice and discrimination that has made blacks second-class citizens. The immediate appeal of the black liberation movement and its initial, if limited, success made it a model for other oppressed groups to follow. We became familiar with liberation movements for Spanish-Americans, gay people, and a variety of other minorities. When a majority group — women — began their campaign, some thought we had come to the end of the road. Discrimination on the basis of sex, it has been said, is the last universally accepted form of discrimination, practiced without secrecy or pretense even in those liberal circles that have long prided themselves on their freedom from prejudice against racial minorities.

One should always be wary of talking of "the last remaining form of discrimination." If we have learnt anything from the liberation movements, we should have learnt how difficult it is to be aware of latent prejudice in our attitudes to particular groups until this prejudice is forcefully pointed out.

A liberation movement demands an expansion of our moral horizons and an extension or reinterpretation of the basic moral principle of equality. Practices that were previously regarded as natural and inevitable come to be seen as the result of an unjustifiable prejudice. Who can say with confidence that all his or her attitudes and practices are beyond criticism? If we wish to avoid being numbered amongst the oppressors, we must be prepared to re-think even our most fundamental attitudes. We need to consider them from the point of view of those most disadvantaged by our attitudes, and the practices that follow from these attitudes. If we can make this unaccustomed mental switch we may discover a pattern in our attitudes and practices that consistently operates so as to benefit one group — usually the one to which we ourselves belong — at the expense of another. In this way we may come to see that there is a case for a new liberation movement. My aim is to advocate that we make this mental switch in respect of our attitudes and practices towards a very large group of beings: members of species other than our own — or, as we popularly though misleadingly call them, animals. In other words, I am urging that we extend to other species the basic principle of equality that most of us recognize should be extended to all members of our own species.

All this may sound a little far-fetched, more like a parody of other liberation movements than a serious objective. In fact, in the past the idea of "The Rights of Animals" really has been used to parody the case for women's rights. When Mary Wollstonecroft, a forerunner of later feminists, published her *Vindication of the Rights of Woman* in 1792, her ideas were widely regarded as absurd, and they were satirized in an anonymous publication entitled *A Vindication of the Rights of Brutes*. The author of this satire (actually Thomas Taylor, a distinguished Cambridge philosopher) tried to refute Wollstonecroft's reasonings by showing that they could be carried one stage further. If sound when applied to women, why should the arguments not be applied to dogs, cats, and horses? They seemed to hold equally well for these "brutes"; yet to hold that brutes had rights was manifestly absurd; therefore the reasoning by which this conclusion had been reached must be unsound, and if unsound when applied to brutes, it must also be unsound when applied to women since the very same arguments had been used in each case.

One way in which we might reply to this argument is by saying that the case for equality between men and women cannot validly be extended to nonhuman animals. Women have a right to vote, for instance, because they are just as capable of making rational decisions as men are; dogs, on the other hand, are incapable of understanding the significance of voting, so they cannot have the right to vote. There are many other obvious ways in which men and women resemble each other closely, while humans and other animals differ greatly. So, it might be said, men and women are similar beings, and should have equal rights, while humans and nonhumans are different and should not have equal rights.

The thought behind this reply to Taylor's analogy is correct up to a point, but it does not go far enough. There *are* important differences between humans and other animals, and these differences must give rise to *some* differences in the rights that each have. Recognizing this obvious fact, however, is no barrier to the case for extending the basic principle of equality to nonhuman animals. The differences that exist between men and women are equally undeniable, and the supporters of Women's Liberation are aware that these differences may give rise to different rights. Many feminists hold that women have the right to an abortion on request. It does not follow that since these same people are campaigning for equality between men and women they must support the right of men to have abortions too. Since a man cannot have an abortion, it is meaningless to talk of his right to have one. Since a pig can't vote, it is meaningless to talk of its right to vote. There is no reason why either Women's Liberation or Animal Liberation should get involved in such nonsense. The extension of the basic principle of equality from one group to another does not imply that we must treat both groups in exactly the same way, or grant exactly the same rights to both groups. Whether we should do so will depend on the nature of the members of the two groups. The basic principle of equality, I shall argue, is equality of consideration; and equal consideration for different beings may lead to different treatment and different rights.

So there is a different way of replying to Taylor's attempt to parody Wollstonecroft's arguments, a way which does not deny the differences between humans and nonhumans, but goes more deeply into the question of equality, and concludes by finding nothing absurd in the idea that the basic principle of equality applies to so-called "brutes." I believe that we reach this conclusion if we examine the basis on which our opposition to discrimination on grounds of race or sex ultimately rests. We will then see that we would be on shaky ground if we were to demand equality for blacks, women, and other groups of oppressed humans while denying equal consideration to nonhumans.

When we say that all human beings, whatever their race, creed or sex, are equal, what is it that we are asserting? Those who wish to defend a hierarchical, inegalitarian society have often pointed out that by whatever test we choose, it simply is not true that all humans are equal. Like it or not, we must face the fact that humans are equal. Like it or not, we must face the fact that humans come in different shapes and sizes; they come with differing moral capacities, differing intellectual abilities, differing amounts of benevolent feeling and sensitivity to the needs of others, differing abilities to communicate effectively, and differing capacities to experience pleasure and pain. In short, if the demand for equality were based on the actual equality of all human beings, we would have to stop demanding equality. It would be an unjustifiable demand.

Still, one might cling to the view that the demand for equality among human beings is based on the actual equality of the different races and sexes. Although humans differ as individuals in various ways, there are no differences between the races and sexes as *such*. From the mere fact that a person is black, or a woman, we cannot infer anything else about that person. This, it may be said, is what is wrong with racism and sexism. The white racist claims that whites are superior to blacks, but this is false — although there are differences between individuals, some blacks are superior to some whites in all of the capacities and abilities that could conceivably be relevant. The opponent of sexism would say the same: a person's sex is no guide to his or her abilities, and this is why it is unjustifiable to discriminate on the basis of sex.

This is a possible line of objection to racial and sexual discrimination. It is not, however, the way that someone really concerned about equality would choose, because taking this line could, in some circumstances, force one to accept a most inegalitarian society. The fact that humans differ as individuals, rather than as races or sexes, is a valid reply to someone who defends a hierarchical society like, say, South Africa, in which all whites are superior in status to all blacks. The existence of individual variations that cut across the lines of race or sex, however, provides us with no defence at all against a more sophisticated opponent of equality, one who proposes that, say, the interests of those with I.Q. ratings above 100 be preferred to the interests of those with I.Q.s below 100. Would a hierarchical society of this sort really be so much better than one based on race or sex? I think not. But if we tie the moral principle of equality to the factual equality of the different races or sexes, taken as a whole, our opposition to racism and sexism does not provide us with any basis for objecting to this kind of inegalitarianism.

There is a second important reason why we ought not to base our opposition to racism and sexism on any kind of factual equality, even the limited kind which asserts that variations in capacities and abilities are spread evenly between the different races and sexes: we can have no absolute guarantee that these abilities and capacities really are distributed evenly, without regard to race or sex, among human beings. So far as actual abilities are concerned, there do seem to be certain measurable differences between both races and sexes. These differences do not, of course, appear in each case, but only when averages are taken. More important still, we do not yet know how much of these differences is really due to the different genetic endowments of the various races and sexes, and how much is due to environmental differences that are the result of past and continuing discrimination. Perhaps all of the important differences will eventually prove to be environmental rather than genetic. Anyone opposed to racism and sexism will certainly hope that this will be so, for it will make the task of ending discrimination a lot easier; nevertheless it would be dangerous to rest the case against racism and sexism on the belief that all significant differences are environmental in origin. The opponent of, say, racism who takes this line will be unable to avoid conceding that if differences in ability did after all prove to have some genetic connection with race, racism would in some way be defensible.

It would be folly for the opponent of racism to stake his whole case on a dogmatic commitment to one particular outcome of a difficult scientific issue which is still a long way from being settled. While attempts to prove that differences in certain selected abilities between races and sexes are primarily genetic in origin have certainly not been conclusive, the same must be said of attempts to prove that these differences are largely the result of environment. At this stage of the investigation we cannot be certain which view is correct, however much we may hope it is the latter.

Fortunately, there is no need to pin the case for equality to one particular outcome of this scientific investigation. The appropriate response to those who claim to have found evidence of genetically-based differences in ability between the races or sexes is not to stick to the belief that the genetic explanation must be wrong, whatever evidence to the contrary may turn up: instead we should make it quite clear that the claim to equality does not depend on intelligence, moral capacity, physical strength, or similar matters of fact. Equality is a moral ideal, not a simple assertion of fact. There is no logically compelling reason for assuming that a factual difference in ability between two people justifies any difference in the amount of consideration we give to satisfying their needs and interests. The principle of the equality of human beings is not a description of an alleged actual equality among humans: it is a prescription of how we should treat humans.

Jeremy Bentham incorporated the essential basis of moral equality into his utilitarian system of ethics in the formula: "Each to count for one and none for more than one." In other words, the interests of every being affected by an action are to be taken into account and given the same weight as the like interests of any other being. A later utilitarian, Henry Sidgwick, put the point in this way: "The good of any one individual is of no more importance, from the point of view (if I may say so) of the Universe, than the good of any other."[1] More recently, the leading figures in contemporary moral philosophy have shown a great deal of agreement in specifying as a fundamental presupposition of their moral theories some similar requirement which operates so as to give everyone's interests equal consideration — although they cannot agree on how this requirement is best formulated.[2]

It is an implication of this principle of equality that our concern for others ought not to depend on what they are like, or what abilities they possess — although precisely what this concern requires us to do may vary according to the characteristics of those affected by what we do. It is on this basis that the case against racism and the case against sexism must both ultimately rest; and it is in accordance with this principle that speciesism is also to be condemned. If possessing a higher degree of intelligence does not entitle one human to use another for his own ends, how can it entitle humans to exploit nonhumans?

Many philosophers have proposed the principle of equal consideration of interests, in some form or other, as a basic moral principle; but, as we shall see in more detail shortly, not many of them have recognised that this principle applies to members of other species as well as to our own. Bentham was one of the few who did realize this. In a forward-looking passage, written at a time when black slaves in the British dominions were

1. *The Methods of Ethics* (7th Ed.), p. 382.
2. For example, R. M. Hare, *Freedom and Reason* (Oxford, 1963) and J. Rawls, *A Theory of Justice* (Harvard, 1972); for a brief account of the essential agreement on this issue between these and other positions, see R. M. Hare, "Rules of War and Moral Reasoning," *Philosophy and Public Affairs*, vol. I, no 2 (1972).

still being treated much as we now treat nonhuman animals, Bentham wrote:

> The day *may* come when the rest of the animal creation may acquire those rights which never could have been witholden from them but by the hand of tyranny. The French have already discovered that the blackness of the skin is no reason why a human being should be abandoned without redress to the caprice of a tormentor. It may one day come to be recognized that the number of the legs, the villosity of the skin, or the termination of the *os sacrum*, are reasons equally insufficient for abandoning a sensitive being to the same fate. What else is it that should trace the insuperable line? Is it the faculty of reason, or perhaps the faculty of discourse? But a full-grown horse or dog is beyond comparison a more rational, as well as a more conversable animal, than an infant of a day, or a week, or even a month, old. But suppose they were otherwise, what would it avail? The question is not, Can they reason? nor Can they *talk?* but, *Can they suffer?*[3]

In this passage Bentham points to the capacity for suffering as the vital characteristic that gives a being the right to equal consideration. The capacity for suffering — or more strictly, for suffering and/or enjoyment or happiness — is not just another characteristic like the capacity for language, or for higher mathematics. Bentham is not saying that those who try to mark "the insuperable line" that determines whether the interests of a being should be considered happen to have selected the wrong characteristic. The capacity for suffering and enjoying things is a pre-requisite for having interests at all, a condition that must be satisfied before we can speak of interests in any meaningful way. It would be nonsense to say that it was not in the interests of a stone to be kicked along the road by a schoolboy. A stone does not have interests because it cannot suffer. Nothing that we can do to it could possibly make any difference to its welfare. A mouse, on the other hand, does have an interest in not being tormented, because it will suffer if it is.

If a being suffers, there can be no moral justification for refusing to take that suffering into consideration. No matter what the nature of the being, the principle of equality requires that its suffering be counted equally with the like suffering — in so far as rough comparisons can be made — of any other being. If a being is not capable of suffering, or of experiencing enjoyment or happiness, there is nothing to be taken into account. This is why the limit of sentience (using the term as a convenient, if not strictly accurate, shorthand for the capacity to suffer or experience enjoyment or hap-

---

3. *Introduction to the Principles of Morals and Legislation*, ch. XVII.

piness) is the only defensible boundary of concern for the interests of others. To mark this boundary by some characteristic like intelligence or rationality would be to mark it in an arbitrary way. Why not choose some other characteristic, like skin color?

The racist violates the principle of equality by giving greater weight to the interests of members of his own race, when there is a clash between their interests and the interests of those of another race. Similarly the speciesist allows the interests of his own species to override the greater interests of members of other species.[4] The pattern is the same in each case. Most human beings are speciesists. I shall now very briefly describe some of the practices that show this.

For the great majority of human beings, especially in urban, industrialized societies, the most direct form of contact with members of other species is at meal-times: we eat them. In doing so we treat them purely as means to our ends. We retard their life and well-being as subordinate to our taste for a particular kind of dish. I say "taste" deliberately — this is purely a matter of pleasing our palate. There can be no defence of eating flesh in terms of satisfying nutritional needs, since it has been established beyond doubt that we could satisfy our need for protein and other essential nutrients far more efficiently with a diet that replaced animal flesh by soy beans, or products derived from soy beans, and other high-protein vegetable products. . . .

. . . The same form of discrimination may be observed in the widespread practice of experimenting on other species in order to see if certain substances are safe for human beings, or to test some psychological theory about the effect of severe punishment on learning, or to try out various new compounds just in case something turns up. . . .

In the past, argument about vivisection has often missed [the] point, because it has been put in absolutist terms: Would the abolitionist be prepared to let thousands die if they could be saved by experimenting on a single animal? The way to reply to this purely hypothetical question is to pose another: Would the experimenter be prepared to perform his experiment on an orphaned human infant, if that were the only way to save many lives? (I say "orphan" to avoid the complication of parental feelings, although in doing so I am being overfair to the experimenter, since the nonhuman subjects of experiments are not orphans.) If the experimenter is not prepared to use an orphaned human infant, then his readiness to use nonhumans is simple discrimination, since adult apes, cats, mice and other mammals are more aware of what is happening to them, more self-directing and, so far as we can tell, at least as sensitive to pain, as any human infant. There seems to be no relevant characteristic that human infants possess that adult mammals do not have to the same or a higher degree.

---

4. I owe the term "speciesism" to Richard Ryder.

(Someone might try to argue that what makes it wrong to experiment on a human infant is that the infant will, in time and if left alone, develop into more than the nonhuman, but one would then, to be consistent, have to oppose abortion, since the fetus has the same potential as the infant — indeed, even contraception and abstinence might be wrong on this ground, since the egg and sperm, considered jointly, also have the same potential. In any case, this argument still gives us no reason for selecting a nonhuman, rather than a human with severe and irreversible brain damage, as the subject for our experiments.)

The experimenter, then, shows a bias in favor of his own species whenever he carries out an experiment on a nonhuman for a purpose that he would not think justified him in using a human being at an equal or lower level of sentience, awareness, ability to be self-directing, etc. No one familiar with the kind of results yielded by most experiments on animals can have the slightest doubt that if this bias were eliminated the number of experiments performed would be a minute fraction of the number performed today.

Experimenting on animals, and eating their flesh, are perhaps the two major forms of speciesism in our society. By comparison, the third and last form of speciesism is so minor as to be insignificant, but it is perhaps of some special interest to those for whom this article was written. I am referring to speciesism in contemporary philosophy.

Philosophy ought to question the basic assumptions of the age. Thinking through, critically and carefully, what most people take for granted is, I believe, the chief task of philosophy, and it is this task that makes philosophy a worthwhile activity. Regrettably, philosophy does not always live up to its historic role. Philosophers are human beings and they are subject to all the preconceptions of the society to which they belong. Sometimes they succeed in breaking free of the prevailing ideology: more often they become its most sophisticated defenders. So in this case, philosophy as practiced in the universities today does not challenge anyone's preconceptions about our relations with other species. By their writings, those philosophers who tackle problems that touch upon the issue reveal that they make the same unquestioned assumptions as most other humans, and what they say tends to confirm the reader in his or her comfortable speciesist habits.

I could illustrate this claim by referring to the writings of philosophers in various fields — for instance, the attempts that have been made by those interested in rights to draw the boundary of the sphere of rights so that it runs parallel to the biological boundaries of the species *homo sapiens*, including infants and even mental defectives, but excluding those other beings of equal or greater capacity who are so useful to us at mealtimes and in our laboratories. I think it would be a more appropriate conclusion to this article, however, if I concentrated on the problem with which we have been centrally concerned, the problem of equality.

It is significant that the problem of equality, in moral and political philosophy, is invariably formulated in terms of human equality. The effect of this is that the question of the equality of other animals does not confront the philosopher, or student, as an issue itself — and this is already an indication of the failure of philosophy to challenge accepted beliefs. Still, philosophers have found it difficult to discuss the issue of human equality without raising, in a paragraph or two, the question of the status of other animals. The reason for this, which should be apparent from what I have said already, is that if humans are to be regarded as equal to one another, we need some sense of "equal" that does not require any actual, descriptive equality of capacities, talents or other qualities. If equality is to be related to any actual characteristics of humans, these characteristics must be some lowest common denominator, pitched so low that no human lacks them — but then the philosopher comes up against the catch that any such set of characteristics which covers *all* humans will not be *possessed only by humans*. In other words, it turns out that in the only sense in which we can truly say, as an assertion of fact, that all humans are equal, at least some members of other species are also equal — equal, that is, to each other and to humans. If, on the other hand, we regard the statement "All humans are equal" in some non-factual way, perhaps as a prescription, then, as I have already argued, it is even more difficult to exclude non-humans from the sphere of equality.

This result is not what the egalitarian philosopher originally intended to assert. Instead of accepting the radical outcome to which their own reasonings naturally point, however, most philosophers try to reconcile their beliefs in human equality and animal inequality by arguments that can only be described as devious.

As a first example, I take William Frankena's well-known article "The Concept of Social Justice." Frankena opposes the idea of basing justice on merit, because he sees that this could lead to highly inegalitarian results. Instead he proposes the principle that

> . . . all men are to be treated as equals, not because they are equal, in any respect, but simply because they are human. They are human because they have emotions and desires, and are able to think, and hence are capable of enjoying a good life in a sense in which other animals are not.[5]

But what is this capacity to enjoy the good life which all humans have, but no other animals? Other animals have emotions and desires, and appear to be capable of enjoying a good life. We may doubt that they can think — although the behavior of some apes, dolphins and even dogs sug-

5. In R. Brandt (ed.) *Social Justice* (Prentice-Hall, Englewood Cliffs, 1962), p. 19.

gests that some of them can — but what is the relevance of thinking? Frankena goes on to admit that by "the good life" he means "not so much the morally good life as the happy or satisfactory life," so thought would appear to be unnecessary for enjoying the good life; in fact to emphasise the need for thought would make difficulties for the egalitarian since only some people are capable of leading intellectually satisfying lives, or morally good lives. This makes it difficult to see what Frankena's principle of equality has to do with simply being *human*. Surely every sentient being is capable of leading a life that is happier or less miserable than some alternative life, and hence has a claim to be taken into account. In this respect the distinction between humans and nonhumans is not a sharp division, but rather a continuum along which we move gradually, and with overlaps between the species, from simple capacities for enjoyment and satisfaction, or pain and suffering, to more complex ones.

Faced with a situation in which they see a need for some basis for the moral gulf that is commonly thought to separate humans and animals, but can find no concrete difference that will do the job without undermining the equality of humans, philosophers tend to waffle. They resort to high-sounding phrases like "the intrinsic dignity of the human individual";[6] They talk of the "intrinsic worth of all men" as if men (humans?) had some worth that other beings did not[7] or they say that humans, and only humans, are "ends in themselves," while "everything other than a person can only have value for a person."[8]

This idea of a distinctive human dignity and worth has a long history; it can be traced back directly to the Renaissance humanists, for instance to Pico della Mirandola's *Oration on the Dignity of Man*. Pico and other humanists based their estimate of human dignity on the idea that man possessed the central, pivotal position in the "Great Chain of Being" that led from the lowliest forms of matter to God himself; this view of the universe, in turn, goes back to both classical and Judeo-Christian doctrines. Contemporary philosophers have cast off these metaphysical and religious shackles and freely invoke the dignity of mankind without needing to justify the idea at all. Why should we not attribute "intrinsic dignity" or "intrinsic worth" to ourselves? Fellow-humans are unlikely to reject the accolades we so generously bestow on them, and those to whom we deny the honor are unable to object. Indeed, when one thinks only of humans, it can be very liberal, very progressive, to talk of the dignity of all human beings. In so doing, we implicitly condemn slavery, racism, and other violations of human rights. We admit that we ourselves are in some fundamental sense on a par with the poorest, most ignorant members of our own

6. Frankena, *op. cit.*, p. 23.

7. H. A. Bedau, "Egalitarianism and the Ideal of Equality" in *Nomos IX: Equality*, ed. J. R. Pennock and J. W. Chapman, New York, 1967.

8. G. Vlastos, "Justice and Equality" in Brandt, *Social Justice*, p. 48.

species. It is only when we think of humans as no more than a small sub-group of all the beings that inhabit our planet that we may realize that in elevating our own species we are at the same time lowering the relative status of all other species.

The truth is that the appeal to the intrinsic dignity of human beings appears to solve the egalitarian's problems only as long as it goes unchallenged. Once we ask *why* it should be that all humans — including infants, mental defectives, psychopaths, Hitler, Stalin and the rest — have some kind of dignity or worth that no elephant, pig, or chimpanzee can ever achieve, we see that this question is as difficult to answer as our original request for some relevant fact that justifies the inequality of humans and other animals. In fact, these two questions are really one: talk of intrinsic dignity or moral worth only takes the problem back one step, because any satisfactory defence of the claim that all and only humans have intrinsic dignity would need to refer to some relevant capacities or characteristics that all and only humans possess. Philosophers frequently introduce ideas of dignity, respect and worth at the point at which other reasons appear to be lacking, but this is hardly good enough. Fine phrases are the last resource of those who have run out of arguments.

Questions and Exercises

1. Write in one sentence Singer's principle of equality.

2. What is the definition of "speciesism"?

3. List the three examples Singer gives of speciesism.

4. Taylor tried to ridicule Wollstonecraft's advocacy of equality for women by a logical analogy. Express this analogy in your own words. What is Singer's position on the analogy? Does he accept it?

5. Compare the treatment of equality by Mary Wollstonecraft (pp. 107 – 110) with that by Singer. What differences in the attitude to human equality can you see?

6. How does Singer use the case of an orphaned human infant to condemn experiments on animals?

7. Take the general topic, animal. Write questions about animals that might be posed by a psychologist, a theologian, a biologist, an economist, an artist, an historian, and a lawyer.

8. Singer argues, "Equality is a moral ideal, not a simple assertion of fact." Explain his meaning. How does he use that principle to argue that equal treatment should not depend on a factual equality.

9. In small groups, discuss what Singer means by saying that for him equality is prescriptive rather than descriptive.

10. Singer argues that if animals are to be excluded from the requirement of equal treatment, we must find some characteristic that all human beings share and only human beings share. In small groups, discuss characteristics that might serve the purpose of distinguishing human from animal? Try to come to consensus.

11. The Jewish religion provides a set of rituals for the humane slaughter of animals. In order for meat to be kosher, the animal must have been killed as painlessly as possible. In small groups discuss the following questions: How do kosher slaughtering techniques reflect an awareness of animal rights? How do they not?

12. For Hobbes, in the state of nature human beings are actually equal. Does Hobbes fall into the trap of defending equal treatment on the basis of a factual equality? Write notes on this question. Meet in small groups to discuss it. Draft a paper addressed to undergraduates who have read the selections by Hobbes and Singer.

13. Singer gives animal experimentation and eating animals as examples of speciesism. Speculate on what he might say about humans keeping animals as pets. Draft a paper on this subject for an audience of undergraduates who have not read Singer's essay.

14. Draft a paper comparing Singer's and King's use of analogy. Assume that your readers are classmates who have read both essays in this anthology but who have not thought about this comparison.

Man's World, Woman's Place

ELIZABETH JANEWAY

Students of the humanities, like Peter Singer in the preceding essay and Elizabeth Janeway in the selection that follows, think critically about unexamined assumptions. Elizabeth Janeway begins *Man's World, Woman's Place: A Study in Social Mythology*, with two familiar old sayings, "It's a man's world," and "Woman's place is in the home." She then devotes twenty chapters to examining these clichés. Why do people take such sayings for granted? What does it mean for a society to divide the world by sexes, to assign to women a place and to men the world itself? Can people be trapped by a proverb? Janeway's purpose is not to force her opinion on her readers, but to explore the beliefs and dynamics of society. Antonia Fraser might call Janeway a "Whatter." Like Fraser, who refuses to stereotype Charles II as the Merry Monarch, Janeway refuses to accept stereotypes of women.

In 1971, when *Man's World, Woman's Place* was first published, American society was in a state of upheaval. The second wave of feminism (the first having crested in 1919 with women's suffrage) was provoking a great deal of attention from the media. In this atmosphere Janeway produced a calm, rational examination of the social context that produced the women's movement.

The following selection comes from *Man's World, Woman's Place*, Chapter 10, in which Janeway discusses two deviant images assigned to women: the shrew and the witch. These images, according to Janeway, are shadows of their counterpart positive roles: the pleasing woman and the loving mother. Janeway's idea is that it is easier for people to do and see the opposite of what was done before than to create something new. If society believes in the stereotype of the pleasing woman, then when a woman deviates from compliant behavior, she reverses the role and becomes a shrew. Each positive role has its negative. "Negative roles," says Janeway, "are reactions, not actions."

The nurturing mother casts the dark shadow of the witch. To develop her thesis, Janeway presents examples from history, anthropology, folklore, and daily life. Writing an extended, cogent argument was new to Janeway as she composed *Man's World, Woman's Place*. She came to the project with extensive experience as a novelist and as a writer of children's literature but with no experience in the composition of a long sustained work of exposition.

Elizabeth Janeway wrote us a letter in which she reflected upon the experience of composing for the first time in a new genre. We reprint her letter here because we think that all writers can take heart from the confessions and suggestions of this accomplished prose stylist.

August 14, 1980

Dear Elaine Maimon:

Thank you for your letter about the anthology, *Readings in the Arts and Sciences*, which you are editing. How nice to have word from Gail Haslett Hearn, even indirectly! Do give her my warm regards.

I well remember the composition of *Man's World, Woman's Place*. It was my first book of non-fiction for adult readers and thus it was really my second "first book." I had to face the task of writing a long sustained work without the resources of fiction on which I had previously been able to rely. These resources include narrative suspense, arresting characters, gripping or amusing dialogue — in short the many ways in which fiction can involve the emotions of the reader. I really felt like an amputee, as I struggled to sustain the reader's interest simply through the development of cogent argument and examples from daily life.

If I succeeded, I believe it's because I did not know exactly where I was going. Against all the injunctions advanced by professors of writing, I wrote this long non-fiction without an outline and without a plan that had been consciously arrived at. This could well be a recipe for disaster and I am not at all sure that I would recommend it to anyone else. The only advantage of this method is that it keeps the writer alert and interested, with her emotions fully engaged. I believe it is possible to convey the excitement that a writer feels as she finds solutions and answers to questions and that this may excite the reader as well.

I suppose that the discipline of writing novels and books for children without outlines was necessary for me to be able to do this with non-fiction. I have always had a sense of the shape and structure of a book and I have trusted the capacity of the subconscious mind to keep me on the track. The penalty is that a great deal of rewriting has to be done. I pay this penalty because I simply can't structure a book until I am right at the point of getting my ideas down on paper. In some way I find that the whole self must be brought to bear on the material and the act of writing.

I hope these comments are helpful to you and I wish you good luck with the anthology.

Elizabeth Janeway

Man's World, Woman's Place
ELIZABETH JANEWAY

The most familiar negative role of all is the witch. If the shrew is the opposite and shadow of the ideal pleasing woman, the witch is the shadow and opposite of the loving mother. Here too it is the power that is feared, but in this case it is magic power. It is easy to see why if we think again of the early mother-child relationship from the point of view of the child. The mother's power to give or to withhold comfort seems magical to the child, because he experiences it long before he can understand the whys and wherefores of the gift or the denial. It antedates language and logic. The child learns to trust and to love the huge creature who comes and goes, gives and denies, and changes the world around him before he and she have any words with which to communicate. Things happen magically, in mysterious ways. The witch retains the magical power of the woman who can effect these mysterious changes, but she has forfeited the trust of her partner-child. Joan of Arc thus was accused of witchcraft by the English because they couldn't deny her power, for she had beaten them in the field, but they couldn't permit themselves to think that such a defeat by a woman was normal. It had to be magical.

The witch, in short, is the bad mother — or, rather, the mother who seems to the child to be bad, for every child must be frustrated and left wailing by his mother at some point, since his desires begin by being total and what he really wants is omnipotence. Because the mother-child duality begins before any sort of behavior can be expected or any explanations offered, every thwarted child has had a glimpse of the witch behind the beloved face of his mother: this figure is really universal. She turns up everywhere, in any number of forms. The witch who caught Hansel and Gretel is (in psychological terms) the mother who might punish them for running away. . . . In Chicago only the other day (so to speak) Bruno Bettelheim found that one of the schizophrenic children he was treating "was convinced that her mother wanted to bake her in the oven and eat her," just as Hansel's witch was planning to bake him.[1] A nursing child, we might remember, "eats" its mother. Anger and fear of the mother, dating back to those early days, might well bring forth the idea that the guilty child may expect a reversal of the process: it will be eaten by the witch-mother. Among the Pueblo Indians, a cure for any disease which the patient believes to be caused by witchcraft is for the sick man or woman to be adopted into another clan. This effectively provides him with a *new mother* and breaks the link with the old one, now turned into a witch.

These negative roles are all associated with the abuse of power and, as Lifton suggests, with social change, for we often find that social change permits and increases this abuse: when traditional hierarchies break down, power is no longer bound by customary limits. The breakdown calls for new approaches — that is, for new roles — and at the same time it makes it harder for people to understand what the central role-player is trying to do: custom no longer helps to explain his actions. Lifton noted the appearance of the shrew in modern China and in Elizabethan England. The latter period was one in which we also find another deviant type, the witch, on the rise. Hugh Trevor-Roper, the English historian, has recently documented a recrudescence of the witch craze in the 1560s at a time when religious wars were turning Europe upside down.[2] The witch hunts which became so frequent then lasted well into the seventeenth century and, as we all remember, reached as far as Salem, Massachusetts.

In India today social change continues to produce witches. There is a section of Mysore where irrigation has recently been introduced. With it has come a sudden prevalence of witches. The increase in the quantity and the variety of agricultural products had brought this backward region

1. Bettelheim, Bruno, *The Empty Fortress.* New York: The Free Press, 1967, p. 71.
2. Trevor-Roper, Hugh, "The Witch Craze," *Encounter,* London, May and June, 1967.

into a money economy and women have overnight become moneylenders. In the past, such few advances of credit as were made came from rich landholders to their clients, were long-term, and were hedged about with traditional safeguards which prevented the ruin of the borrowers. The new women moneylenders, however, are not inhibited by such considerations, and they are often hard and demanding. Their driven clients tend to react by accusing them of witchcraft.

For these women are violating the role expected of them. The anthropologist who reports the case, Scarlett Epstein, remarks that they are not only being condemned for their greed, but that "such a condemnation is a reaffirmation of the traditional social structure in which women did not enter the field of money lending. . . . The ideal peasant woman . . . was a woman who worked hard on the lands of her husband and in the house, who bore many children, particularly many sons, and who was obedient to her husband . . . and generous to his kin." Summing up, Dr. Epstein adds, "A sociological function of witch beliefs widely recognized in anthropological literature is their tendency to support the system of values and thus to sustain the social structure."[3] In other words, negative roles work to support the order of the universe just as positive roles do. The latter are promises, the former threats.

Dr. Field's work in West Africa reveals another aspect of the witch role: the acceptance by the woman of the role. Social change has been endemic for a generation in this part of the world. Dr. Field is both an anthropologist and a practicing psychiatrist, who first went to Ghana in the 1930s and returned in 1955 to practice there. She is thus familiar both with the colonial period and with the effect of independence on the population. Aside from these political changes, both of which broke old tribal patterns, economic change has had repercussions.

In her practice, Dr. Field finds a regular tendency among women who are suffering from depression — that is, from an overwhelming sense of failure and weakness in their real lives — to accuse themselves of witchcraft, often including the murder of their children. They may fear this identification and struggle against it, and yet accept it because it seems to offer the only possible explanation for the course of their lives. Any identification, it seems, is better than the baffling confusion of not knowing where one is or what is to happen next. In addition, of course, the witch role permits the woman to imagine that she can exercise some sort of power, even if it is evil power; and no doubt it recalls the time when, as the mother of young children, she really did enjoy power. Thus, in her need for some understanding of, and control over, the world, she accepts

3. Epstein, Scarlett, "A Sociological Analysis of Witch Beliefs," in *Magic, Witchcraft and Curing*, Middleton, John, ed. New York: The Natural History Press, p. 144.

and even courts (while still fearing) the dark role that shadows the mother role which once was hers.

Questions and Exercises

1. Janeway writes about the negative shadows of positive images. To what positive images might the following relate: the ogre, the harlot, the fool, the beast, the henpecked husband?

2. Janeway believes that times of social upheaval exaggerate the split between a role and its shadow. What social changes were happening in the sixties? How did these changes affect the ability of Americans to deal with conventional roles?

3. Recall an instance when you idealized someone who then disappointed you. Write privately about your new image of that person.

4. Read Hugh Trevor-Roper's "The Witch Craze" (cited in footnote 2). Speculate on the influence of this article on Elizabeth Janeway's thinking about witches.

5. In small groups, discuss the following questions: Why do people need to see each other in terms of roles? What useful function do roles serve in a society?

6. Divide into small groups, with each group assigned to find references to historical and literary examples of cultural images: witches, saints, shrews, loving mothers. In your groups, discuss the individual examples and then report to the class as a whole about the patterns you have discovered.

7. We are suggesting that Janeway's approach is philosophical. Do you agree? How might a psychologist address the issue of "man's world, woman's place"? A sociologist? Meet in small groups to discuss these three different disciplinary approaches to the issue at hand.

8. Draft an essay on the shrew as the negative shadow of the pleasing woman. Assume that your audience includes undergraduates who have not read Janeway's essay.

9. Read a biographical account of Joan of Arc. Draft an essay explaining why the English viewed Joan as a witch. Assume that your audience includes undergraduates who have not read Janeway's essay.

10. Elizabeth Janeway wrote a book to examine a cliché. List a number of other clichés, for example, "Like father, like son"; "a woman's work is never done." Draft an essay exploring the implications of the saying. Assume that your audience includes undergraduates who have not read Janeway's essay.

Climates of Opinion

CARL BECKER

from *The Heavenly City of the Eighteenth-Century Philosophers*

Although Carl Becker was an historian, he once admitted that "the art of writing has been the most persistent and absorbing interest of my life."[1] He was one of this century's pioneers of the "new history," an approach in which historians explicitly interpret the past instead of merely reporting it. The new imperative, accordingly, was to develop opinions and present points of view, and this openly interpretive stance, in turn, put a new emphasis on clear and persuasive writing. Becker argued that if his opinions were worth anything, it was because of his ability to express them capably.

Becker set down his carefully considered views on writing in an essay entitled, "The Art of Writing." His basic thesis is that clear writing begins with clear thinking, and that good style is developed by "not trying to cultivate it apart from thought" because effective writing is not a matter of "happy phrasing alone or primarily, but of clear and logical thinking."[2] Moreover, writing not only expresses ideas; it helps to develop them. "There is," he wrote, "no better way of developing whatever native intelligence one has, or of organizing what knowledge one may have acquired, than by persistently trying to put into written form what one has to say."[3]

What then is good writing to Becker? It is writing which "fully and effectively conveys the fact, the idea, or the emotion which the writer wishes to convey."[4] How is good writing learned? Becker believes that to learn to write well a person has to write. "Writing is after all, an act — something that has to be done; and it is better to approach the teaching of it from the point of view of the created process. . . ."[5]

These opinions, offered in 1942, reflect Becker's own experience. In fact, when he left his father's farm in 1893 to attend the University of Wisconsin, he wanted to be a writer. As an undergraduate he kept journals, which he called his "Wild Thoughts Notebooks," and recorded in them the observations that were supposed to make their way into the novels he planned to write. He described people, tried to record dialects, created characters, and recorded words and phrases from his reading. He also developed his own careful method of composition, which began with a longhand draft that he then converted into a typed second draft. "He altered the typewritten copy in longhand, interlining and writing inserts on new sheets or on the back. The corrected copy was typed again in

---

1. Carl Becker, "The Art of Writing," an address at Smith College, 1942, in *Detachment and the Writing of History*, ed. Phil Snyder (Cornell University Press, 1958), p. 121.
2. *Ibid.*, p. 132.
3. *Ibid.*, p. 131.
4. *Ibid.*, p. 127.
5. *Ibid.*

whole or in part. The process was repeated over and over until the final draft was sent to the printer."[6] The evidence suggests that as he wrote his successive drafts, he worked primarily at the level of ideas and organization, and to achieve clarity of expression. His manuscripts, even those he submitted for publication, "always needed a great deal of editing" because his punctuation and spelling were, as one biographer said, "rather casual."[7]

Carl Becker influenced generations of history students at Cornell University; he told his graduate students to expect to rewrite everything at least twelve times,[8] and gave almost as much attention to teaching writing as to teaching history. Historians could not be developed any other way for, as Becker once wrote, "It is a favorite notion of mine that in literary discourse, form and content are but two aspects of the same thing."[9]

The following selection is from the introduction to *The Heavenly City of the Eighteenth-Century Philosophers*. An example of the "new history," this small book marked a milestone in history writing, for Becker not only advances a strong and definite line of argument, he attacks a long-held assumption. Most history textbooks before Becker took for granted that the French philosophers of the Enlightenment (the *Philosophes*) were modern in their thought and sensibilities. Becker, however, argues that the *Philosophes* were not modern at all. By presenting this case, Becker not only redefines the role of the *Philosophes*, he redefines modernism.

Comparing his book to the accepted rules of history writing of the age, he wrote: "This certainly isn't history. I hope it's philosophy, because if it's not it's probably moonshine — or would you say that the distinction is over subtle?" Its purpose was not just to convey facts, but to teach, to help people find "enduring values amid perishing occasions."[10]

As you read this essay watch for those characteristics in form and content that illustrate aspects of the "new history." Becker's style is personal and argumentative. Look for examples of his distinctive style.

Climates of Opinion
CARL BECKER

... I have chosen to say something about the political and social thought of the eighteenth century, something about the *Philosophes*. If I could stand on high and pronounce judgment on them, estimate authoritatively

6. Charlotte Wathers Smith, *Carl Becker: On History and the Climate of Opinion* (Cornell University Press, 1956), p. 158.

7. *Ibid.*

8. *Ibid.*

9. Carl Becker, *The Declaration of Independence* (New York: Alfred Knopf, 1956), p. xiii.

10. As quoted in Charlotte Wathers Smith, p. 212.

From "Climates of Opinion," pages 28–31, of Carl Becker's *The Heavenly City of the Eighteenth-Century Philosophers*, 1932, Yale University Press. Reprinted by permission of Yale University Press.

the value of their philosophy, tell wherein it is true, wherein false — if I could only do all this it would be grand. But this, unfortunately, is not possible. Living in the twentieth century, I am limited by the preconceptions of my age. It was therefore inevitable that I should approach the subject from the historical point of view; and if I have been at great pains to contrast the climate of opinion of Dante's time with that of our own, it is merely in order to provide the historical setting in which the ideas of the *Philosophes* may be placed. Before the historian can do anything with Newton and Voltaire, he has to make it clear that they came, historically speaking, after Dante and Thomas Aquinas and before Einstein and H. G. Wells. I assume that it will be worth while to place them in this relation, to look at them in this pattern, because the modern mind has a predilection for looking at men and things in this way; it finds a high degree of mental satisfaction in doing it; and mental satisfaction is always worth while, for the simple reason that when the mind is satisfied with the pattern of the things it sees, it has what it calls an "explanation" of the things — it has found the "cause" of them. My object is, therefore, to furnish an explanation of eighteenth-century thought, from the historical point of view, by showing that it was related to something that came before and to something else that came after.

We are accustomed to think of the eighteenth century as essentially modern in its temper. Certainly, the *Philosophes* themselves made a great point of having renounced the superstition and hocus-pocus of medieval Christian thought, and we have usually been willing to take them at their word. Surely, we say, the eighteenth century was preëminently the age of reason, surely the *Philosophes* were a skeptical lot, atheists in effect if not by profession, addicted to science and the scientific method, always out to crush the infamous, valiant defenders of liberty, equality, fraternity, freedom of speech, and what you will. All very true. And yet I think the *Philosophes* were nearer the Middle Ages, less emancipated from the preconceptions of medieval Christian thought, than they quite realized or we have commonly supposed. If we have done them more (or is it less?) than justice in giving them a good modern character, the reason is that they speak a familiar language. We read Voltaire more readily than Dante, and follow an argument by Hume more easily than one by Thomas Aquinas. But I think our appreciation is of the surface more than of the fundamentals of their thought. We agree with them more readily when they are witty and cynical than when they are wholly serious. Their negations rather than their affirmations enable us to treat them as kindred spirits.

But, if we examine the foundations of their faith, we find that at every turn the *Philosophes* betray their debt to medieval thought without being aware of it. They denounced Christian philosophy, but rather too much, after the manner of those who are but half emancipated from the "superstitions" they scorn. They had put off the fear of God, but maintained a respectful attitude toward the Deity. They ridiculed the idea that the universe had been created in six days, but still believed it to be a beautifully articulated machine designed by the Supreme Being according to a rational plan as an abiding place for mankind. The Garden of Eden was for them a myth, no doubt, but they looked enviously back to the golden age of Roman virtue, or across the waters to the unspoiled innocence of an Arcadian civilization that flourished in Pennsylvania. They renounced the authority of church and Bible, but exhibited a naïve faith in the authority of nature and reason. They scorned metaphysics, but were proud to be called philosophers. They dismantled heaven, somewhat prematurely it seems, since they retained their faith in the immortality of the soul. They courageously discussed atheism, but not before the servants. They defended toleration valiantly, but could with difficulty tolerate priests. They denied that miracles ever happened, but believed in the perfectibility of the human race. We feel that these Philosophers were at once too credulous and too skeptical. They were the victims of common sense. In spite of their rationalism and their humane sympathies, in spite of their aversion to hocus-pocus and enthusiasm and dim perspectives, in spite of their eager skepticism, their engaging cynicism, their brave youthful blasphemies and talk of hanging the last king in the entrails of the last priest — in spite of all of it, there is more of Christian philosophy in the writings of the *Philosophes* than has yet been dreamt of in our histories.

In the following lectures I shall endeavor to elaborate this theme. I shall attempt to show that the underlying preconceptions of eighteenth-century thought were still, allowance made for certain important alterations in the bias, essentially the same as those of the thirteenth century. I shall attempt to show that the *Philosophes* demolished the Heavenly City of St. Augustine only to rebuild it with more up-to-date materials.

Questions and Exercises

1. What cues in the writing tell you the selection is taken from an introduction to a larger plan?

2. Where is Becker's thesis? What is it? How can you tell it is his thesis? Does everyone agree on one way of stating Becker's thesis? If not, what is the basis of the disagreement?

3. Define explanation, according to Becker (p. 233). Review Darwin's account of natural selection (pp. 132–39). Is it an explanation in Becker's sense?

4. What is the purpose of the long theoretical first paragraph? How does it fit what you infer to be the author's general goals?

5. In the third paragraph Becker states the evidence favoring the modernist interpretation of the *Philosophes*, and then an opposing interpretation. Take this paragraph and write up two lists, one headed "Evidence Favoring the Modernist Interpretation" and the other headed

"Evidence Favoring the Medievalist Interpretation." Use key words to itemize the evidence on each side, for example:

Modernist	Medievalist
denounced Christianity	but too much
rejected fear of God	but respected God

6. After you have written the lists for question 5, use each list to infer definitions of modernism and medievalism; that is, if Becker attributes these characteristics to each interpretation, what must he mean by modernism and medievalism (beginning, "A person can be classified as modern if . . .)? Meet in small groups to read and discuss the definitions that you have derived.

7. What exactly do you *know* of the *Philosophes* after reading this selection from Becker? Contrast what you know with what you suspect. Draft a statement addressed to fellow students who have also read the Becker essay.

8. In the library, look in other intellectual histories of eighteenth-century France to find the names, dates, and nationalities of four philosophers of the period and a description of what makes each one a philosopher. What does your research add to your reading and understanding of Becker? Draft a statement addressed to fellow students who have read Becker's essay but who have not read the outside sources.

The Myth of Mental Illness

THOMAS S. SZASZ

from *American Psychologist*

Although psychiatrists are trained as scientists, they often draw on humanistic modes of thought. Just as philosophers or historians use the scientific method in their own fields, so can natural and social scientists function as humanists by posing questions about ethics and human values. Thomas S. Szasz is a psychiatrist who, in the essay reproduced here, is acting as a humanist. While his major topics — psychiatry and mental illness — are usually thought to be social science topics, he studies them from the perspective of the humanist. He is interested in the moral questions raised by the use of the term *mental illness*, the ideological implications of the concept, and the effects on human freedom. This essay, therefore, is a humanistic inquiry into human behavior in the field of mental health.

Szasz is a psychiatrist who is critical of psychiatry as it is practiced today. The purpose of this essay is to demonstrate that psychiatry is not a "medical healing art," but "an ideology and technology for the radical remaking of man." It is surprising to find a psychiatrist arguing that we should abandon a medical explanation for mental illness. Despite his medical school education, Szasz believes that mental illness should not be treated with drugs, with surgery, or with the standard therapies provided in mental institutions. He recognizes that abnormal behavior exists, but he does not see that behavior as a medical problem.

Szasz defines mental illness as "problems in living" that we all have to some degree because of "the stresses and strains inherent in the social intercourse of complex human personalities." When we explain deviant behavior in medical terms, we permit psychiatrists to make moral and personal value judgments for us.

This essay was first published in a professional journal — the *American Psychologist* — that is read by psychologists and psychiatrists. Szasz must have been aware that his argument threatened fundamental assumptions held by his readers. Consequently, he takes the precautions that a writer must take when addressing a hostile audience: He writes technically and carefully. He defines and analyzes key terms. He refers to authorities and develops his arguments logically, anticipating counterarguments. Consequently, the article is not easy reading. Because he writes for an audience of specialists, his vocabulary and sentence structure are quite sophisticated. You will need to read carefully to follow the development of his case. You may find it useful to make a list of major points, or an outline, or a tree-diagram to maintain a sense of the whole as he leads you through the parts of his argument. Working your way through Szasz's essay will prepare you for reading scholarly journals, the life-blood of the academic disciplines.

As it turned out, Szasz's audience responded with the hostility that he had expected. Many of his original readers charged Szasz with being unscientific and potentially dangerous. Others countered that his opinions represented wisdom long overdue. Decide as you read whether you are persuaded by his argument. Why or why not?

The Myth of Mental Illness

THOMAS S. SZASZ

My aim in this essay is to raise the question "Is there such a thing as mental illness?" and to argue that there is not. Since the notion of mental illness is extremely widely used nowadays, inquiry into the ways in which this term is employed would seem to be especially indicated. Mental illness, of course, is not literally a "thing" — or physical object — and hence it can "exist" only in the same sort of way in which other theoretical concepts

From "The Myth of Mental Illness" by Thomas Szasz, *The American Psychologist*, Vol. 15, pp. 113–118. Copyright 1960 by the American Psychological Association. Reprinted by permission of the American Psychological Association and Dr. Thomas Szasz.

exist. Yet, familiar theories
least to those who come
"facts"). During certain h
deities, witches, and mi
self-evident *causes of a*
illness is widely rega
cause of innumerabl
cent use of the noti
nomenon, theory,
it is asserted that

In what follo
cept of mental
lived whateve
merely as a c

nervous system
belief in Chr
organs are
be explain
this sort
and d
else

Mental Illness as a

The notion of mental illnes
ena as syphilis of the brain or ac.
instance — in which persons are known to
or disorders of thinking and behavior. Correctly spe
are diseases of the brain, not of the mind. According to
thought, *all* so-called mental illness is of this type. The assumption i.
that some neurological defect, perhaps a very subtle one, will ultimately
be found for all the disorders of thinking and behavior. Many contemporary psychiatrists, physicians, and other scientists hold this view. This position implies that people *cannot* have troubles — expressed in what are
now called "mental illnesses" — because of differences in personal needs,
opinions, social aspirations, values, and so on. *All problems in living* are
attributed to physicochemical processes which in due time will be discovered by medical research.

"Mental illnesses" are thus regarded as basically no different than all
other diseases (that is, of the body). The only difference, in this view,
between mental and bodily diseases is that the former, affecting the brain,
manifest themselves by means of mental symptoms; whereas the latter,
affecting other organ systems (for example, the skin, liver, etc.), manifest
themselves by means of symptoms referable to those parts of the body.
This view rests on and expresses what are, in my opinion, two fundamental errors.

In the first place, what central nervous system symptoms would correspond to a skin eruption or a fracture? It would *not* be some emotion or
complex bit of behavior. Rather, it would be blindness or a paralysis of
some part of the body. The crux of the matter is that a disease of the brain,
analogous to a disease of the skin or bone, is a neurological defect, and not
a problem in living. For example, a *defect* in a person's visual field may be
satisfactorily explained by correlating it with certain definite lesions in the

On the other hand, a person's *belief* — whether this be a ~~Chri~~stianity, in Communism, or in the idea that his internal ~~organs are r~~otting" and that his body is, in fact, already "dead" — cannot ~~be explain~~ed by a defect or disease of the nervous system. Explanations of ~~this sort~~ of occurrence — assuming that one is interested in the belief itself ~~and do~~es not regard it simply as a "symptom" or expression of something ~~else t~~hat is *more interesting* — must be sought along different lines.

The second error in regarding complex psychosocial behavior, consisting of communications about ourselves and the world about us, as mere symptoms of neurological functioning is *epistemological*. In other words, it is an error pertaining not to any mistakes in observation or reasoning, as such, but rather to the way in which we organize and express our knowledge. In the present case, the error lies in making a symmetrical dualism between mental and physical (or bodily) symptoms, a dualism which is merely a habit of speech and to which no known observations can be found to correspond. Let us see if this is so. In medical practice, when we speak of physical disturbances, we mean either signs (for example, a fever) or symptoms (for example, pain). We speak of mental symptoms, on the other hand, when we refer to a patient's *communications about himself, others, and the world about him*. He might state that he is Napoleon or that he is being persecuted by the Communists. These would be considered mental symptoms *only* if the observer believed that the patient was *not* Napoleon or that he was *not* being persecuted by the Communists. This makes it apparent that the statement that "X is a mental symptom" involves rendering a judgment. The judgment entails, moreover, a covert comparison or matching of the patient's ideas, concepts, or beliefs with those of the observer and the society in which they live. The notion of mental symptom is therefore inextricably tied to the *social* (including *ethical*) *context* in which it is made in much the same way as the notion of bodily symptom is tied to an *anatomical* and *genetic context* (Szasz, 1957a, 1957b).

To sum up what has been said thus far: I have tried to show that for those who regard mental symptoms as signs of brain disease, the concept of mental illness is unnecessary and misleading. For what they mean is that people so labeled suffer from diseases of the brain; and, if that is what they mean, it would seem better for the sake of clarity to say that and not something else.

Mental Illness as a Name for Problems in Living

The term "mental illness" is widely used to describe something which is very different than a disease of the brain. Many people today take it for granted that living is an arduous process. Its hardship for modern man, moreover, derives not so much from a struggle for biological survival as from the stresses and strains inherent in the social intercourse of complex human personalities. In this context, the notion of mental illness is used to identify or describe some feature of an individual's so-called personality.

Mental illness — as a deformity of the personality, so to speak — is then regarded as the *cause* of the human disharmony. It is implicit in this view that social intercourse between people is regarded as something *inherently harmonious*, its disturbance being due solely to the presence of "mental illness" in many people. This is obviously fallacious reasoning, for it makes the abstraction "mental illness" into a *cause*, even though this abstraction was created in the first place to serve only as a shorthand expression for certain types of human behavior. It now becomes necessary to ask: "What kinds of behavior are regarded as indicative of mental illness, and by whom?"

The concept of illness, whether bodily or mental, implies *deviation from some clearly defined norm*. In the case of physical illness, the norm is the structural and functional integrity of the human body. Thus, although the desirability of physical health, as such, is an ethical value, what health is can be stated in anatomical and physiological terms. What is the norm deviation from which is regarded as mental illness? This question cannot be easily answered. But whatever this norm might be, we can be certain of only one thing: namely, that it is a norm that must be stated in terms of *psychosocial, ethical,* and *legal* concepts. For example, notions such as "excessive repression" or "acting out an unconscious impulse" illustrate the use of psychological concepts for judging (so-called) mental health and illness. The idea that chronic hostility, vengefulness, or divorce are indicative of mental illness would be illustrations of the use of ethical norms (that is, the desirability of love, kindness, and a stable marriage relationship). Finally, the widespread psychiatric opinion that only a mentally ill person would commit homicide illustrates the use of a legal concept as a norm of mental health. The norm from which deviation is measured whenever one speaks of a mental illness is a *psychosocial and ethical one*. Yet, the remedy is sought in terms of *medical* measures which — it is hoped and assumed — are free from wide differences of ethical value. The definition of the disorder and the terms in which its remedy are sought are therefore at serious odds with one another. The practical significance of this covert conflict between the alleged nature of the defect and the remedy can hardly be exaggerated.

Having identified the norms used to measure deviations in cases of mental illness, we will now turn to the question: "Who defines the norms and hence the deviation?" Two basic answers may be offered: (a) It may be the person himself (that is, the patient) who decides that he deviates from a norm. For example, an artist may believe that he suffers from a work inhibition; and he may implement this conclusion by seeking help *for* himself from a psychotherapist. (b) It may be someone other than the patient who decides that the latter is deviant (for example, relatives, physicians, legal authorities, society generally, etc.). In such a case a psychiatrist may be hired by others to do something to the patient in order to correct the deviation.

These considerations underscore the importance of asking the question

"Whose agent is the psychiatrist?" and of giving a candid answer to it (Szasz, 1956, 1958). The psychiatrist (psychologist or nonmedical psychotherapist), it now develops, may be the agent of the patient, of the relatives, of the school, of the military services, of a business organization, of a court of law, and so forth. In speaking of the psychiatrist as the agent of these persons or organizations, it is not implied that his values concerning norms, or his ideas and aims concerning the proper nature of remedial action, need to coincide exactly with those of his employer. For example, a patient in individual psychotherapy may believe that his salvation lies in a new marriage; his psychotherapist need not share his hypothesis. As the patient's agent, however, he must abstain from bringing social or legal force to bear on the patient which would prevent him from putting his beliefs into action. If his *contract* is with the patient, the psychiatrist (psychotherapist) may disagree with him or stop his treatment; but he cannot engage others to obstruct the patient's aspirations. Similarly, if a psychiatrist is engaged by a court to determine the sanity of a criminal, he need not fully share the legal authorities' values and intentions in regard to the criminal and the means available for dealing with him. But the psychiatrist is expressly barred from stating, for example, that it is not the criminal who is "insane" but the men who wrote the law on the basis of which the very actions that are being judged are regarded as "criminal." Such an opinion could be voiced, of course, but not in a courtroom, and not by a psychiatrist who makes it his practice to assist the court in performing its daily work.

To recapitulate: In actual contemporary social usage, the finding of a mental illness is made by establishing a deviance in behavior from certain psychosocial, ethical, or legal norms. The judgment may be made, as in medicine, by the patient, the physician (psychiatrist), or others. Remedial action, finally, tends to be sought in a therapeutic — or covertly medical — framework, thus creating a situation in which *psychosocial, ethical, and/ or legal deviations* are claimed to be correctible by (so-called) *medical action.* Since medical action is designed to correct only medical deviations, it seems logically absurd to expect that it will help solve problems whose very existence had been defined and established on nonmedical grounds. I think that these considerations may be fruitfully applied to the present use of tranquilizers and, more generally, to what might be expected of drugs of whatever type in regard to the amelioration or solution of problems in human living.

The Role of Ethics in Psychiatry

Anything that people *do* — in contrast to things that *happen* to them (Peters, 1958) — takes place in a context of value. In this broad sense, no human activity is devoid of ethical implications. When the values underlying certain activities are widely shared, those who participate in their pursuit may lose sight of them altogether. The discipline of medicine, both as a pure science (for example, research) and as a technology (for example, therapy), contains many ethical considerations and judgments. Unfortunately, these are often denied, minimized, or merely kept out of focus; for the ideal of the medical profession as well as of the people whom it serves seems to be having a system of medicine (allegedly) free of ethical value. This sentimental notion is expressed by such things as the doctor's willingness to treat and help patients irrespective of their religious or political beliefs, whether they are rich or poor, etc. While there may be some grounds for this belief — albeit it is a view that is not impressively true even in these regards — the fact remains that ethical considerations encompass a vast range of human affairs. By making the practice of medicine neutral in regard to some specific issues of value need not, and cannot, mean that it can be kept free from all such values. The practice of medicine is intimately tied to ethics; and the first thing that we must do, it seems to me, is to try to make this clear and explicit. I shall let this matter rest here, for it does not concern us specifically in this essay. Lest there be any vagueness, however, about how or where ethics and medicine meet, let me remind the reader of such issues as birth control, abortion, suicide, and euthanasia as only a few of the major areas of current ethicomedical controversy.

Psychiatry, I submit, is very much more intimately tied to problems of ethics than is medicine. I use the word "psychiatry" here to refer to that contemporary discipline which is concerned with *problems in living* (and not with diseases of the brain, which are problems for neurology). Problems in human relations can be analyzed, interpreted, and given meaning only within given social and ethical contexts. Accordingly, it *does* make a difference — arguments to the contrary notwithstanding — what the psychiatrist's socioethical orientations happen to be; for these will influence his ideas on what is wrong with the patient, what deserves comment or interpretation, in what possible directions change might be desirable, and so forth. Even in medicine proper, these factors play a role, as for instance, in the divergent orientations which physicians, depending on their religious affiliations, have toward such things as birth control and therapeutic abortion. Can anyone really believe that a psychotherapist's ideas concerning religious belief, slavery, or other similar issues play no role in his practical work? If they do make a difference, what are we to infer from it? Does it not seem reasonable that we ought to have different psychiatric therapies — each expressly recognized for the ethical positions which they embody — for, say, Catholics and Jews, religious persons and agnostics, democrats and communists, white supremacists and Negroes, and so on? Indeed, if we look at how psychiatry is actually practiced today (especially in the United States), we find that people do seek psychiatric help in accordance with their social status and ethical beliefs (Hollingshead & Redlich, 1958). This should really not surprise us more than being told that practicing Catholics rarely frequent birth control clinics.

The foregoing position which holds that contemporary psychotherapists deal with problems in living, rather than with mental illnesses and their cures, stands in opposition to a currently prevalent claim, according to which mental illness is just as "real" and "objective" as bodily illness. This is a confusing claim since it is never known exactly what is meant by such words as "real" and "objective." I suspect, however, that what is intended by the proponents of this view is to create the idea in the popular mind that mental illness is some sort of disease entity, like an infection or a malignancy. If this were true, one could *catch* or *get* a "mental illness," one might *have* or *harbor* it, one might *transmit* it to others, and finally one could get *rid* of it. In my opinion, there is not a shred of evidence to support this idea. To the contrary, all the evidence is the other way and supports the view that what people now call mental illnesses are for the most part *communications* expressing unacceptable ideas, often framed, moreover, in an unusual idiom. The scope of this essay allows me to do no more than mention this alternative theoretical approach to this problem (Szasz, 1957c).

This is not the place to consider in detail the similarities and differences between bodily and mental illnesses. It shall suffice for us here to emphasize only one important difference between them: namely, that whereas bodily disease refers to public, physicochemical occurrences, the notion of mental illness is used to codify relatively more private, sociopsychological happenings of which the observer (diagnostician) forms a part. In other words, the psychiatrist does not stand *apart* from what he observes, but is, in Harry Stack Sullivan's apt words, a "participant observer." This means that he is *committed* to some picture of what he considers reality — and to what he thinks society considers reality — and he observes and judges the patient's behavior in the light of these considerations. This touches on our earlier observation that the notion of mental symptom itself implies a comparison between observer and observed, psychiatrist and patient. This is so obvious that I may be charged with belaboring trivialities. Let me therefore say once more that my aim in presenting this argument was expressly to criticize and counter a prevailing contemporary tendency to deny the moral aspects of psychiatry (and psychotherapy) and to substitute for them allegedly value-free medical considerations. Psychotherapy, for example, is being widely practiced as though it entailed nothing other than restoring the patient from a state of mental sickness to one of mental health. While it is generally accepted that mental illness has something to do with man's social (or interpersonal) relations, it is paradoxically maintained that problems of values (that is, of ethics) do not arise in this process.[1] Yet, in one sense, much of psycho-

1. Freud went so far as to say that: "I consider ethics to be taken for granted. Actually I have never done a mean thing" (Jones, 1957, p. 247). This surely is a strange thing to say for someone who has studied man as a social being as closely as did Freud. I mention it here to show how the notion of "illness" (in the case of psychoanalysis, "psychopathology," or "mental illness") was used by Freud — and by most of his followers — as a means for classifying certain forms of human behavior as falling within the scope of medicine, and hence (by fiat) outside that of ethics!

therapy may revolve around nothing other than the elucidation and weighing of goals and values — many of which may be mutually contradictory — and the means whereby they might best be harmonized, realized, or relinquished.

The diversity of human values and the methods by means of which they may be realized is so vast, and many of them remain so unacknowledged, that they cannot fail but lead to conflicts in human relations. Indeed, to say that human relations at all levels — from mother to child, through husband and wife, to nation and nation — are fraught with stress, strain, and disharmony is, once again, making the obvious explicit. Yet, what may be obvious may be also poorly understood. This I think is the case here. For it seems to me that — at least in our scientific theories of behavior — we have failed to *accept* the simple fact that human relations are inherently fraught with difficulties and that to make them even relatively harmonious requires much patience and hard work. I submit that the idea of mental illness is now being put to work to obscure certain difficulties which at present may be inherent — not that they need be unmodifiable — in the social intercourse of persons. If this is true, the concept functions as a disguise; for instead of calling attention to conflicting human needs, aspirations, and values, the notion of mental illness provides an amoral and impersonal "thing" (an "illness") as an explanation for *problems in living* (Szasz, 1959). We may recall in this connection that not so long ago it was devils and witches who were held responsible for men's problems in social living. The belief in mental illness, as something other than man's trouble in getting along with his fellow man, is the proper heir to the belief in demonology and witchcraft. Mental illness exists or is "real" in exactly the same sense in which witches existed or were "real."

Choice, Responsibility, and Psychiatry

While I have argued that mental illnesses do not exist, I obviously did not imply that the social and psychological occurrences to which this label is currently being attached also do not exist. Like the personal and social troubles which people had in the Middle Ages, they are real enough. It is the labels we give them that concern us and, having labelled them, what we do about them. While I cannot go into the ramified implications of this problem here, it is worth noting that a demonologic conception of problems in living gave rise to therapy along theological lines. Today, a belief in mental illness implies — nay, requires — therapy along medical or psychotherapeutic lines.

What is implied in the line of thought set forth here is something quite different. I do not intend to offer a new conception of "psychiatric illness" nor a new form of "therapy." My aim is more modest and yet also more ambitious. It is to suggest that the phenomena now called mental illnesses be looked at afresh and more simply, that they be removed from the category of illnesses, and that they be regarded as the expressions of man's struggle with the problem of *how* he should live. The last mentioned problem is obviously a vast one, its enormity reflecting not only man's inability to cope with his environment, but even more his increasing self-reflectiveness.

By problems in living, then, I refer to that truly explosive chain reaction which began with man's fall from divine grace by partaking of the fruit of the tree of knowledge. Man's awareness of himself and of the world about him seems to be a steadily expanding one, bringing in its wake an ever larger *burden of understanding* (an expression borrowed from Susanne Langer, 1953). *This burden, then, is to be expected and must not be misinterpreted.* Our only *rational* means for lightening it is *more understanding*, and appropriate *action* based on such understanding. The main alternative lies in acting as though the burden were not what in fact we perceive it to be and taking refuge in an outmoded theological view of man. In the latter view, man does not fashion his life and much of his world about him, but merely lives out his fate in a world created by superior beings. This may logically lead to pleading nonresponsibility in the face of seemingly unfathomable problems and difficulties. Yet, if man fails to take increasing responsibility for his actions, individually as well as collectively, it seems unlikely that some higher power or being would assume this task and carry this burden for him. Moreover, this seems hardly the proper time in human history for obscuring the issue of man's responsibility for his actions by hiding it behind the skirt of an all-explaining conception of mental illness.

Conclusions

I have tried to show that the notion of mental illness has outlived whatever usefulness it might have had and that it now functions merely as a convenient myth. As such, it is a true heir to religious myths in general, and to the belief in witchcraft in particular; the role of all these belief-systems was to act as *social tranquilizers*, thus encouraging the hope that mastery of certain specific problems may be achieved by means of substitutive (symbolic-magical) operations. The notion of mental illness thus serves mainly to obscure the everyday fact that life for most people is a continuous struggle, not for biological survival, but for a "place in the sun," "peace of mind," or some other human value. For man aware of himself and of the world about him, once the needs for preserving the body (and perhaps the race) are more or less satisfied, the problem arises as to what he should do with himself. Sustained adherence to the myth of mental illness allows people to avoid facing this problem, believing that mental health, conceived as the absence of mental illness, automatically insures the making of right and safe choices in one's conduct of life. But the facts are all the other way. It is the making of good choices in life that others regard, retrospectively, as good mental health!

The myth of mental illness encourages us, moreover, to believe in its logical corollary: that social intercourse would be harmonious, satisfying, and the secure basis of a "good life" were it not for the disrupting influences of mental illness or "psychopathology." The potentiality for universal human happiness, in this form at least, seems to me but another example of the I-wish-it-were-true type of fantasy. I do not believe that human happiness or well-being on a hitherto unimaginably large scale and not just for a select few, is possible. This goal could be achieved, however, only at the cost of many men, and not just a few being willing and able to tackle their personal, social, and ethical conflicts. This means having the courage and integrity to forego waging battles on false fronts finding solutions for substitute problems — for instance, fighting the battle of stomach acid and chronic fatigue instead of facing up to a marital conflict.

Our adversaries are not demons, witches, fate, or mental illness. We have no enemy whom we can fight, exorcise, or dispel by "cure." What we do have are *problems in living* — whether these be biologic, economic, political, or sociopsychological. In this essay I was concerned only with problems belonging in the last mentioned category, and within this group mainly with those pertaining to moral values. The field to which modern psychiatry addresses itself is vast, and I made no effort to encompass it all. My argument was limited to the proposition that mental illness is a myth, whose function it is to disguise and thus render more palatable the bitter pill of moral conflicts in human relations.

References

Hollingshead, A. B., & Redlich, F. C. *Social class and mental illness.* New York: Wiley, 1958.

Jones, E. *The life and work of Sigmund Freud.* Vol. III. New York: Basic Books, 1957.

Langer, S. K. *Philosophy in a new key.* New York: Mentor Books, 1953.

Peters, R. S. *The concept of motivation.* London: Routledge & Kegan Paul, 1958.

Szasz, T. S. Malingering: "Diagnosis" or social condemnation? *AMA Arch Neurol. Psychiat.,* 1956, 76, 432–443.

Szasz, T. S. *Pain and pleasure: A study of bodily feelings.* New York: Basic Books, 1957. (a)

Szasz, T. S. The problem of psychiatric nosology: A contribution to a situational analysis of psychiatric operations. *Amer. J. Psychiat.,* 1957, 114, 405–413. (b)

Szasz, T. S. On the theory of psychoanalytic treatment. *Int. J. Psycho-Anal.,* 1957, 38, 166–182. (c)

Szasz, T. S. Psychiatry, ethics and the criminal law *Columbia law Rev.,* 1958, 58, 183–198.

Szasz, T. S. Moral conflict and psychiatry, *Yale Rev.,* 1959, in press. [Vol. 49, pp. 555–566.]

Questions and Exercises

1. Summarize each of the six sections of this article in one sentence each. Make sure that a person who has not read the article would be able to understand the general idea from your six sentences.

2. List the words and phrases that are in italics, that is, those emphasized by the author. Why do you think that he uses this device so much? Play with the words in your list to see if any patterns develop.

3. Compare the first sentence of this article with the first sentence of the article by D. L. Rosenhan (p. 298). How are the sentences similar? How are they different?

4. What does Szasz mean when he writes that mental illness is not a fact but a metaphor? What is mental illness a metaphor for? Make a list of other conditions, (for example, hunger, drunkenness, and so on) that might be considered metaphors. Choose one condition and record some ideas about its possible metaphoric significance. Meet in small groups to read and discuss your list of conditions. In what way are they facts? In what way metaphors?

5. In small groups discuss the concept of "norms" as Szasz uses the term. First, each group member should write a definition of normal behavior. Then the group should compare definitions. Can you reach consensus? Do your findings support or refute Szasz's argument?

6. Pretend that you are an outraged psychiatrist. Write a letter to the editor in response to Szasz's essay. Concentrate on what you consider to be the major fallacies and weaknesses in Szasz's argument.

7. Look up "ethics" in the *Encyclopedia of Philosophy* and write a paragraph explaining what "ethical problems" are. Draft a defense or refutation of Szasz's assertion that "Psychiatry . . . is more intimately tied to problems of ethics than is medicine." Your audience includes undergraduates who have not read Szasz's essay.

Five Articles on Justice and Discrimination

from *Analysis*

Each of the five articles presented in this group represents the kind of short paper that students in philosophy, history, literature, and other humanities subjects are often asked to write. They are examples of "puzzle" papers, that is, papers that require you to think through a possible answer to a problem for which there may be no single right answer. We have reproduced several on the same topic, from the same journal, *Analysis*, to permit you to see different perspectives on a problem that is representative of the type humanists think about. Conflicting interpretations of complex human problems compete for a reader's attention. You are asked, in effect, to accept or reject each position in this type of writing on the basis of how persuasive or convincing the arguments are.

The controversy with which these papers deal is the issue of "reverse discrimination" — a term that is applied to various forms of preferential treatment benefitting persons or groups who normally are or have been discriminated against. An example is the policy the United States Government calls "affirmative action," which requires that institutions such as schools and colleges adopt special procedures to ensure that members of groups which have traditionally been victims of discrimination will gain access to the institutions. Philosophers, so as not to prejudge the action, generally refer to it as "preferential consideration" rather than the more controversial and morally loaded term "reverse discrimination."

James Nickel started the controversy in *Analysis* by exploring the grounds on which the logic of reverse discrimination could be attacked. Some might argue, he says, that if it is morally wrong to discriminate against people on the basis of their race, then it is equally wrong to discriminate in their favor on the basis of their race. This argument claims that it is unfair when individuals or groups are singled out for special treatment — negative or positive — because of characteristics that are irrelevant to the purpose of the treatment. Nickel then examines the assumptions behind that argument. His essay is followed by that of J. L. Cowan, who responds directly to Nickel; then Shiner responds to Cowan, and Bayles argues against both Nickel and Cowan. (P. W. Taylor, in an article we have not reprinted, also enters the discussion.) The last selection is Nickel's response to Cowan and to Bayles.

As examples of philosophical writing, these papers have some distinctive characteristics. Above all, none of these authors explicitly concludes that preferential consideration is acceptable, although most imply their agreement with the policy. Rather, the issue in contention is a particular argument against preferential consideration. Their interest is in the logic of the argument rather than in the conclusion. Thus, as you will notice, Bayles disagrees with Nickel's handling of the argument, but they both seem to favor preferential treatment of minority groups. It is typical of philosophical controversy that the object of attack is the argument given by your opponent rather than the conclusion he or she draws from the argument. Secondly, notice that all the papers establish context at the beginning by repeating what they understand the previous paper to have said. In each case, they summarize the important claims to which they are responding. This practice is not to remind the audience of what has already been said, but to explain the current writer's understanding of the position that he is about to attack or defend. Lastly, compare Nickel's two articles, especially his second formulation of the problem with his original formulation. Although he disagrees with the criticisms made by the others, the statement of his second position has become substantially clearer. His own thinking seems to have benefitted enormously from the need to deal with the objections of others.

Discrimination and Morally Relevant Characteristics

JAMES W. NICKEL

Suppose that a characteristic which should be morally irrelevant (for example, race, creed or sex) has been treated as if it were morally relevant over a period of years, and that injustices have resulted from this. When such a mistake has been recognized and condemned, when the morally irrelevant characteristic has been seen to be irrelevant, can this characteristic *then* properly be used as a relevant consideration in the distribution of reparations to those who have suffered injustices? If we answer this question in the affirmative, we will have the strange consequence that a morally irrelevant characteristic can become morally relevant if its use results in injustices.

The context in which this difficulty is likely to arise is one in which a group has been discriminated against on the basis of morally irrelevant properties, but in which this discrimination has been recognized and at least partly come to an end; and the question at hand concerns how the members of this group should now be treated. Should they now be treated like everyone else, ignoring their history, or should they be given special advantages because of past discrimination and injustices? There are a variety of considerations which are pertinent in answering this question, and I will deal with only one of these, the reverse-discrimination argument. This argument claims that to extend special considerations to a formerly oppressed group will be to persist in the mistake of treating a morally irrelevant characteristic as if it were relevant. For if we take a morally irrelevant characteristic (namely the characteristic which was the basis for the original discrimination) and use it as the basis for granting special consideration or reparations, we will be treating the morally irrelevant as if it were relevant and still engaging in discrimination, albeit reverse discrimination. And hence, it is argued, the only proper stance toward groups who have suffered discrimination is one of strict impartiality.

To state the argument in a slightly different way, one might say that if a group was discriminated against on the basis of a morally irrelevant characteristic of theirs, then to award extra benefits now to the members of this group because they have this characteristic is simply to continue to treat a morally irrelevant characteristic as if it were relevant. Instead of the original discrimination *against* these people, we now have discrimination *for* them, but in either case we have discrimination since it treats the irrelevant as relevant. Hence, to avoid discrimination we must now completely ignore this characteristic and extend no special considerations whatsoever.

Discrimination and Morally Relevant Characteristics. From *Analysis* 32:3 March 1972. Reprinted by permission of Basil Blackwell Publisher Limited.

The objection which I want to make to this argument pertains to its assumption that the characteristic which was the basis for the original discrimination is the same as the one which is used as the basis for extending extra considerations now. I want to suggest that this is only apparently so. For if compensation in the form of extra opportunities is extended to a black man on the basis of past discrimination against blacks (I do not mean to imply that we are in this situation, where discrimination against blacks is a thing of the past. We are not.) the basis for this compensation is not that he is a black man, but that he was previously subject to unfair treatment because he was black. The former characteristic was and is morally irrelevant, but the latter characteristic is very relevant if it is assumed that it is desirable or obligatory to make compensation for past injustices. Hence, to extend special considerations to those who have suffered from discrimination need not involve continuing to treat a morally irrelevant characteristic as if it were relevant. In such a case the characteristic which was the basis for the original discrimination (for example, being a black person) will be different from the characteristic which is the basis for the distribution of special considerations (for example, being a person who was discriminated against because he was black).

My conclusion is that this version of the reverse-discrimination argument has a false premise, since it assumes that the characteristic which was the basis for the original discrimination is the same as that which is the basis for the granting of special considerations. And since the argument has a false premise, it does not succeed in showing that to avoid reverse discrimination we must extend no special considerations whatsoever.

Inverse Discrimination

L. J. COWAN

The justice or injustice of "inverse discrimination" is a question of pressing social importance. On the one hand it is argued that when a morally irrelevant characteristic such as race, creed or sex has been treated as morally relevant and injustices have resulted, it is then proper to treat that characteristic as morally relevant in order to make reparations. On the other hand it is argued that if the characteristic in question is morally irrelevant, its use even in this manner would still constitute discrimination, discrimination now in favor of those possessing the characteristic and against those not, but unjust discrimination still.

Public discussion of this issue all too rarely goes far beyond the level of the arguments as given. Yet the logic of these arguments is murky, to say the least. It is therefore to be hoped that the analytical skills supposedly

Inverse Discrimination. From *Analysis* 33:1 October 1972. Reprinted by permission of Basil Blackwell Publisher Limited.

characteristic of philosophers might here play a valuable social role, and we are indebted to J. W. Nickel for beginning such a clarification. I should like here to try to continue it.

Nickel maintains that the argument against inverse discrimination given above goes wide of the mark since the characteristic which is now operative is not actually the original morally irrelevant one. "For if compensation in the form of extra opportunities is extended to a black man on the basis of past discrimination against blacks, the basis for this compensation is not that he is a black man, but that he was previously subject to unfair treatment because he was black ... in such a case the characteristic which was the basis for the original discrimination (for example, being a black person) will be different from the characteristic which is the basis for the distribution of special considerations (for example, being a person who was discriminated against because he was black)."

The problem is that Nickel does not make it entirely clear just what he is about here. He may simply be pointing out that if a person has suffered injustice through morally unjustified discrimination, then reparation to that person will be appropriate. But surely it was not against this relatively uncontroversial point that the original argument was directed. And Nickel's formulation leaves open the possibility that he is actually trying to support the far more questionable claim that was the original target of that argument.

"Being discriminated against because he was black" is clearly a complex predicate. What I would like to suggest is that the portion of it which was morally irrelevant in independence remains so within the complex and is thus mere excess baggage. The reason why he was discriminated against is not what should now ground reparation, but rather simply the fact that, and extent to which, he was unjustly discriminated against for whatever reason. Thus, assuming that the discrimination is otherwise the same, we would presumably not wish to say that Jones, who has been discriminated against as a black, should now be favored over Smith, who has been equally discriminated against as a woman or a Jew or whatever. We are therefore left without a moral relevance for blackness, and thus without a moral basis for inverse discrimination based on blackness, as opposed to discriminatory injustice per se.

Nickel's reasoning thus does not really, as it might be taken to do, provide any support at all for the kind of self-contradictory thinking the original argument was surely intended to rebut. This is the reasoning that since blacks, to retain this example, have suffered unjust discrimination we should now give them special treatment to make it up to them. Once again there is no problem insofar as this simply means that where individual blacks have suffered injustice it should, as with anyone else, insofar as possible be made up to those individuals who have so suffered. The fallacy arises when, rather than individuals, it is the group which is intended, and individuals are regarded merely as members of that group rather than in their individuality. This creates a contradiction since the original premise of the moral irrelevance of blackness on the basis of which the original attribution of unjust discrimination rests implies that there is and can be no morally relevant group which could have suffered or to which retribution could now be made. Thus those who would argue that since "we" brutally kidnapped "the" blacks out of Africa and subjected "them" to the abominations of slavery, or that since "we" have exploited and degraded "women" since Eve, "we" therefore now owe retribution to our neighbor who happens to be black or a woman, are involved in inextricable self-contradiction. Except to the extent he or she as an individual has unjustly suffered or will unjustly suffer from this history while we as individuals have unjustly profited or will unjustly profit there can be no such obligation.

Nickel's original formulation is thus ambiguous. "The context in which this difficulty is likely to arise is one in which a group has been discriminated against on the basis of morally irrelevant properties, but in which this discrimination has been recognized and at least partly come to an end; and the question at hand concerns how the members of this group should now be treated. Should they now be treated like everyone else, ignoring their history, or should they be given special advantages because of past discrimination and injustices?" Once the question is unambiguous the answer is clear. They should most certainly be treated like everyone else. But this does not mean "their" individual histories should be ignored. As with anyone else, injustices done "them" as individuals should be prevented or rectified insofar as possible. But past or future discrimination and injustice done "them" as a group and special advantages to them as a group are both out of the question, since in the moral context there is no such group.

Individuals, Groups and Inverse Discrimination
ROGER A. SHINER

Many morally sensitive people find themselves faced with the following dilemma. On the one hand, they are persuaded by the argument that if being black, for example, is morally irrelevant, then it is morally irrelevant and no more justifies favorable inverse discrimination than it justifies unfavorable discrimination. On the other hand, this move seems to open the way to neglect, whether benign or malign, of genuine social injustices. James W. Nickel and J. L. Cowan have done much to bring the logic of this situation to the surface. I shall not resist their general strategy of showing that the above is a false dilemma. My concern is with Cowan's diagnosis of the trouble as consisting in the illegitimacy of the thought that

Individuals, Groups and Inverse Discrimination. From *Analysis* 33:6 June 1973. Reprinted by permission of Basil Blackwell Publisher Limited.

blacks *as a group* deserve inverse discrimination. His view is that one cannot argue that blacks as a group deserve retribution without also implying that blackness as such is a morally relevant characteristic. This is false.

In the first place, it simply is not true that sense can never be made of the thought that a group as such deserves inverse discrimination. Consider these cases. (1) The Illyrians, through the incompetence of their negotiators, entered the European Economic Community under extremely unfair conditions. Later on, an EEC Council member argues, "We ought now to give the Illyrians especially favorable consideration," and recommends inverse discrimination. (2) Form 3B is not allowed to go on the school outing because there are thirty-five in the class — or so they are told, and this is not a matter of the school bus size or the tickets available. The form master argues later, "3B should be given special consideration," and recommends inverse discrimination.

The objection might be raised that Form 3B is not really a group in a sense relevant to the problem at issue. It is an individual member of the group "classes in elementary schools," and an individual school class may deserve inverse discrimination because of unfair treatment in the same way as an individual black or woman. However, there are many educators who argue that a disproportionate amount of money has been spent in recent years on secondary and postsecondary education, and that we now need to spend an equally disproportionate amount of money on elementary schools and schoolchildren as a group. But my argument need not turn on the accuracy of this remark, for the Illyrians are not a closed, formally defined group as is Form 3B, nor are they members of some wider group.

Now it might be said that statements about Illyria or the Illyrian nation are reducible without remainder to statements about individual Illyrians. So I still have not presented a counterexample to the thesis that a group as such cannot deserve inverse discrimination. But this is a highly contentious philosophical thesis, and the debate about whether it is true remains unresolved. It cannot be that the present question about inverse discrimination is simply this old chestnut in a new guise, and indeed Cowan does not talk as though this is what he has in mind. Those who wish to support inverse discrimination draw on the stock of available collective nouns, and frequently speak of the black/Indian/Jewish nation/race/people and of the female sex.

These points show, then, I submit, that talk about groups deserving inverse discrimination, as opposed to similar talk about individuals, cannot be simply ruled out as nonsensical, nor will it do to rule it in purely on the basis of some reductionist theory about nations. If we are to get at what is peculiar about the thought that blacks as a group deserve inverse discrimination, we must try a different tack.

Consider these remarks — (3) "My car ought to go in for repair, because it is a 1970 Ford"; (4) "George deserves inverse discrimination, because he is black." Cowan and Nickel are upset about (4), because it is logically of a piece with (5) "George deserves to be discriminated against, because he is black," and we want to reject that inference, on the grounds that the feature mentioned is irrelevant. But why should my car's being a 1970 Ford and just exactly that mean that it ought to go in for repair? We explain a case like (3) by treating it as an elliptical argument, with a missing premise (3*) to the effect that all 1970 Fords have been recalled by the maker and ought to go in for repair. We can then underpin (4) in the same way, by supplying a premise (4*) to the effect that all blacks have been discriminated against unjustly in the past and and deserve discrimination now.

This is pretty clearly the kind of point Cowan wants to make, but to show that (4) won't do unless underpinned with (4*) is not to show what, if anything, is wrong with (4') "Blacks as a group deserve inverse discrimination," still less that it is the introduction of the notion of a group deserving inverse discrimination that is problematic. As I have implied, to get from the need for (4*) to the illegitimacy of (4'), we will at least need to grapple with the reductionist position outlined above.

Nonetheless, the need for (4*) will enable us to get a correct picture of the peculiarity of the bold inference (4). Compare (3)/(3*) and (4)/(4*) with (6) "This figure is a rectangle, because it has equal diagonals." (6) to the same degree seems to need (6*) "All figures with equal diagonals are rectangles." However, although the (3) and (4) sets and the (6) set are in this respect structurally similar, there is an important difference in their content. (3*) and (4*) are, if true, then a posteriori, true. (6*), on the other hand, is true and moreover a priori true. Thus, the arguments constituted by the (3) set and the (4) set will only be sound as well as valid if (3*) and (4*) are as a matter of empirical fact true. The difference between the (6) set and the (3) set and (4) sets is that there is an a priori and conceptual connection between being a rectangle and having equal diagonals, whereas there is *no* a priori and conceptual connection between being a 1970 Ford and needing to go in for repair, nor between being a black and deserving inverse discrimination.

This, then, I take to be the fundamental point about the moral irrelevancy of the characteristic of being a black. It is not a matter of whether it is a group or an individual that is held to have the characteristic. It is instead a matter of the kind of link that exists between the possession of that characteristic and the possession of some other moral characteristic. The moral irrelevancy of being a black is a matter of the absence of the appropriate a priori link. Contrast (7) "Fred deserves inverse discrimination, because he is socioeconomically disadvantaged," and the corresponding (7*) "The socioeconomically disadvantaged deserve inverse discrimination." In this case, many philosophers would be prepared to concede that, if (7*) were part of a plausible moral theory, for example, a la Rawls, (7*) would state a conceptual connection.

In short, my thesis in this paper is that, if we want to get clear why being a black is morally irrelevant though blacks deserve inverse discrimination, then the individual/group distinction is a red herring. We need instead the a posteriori connection/a priori connection distinction. The absence of the latter connection means that any claim to the effect that blacks, whether as a group or as individuals, deserve inverse discrimination must stand, not simply on their being blacks, but on the facts of history. If, that is to say, blacks as a group deserve inverse discrimination, it will be because some claim like (4*) is true. But if (4*) is true, then one can reasonably argue that blacks as a group deserve retribution *without* also implying blackness as such is a morally relevant characteristic. I suspect the facts of history can stand the weight thus put on them.

Reparations to Wronged Groups

MICHAEL D. BAYLES

If a group of people (blacks, women) has been wronged by its members' being discriminated against on the basis of a morally irrelevant characteristic, is it morally permissible to use that characteristic as a basis for providing special considerations or benefits as reparations? It is frequently argued that since the characteristic is morally irrelevant, its use as a basis for providing reparations must also constitute wrongful discrimination.

James W. Nickel contends that such reparations are not wrong because they are not based on the morally irrelevant characteristic. Being black, for example, is a morally irrelevant characteristic for discriminating against or for a person. However, Nickel claims that if a black man receives special consideration as reparation for past discrimination the basis is not the morally irrelevant characteristic of his being black. Instead, it is the morally relevant one of his having been "subject to unfair treatment because he was black."

J. L. Cowan criticizes Nickel for even including the morally irrelevant characteristic as part of the complex predicate on the basis of which reparations are given. It is not a man's having been subject to unfair treatment because he was black which is the basis of reparation, Cowan contends, "but simply the fact that, and the extent to which, he was unjustly discriminated against for whatever reason." We would not, Cowan points out, wish to favor a person who has been discriminated against for being Jewish. He further claims that the problem of using a morally irrelevant characteristic as the basis for reparation "arises when rather than individuals it is the group which is intended, and individuals are regarded merely as members of that group rather than in their individuality. This creates a contradiction since the original premise of the moral irrelevance of blackness on the basis of which the original attribution of unjust discrimination

Reparations to Wronged Groups. From *Analysis* 33:6 June 1973. Reprinted by permission of Basil Blackwell Publisher Limited.

rests implies that there is and can be no morally relevant group which could have suffered or to which retribution could now be made."

The solution of the problem proposed by Nickel and Cowan, that the reparation is based on a characteristic other than the morally irrelevant one, is spurious. By parallel reasoning it can be argued that the original discrimination was not on the basis of a morally irrelevant characteristic. Racists do not discriminate against blacks simply because they are black. Rather they claim that blacks as a class are inferior in certain relevant respects, that is, they lack certain abilities and virtues such as industriousness, reliability and cleanliness. Thus, reasoning similarly to Nickel and Cowan, racists could contend that they do not discriminate on the basis of a morally irrelevant characteristic, but the morally relevant ones which are thought to be associated with being black. Further, a reformed racist could contend that he was mistaken to believe blacks lacked such abilities and virtues. But, since it was a *mistaken* belief which was the basis of his discrimination, he was not responsible and owes no reparations. In short, if being black is not the basis for reparations, it was not the basis for the original discrimination.

However, there need be no contradiction involved in claiming that being black is both morally irrelevant for discriminating against people and morally relevant in discriminating in favor of people to provide reparations. One may simply hold that there is no justifiable moral rule which, when correctly applied, supports discriminating against blacks, but there is one which supports discriminating in favor of them. One may hold that people have an obligation to give reparations to groups they have wronged. By using the characteristic of being black as an identifying characteristic to discriminate against people, a person has wronged the group, blacks. He thus has an obligation to make reparations to the group. Since the obligation is to the group, no specific individual has a right to reparation. However, since the group is not an organized one like a state, church, or corporation, the only way to provide reparations to the group is to provide them to members of the group.

Being black can, thus, become morally relevant in distinguishing between those individuals who are members of the group to whom reparations are owed and those who are not. But being black is only derivatively morally relevant. It is not mentioned as a morally relevant characteristic in the rule requiring one to provide reparations to groups one has wronged. Instead, it becomes relevant by being the identifying characteristic of the group wronged. The way in which it is an identifying characteristic here differs from the way in which it is an identifying characteristic for the racist. Being black is an identifying characteristic for the racist only because he thinks it is contingently connected with other characteristics. But being black is not contingently connected with the group one has wronged. Rather, it is logically connected as the defining characteristic of members of the group.

Cowan has failed to distinguish the relevance of being black as applied to groups and individuals. One may hold that one owes reparations to the group, blacks, not because the group is the group of blacks, but because the group has been wronged. But with respect to individuals, one may, as reparation, discriminate in their favor on the basis of their being black. One discriminates in favor of individuals because they are black, but one owes reparations to the group, blacks, because it has been wronged. Nor does such a position commit one to favoring individual blacks over individuals who belong to another wronged group, for example, women. One has a morally relevant reason to favor each on the basis of their being black and female respectively. It does not follow that either should be preferred over the other.

Nothing has been said to support accepting any moral rules or principles applying to groups. (As a matter of fact, most people appear to accept one such rule, namely, that genocide is wrong.) Nor has anything been said to support accepting the rule that one has an obligation to provide reparations to groups one has wronged. These remarks have only indicated how being black can derivatively be a morally relevant characteristic for discriminating in favor of individuals if such a role is accepted.

Should Reparations Be to Individuals or to Groups?
JAMES W. NICKEL

The discussion occasioned by my note, "Discrimination and Morally Relevant Characteristics," has helped to clarify some of the available positions on the justification of special benefits for victims of discrimination. J. L. Cowan agrees that the justification for special help lies in the fact that one has been wronged, not in the fact, say, that one is black. But he thinks that it is important to emphasize that the special benefits which are due to many blacks are due only because they are individuals who have been wronged, not because of any fact relating to their race. On his view, "reparations for blacks" must be understood as "reparations for wronged individuals who happen to be black." P. W. Taylor and M. D. Bayles criticize my approach from the opposite direction. They think that my approach pays insufficient attention to the moral status of wronged groups. In what follows I shall attempt to point out some weaknesses in my critics' positions and to elaborate further my own.

The "reverse-discrimination argument" alleges that special benefits for blacks are unjust because they continue to base special treatment on an

Should Reparations Be to Individuals or to Groups? From *Analysis* 34:5 April 1974. Reprinted by permission of Basil Blackwell Publisher Limited.

irrelevant characteristic (namely, being black) and hence continue to discriminate. The counterargument that I offered has two premises:

P₁: For differential treatment to be discriminatory (and unjust for that reason) it must be based on a morally irrelevant characteristic.

P₂: Differential treatment of blacks for purposes of reparations is not based on an irrelevant characteristic (as it would be if it were based on race instead of the fact of having been wronged).

From these premises I drew the conclusion that differential treatment of blacks for purposes of reparations is not unjust on account of being discriminatory.

Cowan's criticism is that the formation of the argument is ambiguous because it fails to make clear whether it is defending special help to individuals or special help to groups:

> Nickel's reasoning thus does not really, as it might be taken to do, provide any support at all for the kind of self-contradictory thinking the original argument was surely intended to rebut. This is the reasoning that since blacks . . . have suffered unjust discrimination we should now give them special treatment to make it up to them. Once again there is no problem insofar as this simply means that where individual blacks have suffered injustice it should, as with anyone else, insofar as possible be made up to those individuals who have so suffered. The fallacy arises when rather than individuals it is the group which is intended, and individuals are regarded merely as members of that group rather than in their individuality.

But it was indeed my intention to provide support for the kind of thinking that Cowan finds contradictory. I intended to suggest that since almost all American blacks have been victimized by discrimination it would be justifiable to design and institute programs of special benefits for blacks. Such programs, which are probably the only effective and administratively feasible way to provide reparations to blacks, would be justified in terms of the injuries that almost all of the recipients have suffered — not in terms of the race of the recipients. To make this clearer one needs to distinguish between the justifying and the administrative basis for a program. The justifying basis for such a program would be the injuries that many blacks suffer and the special needs that many blacks have because of discrimination. The administrative basis for distributing the program's benefits might be the presence in an individual of these needs and injuries, but it is more likely that it would be some other characteristics (such as race and present income) which were easier to detect and which were highly correlated with the justifying basis. My assumption here is that it is sometimes justifiable for reasons of administrative efficiency to use as part of the administrative basis for a program of benefits a characteristic such as race which would be implausible as a justifying basis. Cowan argues that special advantages to blacks as a group are "out of the question since in the moral context there is no such group." I agree with the premise that there is no such group insofar as this means that race or ancestry can never be a justifying basis for differential treatment. But I do not agree that race or ancestry can never serve as a morally acceptable administrative basis for a program of differential treatment which provides compensation for past wrongs, and hence I reject the unqualified conclusion that special advantages to blacks as a group are out of the question.

Bayles and Taylor want to go further than this. They want to give direct moral status to the defining characteristics of wronged groups, and argue that special help to blacks as a group can be justified in terms of a principle requiring reparations to wronged groups. They hold the view, paradoxical but not contradictory, that although race is irrelevant in a context where persons of a given race are being unjustly harmed, it is not irrelevant in a context where the obligation to give reparations to wronged groups is being met. Bayles, unlike Taylor, does not offer positive grounds for his own view; he simply offers it as an alternative to my approach — which he thinks can be discredited by refutation by analogy. In response to my claim that having been wronged rather than being black is the justifying basis for special help, he says:

> By parallel reasoning it can be argued that the original discrimination was not on the basis of a morally irrelevant characteristic. Racists do not discriminate against blacks simply because they are black. Rather they claim that blacks as a class are inferior in certain relevant respects, e.g., they lack certain abilities and virtues such as industriousness, reliability and cleanliness. Thus, reasoning similarly to Nickel and Cowan, racists could contend that they do not discriminate on the basis of a morally irrelevant characteristic, but the morally relevant ones which are thought to be associated with being black.

Bayles' complaint is that if those who favor reparations can use this argument, then so can racists. He thinks that if it works for the one then it will work for the other. And since it is obvious that it won't work for the racist as a way of showing that he doesn't discriminate, he concludes that it won't work for those who favor reparations.

One response to this complaint is to argue that the second premise of my counterargument to the reverse-discrimination argument would not be true when used by the racist. The racist's version of the second premise would be:

RP₂: My differential treatment of blacks is not based on an irrelevant characteristic (as it would be if it were based on race instead of the fact of being lazy, unreliable and unclean).

In most cases this would not be, I submit, a true claim. It would, rather, be a self-serving rationalization. In B. A. O. Williams' words, the racist is "paying, in very poor coin, the homage of irrationality to reason." Most racists could not use this defense of their differential treatment of blacks because its premise about their real reasons would not be true.

But to avoid being doctrinaire about this we must allow that some racists might be able to make this claim about their real reasons without falsehood and rationalization. And Bayles is right in suggesting that this possibility requires me to modify or give up my counterargument. Bayles' approach is to give up this defense and use a much stronger principle about reparations to wronged groups to defend programs of reparations to blacks from the charge of unjust discrimination. But before adopting Bayles' approach we will do well, I think, to consider modifying the first premise of my counterargument. This premise holds that for differential treatment to be discriminatory (and unjust for that reason) it must be based on an irrelevant characteristic. But it should be changed to one which holds that for differential treatment to be discriminatory (and unjust for that reason) it is necessary that it be based on an irrelevant characteristic or on a false claim about the correlation between characteristics. This is, in effect, to modify one's definition of *discrimination*. When this modification is made, the defender of reparations is not able to move directly from the fact that preferential treatment was not based on an irrelevant characteristic to the conclusion that it was not unjustly discriminatory. To get to this conclusion, he would also have to show that there was in fact a very high correlation between being an American black and being a victim of discriminatory and harmful treatment. I think that the defender of reparations can do this, but the racist cannot make the analogous move. He cannot show that there is in fact a high correlation between being black and lacking industry, reliability and cleanliness, and hence his actions are based on false beliefs about correlations between characteristics and can — under the modified premise — be condemned as discriminatory. Hence the defender of reparations can use this defense without making an equally good defense available to the racist. . . .

Questions and Exercises

1. For each of the first three papers, record the one sentence which best expresses your understanding of the most important idea.

2. Write a short summary of Nickel's first paper. Then compare it to Bayles's summary in the second paragraph of his paper. If you see Nickel's main points differently from Bayles, explain why.

3. Write a short summary of Cowan's paper, and compare your summary with the summary given by Bayles (in his third paragraph) and the summary given by Nickel in the first paragraph of his second paper.

4. Reread one of the papers and take notes on the function of each paragraph in the developing argument. For example, in his first paper, Nickel (1) states a general problem, (2) states a specific application of the problem, (3) states the problem in another way, (4) suggests a solution to the problem, and (5) summarizes the solution.

5. Look up "discriminate" in a good desk dictionary. Is it always wrong to be discriminatory?

6. In this collection of papers, what issues are introduced after the first paper? What has happened to the issue at the end — is it resolved or ignored?

7. Nickel distinguishes between the administrative basis of a program and its justifying basis. What is the distinction? How does he use it? In small groups, try to reach a consensus on the meaning and use of the terms.

8. The authors of these papers are concerned primarily with the logic of arguments defending reverse discrimination. Consider each author and make a judgment as to whether he favors reverse discrimination. Be specific about what evidence you use for your judgment. Divide into groups; each group should be responsible for one of the essays.

9. How would you decide if something is morally relevant as the basis of differential treatment? When someone applies for a job in a police department, is the sex of that person relevant? Is age relevant to whether one may be permitted to buy alcohol? Is size relevant in the choice of a football player? Is intelligence relevant to the right to vote? Draft your own short essay (three to five pages) on one of these questions. Your readers are undergraduates who have read many essays of the sort in this section and who therefore expect closely reasoned arguments.

10. Trace through these papers what happens to the issue of whether a group can be said to have rights. Take notes from each article on the issue and use these notes to draft your own short essay (three to five pages) on the problem. In your essay you may wish to consider animal rights (see Singer's essay on pp. 214–24) or the rights of particular groups in human society (see Wollstonecraft pp. 107–110 and King pp. 152–67). Your readers are undergraduates who may not have read the specific material you have read but who do expect logically consistent argument.

The Sciences

Political scientists, psychologists, biologists, and chemists often pose questions about the ethics (right and wrong), epistemology (knowledge), aesthetics (principles of beauty), and metaphysics (causes and purposes) of their fields. Some of the reading and writing that you will do in social and natural science courses will, therefore, be humanistic, according to the definition we are using in this anthology. Similarly, a professor of history or linguistics, subjects we usually categorize as humanities — may ask you to observe phenomena systematically, meticulously record what you see, formulate hypotheses about your observations, design objective tests of your hypotheses, quantify the results when you can, and then draw inferences from your quantifications. In other words, the divisions between disciplines are not fixed barriers. The college curriculum at most schools, nevertheless, is divided into the sciences and the humanities, so that students will be sure to pursue with some thoroughness different processes for understanding experience.

Although most schools divide the sciences into two broad categories, the social and the natural (or physical), we believe that there are more important similarities than differences between the social and natural sciences; thus, we have decided to introduce the sciences as a whole. The major difference between the social and natural sciences is in subject matter rather than in approach. Social scientists usually study people and how they behave and live together as families, tribes, communities, and nations. Natural scientists study (among other things) atoms, molecules, compounds, cells, hormones, vital organs, planets, quarks, and humpback whales. Because the behavior of human beings makes systematic study difficult, even perilous at times, social scientists often seem to be engaging in activities that look very different from those of the natural scientists, whose specimens usually wait patiently in the laboratory for the next day's study. Social scientists often observe, videotape, and interview. Natural scientists often feed, withhold food, heat, freeze, liquefy, and dehydrate.

Still, both groups of scientists are committed to following the scientific method to explain the nature of the universe.

The scientific method is a way of seeking knowledge through observation and experimentation. Scientists formulate hypotheses — propositions tentatively articulated to provide a basis for further investigation. They design carefully controlled trials — experiments — to test their hypotheses. They record the results objectively and dispassionately, and study those results by tabulating, categorizing, adding, subtracting, dividing, graphing, and computing them. They then draw inferences — rejecting their original hypotheses if the results so indicate. The rejection of an hypothesis is not a failure; it is an expected step in scientific progress, leading to the formulation of a more plausible hypothesis that reflects the broader experience of the experimenter. The experiments may be based on large numbers of human or nonhuman subjects, plants, or chemicals. Changes may, in contrast, be traced in very few units over a long period of time or as affected by varied environmental factors.

The stereotype of the scientist working alone in a laboratory is a false image. Scientists are a tightly knit community, each one eager for word about the work of colleagues in the same laboratory or about similar work at another institution. The scientific method requires publication. Other scientists want precise information about subjects, equipment, and procedures. They may wish to try the experiment again themselves to see if they can replicate the original results. All scientists know that research is not complete until it is reported.

Scientists usually report their research in specialized journals, which are written for other scientists, not for the general public. When you, as an undergraduate student of science, first read one of these technical articles, you may feel as if you have wandered into a meeting of a secret society. Scientists need a place to report their work quickly and concisely to other scientists; to do so, they often use the kinds of shortcuts that close friends use when communicating with each other. Members of the scientific community, like close friends, communicate within a framework of shared experience and knowledge. This shared context identifies insiders to each other but may intimidate or even offend those outside.

Undergraduates who work as scientists will gradually develop the experience to gain full membership in the scientific community. Undergraduates who study science to enhance their general knowledge may never publish an article in a specialized journal or even read very many such articles after they finish school. However, we believe that all members of the liberally educated community should, when necessary, be able to seek information from specialized sources.

In this anthology we present a few examples of the scientific writing that was originally intended for an audience of specialists. The articles by Rosenhan, by Payne and McVay, and by Clark and Clark fall into this category. You may find these articles somewhat intimidating because you are in a sense eavesdropping on a conversation among research scientists. Since they are talking to each other and not to you, you should not expect to understand every word or to pick up every reference.

You will get the gist of the conversation because in each case we match the technical articles with essays on the same subject written for a more general audience. A *Newsweek* story precedes Rosenhan's study of the effects of mental institutions on the certifiably sane. Payne and McVay's difficult review article and Clark and Clark's research report, both from *Science*, are placed in the context of other articles about the songs of humpback whales, each written for a somewhat different audience: the general readers of *Newsweek* and *National Geographic* and the more scientifically inclined lay readers of *Science News*. In addition to providing you with the background you need to understand the specialized material, these sets of articles on the same subjects will allow you to study the effects of an imagined audience on a writer's prose style.

Other material in this section is written to be accessible to generally educated people. The selection by Mausner originally appeared in a textbook written to introduce the social sciences to adults. Dethier and Thomas wrote their essays to explain scientific concepts to the intellectually curious and to connect these concepts to the general concerns of daily life. Mausner, Dethier, and Thomas believe that scientists have a responsibility to communicate to the public at large. All three have published important research reports in the style expected of scientists writing to each other; all three also write books and articles to explain scientific concepts in a style accessible to readers who are not scientists. If more scientists learn this stylistic flexibility, then the public at large will be able to participate, at least modestly, in the scientific conversation — a conversation that may mean life or death in these latter years of the twentieth century.

In "Visual Thinking in Overview," Rudolph Arnheim, an experimental psychologist, is writing for a multidisciplinary audience of educators, art historians, and other psychologists. He is not popularizing the concepts he conveys; he is instead drawing on the specialized interests of people in a number of disciplines to promote his argument about thinking in pictures. Klockars and Bettelheim are also not popularizers; both of these researchers have chosen the difficult task of reporting their original research to the scientific community and, at the same time, to the public at large. Their books not only are respected by specialists in their fields but widely read and understood by the general public.

Peter Woodford in "Sounder Thinking Through Clearer Writing" proposes that all scientists, whether they are writing just for each other or for a wider audience, should write with logic, precision, and clarity. We agree with him in regarding writing as the outward and visible form of thinking. Scientific writing should be logical, precise, and clear because it is intended to give visible form to the scientific method. We believe that all liberally educated people should understand the traditions of science and the elegant methods developed to pose questions about the physical world and then to suggest possible answers based on empirical investigation.

5

Readings in the Social Sciences

The Nature of Social Science

BERNARD MAUSNER

from *A Citizen's Guide to the Social Sciences*

Bernard Mausner, the author of the following selection, writes of the social sciences as one road to human understanding. Mausner is himself a highly cultured individual who enjoys seeing the aesthetic treatment of human problems in plays or in operas as much as he values a more scientific perspective on human behavior. To clarify the social scientist's perspective, Mausner chooses an artistic work, Eugene O'Neill's *Mourning Becomes Electra*, and then shows how the various social science disciplines might approach the material of the play. Mausner's explanation clarifies a point we have been making throughout this anthology: writers in the various disciplines of the arts and sciences play different roles as they write. These shifting perspectives are reflected in the different questions that are important to writers in different disciplines. As a reader of the writing produced from these varying disciplinary perspectives, you should read with appropriate questions in mind. Mausner's article helps to set the context for conversations appropriate to the social sciences and to the humanities.

The article was written originally as the introduction to a book designed to present an overview of the social science disciplines to an audience of mature adults enrolled in continuing education courses. Although readers of Mausner's book, *A Citizen's Guide to the Social Sciences*, read this introduction first, Mausner did not write it first. The book originally began with what is now the second chapter. Mausner wrote the chapter reprinted here only after reviewers read the first third of the book and suggested that his intended audience might need a more accessible way into the text.

Mausner did not sit right down at his desk and immediately come up with the current solution. He wrote and thought, and he mulled over several ideas. He also went on with the normal routine of his life, which included attendance at plays and other cultural events. While watching a performance of O'Neill's *Mourning Becomes Electra*, he suddenly realized how the different social sciences might be used to explain the play and how he could shape that inspiration into an ideal introduction for the book.

A period of incubation followed by insight and reformulation is typical of Mausner's composing process. In an interview with us, Mausner described this process as including a lengthy period of germination, in which he walks around for a long time sorting out his ideas and shaping sentences in his head. When he is ready to commit his thoughts to paper, the process is like "spilling out of a computer," although he makes revisions after that stage. He acknowledges that his method requires a good memory and a facility with language. Not only is Mausner an experienced writer, he also speaks and reads several different languages.

Mausner suggests that for students who are beginning writers, his stage of carrying full sentences around in his head might be transformed into brainstorming on paper. Years ago, before his present method of composing evolved, Mausner used a dictating machine to get started on a writing project. He would compose out loud and ask a secretary to type up his notes. That version was never really finished enough to be called a first draft; it was still in the messy state that we call brainstorming.

Since students rarely have secretaries available to transcribe their brainstorming, you may have to reconcile yourself to taping or writing your own messy notes and then transcribing them on your own. Still you may find it reassuring to know that Mausner's lucidly presented selection resulted from the writer's long struggle to make words convey his meaning.

The Nature of Social Science
BERNARD MAUSNER

Most of us are intensely curious about why people do the things they do. We try to unravel the motives of our friends, our families; often enough our own behavior needs explanation. The daily papers are filled with mysteries, with unexplained violence in the streets and between countries, with odd acts by obscure citizens and great leaders.

Some of the things that people do can be understood without much difficulty. They sleep when they are tired, eat when they are hungry, seem to enjoy beautiful things and good company. But there are so many paradoxes. Why do fathers and sons so rarely understand each other? Why do great men, cheat, lie, compete for petty advantage? Why is it that the same person can be gentle and helpful at one time, cruel and destructive at another?

People turn to many sources for solutions to these puzzles. For some, the solutions come from the great religious systems. Religion often derives motives from warring spirits of good and evil. It is the devil who is responsible for human wickedness, God who leads us to doing good. For others, the answers may be found in the writings of humanists and philosophers. For yet others, the answers may be found in literature. As they read the works of Plato or Shakespeare, they find ideas that help them to understand the human condition, to predict and perhaps even control human behavior.

The social sciences represent yet another attempt to solve the puzzles inherent in the situation of man in society. This book is an attempt to present some of the basic ideas of the social sciences and the sources of these ideas. At no point do I want to pretend that the social sciences offer wisdom superior to that of so-called humanistic thinking found in literature, religion, philosophy, or the visual and musical arts. Let us say that there are many roads to human understanding, and the social scientist has chosen one of these roads.

In order to explore the differences between the humanistic and the scientific approach to the human condition, it might be worthwhile to examine a particular work of art, discuss the ideas about the nature of man presented by that work, and contrast these ideas with the results that would be obtained from tackling similar problems within the framework of the social sciences. I have chosen a great play by Eugene O'Neill, *Mourning Becomes Electra,* for this comparison. The play is a good one for this purpose because it not only provides an extremely vivid representation of a story set in a particular time and place, but also represents a retelling of an ancient legend in modern terms. It was intended to be a broad reflection on humanity and so gives a clear illustration of the scope of ideas and generalizations about human behavior that can be derived from the thoughts of a great writer.

O'Neill set his play in a small town in New England at the close of the Civil War. The action takes place in the mansion of the Mannon family, a great house of the kind you may still see in old sections of New England towns. It has broad lawns and gardens, a fine porch with Greek pillars. The rooms in the interior are large, hung with ancestral portraits, dark and richly furnished.

As the play opens, Christine Mannon and her daughter Lavinia are awaiting the return of Christine's husband, General Mannon, and her son Orin from the Civil War. The audience learns from conversation among some town people that the Mannons are a wealthy family of ship owners who have lived in the town and dominated it for several hundred years. General Mannon is not only a military leader, he has also been mayor of the town and the owner of its main industry. It becomes obvious that

Christine is deeply disaffected, hates her husband, and has betrayed him with a sea captain, Captain Brant, a relative of the Mannons. Brant is the son of General Mannon's uncle and a beautiful French-Canadian maid. Many years before, Captain Brant's father had seduced the maid, then married her. But General Mannon's father, who had himself been attracted toward the exotic maid, had expelled the couple from the household.

Lavinia accuses her mother of adultery with Brant and threatens to inform her father unless the adulterous relationship is broken. It is clear from much of this discussion that Lavinia is deeply attached to her father and hates her mother with intensity. It is also made apparent that Orin, her brother, is a dependent young man, very much attached to his mother, who went off to war reluctantly under pressure from his sister and father.

Captain Brant appears and tries to mask his affair with Christine by seeming to pay court to Lavinia. She is clearly both attracted and repelled by him. Much is made of the fact that Captain Brant looks like a Mannon and may remind Lavinia of her father. When Christine and Captain Brant meet alone, they plot to kill General Mannon.

General Mannon returns home. He has been touched by his experience of death in the war. He describes himself as having been unhappy because he felt rejected by his wife. He had turned to public affairs and to business because he felt unloved; he now wants to reestablish a loving relation with his wife. She is still repelled by him. Her reactions of disgust are never completely explained, although it is suggested they arise from revulsion over the physical aspects of sex during the first weeks of their marriage.

After a night of joyless lovemaking, General Mannon has an attack of angina; he has had warnings of heart disease. Christine gives her husband poison instead of medicine. Lavinia is attracted into the room by her father's cries and hears him denounce her mother before he dies. She discovers the poison.

Orin, who has been wounded in the war, now returns. We watch him revert to the intensely dependent relation he had with his mother. But when Lavinia informs him of Christine's liaison with Captain Brant, he explodes with fury. Orin and Lavinia trick their mother into going to the captain's ship. They overhear Christine confess to Brant that she has murdered their father. After she leaves, Lavinia and Orin murder Captain Brant. Orin tells about a fantasy he had during the war: he imagined, as he killed one man after another, that he was killing himself and his father. And then he sees the resemblance between Captain Brant and his father. It is almost as if he had actually killed his father.

When Christine is informed of Captain Brant's death, she commits suicide. Orin and Lavinia go for a long voyage to the South Seas and to China. Captain Brant had told both Lavinia and Christine about the joyous life of the natives in the South Seas. He had described the islands as a kind of paradise in which man can live free of a sense of guilt and enjoy the pleasures of love. When Orin and Lavinia return from their voyage, they are both transformed. Lavinia, who had been sexless and sticklike, now has become seductive — almost as if she had taken on her mother's character. She had worn black; now she wears bright colors. Orin, on the other hand, is no longer an engaging and impulsive boy. Instead, he is still and brooding, almost as if he had become his father. Orin feels haunted by the murder of Captain Brant and by the responsibility for his mother's suicide. He first tries to confess these deeds to two childhood friends, a brother and sister to whom Orin and Lavinia had been engaged. Confession does not dispel Orin's self-hatred. Consumed by his need for expiation of guilt, he commits suicide. As the play ends, Lavinia rejects life and goes into the great house. She closes the shutters behind her and prepares to live out her days in the dark, in perpetual confrontation with the sin and guilt of her parents' deaths.

A Humanistic Analysis

The play is about a single family, but it is also about all of mankind. O'Neill's message is that all of us live in a state of sin and consequent guilt. The sin and guilt arise from the relationship between father and daughter, mother and son. But the Mannons are cursed with a guilt that is greater than usual. They suffer from a strange combination of greed, lust, and pride of position in society. These forces lead to an inescapable descent into self-destruction. The sense of sin and guilt is contrasted with the free life of the South Sea islanders. These islands are referred to constantly in the play as a paradise of guiltless hedonism. But this is not only an external paradise. The islands also stand for that part of all of us that possesses the potential of living for love without the constraints of traditional morality. It is only because she has this potential within her that Lavinia could blossom as she does in her year in the islands. In that sense, the experience of life in the islands sharpens the internal conflicts that make life for the Mannons in Puritan New England so much of a hell.

O'Neill's work parallels the ancient Greek plays from which he drew the story. As you may have recognized, the story of the Mannons is based on that of Agamemnon and Clytemnestra, the ancient Greek king and queen, their son Orestes and their daughter Electra. Agamemnon was away from home at the siege of Troy for many years. His wife, angered over Agamemnon's sacrifice of their daughter Iphigenia to gain favorable winds on the voyage to Troy, has betrayed him with Aegisthus. The guilty lovers murder Agamemnon when he returns. Electra and Orestes kill their mother and her lover. Orestes is doomed to a life of guilty wandering haunted by avenging gods called the Furies.

The Greek plays, although they do deal with universal themes, are intensified because their characters are kings and queens, princes and heroes. In O'Neill as in the Greeks, it is the pride the Greeks called *hubris*, the defiance of the gods, that leads to the downfall of tragic heroes. The fact that the Mannons live on an exalted plane makes their relationships much more intense, their sin and guilt more unbearable, and their final tragedy so terrible. Still, despite the heroic size of the characters, one does have the feeling that General Mannon is, to some degree, a representative of all fathers, just as the tragedy of Orin is shared by all sons. And all mothers, like Christine, love their sons a little bit too much and feel rivalry toward their daughters.

It seems fairly certain that O'Neill's goals go beyond the telling of this particular story. He is trying to make the audience identify with the characters. He tries to impart an intuitive understanding of the conflicts among all fathers and sons, mothers and daughters, brothers and sisters as he draws his audience into the tragedy of the Mannons. In so doing, he achieves that purging through pity and terror, identified by Aristotle as the goal of drama, through which a work of theater reaches the universality of all great works of art.

The Theme of Mourning Becomes Electra *Illuminated by the Social Sciences*

The next few pages are devoted to a preliminary look at the way some of the questions raised by the play would be approached by social scientists. We examine particular studies and approaches drawn from psychoanalysis, social psychology, anthropology, sociology, political science, and economics. While the overlap among these areas is considerable, each has a core of its own. The next section tries to use the themes of the play for a first look at the orientations of these fields.

A Psychoanalytic (Freudian) Perspective. Why the intense emotion released by the relation of Orin to his father, Lavinia to her mother, each to the parent of the opposite sex? Is this a peculiar quirk of the Mannon family or a kind of feeling shared by many people? The ideas of *psychoanalysis*, developed by Sigmund Freud during the last part of the nineteenth and early part of the twentieth century, are ideally suited to a discussion of such a question. Besides, it is very likely that O'Neill was quite familiar with Freud. . . . [A] brief review of some of the basic concepts of psychoanalytic theory directly relevant to *Mourning Becomes Electra* might be a good way to start our survey.

Central to Freud's system is his picture of the emotional development of children. He based this picture on recollections, dreams, and free associations given him by his patients as they underwent analysis of their psychological problems. Freud proposed that when children are three or four they first begin to feel sexual attraction to others. The persons to whom sexual feelings are most frequently directed are the parents of the opposite sex. Thus, sons are drawn to their mothers, daughters to their fathers. A concomitant of love for the parent of the opposite sex is a feeling of rivalry and jealousy towards the parent of the same sex. The Greek legend of Oedipus, who killed his father and married his mother, was used by Freud to symbolize a supposedly universal pattern. The story of Electra, the source of O'Neill's play, describes the parallel pattern among girls.

The tensions of this period of development, the period of Oedipal conflicts, must be resolved before a child can go through successful emotional development. To Freud, the resolution occurs when the child, unable to possess his or her parent of the opposite sex and dispose of the rival, achieves a symbolic conquest by becoming as much like the parent of the same sex as possible. This process is called *identification*. There are two kinds of identification. The first is based on events that are almost inevitable in any child's life. Parents are usually warm and accepting towards their children. But sometimes a parent is distracted, feels ill or out of sorts, and then acts cold and rejecting. The child then feels under great pressure to regain the parents' love; after all, a three-year-old can hardly know that the change in atmosphere is purely temporary. One way to recapture love is by showing that you are worthy to be loved, that you are really a copy of the one you love. Thus the origins of one kind of identification.

The second kind of identification, according to Freud, occurs only among boys. As I said earlier, Freud really felt that little boys respond to their mothers with a very sexual, biological kind of feeling. Fathers are rivals; a boy's reaction to his father is a mixture of jealousy, fear that he will be punished (by being castrated) for his rivalry, and worship of a remote and authoritative figure. One way of reducing fear of being punished for rivalry with father is to become like him. This kind of identification is a defense against fear.

O'Neill's play lends itself to a Freudian analysis almost too easily. Lavinia tells about her feeling of having lost her mother's love. Her first reaction is hatred. After her mother's death, Lavinia clearly identifies with Christine, even to dressing like her. Orin fears his father's anger, has fantasies of killing him, and finally does kill a father-like figure, his mother's lover, Captain Brant. Orin, too, in the later scenes is shown carrying himself like his father, wearing similar clothes.

The contrast between O'Neill and Freud lies not only in the latter's systematic exploitation of enormous amounts of clinical experience, but also in Freud's explicit statements of general ideas about humanity. With O'Neill, the artist, we have to make our own generalizations on the basis of the implications of his work. We can see the process of identification vividly in the persons of Lavinia and Orin, but it takes a Freud to name the process and define its origins and consequences in terms applicable to all of us.

An Experimental Approach to Identification. Freud's ideas about parents and children are interesting, and they certainly help us in understanding the play. But the evidence for Freud's formulation is shaky. It is confined to the analysis of individual reports of childhood experiences from adults who came to Freud to be treated for emotional problems. Contemporary psychologists, characteristically, try to develop relatively simple experiments that they can carry out in the laboratory. In these experiments, they try to sort out the factors related to a phenomenon like identification and nail down the relations among them. Typical of this is the work of American psychologist Albert Bandura. He has been studying a process he calls *modeling*, the way in which children learn to imitate the behavior of others.

One kind of modeling that has been examined in Bandura's laboratory is the imitation of aggression. Bandura found that children imitated a model whose aggression was followed by reward more often than a model whose aggression was not followed by reward. However, when the child was placed in a situation in which his or her own aggression was rewarded, even those children who had observed an unrewarded aggressive model showed that they had learned how to express aggression. Bandura's work and that of other psychologists has been especially important because they have found that children imitate aggressive behavior, not only from live models, but also from films of live or even cartoon figures. The notion that the aggression in children's programs on television is harmless is placed in real question by the results of this research.

Bandura describes the process of identification as consisting of several components. First you have to watch what the model is doing. Then you have to make a kind of verbal code for the model's acts. So, for example, when a child watches a cartoon figure or an adult hit out against an animal, he might say to himself, "Gee, he's hitting the animal." This might be followed by his thinking, "Hitting animals must be okay." When the child is placed in a situation in which he can hit out against an animal, the fact that he has seen an adult model carry out the aggression is recalled and, especially if he can put the experience into words, he may act in a way similar to the model.

If Bandura is right, parents are not the only source of identification. Children obviously can model other children, especially older brothers and sisters. They can also model persons seen on TV, teachers, and other significant figures. Bandura's work also suggests that Freud was wrong in saying that the model necessarily has to be a source of support or warmth first, although the quality of the relationship obviously does have an effect. Note that Bandura uses *modeling* to denote single acts of imitation, *identification* a general tendency to imitate.

What does this kind of experimentation and theorizing tell us about *Mourning Becomes Electra?* It really does not add too much to the intuitive understanding we get from O'Neill about the way Orin and Lavinia model themselves on their parents. But it does suggest the history of rewards and punishments that shaped the young Mannons into adults. Even more important, it extends the pattern of development from the particular characters in the play to people in general. As we said before, this is also one of the roles of the artist. But the artist relies on each reader's or viewer's emotional reaction; the social scientist uses the force of objective evidence. Both tell us something about parents and children.

An Anthropologist Examines the Legend. We said before that one of the things that make O'Neill's play especially interesting is the fact that the theme occurs in legends from many parts of the world. To Freud, the legend and the family pattern it describes represent a reflection of a universal family constellation. However, as social scientists have studied societies other than our own, it has become apparent that this pattern is far from universal.

One of the first social scientists to discover this was the Polish-born English anthropologist Bronislav Malinowski. During the early twenties, he studied a group of people living on a South Sea island very much like the paradise described in O'Neill's play. Malinowski's people, the Trobrianders, have a family pattern completely different from that found in most Western societies. The Trobriander family revolves around the mother rather than the father; the society is therefore called *matriarchal* (from the Latin *mater*, for "mother"). In this society, family authority lies in the mother's brothers and father rather than in the man who is husband and father. Although a mother and father live in the father's village, the children are not under the father's discipline. The father is a kind of chum who gives the children presents and helps them learn how to hunt and fish and play games. But he is not an idealized figure, and, even more importantly, he has no control over the children.

If guilt over sexuality is a product of the conflict between a growing child and his father, who is hated and feared because he prevents consummation of the boy's love for his mother, then the Trobrianders' family arrangements may be responsible for their lack of a sense of sin over sex. They engage in sexual games before they reach puberty and indulge in intercourse quite regularly afterwards. There is, however, a clear transition from the fun and games of adolescence to the serious business of adulthood, marriage, and the rearing of children.

Since there is no sense of sin or guilt over sexuality, and since the child's father is not a source of authority, the Oedipal and Electra complexes described by both O'Neill and Freud are not known in Trobrianders. That is, boys do not feel rivalry with their biological fathers, nor are girls sexually attracted towards their fathers. There must be a strong, if unlawful, attraction between brothers and sisters, because the rules of this group forbid sexual relations between them; it is the Trobrianders' most powerful taboo.

One of Freud's supports for the notion that boys love (literally) their mothers and view their fathers as rivals is his report of a common dream in which a boy experiences his father's death and goes to his funeral. Trobrianders, according to Malinowski, never dream of their *father's* death but do occasionally see their mother's brother die in their dreams. And they do not seem to have dreams about their mother; rather, they report dreams of a sexual kind about their sisters.

Anthropologists like Malinowski broaden our perspectives. If we had thought that O'Neill's plot described a universal human problem, the study of other societies would correct this idea. The Trobrianders would write the story differently. They do not have tyrannical, hated, and loved fathers or seductive and possessive mothers. Of course, there are authority figures and mothering figures, but the force of emotion cannot but be thinned when it has to be spread among a number of uncles and grandfathers, aunts and elder sisters.

Clearly, in order to understand the human condition, we will have to look at people, not only in one particular society, but in a variety of societies. . . .

An Analysis of Social Setting. Even within one society such as our own, there are great differences in the way people live. To understand a family like the Mannons, we have to place them in a particular time and a particular social level. The play does that for us. It sets the time at the end of the Civil War. The Mannons are a prosperous family who dominate the life of their town. They have enormous pride, not only in their present social position, but, even more, in the traditions of their family. The play demands a social system in which people have maintained such traditions for generations. It would be hard to imagine the tragedy of the Mannons played against the shifting social scene of a suburb of Los Angeles.

Again, social scientists are able to provide us with hard evidence on which to base a picture of the social structure of a town. As it happens, there is a well-known classic of the social sciences that describes a town very much like the community in which O'Neill set his play. This is the study of "Yankee City" by a team headed by W. Lloyd Warner. Warner's work was carried out almost eighty years after the time period of the play. But New England towns change slowly. And so, Warner's intimate picture of his town is not only useful as an illustration of the techniques and theory of social science, but it also provides invaluable background for an understanding of the complex human problems presented in O'Neill's play.

Warner's method of studying his town was very different from the intuitive procedures of a novelist or playwright. Warner's investigators talked to a great many people living in various parts of the town. They tried to find out who worked with whom, who visited with whom, who belonged to the same clubs, who participated with whom in various kinds of social activities. From this careful investigation, a picture of the social structure of the town slowly emerged. Warner described a class system in which the descendents of ship owners and shipbuilders like the Mannons formed an upper class. Everyone in Yankee City was aware both of the superior position of this upper class and of the layers beneath composed of professionals and businessmen, white-collar workers, blue-collar workers, and, finally, "the people on the wrong side of the tracks." . . .

In O'Neill's play, the tragedy of the Mannons seems to arise inevitably from their position in the community. The Mannons have a set of ideas about themselves and about what is "right" for a Mannon to do that leads to an explosive clash between human desires and social customs. The original expulsion of Captain Brant's father and mother from the tight world of the Mannons came about because Captain Brant's father had stepped over class lines in choosing a mate. The wild desire for revenge that Captain Brant brought back with him arose from his fury over the elder Mannon's treatment of his mother. He tells how his mother had asked for help from General Mannon and had been refused, even though General Mannon was very wealthy and Captain Brant's mother was ill and destitute. In many societies, it would have been unthinkable that a member of a family be refused assistance under these circumstances. Only an upper-upper-class New England family with a powerful sense of pride in its social position could have been so heedlessly cruel.

The Mannons would fit beautifully into the upper-upper-class of Yankee City as it was described by Warner. In the 1930s and probably also today, as in the 1860s of O'Neill's play, life in the class of great merchants and ship owners was dominated by family tradition. The ultimate sanction is, "What would grandmother have said?" Of course, the tragedy of father and son, mother and daughter transcends the particulars of class and position. And yet, the details of this tragedy are worked out in a way peculiar to the circumstances of the time and place.

The contrast between the social scientist Warner and the playwright is not primarily in the outcome of their work. When you read Warner's account of life in his New England town, you get much the same sense of a rigid, class-haunted community that you do from the play. The difference is in method and language. Warner engages in systematic surveys of the community; O'Neill writes on the basis of his intuition and his own experiences. Warner uses a rigorous system of theoretical labels; O'Neill uses poetic language. To understand fully the strange story of the Mannons, it would be desirable to have the kind of experiences that O'Neill brought to the writing of the play. But, if you do not, systematic observations and theoretical discussions of the social scientist provide something of a substitute. . . .

Power and Politics. O'Neill's story derives some of its scope and grandeur from the wealth and power of the Mannon family. The townspeople form a kind of chorus, commenting on the action. Their comments place the Mannons in the social system. Their reactions give vivid evidence of the Mannons' influence. In telling the story of the play I noted that General Mannon is not only a military leader. He has been the mayor and owns one of the major sources of livelihood in the town. To understand the complex interweaving of the Mannons' story with the life of the town, one must be able to describe the political and economic system in which they exercised power.

The study of power is a central theme in many of the social sciences, but it is especially important in political science. In fact, some political scientists have defined their field as an examination of the sources of power and of the way in which power is exercised in the community. Political scientists use two empirical approaches to study power. The first is an analysis of social organization, and, more particularly, of forms of government. The second is a survey technique in which questionnaires are administered to samples of the population who are asked for their opinions about issues of political importance.

A political scientist named Robert A. Dahl has done an intensive study of a small New England city not very different from the one in which the Mannons lived. His study, reported in a book entitled *Who Governs*, looks at the way in which the city of New Haven, Connecticut, is run today but also includes some background historical material relevant to our examination of O'Neill's play. Dahl discovered that, in the New Haven of the mid-nineteenth century, the governing figures were very much like the Mannons. That is, they were people who had acquired great wealth through shipbuilding and other industry or the ownership of fleets of ships. They undertook a role in government as a result of a feeling that they owed it to the community to give it leadership. An unstated motive, perhaps not quite so praiseworthy, might have been a desire to maintain control of the community and to profit from their position of leadership. A man from this "aristocratic" group could move easily from his office in the shipbuilding companies into the mayor's offices and from those into command posts in the army. He would be used to wielding authority in a manner that would permit little questioning. The unofficial rules, if not the legal formalities, permitted this authoritarian system to operate; the New England town maintained the outward appearance but not the substance of democracy.

Certainly General Mannon fits this mold. He expects the unquestioning obedience of the townspeople, of the members of his family — especially his son — and of the common soldiers serving under his command. If tyranny invites revolt, then such organization of power both in the community and in the family invites the kind of rebellion shown by members of General Mannon's family, especially his wife. And the barely concealed hostility that the son feels towards the father and expresses indirectly by murdering Captain Brant may also flow from that power structure of the family, and, more remotely, the community.

Much of this is suggested rather than directly stated in O'Neill's description of the Mannons' story. The playwright sketches General Mannon's role as lawyer, judge, mayor, general by means of a few vivid comments by the characters in the play. From these you learn something about the exercise of power in mid-nineteenth-century New England. Dahl's study is more precise but less moving. He lists mayors, tabulates their occupations and social origins. He digs out documents that demonstrate the forces that determined the character of public life. From these he draws general conclusions about the exercise of power.

Economic Organization. It might seem that economics is pretty remote from the Mannons' story. But economic factors do play a critical role. If the Mannons had not become very wealthy through their shipbuilding and trading, they would not have been able to exercise the power that is the source of their tragedy. And they would not have had the freedom to take political office.

There are all sorts of ways in which economic power is crucial to the play. Orin and Lavinia are sufficiently properous to take a year to travel around the world. The Mannons' wealth and, even more, their economic power as ship owners allow Lavinia to threaten her mother and Captain Brant with the loss of his present job as a ship's master and with disbarment from the possibility of ever getting a new place. We are never allowed to forget the wealth and power of the Mannons; the haunting mansion with its great halls and ancestral portraits, its gardens, its pillared porch are an ever-present reminder.

But the Mannons, whose wealth was based on a living industry in the first part of the nineteenth century, represent a way of life that was dying at the time of the play's action. O'Neill tells us this in a vivid incident in which a sailor comes stumbling drunkenly into the scene just before Captain Brant meets with Christine. The sailor is a chanteyman; his job was to sing the rhythmic songs that paced the work of men on the clipper ships. However, he cannot find work now because sail is being replaced by steam, and he tells a sad, if drunken, story of the squat, ugly steamers whose coming foretells a new way of life in which he will have no place.

The Mannons also cannot adjust to the new world of factories, railroads, and steamships. In a way, Lavinia's withdrawal into her sunless mansion is a symbol, not only of the death of family tradition, but also of a retreat from the nasty, brawling, but explosively productive economic world of post–Civil War America. To be able to contrast the world the Mannons dominated and the world of today, you have to be able to describe the ways people work, exchange the products of their labor, and use money as a vehicle for these exchanges. It may seem farfetched, but one could argue that a study of the economics of nineteenth-century New England is essential for a grasp of the significance of the particular events of *Mourning Becomes Electra*. But it works the other way too. Reading the play could certainly enrich one's appreciation of the impact of economics on life.

Summary

In this first chapter, I have tried to sketch some general ideas about the ways in which social scientists approach human problems. We started with a special set of problems suggested by a great play and then contrasted the methods of the playwright with those of various kinds of social scientists. As we go on in the book, you will see how the analysis of dreams in the Freudian tradition, the laboratory studies of the psychologist or sociologist, the questionnaires, the reports from exotic places and peoples, the statistical breakdowns, the analysis of documents all contribute to a picture of humanity.

Before we go on to the substance of the social sciences, we must clarify some basic issues in their methods. The most important issues arise from the ways most social scientists organize their ideas into systematic sets of concepts called theories. In addition to defining what social scientists mean by theory, we should examine the relation between theory and the empirical investigation that is the major enterprise of every science. Lastly, we should look at some of the specific problems that make the work of the social scientist difficult. Among these are the difficulties that come from the relation of ethical and social values, the search for ways of handling the individuality of particular men and women in a scientific system, and the questions posed by interrelations among the various fields within social science.

Questions and Exercises

1. Read *Mourning Becomes Electra*. From the vantage point of any relevant course you are now taking — social science, humanities, or business — pose questions appropriate to the disciplines and then address these questions.

2. Name the social sciences Mausner uses in his analysis and define the type of behavior each one studies. Compare your definitions with those in the *International Encyclopedia of Social Sciences*. Check your college catalogue to see what other social sciences might be listed. Meet in small groups to compare notes on the areas of inquiry in each social science.

3. Draft an analysis of a popular television program from the view of the disciplines used by Mausner. Meet in small groups. Change the names of the characters in the program and see whether your classmates can guess which program you are analyzing.

4. *Mourning Becomes Electra* was written when Freudian theory was a more dominant influence on psychology than it is now. After reading the play and the two analyses from psychology — Freudian and experimental — find further support in the play for either of the two approaches. Compare notes with your classmates.

5. Reread "Araby" on pp. 176–80 of this anthology. Considering the courses you are now taking, pose questions about "Araby" that are similar to the questions which Mausner poses about *Mourning Becomes*

Electra. Choose one of the disciplinary perspectives. Draft an analytic paper addressed to undergraduates who have read "Araby" but who have not necessarily read Mausner's article.

Running a Fencing Business: Wheelin' and Dealin'

CARL KLOCKARS

from *The Professional Fence*

In the social sciences the observation of behavior is basic to other, more sophisticated skills. Psychologists, sociologists, anthropologists, and political scientists are trained observers and recorders of the behavior of individuals and groups. They know how to see detail and to record what they see with great accuracy. When you read case studies with an understanding of how and why they were written, you will get a better feeling for the important characteristics of the social sciences.

Carl Klockars, Associate Professor of Criminology at the University of Delaware, wrote the following case study because he became intrigued by the fact that among criminologists there was virtually no reliable information about "fences" — criminals who specialize in buying and selling goods stolen by someone else. A great deal was known about thieves, who constitute a more numerous and visible group. But fences inhabit a sort of twilight zone between criminality and respectability. They often have strong contacts with respectable people, who do not regard fences in quite the same disapproving way they see thieves. Fences do not break into houses, mug people, or embezzle. They act as middlemen between street criminals and people who, rationalizing to themselves that they are merely purchasing discounted merchandise, are prepared to buy.

When Klockars was in graduate school in Philadelphia, he sought out a fence and found one "Vincent Swaggi," who agreed to be interviewed. The interviews were not tape recorded, but Klockars took extensive notes, which he later verified through a second set of interviews with Swaggi. To double-check the wording, tone, and style of the quotations, Klockars asked Swaggi to read the material aloud. If Swaggi stumbled over any of the wording, Klockars modified the phrasing. After some two years of regular contact with the fence, Klockars wrote his doctoral dissertation on what a fence does and how he survives. He later revised his dissertation and published it as a book, entitled *The Professional Fence*, from which the following excerpt is taken.

Case studies, such as this sociological work, present unique problems as a form of scientific writing. Unlike quantitative studies, descriptions in case studies are vivid in detail and, therefore, are likely to be more readable. The difficulty is that science must seek the general rather than the individual: criminologists wish to know about fences as a criminal class, not about the particular characteristics of one fence. Thus, the burden is on the writer to show that the individual case is a representative one.

The writer of a criminological case study confronts an especially acute problem, for typically the subject of the study must be guaranteed anonymity. Thus, another criminologist has no easy way to check on the objectivity of the description in the study. In experimental science, objectivity is the essence of description. This objectivity is best verified by repeating the study. Another criminologist would have difficulty even finding the subject of this case study, since Klockars's fence is identified only by a pseudonym, Vincent Swaggi. Klockars must convey the genuineness of his description by the richness of detail, by the authoritativeness of his sociological insight, and by the reasonableness of his interpretations. Since no one can check his impressions of Swaggi directly, Klockars must persuade his readers that he notices the factors that a competent sociologist would find significant.

Klockars addresses this article to other sociologists but also to a wider public, who would enjoy Klockars's lively descriptions and Vincent's direct dialogue. But note the techniques Klockars uses to take the writing beyond a piece of investigative journalism. He uses Vincent's monologues (which are set in italics) to exemplify the general behavior of fences. Klockars's interest is in Vincent-as-fence, not just in Vincent the individual. Klockars classifies the people who buy from Vincent — "these contacts follow kinship lines" (p. 285) — and the people who sell to him. These classifications are part of the structure of the relationship between fences and those who deal with them; they are not just an accidental relationship that applies only to Vincent. Klockars uses footnotes, so that other criminologists can check his historical and theoretical sources.

In a letter to us, Carl Klockars explains more about his working methods as a criminologist. Writing is essential to him as a way of clarifying his thought, rather than being just a method of reporting his findings. To Klockars, writing is an extension of his eyes and his mind.

January 7, 1983

Dear Barbara, Barry, Gerry, Gail, and Elaine:

You have asked me to write something about my own experience with writing that would be of interest to the students who will read your forthcoming book. In a nutshell, what I have to say is that, for me, writing is inseparable from thinking. Rarely do I know what I think about anything important until I have written about it. In my work as a field researcher this truth works out as follows:

When I go into the field to study anything — be it dealers in stolen property, detectives, police informants, drug addicts, shoplifters or con artists — I bring with me, as any field researcher

Used by permission of Carl B. Klockars.

does, a whole load of preconceptions, expectations, and other notions about what I am going to see. These notions are a product of my previous experiences, what I've seen and read and been told. For the most part what I observe, ask questions about, and take field notes on during my first few weeks in the field is the way in which what I witness conforms to or differs from these notions.

As my field experience continues I begin to observe other things — ways of working, thinking, behaving, and understanding — that I did not notice earlier. I describe these things in my field notes as best I can, but because I have only a primitive notion of how they fit together or what they mean in context, my notes on them are always defective.

Sometime before my time in the field comes to an end what I try to achieve is an understanding of the world I am studying that is good enough for me to feel comfortable in it. What this means is that I know what to say, how to behave, and pretty much what others will say and how they will behave in most situations. Once I reach that level of understanding about a world I am studying I am ready to write about it.

It is important to appreciate that at this point, the point of being comfortable in the world I am studying, that I only understand that world in an intuitive way. To understand that world in a systematic, organized and principled way I must write. It is in the attempt to write about the world I understand intuitively that I discover what I know about it.

For me, the hardest part of writing is figuring out where to begin. In my work this means coming up with an approach to understanding the world I have studied that is broad enough for me to use to encompass all of what I am going to have to say and rich and powerful enough to allow me to deal with all of the issues I intuitively know I am going to have to address. For example, a book I have been working on for the past six years I have entitled *Criminal Work*. It is a study of detective level policing for which I spent eighteen months as a participant observer in the detective divisions of three different police departments. I settled on the organizing idea of criminal work because it embodies four themes I would have to address in the book. One is that detective work is work — a job, an occupation — and must be understood at least partly in job terms — overtime, salary, promotion, career, hiring, firing, mobility, scheduling and the like. All of these aspects of detective work are critical to those people who do it. Secondly, *Criminal Work* appealed to me because it is an "insiders'" term. It is what detectives in the agencies I studied called their work to distinguish it from the work other police officers did. I had much to say about the inside aspects of this work and this sense of "criminal work" would help me to say it.

Thirdly, I liked "criminal work" because I knew I was going to have to write about the criminal and illegal things detectives are inclined to do in the course of their occupations. Finally, I chose "criminal work" as a place to begin because there is a sense in which it implies that it is criminal, metaphorically speaking, to ask persons to do this kind of work. This sense of the term allowed me to write about certain tragic aspects of the detective's life.

So, the act of writing for me in this book is a matter of pursuing each of these themes through the experiences I have had in the field. By writing about them I come to understand them. I could no more understand them without writing about them than I could add a tall column of four-digit figures in my head. With any grown-up idea — and nothing else is worth thinking about — things get so complicated so quickly that to think about it without writing about it is unthinkable.

Best wishes,
Carl B. Klockars, Ph.D.
Associate Professor

Running a Fencing Business: Wheelin' and Dealin'

CARL KLOCKARS

The Wholesale Trade

As a fence, Vincent is a generalist. This means he is able to sell at a profit, and hence will buy, virtually anything that is offered to him. Unlike the specialist fence, who may be involved in trading only a single variety of merchandise such as jewelry, clothing, or office equipment, Vincent must have a number of buyers in different businesses willing to take what he has to sell. Vincent dislikes discussing just how many wholesale buyers he has and who they are, but I would estimate that at any one time the number doing regular business with him (once a month or more) is less than thirty and the number doing very regular business with him (once a week or more) is less than fifteen. (For Vincent there is never enough to go around to all his buyers.)

The frequency of a given buyer's business with Vincent fluctuates according to the market situation generally and with respect to the type of good involved, the opportunities for theft, which are related to the market situation, and the type of thief patronizing Vincent at the moment. For example, for some months Vincent bought adding machines and typewriters from a thief who stole nothing else. Vincent's buyer, a purchasing agent for a large corporation, traded with him every day. (Vincent suspects that after he bought all his company could use he became an intermediate fence for a typewriter repair and sales shop and a peddler of the machines to the employees of his company.) The thief who supplied Vincent would steal at least one machine a day and often two or three. The purchasing agent would come by at 4:30 P.M. five days a week and at 10:00 A.M. on Sunday (after church). When the thief was finally convicted (Vincent posted his bail and kept the machines coming for two months after his arrest), the typewriter-and-adding-machine trade slowed to a trickle. The purchasing agent now comes by only once a week and then often only to chat because nothing is available.

Sometimes Vincent may slow a thief down rather than have the authorities do so. I met a warehouse worker whom Vincent told not to bring any more electric razors because at the ten-a-day rate he was taking them it would not be long before the management would grow suspicious. The worker complained that he needed the money, so Vincent suggested hot combs, then electric frying pans, and then steam irons. Of course, when Vincent is obliged to suggest such a shift in the flow of items to a thief it naturally affects the availability of certain goods to would-be buyers. Vincent can suggest items to fill the needs of his own or his customers' inventories, but this has its limitations. For example, a shipper in a clothing warehouse simply cannot take cameras.

Because of the work and time involved in setting up deals with buyers, Vincent prefers the rather stable arrangements possible with shippers, drivers, and warehouse-worker thieves to the more irregular flow of merchandise that comes from store and truck thieves. When one has a regular arrangement it is possible to agree on a fixed price with both the buyer and seller as well as on delivery and storage routines.

> About six blocks from me there was this big plumbing supply company. I mean they had a half a city block which was just plumbing supplies. I got to know the guy who was the shipper. He used to come into my store. He knew what I had was hot stuff, so one day I asked him where he worked. He told me, Howard Plumbing, the big warehouse. So I kept talkin' to him and we made a little arrangement: when I put in an order for like a dozen toilets I'd get four dozen. I mean I'd pay for the one dozen but I'd get the three dozen free. He'd get the order in the warehouse and just load the extra on the truck. The driver didn't know nothin' about it.
>
> After we made that arrangement I started to look around for people I could sell plumbing supplies to. Well, before you know it I had half a dozen contractors givin' me orders for sinks, toilets, pipe, solder, everything to do with plumbing. Well, that deal lasted close to a year. They did an inventory and fired everybody in the warehouse. What did the shipper care? I'd say he made easy ten thousand off of me, and who knows how much off of everybody else he was doin' business with.

[I ask, "How much did you pay the shipper on each load?"] He got twenty percent on three for one. It's like this: I order one thing, he sends me four. I pay the company full price on the one and I give him twenty percent on the other three. Say he gives me four items which cost a dollar each. I give the company a dollar and him sixty [cents]. Each piece, averaged out, runs me forty cents. I sell it for eighty [cents] and give my buyer twenty percent off dealer wholesale.[1]

Although Vincent prefers such stable deals, they are never available in the numbers he would be willing to participate in. It is unusual, for one thing, to find a shipper who is willing to trade in the volume described in the above anecdote. Instead, Vincent has perhaps half a dozen arrangements with shippers who will supply him with three or four cartons of goods every few months. Vincent is happy with such arrangements because they almost never involve complications with the law. In the incident above, for example, Vincent enjoyed the possession of a legitimate bill for every item he possessed (although not in the quantity he possessed it), as well as a plausible story were he caught red-handed (shipper error which he was about to correct).

Because of the irregular character of his inflow of merchandise, Vincent's wholesale and retail customers are forever making known to Vincent the kind of merchandise they would be interested in. These requests may be regarded as standing orders. However, Vincent's promise to "keep my eyes open" for what they are looking for is no obligation on his part to fill them. Needless to say, such standing orders are important in affecting Vincent's decisions to buy when opportunities become available.[2]

1. According to this arrangement, if the shipper made $10,000 from Vincent the company lost $50,000 in merchandise.

2. Some sources have considered the practice of telling a fence what one wants as the equivalent of an order to a legitimate dealer. See Bruce Jackson, A Thief's Primer (London: Macmillan and Co., 1969, pp. 86–87. I believe this to be a distortion encouraged by the use of thieves' testimony to find out about fences. From the thieves' point of view the fence may often be seen as making suggestions or expressing interest in one kind of goods or another. From this the impression arises that the fence is filling direct orders. It is an impression that is accurate but incomplete. Actually, Vincent receives dozens of requests each week. They fall less in the "order" category than in the "let me know if you run across. . ." category. Requests to thieves involve not only customer demand but also an estimation of the thief's skills, the profit to be made on the items customers request, the seriousness of the customer's request, and the complications that might arise in attempting to fill a request. Vincent can accept the majority of thieves' offers of stolen property not because he has instructed his thieves to steal but because he has a kind of standing catalogue of requests.

It also bears mention that the fence sacrifices some bargaining advantage when he places an order with a thief. This is so because he creates an obligation to buy, may be obliged to offer an advance price, and divulges his need for the goods.

I suspect that Vincent does most of his trading with only a dozen or so customers. He can do so because a dozen different businesses, if chosen properly, can cover almost the full range of merchandise that is ordinarily brought to him. Indeed, five willing contacts — a small retail store (clothing), a drug store (cosmetics), a medium-size contractor (tools, building supplies), a market or restaurant (food, groceries, dishes, liquor, cigarettes), and an auction (almost anything) — in addition to his own store could satisfy the need for markets for the merchandise that ordinarily becomes available to Vincent. Having a dozen willing customers in different businesses not only covers the usual flow of merchandise but gives Vincent the option to choose whom he will sell to, an option Vincent exercises to "spread the merchandise around" and keep the price level up. In dealing in stolen merchandise as well as in legitimate merchandise one can make higher profits on small amounts than on large ones. . . .

The unwritten catalogue of standing orders is supplemented by information about Vincent's retail customers that may be called upon when quite special merchandise comes along.

> One day this truck thief walks in with two small cartons. He didn't know what they were even, so I got 'em real cheap. I dunno, maybe thirty-five for both. Well, each carton had two dozen dentist drills in it. So I wonder, where am I gonna get rid of this? I remember one of my customers told me his brother owns a dental supply. So I called him and he called his brother. Then his brother come over to see me. You should'a seen him! Was he excited! He gave me a hundred and a half for each case. Oh, I done lots of business with him since then. One time I got teeth, maybe five thousand teeth in one carton. You know, the kind they use for making false teeth. I stole it off the thief and he [the dental-supply-house owner] couldn't buy it fast enough.
>
> You see, you never know what a thief's gonna come up with. I mean the thief don't even know most of the time. So you gotta be ready for anything. You see, I got a buyer for almost anything. I mean we maybe do business once or twice in a year but I know where to go.

Thus, a by-product of Vincent's reputation among his retail customers as a dealer in stolen merchandise is the network of normally quite-removed contacts which he becomes aware of for special items such as those above. More often than not, these contacts follow kinship lines. For example, one of Vincent's customers who noticed a carton of children's ballet slippers on the floor of the store suggested that her cousin might be interested in them because she ran a ballet school. In this case the customer offered to check with her cousin and to report back to Vincent if her cousin were interested. In such a case, the customer is not only selling the merchandise for Vincent but is motivated as well by the possibility of doing a relative a "favor."

An additional advantage of Vincent's reputation as a receiver, and of his friendly associations with retail customers, is his tacit working assumption that they will be willing to act as intermediaries in the sale of stolen goods. Were they not willing to buy stolen merchandise, they probably would not be in his store to begin with. Thus, if he asks about a relative's willingness to buy (as in the dental-supply deal), the possibility that the customer will be offended is extremely remote. More likely the customer will react with enthusiasm at the opportunity to help both Vincent and his relative.

The primary advantage in dealing with Vincent is, of course, his price. Depending on the kind of merchandise and how cheaply Vincent was able to buy it, the wholesale buyer may get anywhere from twenty to eighty percent off the normal wholesale price. The largest discounts are probably given for exotic items (like dentist's drills) and goods that have a very low profit margin (like foods, especially meat). In both these cases, the greater discounts available are more a result of Vincent's bargaining strategy with thieves than of market demand.

There are advantages to dealing with Vincent. One is that one may obtain a bill for what one buys. Because Vincent is a licensed merchant, such a bill serves as a ticket to legitimize the purchase. Even if one doesn't obtain a bill, buying through Vincent places a step between the purchaser and the thief, thus rendering the buyer relatively safe from detection should the thief be captured. Many of the buyers who do not hesitate to deal with Vincent would have absolutely nothing to do with a thief vending the same merchandise.

Paradoxically, another advantage in dealing with Vincent is that no bill and no record of the sale is ever recorded, if the buyer so desires. This means that profits on the subsequent sale of the merchandise will not be declared for business taxation. With business profit tax in the neighborhood of fifty percent this can represent a substantial savings. . . .

Buying Right: Vincent's Trade with Thieves

Those to whom Vincent sells are, for the most part, businessmen who are aware of the intricacies of merchandising and know the market for the goods they buy. Those from whom Vincent buys are frequently inept and usually ignorant of the market for what they have to sell. They have often expended a small amount of energy for what they have, and frequently need money. Furthermore, they may want to get back to work or make a connection for drugs and are aware that they are in some danger so long as they have stolen property in their possession. Consequently, although the trade Vincent enjoys with those he sells to bears some resemblance to conventional market descriptions, the trade with those he buys from is likely to be unintelligible according to standard economic theory.

I do not mean to suggest, however, that trading between fence and thief is random. Rather, certain assumptions made in the analysis of normal economic dealing simply do not fit the fence-thief situation. For example, a norm that has governed the asking price of thieves for centuries says simply, "When you take something to a fence you should try to get a third of the value of the goods."[3]

Why should this norm exist? Why does it survive? What relationship does it bear to the economics of fencing? Let us first look at the simple economic implications of this norm. If the fence buys wholesale merchandise at one-third of its retail value he is quite likely to go broke. A $100 retail item purchased at $33 from a thief is likely to sell for $50 to $60 wholesale in the legitimate market. In order to be competitive the fence must sell below wholesale. Thus, if he sells at 30 percent below wholesale ($35 for a wholesale cost of $50), he will make only $2 on each item. At that rate he would be far better off economically in legitimate business. Consequently, the one-third norm must apply, if at all, only to those items which the fence will himself sell at retail cost.

But why does this norm exist at all? Why does the presumably arbitrary figure of one-third govern? Vincent remarks:

> You see, it's your small thieves who come in expectin' to get a third of the ticket. Boosters, snitches, guys like that. They know they can't get a half so they ask for a third.
> [I ask, "Why can't they get a half?"]
> I can get it wholesale for half. Why should I bother with them if I can do just as good legitimate. So they ask a third.

For centuries thieves have been asking for a third of the ticket price because they couldn't get half of it. I suggest that this is the only tenable argument in support of a norm that has existed for centuries in the trade between fences and thieves. The thief asks for one-third because it is the next simple fraction after one-half. What else would he ask for — two-fifths, three-sevenths, four-ninths? For many small thieves these fractions

3. I do not mean that the fence in fact pays one-third of the retail value of merchandise, but rather that the thief begins his bargaining with this amount. Certain types of goods, certain fences, and certain thieves have stood as exceptions to this "one-third norm," but the literature available on fences' prices supports my assertion. Cf. Danny Ahem, *How to Commit a Murder* (New York: Ives Washburn, 1930), p. 62; [P. Colquhoun], *A Treatise on the Police of The Metropolis* (London: H. Fry for C. Dilly, 1796), p. 188; Edward Crapsey, *The Nether Side of New York* (New York: Sheldon and Co., 1872), p. 90; Frank E. Emerson, "They Can Get It For You Better Than Wholesale," *New York Magazine*, 22 November, 1971, p. 39; Hans Von Hentig, *The Criminal and His Victim* (New Haven: Yale University Press, 1948), p. 401; Leon Radzinowicz, *A History of English Criminal Law and Its Administration from 1750*, vol. 2 (New York: Macmillan Co., 1957), p. 322.

do not exist! Even if they knew about them they would be unable to calculate the proportion of the price they represented. The assumption that there are fractions between one-half and one-third can be made only for sellers more sophisticated than the class of petty thieves who have operated without them for at least two hundred years.

The implication for Vincent is that bargaining need only begin at a third. Any fence can buy at a third; Vincent claims, perhaps more from pride than from calculation, "I never paid a third in my life."

The thief differs from the legitimate consumer of goods in a number of ways that bear importantly on his transactions with a fence. Unlike the legitimate consumer, he may have no real knowledge about the product he has in his possession. If the item is not labeled he may have no idea of its price. Even if it is labeled, he probably will not know if the price marked is competitive. Judgments about quality, market demand, and wholesale mark-up are difficult for the most sophisticated consumer; for the thief they may well be impossible. Finally, with high-cost items marketed to a social class different from his own, or items specific to a particular industry, he may have not only no notion of their price but also no idea of their purpose or use. Vincent is aware of such deficiencies in those who would sell to him and utilizes these deficiencies to his advantage.

Questions and Exercises

1. Reread the first paragraph of the selection. Design a table to show the number of Vincent's customers and the frequency with which they deal with him.

2. Vincent's speech is written to preserve his dialect — "gonna," "talkin'" "gotta'." Why?

3. In a dictionary of slang terms, look up the word "swag." What does this definition tell you about the fence's pseudonym?

4. What information does Klockars give us about himself in this excerpt?

5. On the basis of the information given here, discuss the question of whether Vincent is more like a business person or more like a thief.

6. Meet in small groups and try to reach a consensus about the function of each footnote in this selection. Does it give documentary reference? Does it expand the text? Does it reply to possible objections? In your opinion, why did the author include it?

7. List the advantages to the customers of buying from Vincent. Write an advertisement for Vincent's store based on the information you have, but be careful not to reveal that he is a fence. Meet in small groups to discuss the implication of your advertisements.

8. Why is a thief at such a disadvantage when selling to a fence? Draft a paper explaining this idea to an audience that includes your classmates and instructor.

Love Is Not Enough
BRUNO BETTELHEIM

The following excerpt from Bruno Bettelheim's book, *Love Is Not Enough*, is similar in form to the excerpt from Carl Klockars's book on the *Professional Fence*. Both excerpts are case studies, based on the assumption that the individual cases described are representative of larger questions.

Bruno Bettelheim is a psychologist, a clinician as well as a researcher. His special interest is in emotionally disturbed children, whom he treats in a special resident school, the Orthogenic School of the University of Chicago. *Love Is Not Enough* is an explanation of the philosophy and procedures developed at this school to help autistic children. Autistic children live very much in their own worlds; they are handicapped in their ability to relate to other human beings. Bettelheim planned his school to provide a totally supportive environment for these disturbed children. All activities are designed to support constructive emotions and modes of behavior.

Bettelheim's school is an outgrowth of the psychological theory he developed to explain autism. He believes that parents cause their children to be autistic by rejecting them in various ways. Bettelheim's school provides an alternative, therapeutic environment. According to Bettelheim's theory, an environment of warmth and complete acceptance will be effective in treating autistic children.

Bettelheim's views are controversial. Some of his professional colleagues claim that reports of his positive results may be biased. Parents of autistic children object to being labelled "emotional refrigerators" and charge Bettelheim with misrepresenting their relationships with their children.

In this excerpt, Bettelheim is writing to convince his professional colleagues that his procedures are effective. However, he is also writing for a wider public audience. Bettelheim writes so powerfully that his books are almost always bestsellers. His secondary goal is, therefore, to contribute to the public understanding of emotionally disturbed children.

By presenting a sample therapy session, this selection shows the reader how a therapist at Bettelheim's school makes contact with one student. The exchange is interesting to the general reader for another reason. The theme of this excerpt is jealousy, a basic human emotion, characteristic of those inside and outside special schools. The particular type of jealousy, sibling rivalry, takes an extreme form in the case of the emotionally disturbed child, Richard. Bettelheim knows, however, that most readers will be able to empathize with Richard because in their own homes they may have experienced the emotions that are so vividly described.

Love Is Not Enough
BRUNO BETTELHEIM

Jealousy is another of the problems which lend themselves well to being worked through in individual sessions. Jealousy is unavoidable, of course, in a setting where children must often share the attention of one and the same adult, a person who is important to all of them. Moreover, sibling rivalry has already aggravated the difficulties of most of the children so seriously before they came to the School, that they are driven to re-enact it in their new relationships. This acting out permits us to deal with it constructively, but in order to do so we must be able to help the child recognize it immediately. Otherwise, it can interfere so much with his relation to a significant staff member that the child is no longer able or willing to recognize the origin of his difficulty in the relationship.

Sibling rivalry must be accepted as a legitimate expression of natural emotions. But at the same time, the child must be helped to understand that his jealousy of another child (whom he views as a competing sibling) becomes exaggerated if he bases his relation to a staff member mainly on the fact that the adult also has a relation to another child. We must help the jealous child to understand that having to share the attention of a counselor does not mean he himself is rejected.

In the School this common emotional problem is not reserved for sessions with a therapist who is remote from the center of rivalry; neither is it re-enacted solely by means of dolls, nor expressed only in hammering or kicking games which can at best release nonspecific, unintegrated tension. Instead, we try as much as possible to deal with these emotions within a personal relationship, and in exactly the settings in which they originated.

Richard, for example, felt rejected all his life by a mother who he thought favoured his older brother. He had been seen in individual sessions for some time when he learned that his counselor was also to begin seeing Jerry (another boy in the same group) in individual sessions. We knew it would be difficult for Richard to take, and expected some reaction, though we could not know when or how it might come. It might be while the group was together, or when he ran into his counselor by chance, or perhaps in his next session with her. As it turned out, it was when she saw him the next day, individually.

Richard came on time but as soon as he walked in he turned his back. Then, without speaking to her he edged over to the candy box in a roundabout way, stuffed his pockets with candy, turned his back on her again and began to eat the candy, strewing the wrappers all over the floor. Since this brought no reaction, Richard pretended to stagger about the room and then began to grumble, though his counselor could not make out what he said.

After waiting for some time, hoping he might be able to say what was bothering him, she finally asked, "Richard, why don't you tell me what you're angry about instead of acting this way?" "I'm not angry," he said, but he turned away roughly and looked out of the window. After another short pause he walked toward her very quietly, grabbed the chair over which she had hung her coat (though there were other chairs in the room), pulled it forward as if he meant to sit on it, and managed to have the coat fall to the floor. Once it had fallen he stepped on it heavily and deliberately.

His counselor said, "I wish you'd tell me what you're angry about. You're stepping on my coat but I can't tell from that what's really the matter." He looked up at her, and after a moment's hesitation, he picked up the coat and put it back on the chair. Then he blurted out, "You don't like me anymore, you never do anything with me, you never take me any place, you never give me anything." When she asked him why he thought that, he said, "I don't know." So she asked him again what had made him so angry, and again he replied, "I don't know." She asked what had happened that made him feel he wasn't liked — what had happened that week, the day before. . . . When they came to the preceding day, his "I don't know" was less sure. Then he said, very slowly, "Well . . . I don't know."

By then his counselor felt that he himself had come close enough to the real source of his anger, and had also convinced himself that she still liked him since she hadn't been cross about his ignoring her at the beginning of the session, about his not wanting to have anything to do with her, or his stepping on her symbolically by stepping on her coat. (She was able to accept these things so sympathetically partly because she herself felt bad about starting to see another boy individually when she knew how it would make Richard feel.)

At any rate, it was here that she asked, "What about me starting to see Jerry yesterday." And now Richard was very sure of himself. "Yes," he said, and when she asked what about it, he replied, "You don't like me." But she assured him that her seeing another boy didn't affect her relationship to him, that she liked him just as much as before.

Then Richard asked if he could use the baby bottle again. His counselor said he knew he could, and he asked her to fill it for him. (Previously he had always filled it himself, but he had not been using the baby bottle for some time.) She filled it, put the nipple on for him and he sucked on it for some time, very content, and very much in contact with her. Then he said, "It's a long time since I started seeing you, isn't it? It's been over a year and a half," and he went on sucking the bottle. A few minutes later he said, "Patty, I never had one of these when I was a baby," and he looked at her provocatively. "That was a long time ago," she said, "and pretty hard to remember." He dropped that line then, and said, "Yes, I suppose so. I did use one when I was a baby but I can't remember very much about it."

Richard went on drinking out of the baby bottle for the rest of the session, and before he left he said a very friendly "so long"[1] to her.

It was as if, after first having convinced himself that his counselor was still fully accepting of him in spite of her also seeing Jerry, and after Richard realized that his feeling of no longer being liked was due to his own emotions and not to her actions, that he recalled the many pleasant times he had had with her in individual sessions.

He had convinced himself that even the most primitive satisfaction was still available to him with her and yet he had made one last effort to provoke her; this time not into rejecting him, but into providing him with a very special satisfaction; that is, by pretending that he was much more deprived than anybody else because he had never been allowed to enjoy sucking as a baby, and therefore had very special claims to indulgence.

When she dealt with this last remark realistically, he dropped his provocative behaviour. He was convinced, then, that she accepted his drinking out of the bottle not because she felt guilty about also seeing Jerry individually, or because it was a particular measure that her job obliged her to, but just because he enjoyed it. He believed now that she still liked him and he felt secure again about enjoying childish pleasures in close contact with her.

Questions and Exercises

1. Richard's behavior is described as "provocative." Give a dictionary definition of the word. In a paragraph explain why you think Bettelheim chose that word.

2. What is a participant observer? Look it up in your sociology or psychology textbook. The word is most likely to appear in the methodology section of the text. How could you tell from the selection printed here that Bettelheim's school used participant observers?

3. If you assume that among Bettelheim's audience are people concerned about emotionally disturbed children, including their parents and teachers, and also psychologists and counselors, to which audience do you think his title, *Love Is Not Enough*, is addressed? Who is likely to think love *is* enough?

---

[1] Participant observer: Patty Pickett.

4. Write two lists of words used to describe Richard, one a list of descriptive words and the other a list of interpretive words.

5. As you read the description of Richard's behavior, you may find yourself empathizing with him. What role does empathy play generally in the study of psychology? Is it ever appropriate? Discuss these questions in small groups.

6. Bettelheim relates the resolution of Richard's jealousy to his drinking from the baby bottle. What is the relationship? Bettelheim suggests that Richard could have made two other interpretations of the counselor's acceptance of his desire to drink from the bottle. What are they? Discuss these other interpretations in small groups.

7. If you had observed Richard's interaction with his counselor without the benefit of Bettelheim's interpretation of it as jealousy, would you have interpreted it that way? Enact the scenario in class. Then divide into small groups to discuss your interpretation. Are you still convinced by Bettelheim's explanation? Why or why not?

8. How might psychologists usefully generalize from Bettelheim's anecdote? Discuss the possible theories in small groups.

9. Jealousy is a common emotion, occurring among siblings, roommates, teammates, or co-workers. After jotting down some of your own experiences in your journal, draft a definition of jealousy that encompasses your own experience. How might Bettelheim respond to your definition? Develop these ideas into a draft of an essay defining jealousy for an audience composed of the readers of a feature column in the "Family" section of your local newspaper.

10. Scientific reports usually contain an introduction, a methods section, a results section, and a discussion section. Transform Bettelheim's report into these four sections. (See the introduction to Rosenhan, p. 295, for an explanation of the four sections.)

Sanity in Bedlam

from *Newsweek*

AND

On Being Sane in Insane Places

DAVID L. ROSENHAN

from *Science*

Following are two selections on the same topic written for two entirely different audiences. One is an article from *Science* by David L. Rosenhan, reporting his findings from a psychological experiment. The other selection is an article on Rosenhan's experiment that appeared in the "Medicine" section of *Newsweek* magazine. We reproduce these two articles together to illustrate how writing on the same topic can be directed toward the needs, expectations, and knowledge of different audiences.

Rosenhan's experiment was devised to find out whether normal behavior will be labelled abnormal and, therefore, a symptom of mental illness, when occuring in an environment where the observer expects abnormal behavior. The purpose of the experiment is to discover whether mental illness can be detected and identified as experts detect and identify physical illness. The premise for Rosenhan's experiment is that physical illness, such as measles, has the same or similar symptoms for everyone and can be diagnosed no matter what the situation or context. If mental illness, such as schizophrenia, is like physical illness, then it also should have detectable symptoms no matter what the context. Conversely, if a person is mentally normal, his condition will be recognized and he will be released from a mental hospital.

The experiment that Rosenhan created to test the diagnosis of mental illness illustrates the creativity required of social scientists. He had a group of people pretend to be mentally ill in order to gain admittance to a mental hospital. Once inside, they were instructed to revert to "normal" behavior. Would their absence of symptoms be detected by the hospital staff? Rosenhan hypothesized that the staff of the hospital would expect to see symptoms of mental illness in all the people who were labelled as patients. He wanted to find out if people who acted "normal" would, nonetheless, be labelled mentally ill only because they were in a place where the people were expected to be insane.

Rosenhan's methods differ from the case study techniques used by Klockars and Bettelheim. Rosenhan did not study and record the experiences of a single patient in a mental institution. Instead, he formulated an hypothesis about the expectations of psychiatric professionals and tested that hypothesis by accumulating quantities of evidence in a variety of institutional settings.

The study was reported in *Science*, a highly respected scholarly journal for scientists. Its readership includes professionals and researchers of all kinds, not all of whom are expected to be familiar with technical terms from psychology and psychiatry, so the language, although sophisticated, is not highly technical. However, the tone of the report is formal, fulfilling a basic requirement of scientific writing, that it reflect the objectivity of the research methods used. Note, for example, how Rosenhan creates distance between the experience of the pseudopatients and the report of their experiences. He says that "all pseudopatients took extensive notes publicly," not "we took extensive notes publicly," although, as he tells the reader, he was one of the pseudopatients. This distance, however, does not mean that he writes in generalities. Detailed observations, such as "35 of a total of 118 patients on the admissions ward voiced their suspicions, some vigorously," are the substance of thorough, credible, scientific reporting.

In fact, Rosenhan uses "I" in the last section, "Summary and Conclusions." There he draws inferences from his observations and thus feels free to use a pronoun that reminds us of his first-hand experience.

Articles reporting empirical studies follow a formal structure, usually divided into four sections: introduction, methods, results, and discussion. Readers of *Science* expect to find in the introduction a statement of the purpose and importance of the study and a description of where the study fits into relevant theories and research. They expect the methods section to describe the subjects of the study, the setting, and the procedures used to collect information. The results section is expected to contain the outcome of the study — that is, what actually happened in the experiment. Finally, the discussion section should include comment on the results and their implications. You should be able to identify these four sections in Rosenhan's paper, although Rosenhan integrates results and discussion. Note also that he uses subheadings to direct the reader.

In contrast to this format, the article from *Newsweek* distills Rosenhan's report for a general audience. Several hundred scientific articles, such as Rosenhan's, are published in scholarly journals each week. The editor of the medicine section of *Newsweek* reviews these publications and selects a handful for coverage, selecting the ones of greatest general interest and importance. Articles that are published in *Newsweek* and other popular magazines must be written in lively and readable language and must faithfully report the main idea of the study, relating it to the perspectives of a mass audience. You will notice that the *Newsweek* summary is easier to read than the original article, and that *Newsweek* concentrates heavily on the methods and results sections, while minimizing theory and interpretation.

Other differences in style also offer insight into the perceived audience for each publication. *Newsweek* personalizes the researcher by providing a picture of him along with some comments which he made directly to the *Newsweek* interviewer. *Science* acknowledges the researcher by a terse footnote, which gives only his academic affiliation and some background about previous presentations of the material in the article. The *Newsweek* account also goes beyond the actual report to dramatize the situation. Note, in the fifth paragraph, the disclaimer that the pseudopatients were not exposed to "the squalor and degradation of any modern snake pits." In light of the numerous exposés of state institutions in the popular press, the *Newsweek* article stresses themes with which its readers can identify. In this case, ongoing research in psychology is not as important as the "Catch-22" situation in which patients in mental hospitals find themselves. We present the *Newsweek* article first so that you can bring an overview of the circumstances to your reading of the more difficult article from *Science*.

While you are comparing styles of reporting in the social sciences, read also the earlier selection in this book from *Ideology and Insanity* by

Thomas S. Szasz. Szasz questions whether there is such a thing as mental illness at all, but his approach is quite different from Rosenhan's. Szasz's article, which also appeared in a scholarly professional journal, is not a report of findings, but an argument based on grounds that are philosophical, historical, and conceptual. These two different articles by Szasz and Rosenhan are included in different sections of this book because they discuss the same problem (what factors influence the labelling of someone as mentally ill?) but in two quite different ways.

Sanity in Bedlam

from *Newsweek*

The plight of the normal person who finds himself committed to a mental institution and unable to convince anyone he is not insane is a standard plot for horror fiction. But in a remarkable study last week, Dr. David L. Rosenhan, professor of psychology and law at Stanford University, and seven associates reported just such a nightmare in real life. To find out how well psychiatric professionals can distinguish the normal from the sick, they had themselves committed to mental institutions. Their experiment, reported in the journal Science, clearly showed that once inside the hospital walls, everyone is judged insane.

The "pseudopatients," five men and three women, included three psychologists, a pediatrician, a psychiatrist, a painter and a housewife, all of whom were certifiably sane. In the course of the three-year study, the volunteers spent an average of nineteen days in a dozen institutions, private and public, in New York, California, Pennsylvania, Oregon and Delaware. Each pseudopatient told admitting doctors that he kept hearing voices that said words like "empty," "hollow" and "void," suggesting that the patient found his life meaningless and futile. But beyond falsifying their names and occupations, all the volunteers described their life histories as they actually were. In so doing, they gave the doctors every chance to discern the truth. "I couldn't believe we wouldn't be found out," Rosenhan told NEWS-WEEK's Gerald Lubenow. But they weren't. At eleven hospitals the pseudopatients were promptly diagnosed as schizophrenic and, at the twelfth, as manic-depressive.

As soon as they had gained admission the volunteers studiously resumed normal behavior. They denied hearing voices and worked hard to convince staff members that they ought to be released. But such efforts were to no avail; doctors and nurses interpreted everything the pseudopatients did in terms of the original diagnosis. When some of the volunteers went about taking notes, the hospital staff made such entries in their records as "patient engages in writing behavior." The only people who realized that the experimenters were normal were some of the patients. "You're not crazy," said one patient. "You're a journalist or a professor. You're checking up on the hospital."

Crazy. During a psychiatric interview a pseudopatient noted that he was closer to his mother as a small child, but as he grew up, became more attached to his father. Although this was a perfectly normal alteration of identity figures, it was taken by the psychiatrist as evidence of "unstable relationships in childhood." The hospital, Rosenhan concluded, distorts the perception of behavior. "In a psychiatric hospital," he says, "the place is more important than the person. If you're a patient you must be crazy."

Rosenhan and his colleagues were not exposed to the squalor and degradation of any modern snake pits, but they did witness incidents of abuse and brutality. One patient was beaten for approaching an attendant and saying "I like you."

All this, the Stanford psychologist points out, is part of a pervasive depersonalization and helplessness that afflicts patients in a mental hospital. The experimenters found much additional evidence that the staff didn't regard the patients as people, or even in some cases, acknowledge that they existed. On one occasion a nurse casually opened her blouse to adjust her brassiere in the midst of a ward full of men. "One did not have the sense she was being seductive," said Rosenhan, "She just didn't notice us."

From their fellow patients, the volunteers quickly learned that they were caught up in a kind of Catch-22 paradox. "Never tell a doctor that you're well," said one patient. "He won't believe you. That's called a 'flight into health.' To him you're still sick, but you're feeling a lot better. That's called insight." "You've got to be sick and acknowledge that you're sick," says Rosenhan, "to be considered well enough to be released."

As it was, it took up to 52 days for the volunteers to get out of the hospitals even though most had been admitted voluntarily and the law in many states makes discharge mandatory on request in such instances on 72 hours' notice. Three of the volunteers finally walked out of the hospital. The other nine were ultimately discharged, but with the stigma of the diagnosis "schizophrenia in remission."

Rosenhan bears no ill will against the doctors and nurses who run the institutions he and his associates saw. The staffers' behavior and perceptions, he feels, were controlled by the situation, not by personal malice or stupidity. Perhaps, he hopes, alternate forms of therapy, such as community mental health centers and crisis intervention will increasingly replace the hospital in the treatment of mental illness.

On Being Sane in Insane Places

DAVID L. ROSENHAN

If sanity and insanity exist, how shall we know them?

The question is neither capricious nor itself insane. However much we may be personally convinced that we can tell the normal from the abnormal, the evidence is simply not compelling. It is commonplace, for example, to read about murder trials wherein eminent psychiatrists for the defense are contradicted by equally eminent psychiatrists for the prosecution on the matter of the defendant's sanity. More generally, there are a great deal of conflicting data on the reliability, utility, and meaning of such terms as "sanity," "insanity," "mental illness," and "schizophrenia" (1). Finally, as early as 1934, Benedict suggested that normality and abnormality are not universal (2). What is viewed as normal in one culture may be seen as quite aberrant in another. Thus, notions of normality and abnormality may not be quite as accurate as people believe they are.

To raise questions regarding normality and abnormality is in no way to question the fact that some behaviors are deviant or odd. Murder is deviant. So, too, are hallucinations. Nor does raising such questions deny the existence of the personal anguish that is often associated with "mental illness." Anxiety and depression exist. Psychological suffering exists. But normality and abnormality, sanity and insanity, and the diagnoses that flow from them may be less substantive than many believe them to be.

At its heart, the question of whether the sane can be distinguished from the insane (and whether degrees of insanity can be distinguished from each other) is a simple matter: do the salient characteristics that lead to diagnoses reside in the patients themselves or in the environments and contexts in which observers find them? From Bleuler, through Kretchmer, through the formulators of the recently revised *Diagnostic and Statistical Manual* of the American Psychiatric Association, the belief has been strong that patients present symptoms, that those symptoms can be categorized, and, implicitly, that the sane are distinguishable from the insane. More recently, however, this belief has been questioned. Based in part on theoretical and anthropological considerations, but also on philosophical, legal, and therapeutic ones, the view has grown that psychological categorization of mental illness is useless at best and downright harmful, misleading, and pejorative at worst. Psychiatric diagnoses, in this view, are in

The author is professor of psychology and law at Stanford University, Stanford, California 94305. Portions of these data were presented to colloquiums of the psychology departments at the University of California at Berkeley and at Santa Barbara; University of Arizona, Tucson; and Harvard University, Cambridge, Massachusetts.

the minds of the observers and are not valid summaries of characteristics displayed by the observed (*3–5*).

Gains can be made in deciding which of these is more nearly accurate by getting normal people (that is, people who do not have, and have never suffered, symptoms of serious psychiatric disorders) admitted to psychiatric hospitals and then determining whether they were discovered to be sane and, if so, how. If the sanity of such pseudopatients were always detected, there would be prima facie evidence that a sane individual can be distinguished from the insane context in which he is found. Normality (and presumably abnormality) is distinct enough that it can be recognized wherever it occurs, for it is carried within the person. If, on the other hand, the sanity of the pseudopatients were never discovered, serious difficulties would arise for those who support traditional modes of psychiatric diagnosis. Given that the hospital staff was not incompetent, that the pseudopatient had been behaving as sanely as he had been outside of the hospital, and that it had never been previously suggested that he belonged in a psychiatric hospital, such an unlikely outcome would support the view that psychiatric diagnosis betrays little about the patient but much about the environment in which an observer finds him.

This article describes such an experiment. Eight sane people gained secret admission to 12 different hospitals (*6*). Their diagnostic experiences constitute the data of the first part of this article; the remainder is devoted to a description of their experiences in psychiatric institutions. Too few psychiatrists and psychologists, even those who have worked in such hospitals, know what the experience is like . . . .

Pseudopatients and Their Settings

The eight pseudopatients were a varied group. One was a psychology graduate student in his 20's. The remaining seven were older and "established." Among them were three psychologists, a pediatrician, a psychiatrist, a painter, and a housewife. Three pseudopatients were women, five were men. All of them employed pseudonyms, lest their alleged diagnoses embarrass them later. Those who were in mental health professions alleged another occupation in order to avoid the special attentions that might be accorded by staff, as a matter of courtesy or caution, to ailing colleagues (*7*). With the exception of myself (I was the first pseudopatient and my presence was known to the hospital administrator and chief psychologist and, so far as I can tell, to them alone), the presence of pseudopatients and the nature of the research program was not known to the hospital staffs (*8*).

The settings were similarly varied. In order to generalize the findings, admission into a variety of hospitals was sought. The 12 hospitals in the sample were located in five different states on the East and West coasts. Some were old and shabby, some were quite new. Some were research-oriented, others not. Some had good staff-patient ratios, others were quite understaffed. Only one was a strictly private hospital. All of the others were supported by state or federal funds or, in one instance, by university funds.

After calling the hospital for an appointment, the pseudopatient arrived at the admissions office complaining that he had been hearing voices. Asked what the voices said, he replied that they were often unclear, but as far as he could tell they said "empty," "hollow," and "thud." The voices were unfamiliar and were of the same sex as the pseudopatient. The choice of these symptoms was occasioned by their apparent similarity to existential symptoms. Such symptoms are alleged to arise from painful concerns about the perceived meaninglessness of one's life. It is as if the hallucinating person was saying, "My life is empty and hollow." The choice of these symptoms was also determined by the *absence* of a single report of existential psychoses in the literature.

Beyond alleging the symptoms and falsifying name, vocation, and employment, no further alterations of person, history, or circumstances were made. The significant events of the pseudopatient's life history were presented as they had actually occurred. Relationships with parents and siblings, with spouse and children, with people at work and in school, consistent with the aforementioned exceptions, were described as they were or had been. Frustrations and upsets were described along with joys and satisfactions. These facts are important to remember. If anything, they strongly biased the subsequent results in favor of detecting sanity, since none of their histories or current behaviors were seriously pathological in any way.

Immediately upon admission to the psychiatric ward, the pseudopatient ceased simulating *any* symptoms of abnormality. In some cases, there was a brief period of mild nervousness and anxiety, since none of the pseudopatients really believed that they would be admitted so easily. Indeed, their shared fear was that they would be immediately exposed as frauds and greatly embarrassed. Moreover, many of them had never visited a psychiatric ward; even those who had, nevertheless had some genuine fears about what might happen to them. Their nervousness, then, was quite appropriate to the novelty of the hospital setting and it abated rapidly.

Apart from that short-lived nervousness, the pseudopatient behaved on the ward as he "normally" behaved. The pseudopatient spoke to patients and staff as he might ordinarily. Because there is uncommonly little to do on a psychiatric ward, he attempted to engage others in conversation. When asked by staff how he was feeling, he indicated that he was fine, that he no longer experienced symptoms. He responded to instructions from attendants, to calls for medication (which was not swallowed), and to dining-hall instructions. Beyond such activities as were available to him on the admissions ward, he spent his time writing down his observations about the ward, its patients, and the staff. Initially these notes were written "secretly," but as it soon became clear that no one much cared, they were subsequently written on standard tablets of paper in such public places as the dayroom. No secret was made of these activities.

The pseudopatient, very much as a true psychiatric patient, entered a hospital with no foreknowledge of when he would be discharged. Each was told that he would have to get out by his own devices, essentially by convincing the staff that he was sane. The psychological stresses associated with hospitalization were considerable, and all but one of the pseudopatients desired to be discharged almost immediately after being admitted. They were, therefore, motivated not only to behave sanely, but to be paragons of cooperation. That their behavior was in no way disruptive is confirmed by nursing reports, which have been obtained on most of the patients. These reports uniformly indicate that the patients were "friendly," "cooperative," and "exhibited no abnormal indications."

The Normal Are Not Detectably Sane

Despite their public "show" of sanity, the pseudopatients were never detected. Admitted, except in one case, with a diagnosis of schizophrenia (9), each was discharged with a diagnosis of schizophrenia "in remission." The label "in remission" should in no way be dismissed as a formality, for at no time during any hospitalization had any question been raised about any pseudopatient's simulation. Nor are there any indications in the hospital records that the pseudopatient's status was suspect. Rather, the evidence is strong that, once labeled schizophrenic, the pseudopatient was stuck with that label. If the pseudopatient was to be discharged, he must naturally be "in remission"; but he was not sane, nor, in the institution's view, had he ever been sane.

The uniform failure to recognize sanity cannot be attributed to the quality of the hospitals, for, although there were considerable variations among them, several are considered excellent. Nor can it be alleged that there was simply not enough time to observe the pseudopatients. Length of hospitalization ranged from 7 to 52 days, with an average of 19 days. The pseudopatients were not, in fact, carefully observed, but this failure clearly speaks more to traditions within psychiatric hospitals than to lack of opportunity.

Finally, it cannot be said that the failure to recognize the pseudopatients' sanity was due to the fact that they were not behaving sanely. While there was clearly some tension present in all of them, their daily visitors could detect no serious behavioral consequences — nor, indeed, could other patients. It was quite common for the patients to "detect" the pseudopatients' sanity. During the first three hospitalizations, when accurate counts were kept, 35 of a total of 118 patients on the admissions ward voiced their suspicions, some vigorously. "You're not crazy. You're a journalist, or a professor [referring to the continual note-taking]. You're checking up on the hospital." While most of the patients were reassured by the pseudopatient's insistence that he had been sick before he came in but was fine now, some continued to believe that the pseudopatient was sane throughout his hospitalization (*10*). The fact that the patients often recognized normality when staff did not raises important questions. . . .

The Stickiness of Psychodiagnostic Labels

Beyond the tendency to call the healthy sick — a tendency that accounts better for diagnostic behavior on admission than it does for such behavior after a lengthy period of exposure — the data speak to the massive role of labeling in psychiatric assessment. Having once been labeled schizophrenic, there is nothing the pseudopatient can do to overcome the tag. The tag profoundly colors others' perceptions of him and his behavior. . . .

. . . Once a person is designated abnormal, all of his other behaviors and characteristics are colored by that label. Indeed, that label is so powerful that many of the pseudopatients' normal behaviors were overlooked entirely or profoundly misinterpreted. Some examples may clarify this issue. . . .

As far as I can determine, diagnoses were in no way affected by the relative health of the circumstances of a pseudopatient's life. Rather, the reverse occurred: the perception of his circumstances was shaped entirely by the diagnosis. A clear example of such translation is found in the case of a pseudopatient who had had a close relationship with his mother but was rather remote from his father during his early childhood. During adolescence and beyond, however, his father became a close friend, while his relationship with his mother cooled. His present relationship with his wife was characteristically close and warm. Apart from occasional angry exchanges, friction was minimal. The children had rarely been spanked. Surely there is nothing especially pathological about such a history. Indeed, many readers may see a similar pattern in their own experiences, with no markedly deleterious consequences. Observe, however, how such a history was translated in the psychopathological context, this from the case summary prepared after the patient was discharged.

> This white 39-year-old male . . . manifests a long history of considerable ambivalence in close relationships, which begins in early childhood. A warm relationship with his mother cools during his adolescence. A distant relationship to his father is described as becoming very intense. Affective stability is absent. His attempts to control emotionality with his wife and children are punctuated by angry outbursts and, in the case of the children, spankings. And while he says that he has several good friends, one senses considerable ambivalence embedded in those relationships also. . . .

The facts of the case were unintentionally distorted by the staff to achieve consistency with a popular theory of the dynamics of a schizophrenic reaction (*11*). Nothing of an ambivalent nature had been described in relations with parents, spouse, or friends. To the extent that ambivalence could be inferred, it was probably not greater than is found in all human relationships. . . .

All pseudopatients took extensive notes publicly. Under ordinary circumstances, such behavior would have raised questions in the minds of observers, as, in fact, it did among patients. Indeed, it seemed so certain that the notes would elicit suspicion that elaborate precautions were taken to remove them from the ward each day. But the precautions proved needless. The closest any staff member came to questioning these notes occurred when one pseudopatient asked his physician what kind of medication he was receiving and began to write down the response. "You needn't write it," he was told gently. "If you have trouble remembering, just ask me again."

If no questions were asked of the pseudopatients, how was their writing interpreted? Nursing records for three patients indicate that the writing was seen as an aspect of their pathological behavior. "Patient engages in writing behavior" was the daily nursing comment on one of the pseudopatients who was never questioned about his writing. Given that the patient is in the hospital, he must be psychologically disturbed. And given that he is disturbed, continuous writing must be a behavioral manifestation of that disturbance, perhaps a subset of the compulsive behaviors that are sometimes correlated with schizophrenia.

One tacit characteristic of psychiatric diagnosis is that it locates the sources of aberration within the individual and only rarely within the complex of stimuli that surrounds him. Consequently, behaviors that are stimulated by the environment are commonly misattributed to the patient's disorder. For example, one kindly nurse found a pseudopatient pacing the long hospital corridors. "Nervous, Mr. X?" she asked. "No, bored," he said.

The notes kept by pseudopatients are full of patient behaviors that were misinterpreted by well-intentioned staff. Often enough, a patient would go "berserk" because he had, wittingly or unwittingly, been mistreated by, say, an attendant. A nurse coming upon the scene would rarely inquire even cursorily into the environmental stimuli of the patient's behavior. Rather, she assumed that his upset derived from his pathology, not from his present interactions with other staff members. Occasionally, the staff might assume that the patient's family (especially when they had recently visited) or other patients had stimulated the outburst. But never were the staff found to assume that one of themselves or the structure of the hospital had anything to do with a patient's behavior. One psychiatrist pointed to a group of patients who were sitting outside the cafeteria entrance half an hour before lunchtime. To a group of young residents he indicated that such behavior was characteristic of the oral-acquisitive nature of the syndrome. It seemed not to occur to him that there were very few things to anticipate in a psychiatric hospital besides eating.

A psychiatric label has a life and an influence of its own. Once the impression has been formed that the patient is schizophrenic, the expectation is that he will continue to be schizophrenic. When a sufficient amount of time has passed, during which the patient has done nothing bizarre, he is considered to be in remission and available for discharge. But the label endures beyond discharge, with the unconfirmed expectation that he will behave as a schizophrenic again. Such labels, conferred by mental health professionals, are as influential on the patient as they are on his relatives and friends, and it should not surprise anyone that the diagnosis acts on all of them as a self-fulfilling prophecy. Eventually, the patient himself accepts the diagnosis, with all of its surplus meanings and expectations, and behaves accordingly (5). . . .

. . . [T]here is enormous overlap in the symptoms presented by patients who have been variously diagnosed (12), so there is enormous overlap in the behavior of the sane and the insane. The sane are not "sane" all of the time. We lose our tempers "for no good reason." We are occasionally depressed or anxious, again for no good reason. And we may find it difficult to get along with one or another person — again for no reason that we can specify. Similarly, the insane are not always insane. Indeed, it was the impression of the pseudopatients while living with them that they were sane for long periods of time — that the bizarre behaviors upon which their diagnoses were allegedly predicated constituted only a small fraction of their total behavior. If it makes no sense to label ourselves permanently depressed on the basis of an occasional depression, then it takes better evidence than is presently available to label all patients insane or schizophrenic on the basis of bizarre behaviors or cognitions. It seems more useful, as Mischel (13) has pointed out, to limit our discussions to *behaviors*, the stimuli that provoke them, and their correlates. . . .

The Experience of Psychiatric Hospitalization

. . . There is by now a host of evidence that attitudes toward the mentally ill are characterized by fear, hostility, aloofness, suspicion, and dread (14). The mentally ill are society's lepers.

That such attitudes infect the general population is perhaps not surprising, only upsetting. But that they affect the professionals — attendants, nurses, physicians, psychologists, and social workers — who treat and deal with the mentally ill is more disconcerting, both because such attitudes are self-evidently pernicious and because they are unwitting. Most mental health professionals would insist that they are sympathetic toward the mentally ill, that they are neither avoidant nor hostile. But it is more likely that an exquisite ambivalence characterizes their relations with psychiatric patients, such that their avowed impulses are only part of their entire attitude. Negative attitudes are there too and can easily be detected. Such attitudes should not surprise us. They are the natural offspring of the labels patients wear and the places in which they are found.

Consider the structure of the typical psychiatric hospital. Staff and patients are strictly segregated. Staff have their own living space, including their dining facilities, bathrooms, and assembly places. The glassed quarters that contain the professional staff, which the pseudopatients came to call "the cage," sit out on every dayroom. The staff emerge primarily for caretaking purposes — to give medication, to conduct a therapy or group meeting, to instruct or reprimand a patient. Otherwise, staff keep to themselves almost as if the disorder that afflicts their charges is somehow catching.

So much is patient-staff segregation the rule that, for four public hospitals in which an attempt was made to measure the degree to which staff and patients mingle, it was necessary to use "time out of the staff cage" as the operational measure. While it was not the case that all time spent out of the cage was spent mingling with patients (attendants, for example, would occasionally emerge to watch television in the dayroom), it was the only way in which one could gather reliable data on time for measuring.

The average amount of time spent by attendants outside of the cage was 11.3 percent (range, 3 to 52 percent). This figure does not represent only time spent mingling with patients, but also includes time spent on such chores as folding laundry, supervising patients while they shave, directing ward cleanup, and sending patients to off-ward activities. It was the relatively rare attendant who spent time talking with patients or playing games with them. It proved impossible to obtain a "percent mingling time" for nurses, since the amount of time they spent out of the cage was too brief. Rather, we counted instances of emergence from the cage. On the average, daytime nurses emerged from the cage 11.5 times per shift, including instances when they left the ward entirely (range, 4 to 39 times). Late afternoon and night nurses were even less available, emerging on the average 9.4 times per shift (range, 4 to 41 times)....

Physicians, especially psychiatrists, were even less available. They were rarely seen on the wards. Quite commonly, they would be seen only when they arrived and departed, with the remaining time being spent in their offices or in the cage. On the average, physicians emerged on the ward 6.7 times per day (range, 1 to 17 times). It proved difficult to make an accurate estimate in this regard, since physicians often maintained hours that allowed them to come and go at different times.

The hierarchical organization of the psychiatric hospital has been commented on before (15), but the latent meaning of that kind of organization is worth noting again. Those with the most power have least to do with patients, and those with the least power are most involved with them. Recall, however, that the acquisition of role-appropriate behaviors occurs mainly through the observation of others, with the most powerful having the most influence. Consequently, it is understandable that attendants not only spend more time with patients than do any other members of the staff — that is required by their station in the hierarchy — but also, insofar as they learn from their superiors' behavior, spend as little time with patients as they can. Attendants are seen mainly in the cage, which is where the models, the action, and the power are.

I turn now to a different set of studies, these dealing with staff response to patient-initiated contact. It has long been known that the amount of time a person spends with you can be an index of your significance to him. If he initiates and maintains eye contact, there is reason to believe that he is considering your requests and needs. If he pauses to chat or actually stops and talks, there is added reason to infer that he is individuating you. In four hospitals, the pseudopatient approached the staff member with a request which took the following form: "Pardon me, Mr. [or Dr. or Mrs.] X, could you tell me when I will be eligible for grounds privileges?" (or " . . . when I will be presented at the staff meeting?" or " . . . when I am likely to be discharged?"). While the content of the question varied according to the appropriateness of the target and the pseudopatient's (apparent) current needs the form was always a courteous and relevant request for information. Care was taken never to approach a particular member of the staff more than once a day, lest the staff member become suspicious or irritated. In examining these data, remember that the behavior of the pseudopatients was neither bizarre nor disruptive. One could indeed engage in good conversation with them.

The data for these experiments are shown in Table 1, separately for physicians (column 1) and for nurses and attendants (column 2). Minor

Table 1. Self-initiated contact by pseudopatients with psychiatrists and nurses and attendants, compared to contact with other groups.

Contact	Psychiatric hospitals Psychiatrists (1)	Nurses and attendants (2)	University campus (nonmedical) Faculty (3)	University medical center Physicians (4)	"Looking for a psychiatrist" (5)	"Looking for an internist" (6) No additional comment
Responses						
Moves on, head averted (%)	71	88	0	0	0	0
Makes eye contact (%)	23	10	0	11	0	0
Pauses and chats (%)	2	2	0	11	0	10
Stops and talks (%)	4	0.5	100	78	100	90
Mean number of questions answered (out of 6)	*	*	6	3.8	4.8	4.5
Respondents (No.)	13	47	14	18	15	10
Attempts (No.)	185	1283	14	18	15	10

*Not applicable

differences between these four institutions were overwhelmed by the degree to which staff avoided continuing contacts that patients had initiated. By far, their most common response consisted of either a brief response to the question, offered while they were "on the move" and with head averted, or no response at all.

The encounter frequently took the following bizarre form: (pseudopatient) "Pardon me, Dr. X. Could you tell me when I am eligible for grounds privileges?" (physician) "Good morning, Dave. How are you today?" (Moves off without waiting for a response).

It is instructive to compare these data with data recently obtained at Stanford University. It has been alleged that large and eminent universities are characterized by faculty who are so busy that they have no time for students. For this comparison, a young lady approached individual faculty members who seemed to be walking purposefully to some meeting or teaching engagement and asked them the following six questions.

1) "Pardon me, could you direct me to Encina Hall?" (at the medical school: " . . . to the Clinical Research Center?").

2) "Do you know where Fish Annex is?" (there is no Fish Annex at Stanford).

3) "Do you teach here?"

4) "How does one apply for admission to the college?" (at the medical school: " . . . to the medical school?").

5) "Is it difficult to get in?"

6) "Is there financial aid?"

Without exception, as can be seen in Table 1 (column 3), all of the questions were answered. No matter how rushed they were, all respondents not only maintained eye contact, but stopped to talk. Indeed, many of the respondents went out of their way to direct or take the questioner to the office she was seeking, to try to locate "Fish Annex," or to discuss with her the possibilities of being admitted to the university.

Similar data, also shown in Table 1 (columns 4, 5, and 6), were obtained in the hospital. Here too, the young lady came prepared with six questions. After the first question, however, she remarked to 18 of her respondents (column 4), "I'm looking for a psychiatrist," and to 15 others (column 5), "I'm looking for an internist." Ten other respondents received no inserted comment (column 6). The general degree of cooperative responses is considerably higher for these university groups than it was for pseudopatients in psychiatric hospitals. Even so, differences are apparent within the medical school setting. Once having indicated that she was looking for a psychiatrist, the degree of cooperation elicited was less than when she sought an internist.

Powerlessness and Depersonalization

Eye contact and verbal contact reflect concern and individuation; their absence, avoidance and depersonalization. The data I have presented do not do justice to the rich daily encounters that grew up around matters of depersonalization and avoidance. I have records of patients who were beaten by staff for the sin of having initiated verbal contact. During my own experience, for example, one patient was beaten in the presence of other patients for having approached an attendant and told him, "I like you." Occasionally, punishment meted out to patients for misdemeanors seemed so excessive that it could not be justified by the most radical interpretations of psychiatric canon. Nevertheless, they appeared to go unquestioned. Tempers were often short. A patient who had not heard a call for medication would be roundly excoriated, and the morning attendants would often wake patients with, "Come on, you m-----f-----s, out of bed!

Neither anecdotal nor "hard" data can convey the overwhelming sense of powerlessness which invades the individual as he is continually exposed to the depersonalization of the psychiatric hospital. . . .

Powerlessness was evident everywhere. The patient is deprived of many of his legal rights by dint of his psychiatric commitment (*16*). He is shorn of credibility by virtue of his psychiatric label. His freedom of movement is restricted. He cannot initiate contact with the staff, but may only respond to such overtures as they make. Personal privacy is minimal. Patient quarters and possessions can be entered and examined by any staff member, for whatever reason. His personal history and anguish is available to any staff member (often including the "grey lady" and "candy striper" volunteer) who chooses to read his folder, regardless of their therapeutic relationship to him. His personal hygiene and waste evacuation are often monitored. The water closets may have no doors.

At times, depersonalization reached such proportions that pseudopatients had the sense that they were invisible, or at least unworthy of account. Upon being admitted, I and other pseudopatients took the initial physical examinations in a semipublic room, where staff members went about their own business as if we were not there.

On the ward, attendants delivered verbal and occasionally serious physical abuse to patients in the presence of other observing patients, some of whom (the pseudopatients) were writing it all down. Abusive behavior, on the other hand, terminated quite abruptly when other staff members were known to be coming. Staff are credible witnesses. Patients are not.

A nurse unbuttoned her uniform to adjust her brassiere in the presence of an entire ward of viewing men. One did not have the sense that she was being seductive. Rather, she didn't notice us. A group of staff persons might point to a patient in the dayroom and discuss him animatedly, as if he were not there.

One illuminating instance of depersonalization and invisibility occurred with regard to medications. All told, the pseudopatients were administered nearly 2100 pills, including Elavil, Stelazine, Compazine, and Thorazine, to name but a few. (That such a variety of medications should have been administered to patients presenting identical symptoms is itself worthy of note.) Only two were swallowed. The rest were either pocketed or deposited in the toilet. The pseudopatients were not alone in this. Although I have no precise records on how many patients rejected their medications, the pseudopatients frequently found the medications of other patients in the toilet before they deposited their own. As long as they were cooperative, their behavior and the pseudopatients' own in this matter, as in other important matters, went unnoticed throughout. . . .

The Sources of Depersonalization

What are the origins of depersonalization? I have already mentioned two. First are attitudes held by all of us toward the mentally ill — including those who treat them — attitudes characterized by fear, distrust, and horrible expectations on the one hand, and benevolent intentions on the other. Our ambivalence leads, in this instance as in others, to avoidance.

Second, and not entirely separate, the hierarchical structure of the psychiatric hospital facilitates depersonalization. Those who are at the top have least to do with the patients, and their behavior inspires the rest of the staff. Average daily contact with psychiatrists, psychologists, residents, and physicians combined ranged from 3.9 to 25.1 minutes, with an overall mean of 6.8 (six pseudopatients over a total of 129 days of hospitalization). Included in this average are time spent in the admissions interview, ward meetings in the presence of a senior staff member, group and individual psychotherapy contacts, case presentation conferences, and discharge meetings. Clearly, patients do not spend much time in interpersonal contact with doctoral staff. And doctoral staff serve as models for nurses and attendants. . . .

The Consequences of Labeling and Depersonalization

Whenever the ratio of what is known to what needs to be known approaches zero, we tend to invent "knowledge" and assume that we understand more than we actually do. We seem unable to acknowledge that we simply don't know. The needs for diagnosis and remediation of behavioral and emotional problems are enormous. But rather than acknowledge that we are just embarking on understanding, we continue to label patients "schizophrenic," "manic-depressive," and "insane," as if in those words we had captured the essence of understanding. The facts of the matter are that we have known for a long time that diagnoses are often not useful or reliable, but we have nevertheless continued to use them. We now know that we cannot distinguish insanity from sanity. It is depressing to consider how that information will be used.

Not merely depressing, but frightening. How many people, one wonders, are sane but not recognized as such in our psychiatric institutions? How many have been needlessly stripped of their privileges of citizenship, from the right to vote and drive to that of handling their own accounts?

How many have feigned insanity in order to avoid the criminal consequences of their behavior, and, conversely, how many would rather stand trial than live interminably in a psychiatric hospital — but are wrongly thought to be mentally ill? How many have been stigmatized by well-intentioned, but nevertheless erroneous, diagnoses? ... [An error in] psychiatric diagnosis does not have the same consequences it does in medical diagnosis. A diagnosis of cancer that has been found to be in error is cause for celebration. But psychiatric diagnoses are rarely found to be in error. The label sticks, a mark of inadequacy forever.

Finally, how many patients might be "sane" outside the psychiatric hospital but seem insane in it — not because craziness resides in them, as it were, but because they are responding to a bizarre setting, one that may be unique to institutions which harbor nether people? ...

Summary and Conclusions

It is clear that we cannot distinguish the sane from the insane in psychiatric hospitals. The hospital itself imposes a special environment in which the meanings of behavior can easily be misunderstood. The consequences to patients hospitalized in such an environment — the powerlessness, depersonalization, segregation, mortification, and self-labeling — seem undoubtedly counter-therapeutic. . . .

I and the other pseudopatients in the psychiatric setting had distinctly negative reactions. We do not pretend to describe the subjective experiences of true patients. Theirs may be different from ours, particularly with the passage of time and the necessary process of adaptation to one's environment. But we can and do speak to the relatively more objective indices of treatment within the hospital. It could be a mistake, and a very unfortunate one, to consider that what happened to us derived from malice or stupidity on the part of the staff. Quite the contrary, our overwhelming impression of them was of people who really cared, who were committed and who were uncommonly intelligent. Where they failed, as they sometimes did painfully, it would be more accurate to attribute those failures to the environment in which they, too, found themselves than to personal callousness. Their perceptions and behavior were controlled by the situation, rather than being motivated by a malicious disposition. In a more benign environment, one that was less attached to global diagnosis, their behaviors and judgments might have been more benign and effective.

References and Notes

1. P. Ash, *J. Abnorm. Soc. Psychol.* 44, 272 (1949); A. T. Beck, *Amer. J. Psychiat.* 119, 210 (1962); A. T. Boisen, *Psychiatry* 2, 233 (1938); N. Kreitman, *J. Ment. Sci.* 107, 876 (1961); N. Kreitman, P. Sainsbury, J. Morrisey, J. Towers, J. Scrivener, *ibid.*, p. 887; H. O. Schmitt and C. P. Fonda, *J. Abnorm. Soc. Psychol.* 52, 262 (1956); W. Seeman, *J. Nerv. Ment. Dis.* 118, 541 (1953). For an analysis of these artifacts and summaries of the disputes, see J. Zubin, *Annu. Rev. Psychol.* 18, 373 (1967); L. Phillips and J. G. Draguns, *ibid.* 22, 447 (1971).

2. R. Benedict, *J. Gen. Psychol.* 10, 59 (1934).

3. See in this regard H. Becker, *Outsiders: Studies in the Sociology of Deviance* (Free Press, New York, 1963); B. M. Braginsky, D. D. Braginsky, K. Ring, *Methods of Madness: The Mental Hospital as a Last Resort* (Holt, Rinehart & Winston, New York, 1969); G. M. Crocetti and P. V. Lemkau, *Amer. Sociol. Rev.* 30, 577 (1965); E. Goffman, *Behavior in Public Places* (Free Press, New York, 1964); R. D. Laing, *The Divided Self: A Study of Sanity and Madness* (Quadrangle, Chicago, 1960); D. L. Phillips, *Amer. Sociol. Rev.* 28, 963 (1963); T. R. Sarbin, *Psychol. Today* 6, 18 (1972); E. Schur, *Amer. J. Sociol.* 75, 309 (1969); T. Szasz, *Law, Liberty and Psychiatry* (Macmillan, New York, 1963); *The Myth of Mental Illness: Foundations of a Theory of Mental Illness* (Hoeber-Harper, New York, 1963). For a critique of some of these views, see W. R. Gove, *Amer. Sociol. Rev.* 35, 873 (1970).

4. E. Goffman, *Asylums* (Doubleday, Garden City, N.Y., 1961).

5. T. J. Scheff, *Being Mentally Ill: A Sociological Theory* (Aldine, Chicago, 1966).

6. Data from a ninth pseudopatient are not incorporated in this report because, although his sanity went undetected, he falsified aspects of his personal history, including his marital status and parental relationships. His experimental behaviors therefore were not identical to those of the other pseudopatients.

7. Beyond the personal difficulties that the pseudopatient is likely to experience in the hospital, there are legal and social ones that, combined, require considerable attention before entry. For example, once admitted to a psychiatric institution, it is difficult, if not impossible, to be discharged on short notice, state law to the contrary notwithstanding. I was not sensitive to these difficulties at the outset of the project, nor to the personal and situational emergencies that can arise, but later a writ of habeas corpus was prepared for each of the entering pseudopatients and an attorney was kept "on call" during every hospitalization. I am grateful to John Kaplan and Robert Bartels for legal advice and assistance in these matters.

8. However distasteful such concealment is, it was a necessary first step to examining these questions. Without concealment, there would have been no way to know how valid these experiences were; nor was there any way of knowing whether whatever detections occurred were a tribute to the diagnostic acumen of the staff or to the hospital's rumor network. Obviously, since my concerns are general ones that cut across individual hospitals and staffs, I have respected their anonymity and have eliminated clues that might lead to their identification.

9. Interestingly, of the 12 admissions, 11 were diagnosed as schizophrenic and one, with the identical symptomatology, as manic-depressive psychosis. This diagnosis has a more favorable prognosis, and it was given by the only private hospital in our sample. On the relations between social class and psychiatric diagnosis, see A. deB. Hollingshead and F. C. Redlich, *Social Class and Mental Illness: A Community Study* (Wiley, New York, 1958).

10. It is possible, of course, that patients have quite broad latitudes in diagnosis and therefore are inclined to call many people sane, even those whose behavior is patently aberrant. However, although we have no hard data on this matter, it was our distinct impression that this was not the case. In many instances, patients not only singled us out for attention, but came to imitate our behaviors and styles.

11. For an example of a similar self fulfilling prophecy, in this instance dealing with the "central" trait of intelligence, see R. Rosenthal and L. Jacobson, *Pygmalion in the Classroom* (Holt, Rinehart & Winston, New York, 1968).

12. E. Zigler and L. Phillips, *J. Abnorm. Soc. Psychol.* 63, 69 (1961). See also R. K. Freudenberg and J. P. Robertson, *A.M.A. Arch. Neurol. Psychiatr.* 76, 14 (1956).

13. W. Mischel, *Personality and Assessment* (Wiley, New York, 1968).

14. T. R. Sarbin and J. C. Mancuso, *J. Clin. Consult. Psychol.* 35, 159 (1970); T. R. Sarbin, *ibid.* 31, 447 (1967); J. C. Nunnally, Jr., *Popular Conceptions of Mental Health* (Holt, Rinehart & Winston, New York, 1961).

15. A. H. Stanton and M. S. Schwartz, *The Mental Hospital: A Study of Institutional Participation in Psychiatric Illness and Treatment* (Basic, New York, 1954).

16. D. B. Wexler and S. E. Scoville, *Ariz. Law Rev.* 13, 1 (1971).

17. I thank W. Mischel, E. Orne, and M. S. Rosenhan for comments on an earlier draft of this manuscript.

Questions and Exercises

1. What is the main purpose of Rosenhan's study? Write a one-sentence statement of the hypothesis for the research.

2. Rosenhan believes that being a mental patient causes a person to feel helpless and depersonalized. What evidence does he use to illustrate this phenomenon in the mental hospitals?

3. A patient in a mental hospital has a label that influences the interactions of everyone with whom he or she comes in contact. List the incidents that Rosenhan cites to illustrate the phenomenon of labelling.

4. Find the paragraph that describes the eight pseudopatients. Pretend that a study is being conducted on the composition skills of the members of your composition class. Draft a paragraph describing your class as though they were subjects in this study.

5. What context of theory and other research does Rosenhan offer for his study? Draft a one-paragraph summary of the context.

6. In Rosenhan's article, find instances of specific observations of behavior. Analyze what characteristics of those descriptions make them valuable observations. Meet in small groups to discuss these characteristics and to reach consensus about the function of the descriptions.

7. Study the *Newsweek* and *Science* articles for differences in vocabulary and in length of sentences. After you have prepared notes on these stylistic matters, meet in small groups to compare your findings and to reach consensus on the style of each article.

8. How does the label "student" influence people's perceptions of you? List as many examples as possible of situations in which people have acted toward you as a "student" rather than as an individual. Meet in small groups to compare your lists. Then draft an essay explaining the effects of the label "student" on others' perception of you and on your perception of yourself. Your audience for this essay is composed of your classmates and your professor.

9. Reread Thomas Szasz's essay on pp. 235–45. Draft a letter that Szasz might write to Rosenhan about the connections between their articles.

10. Write a *Newsweek*-type article based on the Woodford article, "Sounder Thinking Through Clearer Writing" (pp. 322–28). Remember that the *Newsweek* audience differs from the *Science* audience.

Visual Thinking in Overview

RUDOLF ARNHEIM

from *Perception and Pictorial Representation*

What is the relationship between thinking and seeing? When we see something are we by definition thinking about it? Social scientists, particularly psychologists, are interested in this question. Perception — the psychological process of gathering information about the external world through the senses — used to be considered a process of a lower order than thinking. Rudolf Arnheim, an experimental psychologist whose study of art spans more than forty years, helped to pioneer the idea that perception and thinking are interdependent processes of equal importance. Productive thinking, according to Arnheim, whether in philosophy or science or art, involves sensory information and visual images. We think in images, says Arnheim; visual thinking gives "flesh and blood to the structural skeletons of ideas."

We usually assume that art historians study paintings and that psychologists study rats, but Arnheim brings social science questions to the realm of the fine arts. How do observers experience works of art? How do individuals create formally arranged visual images? Arnheim's systematic study of cognitive processes identifies him as a social scientist. Humanists also pose questions about seeing, knowing, understanding, and creating, but their questions address matters of aesthetics, value, and interpretation. Arnheim focuses on how the mind works when the eye sees.

Early in his career, Arnheim did theoretical work on how the eye and the mind process works of art. This work led him to the position, explained in the following article, that visual literacy should be encouraged in every child's education. Children need to be taught how to see. The ability to use visual symbols, he says, allows an individual to solve intellectual problems that might go unsolved if left only in verbal form. Arnheim's concern with the educational implications of his theoretical work places much of his writing in another subdivision of the social sciences, art education.

The essay reproduced here was originally part of an invited address delivered to a meeting of educational psychologists. Arnheim's audience, therefore, were well informed about psychology in general but were not necessarily familiar with his theories and ideas. His purpose was to convince this influential audience that their views of the educational needs of their students must be broadened to include visual thinking as part of the general definition of thinking. The members of Arnheim's original audience were not necessarily hostile to his ideas, but they must be thought of as skeptical — that is, they needed to be convinced. As you read, you should pay attention not only to the nature of Arnheim's argument, but also to the examples he uses for support and illustration. These were, obviously, selected carefully to appeal to educational psychologists.

His original address was later modified into the present essay, which appeared as the foreword to a book containing the proceedings of an unusual conference, at which psychologists, philosophers, art critics, and studio artists all presented papers on visual thinking. It is, we think, appropriate that Arnheim's paper linked two interdisciplinary meetings because his career has been devoted to promoting conversations across disciplinary barriers.

Visual Thinking in Overview
RUDOLF ARNHEIM

In recent years, the notion of visual thinking has made its appearance everywhere. This cannot but give me some personal satisfaction (Arnheim 1969). But it also astonishes me because according to the long tradition of Western philosophy and psychology, the two concepts of perception and reasoning do not belong under the same bedcover. One can characterize the traditional view by saying that the two concepts are believed to require but also to exclude each other.

Perceiving and thinking require each other. They complement each other's functions. The task of perception is supposed to be limited to collecting the raw materials for cognition. Once the material has been gathered, thinking enters the scene, at a higher level of the mind, and does the processing. Perception would be useless without thinking; thinking without perception would have nothing to think about.

But according to the traditional view, the two mental functions also exclude each other, since perception, supposedly, can deal only with individual instances. George Berkeley extended this belief to mental images and insisted that nobody can picture in his or her mind an idea such as "man" as a generality: one can visualize only a tall or a short man or a white or a black one but not man as such. Thinking, on the other hand, is said to handle only generalities. It cannot tolerate the presence of particular things. If, for example, to reason about the nature of man, any image of a particular man would lead me astray.

This supposed incompatibility of mental functions, which nevertheless cannot do without each other, has disturbed philosophers throughout the history of the Western world. It led to an underestimation of the senses and promoted thought to a splendid isolation, which threatened it with sterility. In education, it made for a strict distinction between the necessary and honorable study of words and numbers and the luxury of a slightly indecent concern with the senses. When nowadays, the budget for the teaching of the arts is the first to be cut, as soon as the school system of a city is in financial trouble, we are still heirs to the pernicious split that has hampered our educational thinking for so long. . . .

The fact that thinking of this kind must take place in the perceptual realm because there is no other place to go is concealed by the belief that reasoning can only be done through language. I can observe here only that although language is a valuable help in much human thinking, it is neither indispensable nor can it serve as the medium in which thinking takes place (Arnheim 1969, chap 13). It should be obvious that language consists of sounds or visual signs that possess none of the properties of the things to be manipulated in a problem situation. In order to think productively about the nature of, say, liberty, one needs a medium of thought in which the properties of liberty can be represented. Productive thinking is done by means of the things to which language refers — referents that in themselves are not verbal but perceptual. What else could they be?

As a further example, I would like to raise a question that is particularly relevant to psychology, namely, In what medium do we think about mental processes? Sigmund Freud in one of the few diagrams that accompany his theories illustrated the relation between two triads of concepts: id, ego, and superego and unconscious, preconscious, and conscious (Freud 1933). His drawing presents these terms in a vertical section through a bulgy container, a kind of abstract architecture. (See Figure F.1.) The psychological relations are shown as spatial relations, from which we are asked to infer the places and directions of the mental forces that Freud's model is intended to illustrate. These forces, although not represented in the picture, are as perceptual as the space in which they are shown to act. It is well-known that Freud made them behave like hydraulic forces — an image that imposed certain constraints on his thinking.

Note here that Freud's drawing was not a mere teaching device, used in his lectures to facilitate the understanding of processes about which he himself thought in a different medium. No, he portrays them precisely in the medium in which he himself was thinking, well aware though he was that he was thinking in analogies. Whoever hesitates to believe this is invited to ask himself in what other medium Freud — or, for that matter, any other psychologist — could have done his or her reasoning. If the hydraulic model was imperfect, it had to be replaced by a more suitable image, perhaps a more kinesthetic one. But perceptual it had to be. Unless Freud, instead of engaging in productive thinking, had limited himself to trying out new combinations of properties his concepts already possessed, in which case an inexpensive computer would have done equally well. . . .

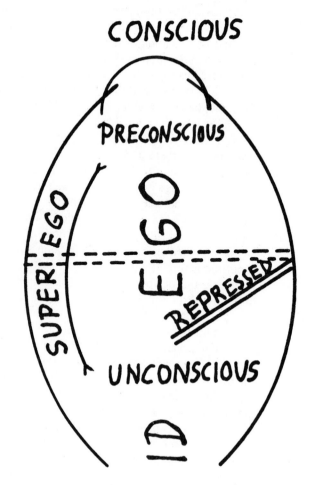

Figure F.1 Sigmund Freud's diagram of the relation between two triads of concepts: id, ego, and superego and unconscious, preconscious, and conscious (after Sigmund Freud *Neue Vorlesungen zur Einführung in die Psychoanalyse*).

... [T]he term "Visual Thinking" refers only to one facet of our subject. It fails to indicate that vision is only one of the senses that serve perception — kinesthesia being another important one. It also does not claim, as it should, that *all* productive thinking (as distinguished from the mechanical manipulation of data) must be perceptual. Once we acknowledge that thinking has a perceptual base, we must also consider the mirror image of this claim, namely, that all perception involves aspects of thought.

These claims cannot but be profoundly relevant to education, and I propose to devote the remainder of this foreword to a few more specific remarks on this subject. The teaching of the arts, an exclusively visual matter, seems to deserve a prominent place here. But this responsibility is not always clearly faced. We hear art educators say that the arts are needed to create a well-rounded person, although it is not obvious that being well rounded is better than being slim. We hear that the arts give pleasure but are not told why and to what useful end. We hear of self-expression and emotional outlets and the liberation of individuality. But rarely is there an emphasis on the art room or studio as a training ground for visual thinking. Yet every art teacher knows from experience that drawing, painting, or sculpture, properly conceived, pose cognitive problems worthy of a good brain and every bit as exacting as a mathematical or scientific puzzle.

How does one render in a picture the characteristic aspects of an object or event? How does not create space, depth, movement; how does one create balance and unity? How do the arts help the young mind comprehend the confusing complexity of the world it is facing? These problems will be productively approached by the students only if the teacher encourages them to rely on their own intelligence and imagination rather than on mechanical tricks. One of the great educational advantages of art work is that a minimum of technical instruction suffices to supply students with the instruments needed for the independent development of their own mental resources.

Art work, intelligently pursued, lets the student take conscious possession of the various aspects of perceptual experience. For example, the three dimensions of space, which are available for practical use in daily life from infancy on, must be conquered, step by step, in sculpture. Such competent handling of spatial relations, acquired in the art room, is of direct professional benefit for such activities as surgery or engineering. The ability to visualize the complex properties of three-dimensional objects in space is needed for artistic, scientific, and technological tasks.

So directly and indirectly connected are the exploration of perceptual space and the categories of theoretical thinking that the former is the best training ground for the latter.... It stands to reason that a person familiar with the intricacies of perceptual relations will be equipped to deal more imaginatively with the properties of theoretical concepts, such as inclusion, exclusion, dependence, interference, channels, barriers, sequence, random arrangement, and so forth.

What, then, are some of the desiderata of visual thinking for the various fields of teaching and learning? Let me mention the consequences for the use of language, an instrument needed by them all. If we look at language with some affectionate attention, we find that many so-called abstract terms still contain the perceivable practical qualities and activities from which they were originally derived. Words are monuments to the close kinship between perceptual experience and theoretical reasoning. They can promote the cross-fertilization between the two when in the use of language, attention is paid to the perceptual matrices from which intellectual terminology is derived. This is the specialty of poets and other writers. They know how to revive the fossils buried in words and, thereby, to make verbal statements come alive. Their services are needed for the survival of productive thinking in the sciences. When we remark regretfully that psychologists today no longer write like William James or Freud, we are not making a merely "aesthetic" complaint. We sense that the desiccation of our language is symptomatic of the pernicious split between the manipulation of intellectual schemata and the handling of live subject matter.

If I were asked to describe my dream university, I would have it organize itself around a central trunk of three disciplines: philosophy, the art studio, and the poetry workshop. Philosophy would be asked to return to the teaching of ontology, epistemology, ethics, and logic in order to remedy the shameful deficiencies of the reasoning now common in the fields of academic specialization. Art education would provide the instruments by which to carry out such thinking. Poetry would make language, our principal medium for communicating thought, fit for thinking in images.

A glance at the practice of secondary and higher education today indicates that imagery has its representatives in the classroom. The blackboard is the venerable vehicle of visual education, and the diagrams drawn in chalk by teachers of social science, grammar, geometry, or chemistry indicate that theory must rely on vision. But a look at these diagrams also reveals that most of them are the products of unskilled labor. They fail to transmit their meaning as well as they should because they are badly drawn. In order to deliver their message safely, diagrams must rely on the rules of pictorial composition and visual order that have been perfected in the arts for some 20,000 years. Art teachers should be prepared to apply these skills not only to the exalted visions of painters fit for museums but to all those practical applications that the arts have served, to their own benefit, in all functioning cultures.

The same consideration holds for the more elaborate visual aids — the illustrations and maps, the slides and films, and the video and television shows. Neither the technical skill of picture making alone nor the faithful realism of the images guarantees that the material explains what it is intended to explain. Here, it seems to me essential to get beyond the traditional notion that pictures provide the mere raw material and that thinking begins only after the information has been received — just as digestion must wait until one has eaten. Instead, the thinking is done by means of structural properties inherent in the image, and therefore, the image must be shaped and organized intelligently in such a way as to make the salient properties visible. Decisive relations between components must show up: cause must aim at effect, correspondences, and symmetries; hierarchies must be clearly presented — an eminently artistic task, even when it is used simply to explain the working of a piston engine or a shoulder joint (Arnheim 1974). . . .

... [V]isual thinking is inevitable. Even so, it will take time before it truly conquers its place in our education. Visual thinking is indivisible: unless it is given its due in every field of teaching and learning, it cannot truly work well in any field. The best intentions of the biology teacher will be hampered by half-ready student minds if the mathematics teacher is not applying the same principles. We need nothing less than a change of basic attitude in all teaching. Until then, those who happen to see the light will do their best to get the ball rolling. The seeing of the light and the rolling ball are good visual images.

References

Arnheim, R. *Visual Thinking*. Berkeley: University of California Press, 1969.
———. *Art and Visual Perception*. Berkeley: University of California Press, 1974.
Berkeley, G. "Introduction." A *Treatise Concerning the Principles of Human Knowledge*. 1710.
Freud, S. "Lecture 31." *Neue Vorlesungen zur Einführung in die Psychoanalyse*. Vienna: Internationaler Psychoanalytisches Verlag, 1933.

Questions and Exercises

1. Find a diagram in your biology, economics, sociology, or other textbook. Study the relationships that are expressed there in visual form. Write a paragraph to translate those relationships into verbal form.

2. How did Freud use the diagram of his theory?

3. When writing an essay for this course or for any other course, sketch appropriate visual symbols in your journal. How does visual thinking help to clarify your own concept of your paper? Would these visual symbols help readers?

4. How does Arnheim describe his dream university? Draft a paragraph describing what you think are the essential components for an ideal college education. Divide into small groups and read these paragraphs to each other. Work toward consensus about the characteristics of a dream college or university.

5. What are the traditional claims for the importance of teaching art in school? How does visual thinking contribute to a person's education outside of art? In a small group, discuss examples of visual thinking that each of you has encountered outside the art class.

6. Construct a diagram of the relationship between the processes of perception and thought. Compare your diagram with those of others in the class.

7. In his essay, Arnheim is trying to persuade his peers in the academic world that his view of visual thinking is valid. What features of this essay indicate his sense of audience? Imagine that you are trying to make the same point to an elementary school PTA meeting. Write a short address for that audience. In what way does your address differ from Arnheim's?

6

Readings in the Natural Sciences

Sounder Thinking Through Clearer Writing

F. PETER WOODFORD

from *Science*

A number of years have passed since 1967, when Peter Woodford wrote this essay. We reprint it here because we think that some science writers still generate the "appalling" products that Woodford colorfully describes in his second paragraph. Woodford writes from the point of view of a research scientist and editor of a distinguished scientific periodical, the *Journal of Lipid Research*. You may not know what the word "lipid" means, but your lack of familiarity with a specialized term does not mean that Woodford himself is using jargon. Lipids are organic compounds that are important components of living cells. No other word would label these compounds so precisely, and Woodford does not advocate the use of loose terminology. Precise terminology indicates precise thinking.

When a scientist is writing for other scientists, the word "lipid" is entirely appropriate. No respectable scientist, however, wants to read about "utilizing a pedestrian relocation," when the writer means "walking to the door." Woodford points out that too many scientists are unable to distinguish between jargon and the necessary use of technical vocabulary. Jargon is language that is inappropriately technical and therefore obscure. Jargon, according to Woodford, is not simply a stylistic flaw, but, more seriously, a sign of woolly thinking.

Woodford adheres to the theory held by many composition teachers — as he puts it, "writing clarifies thought." Not only does a person's writing express the stage of thinking — fuzzy or clear — that the writer is in, but getting something, even something fuzzy, down on paper and then reading it over carefully to seek clarity, can actually help a writer to think more clearly. Scientists too often wait, Woodford says, to "write up" their research. Woodford recommends writing at all stages of the research project, not necessarily to develop more elegant prose, but to produce better scientific research.

Woodford also argues that persistent writing will help scientists to be more effective readers. If scientists view themselves as writers, they will read the work of others more closely. Young scientists just entering the field will be less likely to echo the surface sounds of professional scientific writing. Instead, they will understand that the fundamental qualities of good scientific writing are clarity and objectivity. They will use precise terminology when appropriate, but they will avoid the needless elaboration of simple, everyday phrases.

Some editors of scientific journals now require that the professional scientists who are their contributors write in a style that is clear, direct, and, if at all possible, lively. Editors will often return articles for rewriting. Peter Woodford would agree with us that this policy will set a standard not only for clearer writing but for clearer thinking.

Sounder Thinking Through Clearer Writing
F. PETER WOODFORD

In the linked worlds of experimental science, scientific editing, and science communication many scientists are considering just how serious an effect the bad writing in our journals will have on the future of science.

All are agreed that the articles in our journals — even the journals with the highest standards — are, by and large, poorly written. Some of the worst are produced by the kind of author who consciously pretends to a "scientific scholarly" style. He takes what should be lively, inspiring, and beautiful and, in an attempt to make it seem dignified, chokes it to death with stately abstract nouns; next, in the name of scientific impartiality, he fits it with a complete set of passive constructions to drain away any remaining life's blood or excitement; then he embalms the remains in molasses of polysyllable, wraps the corpse in an impenetrable veil of vogue words, and buries the stiff old mummy with much pomp and circumstance in the most distinguished journal that will take it. Considered either as a piece of scholarly work or as a vehicle of communication, the product is appalling. The question is, Does it matter?

Does the Standard of Writing Matter?

Some editors believe it does, and either work themselves into the ground or employ large staffs to set the writing right. Others regard the correction of an illogical or pompous sentence as tantamount to remodeling the author's thinking, and consequently none of their business. The majority conclude that, if a paper represents sound work and is reasonably intelli-

"Sounder Thinking Through Clearer Writing," by F. Peter Woodford, *Science* Vol. 156, pp. 743-745, 12 May 1967. Copyright 1967 by the American Association for the Advancement of Science. Reprinted by permission of the American Association for the Advancement of Science.

gible, no lasting damage is done if it is published complete with all its blemishes. The blemishes may include ungrammatical constructions, confused thought, ambiguity, unjustifiable interpretation, subspecialty jargon, concealed hedging, inadequate description of statistical treatment, or imperfect controls.

I disagree with the majority conclusion. I am amazed by the patience with which my colleagues read these blemished scientific articles. I think that the spirit in which articles are often written, in which the object seems to be to impress the reader rather than express an idea, is all wrong. I think that we should protest vigorously about poor writing in scientific articles when it occurs, and *not* be indulgent about it. And I think we should take steps to ensure that the standard of scientific writing goes up. I feel strongly enough about it to teach a course on the Principles of Scientific Writing for graduate students, in the hope that when they come to contribute to the literature they will do a better job than we, the scientists of today, seem to have done.

Sometimes a skeptic will ask me, "Do you really think it's so important to improve scientific writing? We know it's usually a bit on the pompous side, but once you get used to the conventions you can zip through it pretty easily and get to the author's meaning." Personally, I *don't* find it so easy to zip through the pretentious constructions, and I think that one all too frequently arrives at a meaning that was not intended. But more telling than either of these reasons for concern is this: I have definite and clear-cut evidence that the scientific writing in our journals exerts a corrupting influence on young scientists — on their writing, their reading, and their thinking.

Decline of Writing, Reading, and Thinking

When science students enter graduate school they often write with admirable directness and clarity of purpose, like this:

> In order to determine the molecular size and shape of A and B, I measured their sedimentation and diffusion constants. The results are given in Table 1. They show that A is a roughly spherical molecule of molecular weight 36,000. The molecular weight of B remains uncertain since the sample seems to be impure. This is being further investigated.

Two years later, these same students' writing is verbose, pompous, full of fashionable circumlocutions as well as dangling constructions, and painfully polysyllabic, like this:

> In order to evaluate the possible significance of certain molecular parameters at the subcellular level, and to shed light on the conceivable role of structural configuration in spatial relationships of

intracellular macromolecules, an integrated approach [see *1*] to the problem of cell diffusivity has been devised and developed. The results, which are in a preliminary stage, are discussed here in some detail because of their possible implication in mechanisms of diffusivity in a wider sphere.

The student can no longer write: he pontificates.

What has brought about the change? Clearly, the students have copied these dreary and pretentious phrases from the scientific literature. They have been dutifully studying it, as they are urged to do, and it has warped their style to the point that they can no longer walk to the door without "utilizing a pedestrian relocation," or sip their coffee without "prior elevation of the containing vessel to facilitate imbibition."

Comcomitantly, something drastic happens to their powers of reading. As one of the assignments in my course, my students had to write an abstract of a published paper. The paper itself was brief, simple, and well written. I was dismayed to find that at least half of my students misread the paper in three major ways. First, they referred to 20-day-old rats, although the age of the animals was never given — the article described 20-gram rats; second, they talked about specific activity of the cholesterol injected, whereas the specific activity was never stated — the figure they had got hold of was actually the number of millicuries injected per kilogram of rat body weight, and they had misread it as mc/mg; last, and most amazing of all, they gave conclusions *directly opposite* to those indicated both by the data and by the authors of the article they were abstracting!

Now these students are by no means numskulls — they are like the rest of us, busy scientists zipping quickly through the literature to get to the authors' meaning. This is where the habit of guesswork leads.

Worst of all, there is a deterioration in the quality of students' *thinking* as they study the scientific literature. In a survey paper by one of my best students, everything was going along nicely, and everybody's head was clear, until we fell into the mire of this sentence:

> A variety of stimulatory hormones, irrespective of their chemical nature, are characterized by their ability to influence the synthesis of messenger RNA as a prerequisite for the secondary biologic events characteristic of the particular target organ.

"What on earth do you mean by that?" I asked. He blushed, and said, "Actually it's a quotation, I forgot to put in the quotation marks." "Well, but what do you suppose it means, anyway?" He couldn't be absolutely sure. It seemed to clinch his argument, and it *sounded impressive*. And when he told me the name of the journal it came from, my spirits sank. How can we hope to have our students think straight if we can't send them to the most celebrated journal in the country without cautioning them about the woolly thinking they will find there? For I cannot be tolerant, as some people are, and say, "Well, great scientists often write badly." You can't get away from it: execrable writing like this is the product of shoddy thinking, of careless condescension, or of pretentiousness. None of these is good for science.

Bringing About Improvement

These, then, are the negative effects of the scientific literature I have observed in the course of teaching scientific writing. I am glad to say that there are also definite positive findings. The most striking observation is that by teaching writing you can actually strengthen students' ability not only to write but also to read more attentively and to think more logically and rigorously.

It is surely no accident that greater lucidity and accuracy in thinking should result from the study of clarity and precision in writing. For writing necessarily uses *words*, and almost all thinking is done with words. One cannot even decide what to have for dinner, or whether to cross town by bus or taxi, without expressing the alternatives to oneself in words. My experience is, and the point of my whole course is, that the discipline of marshaling words into formal sentences, writing them down, and examining the written statement is bound to clarify thought. Once ideas have been written down, they can be analyzed critically and dispassionately; they can be examined at another time, in another mood, by another expert. Thoughts can therefore be developed, and if they are not precise at the first written formulation, they can be made so at a second attempt.

The power of writing as an aid in thinking is not often appreciated. Everyone knows that someone who writes successfully gets his thoughts completely in order before he publishes. But it is seldom pointed out that the very act of writing can help to clarify thinking. Put down woolly thoughts on paper, and their woolliness is immediately exposed. If students come to realize this, they will write willingly and frequently at all stages of their work, instead of relegating "writing up" to the very end and regarding it as a dreadful chore that has very little to do with their "real" work.

In teaching scientific writing it is not difficult to point out the absurdity of the bombastic phraseology discussed above, and to teach students to simplify their writing and make it direct and vigorous. But these stylistic considerations only scratch the surface of what is really at fault in many scientific articles. I am appalled by the frequent publication of papers that describe most minutely what experiments were done, and how, but with no hint of why, or what they mean. Cast thy data upon the waters, the authors seem to think, and they will come back interpreted.

If this approach to publication is to be successfully thwarted by a course on scientific writing, the course should concentrate primarily on clarifying the students' thoughts about the purpose of a piece of research, the conclusions that can justifiably be drawn, and the significance of those conclusions; matters of style are of subsidiary importance. The course should focus on a method for getting these thoughts fully worked out — the technique of writing them down for critical appraisal. The essence of the approach is: Writing clarifies thought.

Considerations in a Scientific Writing Course

A course on scientific writing is best given, perhaps, within the framework of writing a journal article — for the practical reason that students are familiar with this type of publication and know that they will have to produce journal articles in the course of their work. The most receptive students are those who have done some research and who are therefore psychologically ready to consider how they can best present it in a journal.

These are the kinds of questions that should be considered:

"In the work to be described, what was the question asked and what are the answers obtained?" These must be clearly placed before the reader. Students, with their recent results in mind, can often tell you what their *answers* are, but they are not always so sure of what the *question* was. Here is the first opportunity to test the hypothesis that writing clarifies thought. When they write down the questions asked and the answers obtained, students frequently come to see that the answers they have are to questions different from what they had thought. Fortunately, the questions to which they do have the answers are usually valid and important, but the difference from the previous state of affairs is that each student is now able to define the true subject of the paper he is about to write. He will not confuse his readers, or himself, with a paper that does not match its title; on the contrary, he can now commit a fitting title to paper and keep closely to the subject it defines through all the subsequent steps, without wandering off into irrelevancies. In addition, he often perceives what the questions are that he would now *like* to ask, and begins to design experiments to answer them. Writing has clarified thought.

The next questions are, "What was the purpose of the work, and what is the significance of the conclusions?" Purpose and significance should always be stated for the reader. At this point, surprisingly, a storm of protest arises. "The work is descriptive!" the students cry. "The reader who is knowledgeable in the field will grasp the purpose, and draw his own conclusions." They seem to think that in research you don't need to have a clear purpose, or to state the conclusions drawn from your frantic activity; that the technique of Science is to mix A and B, inject C into rats, heat it up, precipitate it, centrifuge it, analyze it — and hope against hope that the results will throw light on some "problem" that has not even been defined. And it's not only raw students who think this: examination of the literature reveals that the attitude is widespread. When, however, the students are made to put the problem *in writing* they see why they did the experiments — and why, perhaps, others would have been more to the point. Their probing into the unknown becomes less haphazard, because it is more disciplined.

Any supervisor of research tries to apply this kind of training, of course. All I would like to do is to systematize the training, and to get writing accepted as a regular part of the apparatus for self-criticism.

Other considerations in a course on scientific writing (2) include methods for separating main issues from side issues and side issues from irrelevancies; the function of publication; methods of search; the nature of scientific proof — essentially, in one guise or another, most of the aspects of scientific method. Lastly, toward the end of such a course, students can be taught to recognize and avoid the sort of clumsy and barbaric sentence constructions with which our literature is strewn. All these points should be made in the name of three things that the budding scientist is bound to have respect for: logic, clarity of thought, and precision.

The process of educating scientists is becoming increasingly complex. The student has to learn more and more facts, study exceedingly complex theories that are out of date before he can master them, and become adept at using more and more machines. We seldom make him, or even let him, write — which is the only way for him to find out if his thoughts are clear or muddled. Surely, the object of a university training is not so much the acquisition of knowledge as the development of the power to think. I believe we can strengthen scientific thinking by teaching scientific writing. If this is so, the teaching of scientific writing should not be, as it is at present, almost entirely neglected, but should be accorded a place at the very heart of a science curriculum.

Much attention is currently being paid to the streamlining and automation of information retrieval and the possible use of computers not merely to compile bibliographies but to enable scientists seated at widely separated consoles to engage in "dialogues." In view of all this it seems, perhaps, slightly old-fashioned to be concerned with precise formulation of thought in written language, composed without haste and considered with care. Yet I am convinced that unless we do concern ourselves with it, unless we do train our students to use the technique of writing to clarify thinking, communication between scientists will degenerate into chaos and scientific thinking will decay into a haze of fruitless intuitive feeling.

Summary

Bad scientific writing involves more than stylistic inelegance: it is often the outward and visible form of an inward confusion of thought. The scientific literature at its present standard distorts rather than forms the graduate student's view of scientific knowledge and thought, and corrupts his ability to write, to read, and to think.

Strong educational measures are needed to effect reform. I advocate a course on scientific writing as an essential feature in every scientist's training. Such a course delves deep into the philosophy and method of science if it deals with logic, precision, and clarity; on how these qualities can be achieved in writing; and on how such achievement strengthens the corresponding faculties in thinking.

Reference and Notes

1. Whenever an "integrated approach" is mentioned (why anyone should use a disintegrated approach passes all comprehension), the reader should steel himself for other tidbits of Fashionable Foundationese: "constellation of ideas," "sophisticated balance of experimentation and ideational material," "man-machine interface."

2. Council of Biology Editors' Committee on Graduate Training in Scientific Writing, "Manual on the Teaching of Scientific Writing," in preparation.

Questions and Exercises

1. Outline the main points of this article. What cues did the author use to alert you to the major subdivisions?

2. In a professional scientific journal, a textbook, a government document, or another source, find a one-paragraph example of pompous, excessively wordy writing and rewrite it in the clear, direct style recommended by Woodford.

3. Woodford notes that the clarity of writing reaches its highest point as science students leave college. Make a graph illustrating this situation. The vertical axis should be "clarity" and the horizontal axis should be "years of schooling." Most scientists spend five to six years in graduate school and many continue their training with a postdoctoral fellowship lasting an additional two or three years. Incorporate all this information into your graph.

4. Go to the library and look up this article in *Science*. Skim through the volume as a whole. How does Woodford's article differ from others in the volume? Write a paragraph characterizing the journal for an undergraduate who has never looked through it.

5. Compare the style of this article with that of the other *Science* articles reprinted in this book: Rosenhan, pp. 298–312; Payne and McVay, pp. 352–59; and Clark and Clark, pp. 371–75. Which articles use a more formal style? What particular features help you identify the level of formality?

6. Many academics, if asked what "good writing" is, will reply that "good writing is clear writing." Is this statement true? To what extent does the impression of clarity depend on the educational background of the audience? Write down a few of your initial ideas in response to these questions. Then discuss these questions in small groups.

7. Imagine that you are a science graduate student concerned about the possible deterioration of your writing skills during graduate school. You have been given permission to make a five-minute presentation to your graduate school's Committee on Academic Policy in support of a new science writing course. You plan to use the graph you prepared in Question 3. Draft notes for this presentation. At what point will you use your graph?

Experiments
VINCENT C. DETHIER

from *To Know a Fly*

Vincent Dethier, the author of the next selection, is a biologist who is famous for his pioneering research on the physiological basis of animal behavior. He established his reputation through his work on the feeding behavior of the blowfly, a slightly larger (and even less attractive) version of the common housefly. In his research Dethier was able to show how the blowfly's nervous system detected the presence of food, directed the fly to feed, and made it recognize when to stop feeding.

Dethier began publishing his research in the 1950s, a time when an animal's desire to eat had to be explained by using vague concepts like "drive" or "motivation." Although scientists realized that the nervous system controlled, for example, the desire to eat or drink, they did not know exactly how the nervous system achieved this control. Therefore, they were forced to speak of a "motivation to drink," or a "drive to eat." Dethier's experiments clarified the nervous system's mechanisms underlying feeding and drinking in one particular animal. In doing so he provided other scientists with a model for how the nervous system controls behavior.

Dethier was already well known among scientists for his excellent teaching when he wrote *To Know a Fly*, the brief and humorous book from which this selection is taken. In the book Dethier recounts experiences from his research on the feeding behavior of flies and adds his observations on the nature of academic research in general. Clever drawings and a variety of quotations make the book delightful reading. Because *To Know a Fly* conveys the excitement of scientific research and the wonder of scientific discovery to readers who are not themselves scientists, it has become a classic. Scientists frequently recommend this book to their not-so-scientific friends or to their undergraduates as a painless source of enlightenment on the pleasures of doing research.

Dethier believes in making connections. He writes about scientific experimentation in humanistic terms: beauty, adventure, and faith. He draws analogies to help the general reader connect the unfamiliar with the known. Dethier shows us that to know a fly is to know a little more about life itself and therefore about ourselves.

Experiments
VINCENT C. DETHIER

A properly conducted experiment is a beautiful thing. It is an adventure, an expedition, a conquest. It commences with an act of faith, faith that the world is real, that our senses generally can be trusted, that effects have causes, and that we can discover meaning by reason. It continues with an observation and a question. An experiment is a scientist's way of asking nature a question. He alters a condition, observes a result, and draws a conclusion. It is no game for a disorderly mind (although the ranks of Science are replete with confused thinkers). There are many ways of going astray. The mention of two will suffice.

The most commonly committed scientific sin is the lack of proper experimental control. The scientist must be certain that the result he obtains is a consequence of the specific alteration he introduced and not of some other coincidental one. . . .

. . . [T]here is the well-known case of the chap who wondered which component of his mixed drink caused his inevitable intoxication. He tried bourbon and water, rum and water, scotch and water, rye and water, gin and water and concluded, since every drink had water as a constant, that water caused his drunkenness. He then gritted his teeth and tried water alone — with negative results. When I last saw him he had concluded that the glass was the intoxicating agent, and he was about to begin another series of experiments employing paper cups.

Of course even controls can be carried to absurd extremes as in the case of the atheistic scientist who seized upon the opportunity afforded by the birth of twins to test the efficacy of religion. He had one baby baptized and kept the other as a control.

Another common fallacy is that of confusing correlation with cause and effect. This is exemplified by the case of the gentleman who was extricated from the rubble of an apartment house immediately after an earthquake. "Do you know what happened?" his rescuers inquired.

"I am not certain," replied the survivor. "I remember pulling down the window shade and it caused the whole building to collapse."

The kind of question asked of nature is a measure of a scientist's intellectual stature. Too many research workers have no questions at all to ask, but this does not deter them from doing experiments. They become enamored of a new instrument, acquire it, then ask only "What can I do with this beauty?" Others ask such questions as "How many leaves are there this year on the ivy on the zoology building?" And having counted them do not know what to do with the information. But some questions can be useful and challenging. And meaningful questions can be asked of a fly.

Between the fly and the biologist, however, there is a language barrier that makes getting direct answers to questions difficult. With a human subject it is only necessary to ask: what color is this? does that hurt? are you hungry? The human subject may, of course, lie; the fly cannot. However, to elicit information from him it is necessary to resort to all kinds of trickery and legerdemain. This means pitting one's brain against that of the fly — a risk some people are unwilling to assume. But then, experimentation is only for the adventuresome, for the dreamers, for the brave....

Extracting information from a fly can be ... challenging. Take the question of taste, for example. Does a fly possess a sense of taste? Is it similar to ours? How sensitive is it? What does he prefer?

The first fruitful experimental approach to this problem began less than fifty years ago with a very shrewd observation; namely, that flies (and bees and butterflies) walked about in their food and constantly stuck out their tongues. The next time you dine with a fly (and modern sanitary practice has not greatly diminished the opportunities), observe his behavior when he gavots across the top of the custard pie. His proboscis, which is normally carried retracted into his head like the landing gear of an airplane, will be lowered, and like a miniature vacuum cleaner he will suck in food. For a striking demonstration of this, mix some sugared water and food coloring and paint a sheet of paper. The first fly to find it will leave a beautiful trail of lip prints, hardly the kind suitable for lipstick ads but nonetheless instructive.

Proboscis extension has been seen thousands of times by thousands of people but few have been either struck by the sanitary aspects of the act or ingenious enough to figure out how they might put the observation to use to learn about fly behavior.

The brilliant idea conceived by the biologist who first speculated on why some insects paraded around in their food was that they tasted with their feet. In retrospect it is the simplest thing in the world to test this idea. It also makes a fine parlor trick for even the most blasé gathering.

The first step is to provide a fly with a handle since Nature failed to do so. Procure a stick about the size of a lead pencil. (A lead pencil will do nicely. So will an applicator stick, the kind that a physician employs when swabbing a throat). Dip one end repeatedly into candle wax or paraffin until a fly-sized gob accumulates. Next anaesthetize a fly. The least messy method is to deposit him in the freezing compartment of a refrigerator for several minutes. Then, working very rapidly, place him backside down on the wax and seal his wings onto it with a hot needle.

Now for the experimental proof. Lower the fly gently over a saucer of water until his feet just touch. Chances are he is thirsty. If so, he will lower his proboscis as soon as his feet touch and will suck avidly. When thirst has been allayed, the proboscis will be retracted compactly into the head. This is a neat arrangement because a permanently extended proboscis might flop about uncomfortably during flight or be trod upon while walking.

Next, lower the fly into a saucer of sugared water. In a fraction of a second the proboscis is flicked out again. Put him back into water (this is the control), and the proboscis is retracted. Water, in; sugar, out. The performance continues almost indefinitely. Who can doubt that the fly can taste with his feet? The beauty of this proboscis response, as it is called, is that it is a reflex action, almost as automatic as a knee jerk. By taking advantage of its automatism, one can learn very subtle things about a fly's sense of taste.

For example, who has the more acute sense of taste, you or the fly? As the cookbooks say, take ten saucers. Fill the first with water and stir in one teaspoon of sugar. Now pour half the contents of the saucer into another which should then be filled with water. After stirring, pour half of the contents of the saucer into another which should then be filled with water. After stirring, pour half of the contents of the second saucer into a third and fill it with water. Repeat this process until you have a row of ten saucers. Now take a fly (having made certain that he is not thirsty) and lower him gently into the most dilute mixture. Then try him in the next and so on up the series until his proboscis is lowered. This is the weakest sugar solution that he can taste.

Now test yourself. If you are the sort of person who does not mind kissing his dog, you can use the same saucers as the fly. Otherwise make up a fresh series. You will be surprised, perhaps chagrined, to discover that the fly is unbelievably more sensitive than you. In fact, a starving fly is ten million times more sensitive.

Questions and Exercises

1. How many ways of going astray in the design of experiments does Dethier mention? What are they?

2. How many different experiments does Dethier suggest? What question is asked in each experiment? What hypothesis is tested? How does the behavior of the fly indicate the answer to the question?

3. Devise a seemingly useless or meaningless research question similar to Dethier's "How many leaves are there this year on the ivy on the zoology building?" Under what circumstances would your question

become meaningful? (For example, the number of ivy leaves might be directly related to winter temperatures, or spring rainfall; in that case, the number might be an important indicator of the environmental stress experienced by plants in that particular geographic area.)

4. Using the *General Science Index* and the card catalogue, locate one of these two research reports written by Dethier in the late 1950s:

Dethier, V. G. 1955. "The Physiology and Histology of the Contact Chemoreceptors of the Blowfly," *Quarterly Review of Biology*, 30: 348–371.

Dethier, V. G., and Bodenstein, D. 1958. "Hunger in the Blowfly," *Zeitschrift fur Tierpsychologie* 15: 129–140. Reprinted in *Readings in Animal Behavior*, ed. T. E. McGill. New York: Holt, Rinehart and Winston, 1965.

Read the professional version of either of the two experiments described in this excerpt. How does the professional version differ in style and in format from the more informal version presented here?

5. For the benefit of your astonished classmates, carry out one of Dethier's fly experiments. Did Dethier provide enough information for you? What additions or changes, if any, did you have to make in the procedures?

6. Who is the audience for this essay? What characteristics of Dethier's writing (word choice, sentence structure, choice of examples) support your answer? Meet in small groups to discuss specific passages and to characterize Dethier's intended audience.

7. Using the card catalogue in your library, locate a copy of the book from which this chapter was taken. Look at the drawings which accompany Chapter 3. In small groups discuss the significance and effect of the drawings.

8. Draft a response to this possible essay examination question: Name several common errors in experimental design and give an example of each. If possible, give examples that are different from the ones mentioned in Dethier's article.

9. Using standard research report (or laboratory report) style and format, write up one of the experiments described by Dethier. What information did you choose to leave out because it was not appropriate for a research or lab report?

10. The book *To Know a Fly* was published in 1962. What research has Dethier done since publishing this book? Check textbooks in the fields of animal behavior, physiological psychology, and comparative physiology for information. Also check the *Science Citation Index* and *Biological Abstracts* for more recent references. Summarize the recent research. Provide appropriate author and date citations. At the end of your summary, include a list of references.

Germs

LEWIS THOMAS

from *Lives of a Cell*

Lewis Thomas, chancellor of the Memorial Sloan-Kettering Cancer Center, originally wrote "Germs" for his regular column in the *New England Journal of Medicine*. His column was intended to keep other physicians up to date on the biological research at the Center, but his essays, as you can tell from this example, were far more than summaries of basic research. Integrating information from scientific research and from his own wide-ranging experience, he writes in a style that nonspecialists can understand. The best of his columns (including this one) have been collected in two books aimed at readers of popular science — *Lives of a Cell*, published in 1974, and *The Medusa and the Snail*, published in 1979. His latest book, *The Youngest Science: Notes of a Medicine-Watcher* (1983) is not a collection of essays but a memoir of his career.

That career began before the First World War in Flushing, N.Y., where Thomas accompanied his father, also a physician, on house calls. *The Youngest Science* presents an account of Thomas's formal medical education and his success as dean of the medical schools at Yale and New York University. On medical education, he writes:

> What I remember now, from this distance, is the influence of my classmates. We taught each other; we may even have set careers for each other without realizing at the time that so fundamental an educational process was even going on.

Lewis Thomas believes in collaborative learning, the sort of learning we encourage you to do when we ask you to meet in small groups to discuss a question.

One of Thomas's medical school friends, Franz Ingelfinger, played an important role in inspiring Thomas's second career as a popular science writer. In the 1970s, Dr. Ingelfinger invited Thomas to write a monthly column for the *New England Journal of Medicine*, which Ingelfinger was then editing. Dr. Ingelfinger's familiarity with his friend's eloquence did not stop the editor from using the occasion of a dinner of the Association of American Physicians to tease Thomas about his "laboratory prose." "He read from several of my scientific papers, which are perfectly dreadful reading," explained Thomas to Joseph Barbato, a reporter for *The Chronicle of Higher Education*. "In that kind of writing, you have to weigh every word, to make sure that whoever reads your paper can do *exactly* what you did without making any errors in procedures and methods. The prose becomes hideous."[1]

---

1. *The Chronicle of Higher Education*, April 20, 1983, pp. 23–24.

Thomas is a good writer, in part, because he understands the different necessities of audience, occasion, and purpose. In "Germs," he is not trying to tell other scientists how to replicate an experiment on microorganisms. He writes so that the general public can learn something about the nature of germs.

If you are a science major and already understand that microorganisms are not demons, you may wonder what Thomas offers you. You may feel impatient at first by what may seem to be elaborate explanations of simple points. If you are already a member of an "in" group, you may not enjoy listening to another group member explain procedures to a newcomer. If you listen carefully to that explanation, however, you may find that you see a new light cast on something that you thought you well understood. Thomas's analogies do something else, even for the experienced scientist. They connect science to a larger world, and that connection is as important for the scientist as it is for the lay public. All educated people need to understand basic concepts in science, and scientists need to see connections between their work and the general realm of human activity. Thomas uses analogies not merely to clarify concepts but to make these important connections.

Although written in a lively manner, the essay does contain, for the lay reader, a host of unfamiliar words. Terms such as "hemolytic" and "pathogenicity" may well slow down your reading, if you let them. Their use reflects an original audience of physicians and researchers to whom the words are not only clear, but precise. *Lives of a Cell*, from which this essay is taken, won the National Book Award, was enthusiastically reviewed in such publications as *The New York Times*, *Time*, and *The New Yorker*, and became a best-seller.

You may wonder, if so few people understand all the terms, why the book is so popular. The answer lies in the quality of Thomas's ideas and the skill of his writing. Readers who are absorbed in the content and pleased with the writing will guess at the general meaning of words from their contexts. Later they may look up some of the specialized terms about which they are particularly curious.

Thomas believes that curiosity is the wellspring of science. In the *Chronicle of Higher Education* article cited earlier, Thomas says:

> I think a lot of people in the intelligent reading public are misled into thinking that the reason for doing science is to get more technology, or to change and improve technology. In fact, science is done because of altogether human curiosity — to find out how nature works. The technology comes more or less by accident.

We have provided a glossary for the scientifically curious reader. We suggest that you read the article once through quickly without consulting the glossary. Simply underline the words that you do not know. On a second reading, use the glossary to learn more about the scientific terms that

Thomas uses. Some readers allow their intimidation by specialized vocabulary to stop them from reading about scientific concepts. That fear prevents the timid from understanding ideas that intimately affect our lives.

As you read, apply the information in the essay to your own life. What is your personal — and perhaps almost unconscious — attitude toward microorganisms? What recent encounters have you had with microorganisms? After reading this essay, do you believe that your attitude, both intellectual and psychological, toward germs is appropriate to the threat they pose? At the end of the essay, Thomas, by using the word, "Pentagon," draws an analogy between the human body's reaction to invasion and the reaction of an entire nation to perceived danger. How does this analogy help you to understand germs? How does it help you to understand foreign policy?

Germs

LEWIS THOMAS

Watching television, you'd think we lived at bay, in total jeopardy, surrounded on all sides by human-seeking germs, shielded against infection and death only by a chemical technology that enables us to keep killing them off. We are instructed to spray disinfectants everywhere, into the air of our bedrooms and kitchens and with special energy into bathrooms, since it is our very own germs that seem the worst kind. We explode clouds of aerosol, mixed for good luck with deodorants, into our noses, mouths, underarms, privileged crannies — even into the intimate insides of our telephones. We apply potent antibiotics to minor scratches and seal them with plastic. Plastic is the new protector; we wrap the already plastic tumblers of hotels in more plastic, and seal the toilet seats like state secrets after irradiating them with ultraviolet light. We live in a world where the microbes are always trying to get at us, to tear us cell from cell, and we only stay alive and whole through diligence and fear.

We still think of human disease as the work of an organized, modernized kind of demonology, in which the bacteria are the most visible and centrally placed of our adversaries. We assume that they must somehow relish what they do. They come after us for profit, and there are so many of them that disease seems inevitable, a natural part of the human condition; if we succeed in eliminating one kind of disease there will always be a new one at hand, waiting to take its place.

These are paranoid delusions on a societal scale, explainable in part by our need for enemies, and in part by our memory of what things used to be like. Until a few decades ago, bacteria were a genuine household threat, and although most of us survived them, we were always aware of the nearness of death. We moved, with our families, in and out of death. We had lobar pneumonia, meningococcal meningitis, streptococcal infections, diphtheria, endocarditis, enteric fevers, various septicemias, syphilis, and, always, everywhere, tuberculosis. Most of these have now left most of us, thanks to antibiotics, plumbing, civilization, and money, but we remember.

In real life, however, even in our worst circumstances we have always been a relatively minor interest of the vast microbial world. Pathogenicity is not the rule. Indeed, it occurs so infrequently and involves such a relatively small number of species, considering the huge population of bacteria on the earth, that it has a freakish aspect. Disease usually results from the inconclusive negotiations for symbiosis, an overstepping of the line by one side or the other, a biologic misinterpretation of borders.

Some bacteria are only harmful to us when they make exotoxins, and they only do this when they are, in a sense, diseased themselves. The toxins of diphtheria bacilli and streptococci are produced when the organisms have been infected by bacteriophage; it is the virus that provides the code for toxin. Uninfected bacteria are uninformed. When we catch diphtheria it is a virus infection, but not of us. Our involvement is not that of an adversary in a straightforward game, but more like blundering into someone else's accident.

I can think of a few microorganisms, possibly the tubercle bacillus, the syphilis spirochete, the malarial parasite, and a few others, that have a selective advantage in their ability to infect human beings, but there is nothing to be gained, in an evolutionary sense, by the capacity to cause illness or death. Pathogenicity may be something of a disadvantage for most microbes, carrying lethal risks more frightening to them than to us. The man who catches a meningococcus is in considerably less danger for his life, even without chemotherapy, than meningococci with the bad luck to catch a man. Most meningococci have the sense to stay out on the surface, in the rhinopharynx. During epidemics this is where they are to be found in the majority of the host population, and it generally goes well. It is only in the unaccountable minority, the "cases," that the line is crossed, and then there is the devil to pay on both sides, but most of all for the meningococci.

Staphylococci live all over us, and seem to have adapted to conditions in our skin that are uncongenial to most other bacteria. When you count them up, and us, it is remarkable how little trouble we have with the relation. Only a few of us are plagued by boils, and we can blame a large part of the destruction of tissues on the zeal of our own leukocytes. Hemolytic streptococci are among our closest intimates, even to the extent of sharing antigens with the membranes of our muscle cells; it is our reaction to their presence, in the form of rheumatic fever, that gets us into trouble. We can carry brucella for long periods in the cells of our reticuloendothelial system without any awareness of their existence; then cyclically, for reasons not understood but probably related to immunologic reactions on our part, we sense them, and the reaction of sensing is the clinical disease.

Most bacteria are totally preoccupied with browsing, altering the configurations of organic molecules so that they become usable for the energy needs of other forms of life. They are, by and large, indispensable to each other, living in interdependent communities in the soil or sea. Some have become symbionts in more specialized, local relations, living as working parts in the tissues of higher organisms. The root nodules of legumes would have neither form nor function without the masses of rhizobial bacteria swarming into root hairs, incorporating themselves with such intimacy that only an electron microscope can detect which membranes are bacterial and which plant. Insects have colonies of bacteria, the mycetocytes, living in them like little glands, doing heaven knows what but being essential. The microfloras of animal intestinal tracts are part of the nutritional system. And then, of course, there are the mitochondria and chloroplasts, permanent residents in everything.

The microorganisms that seem to have it in for us in the worst way — the ones that really appear to wish us ill — turn out on close examination to be rather more like bystanders, strays, strangers in from the cold. They will invade and replicate if given the chance, and some of them will get into our deepest tissues and set forth in the blood, but it is our response to their presence that makes the disease. Our arsenals for fighting off bacteria are so powerful, and involve so many different defense mechanisms, that we are in more danger from them than from the invaders. We live in the midst of explosive devices; we are mined.

It is the information carried by the bacteria that we cannot abide.

The gram-negative bacteria are the best examples of this. They display lipopolysaccharide endotoxin in their walls, and these macromolecules are read by our tissues as the very worst of bad news. When we sense lipopolysaccharide, we are likely to turn on every defense at our disposal; we will bomb, defoliate, blockade, seal off, and destroy all the tissues in the area. Leukocytes become more actively phagocytic, release lysosomal enzymes, turn sticky, and aggregate together in dense masses, occluding capillaries and shutting off the blood supply. Complement is switched on at the right point in its sequence to release chemotactic signals, calling in leukocytes from everywhere. Vessels become hyperreactive to epinephrine so that physiologic concentrations suddenly possess necrotizing properties. Pyrogen is released from leukocytes, adding fever to hemorrhage, necrosis, and shock. It is a shambles.

All of this seems unnecessary, panic-driven. There is nothing intrinsically poisonous about endotoxin, but it must look awful, or feel awful, when sensed by cells. Cells believe that it signifies the presence of gram-negative bacteria, and they will stop at nothing to avoid this threat.

I used to think that only the most highly developed, civilized animals could be fooled in this way, but it is not so. The horseshoe crab is a primitive fossil of a beast, ancient and uncitified, but he is just as vulnerable to disorganization by endotoxin as a rabbit or a man. Bang has shown that an injection of a very small dose into the body cavity will cause the aggregation of hemocytes in ponderous, immovable masses that block the vascular channels, and a gelatinous clot brings the circulation to a standstill. It is now known that a limulus clotting system, perhaps ancestral to ours, is centrally involved in the reaction. Extracts of the hemocytes can be made to jell by adding extremely small amounts of endotoxin. The self-disintegration of the whole animal that follows a systemic injection can be interpreted as a well-intentioned but lethal error. The mechanism is itself quite a good one, when used with precision and restraint, admirably designed for coping with intrusion by a single bacterium: the hemocyte would be attracted to the site, extrude the coagulable protein, the microorganism would be entrapped and immobilized, and the thing would be finished. It is when confronted by the overwhelming signal of free molecules of endotoxin, evoking memories of vibrios in great numbers, that the limulus flies into panic, launches all his defenses at once, and destroys himself.

It is, basically, a response to propaganda, something like the panic-producing pheromones that slave-taking ants release to disorganize the colonies of their prey.

I think it likely that many of our diseases work in this way. Sometimes, the mechanisms used for overkill are immunologic, but often, as in the limulus model, they are more primitive kinds of memory. We tear ourselves to pieces because of symbols, and we are more vulnerable to this than to any host of predators. We are, in effect, at the mercy of our own Pentagons, most of the time.

Glossary

antigen: a foreign (that is, from outside the body) substance that activates the body's immune system and causes the production of special proteins in the blood called antibodies. The antibodies destroy or inactivate the offending antigen.

bacillus: any rod-shaped bacterium.

bacteriophage: a virus that infects bacteria.

brucella: any of a group (genus *Brucella*) of rod-shaped gram-negative bacteria that cause undulant fever (brucellosis) in humans. Brucella can also infect domestic herd animals. The disease, which can be transmitted from farm animals to humans, has rather vague symptoms — aches, chills, and sweating episodes — with a fever that rises and falls. The bacteria multiply in the human reticuloendothelial system causing abscesses in the liver, spleen, bone marrow, and lymph nodes. Tetracycline antibiotics are effective against *Brucella* bacteria.

chloroplasts: subcellular structures (organelles) found in the cytoplasm of plant cells. These rounded, membrane-bound organelles contain the pigment chlorophyll and the photosynthetic machinery that allow plants to trap solar energy as chemical energy. Although chloroplasts are always found inside plant cells, they closely resemble (and may have descended from) small bacteria-sized cells called blue-green algae.

complement: a complex series of enzymatic proteins found in the fluid part of the blood. These proteins break down foreign cells (such as bacterial cells) after they have been attacked by the body's antibodies. Recently, scientists have used bioengineering techniques to produce complement in large quantities because complement may prove to be an anticancer agent.

diphtheria: a human childhood disease caused by the gram-positive rod-shaped bacterium *Corynebacterium diphtheriae*, which releases a poisonous protein (an exotoxin) after it has been infected with a virus. The bacterial infection is usually limited to the throat, where a characteristic whitish membrane forms. Unfortunately, the exotoxin produced by the bacteria is absorbed by the body, where it inhibits protein synthesis and does widespread damage. Degeneration of the heart and kidney becomes evident about a week after infection; muscle weakness and variable paralysis can occur about a month after infection. Since 1923, children have been routinely immunized against diphtheria.

endocarditis: a life-threatening inflammation of the membrane that lines the inside of the heart and forms the heart valves. The disease is often caused by *Streptococcus* bacteria. In people with defective hearts even the small number of bacteria that enter the bloodstream during routine dental procedures can cause endocarditis.

endotoxin: a poisonous lipopolysaccaride substance found imbedded in the outer coat of gram-negative bacteria.

enteric fever: another name for typhoid fever, the most severe of the human gastrointestinal infections. The bacterium *Salmonella typhi* causes the disease, which damages the intestines and spleen. The disease is spread when infected fecal material contaminates food. Severe diarrhea, resulting in a fatal loss of fluid from the body, can lead to death unless fluid replacement therapy is used.

epinephrine: a hormone (also called adrenalin) produced by the adrenal medulla (core of the adrenal glands). Epinephrine produces effects similar to those obtained when the sympathetic nerves are stimulated. These effects, typically elicited in emergency situations, include increased heart rate, wider air passages in the lungs, and decreased intestinal activity.

exotoxin: a poisonous protein released by a bacterial cell into its surrounding medium.

gram-negative bacteria: a category of bacteria that do not retain a particular purple dye used in Gram's method for staining bacteria. These bacteria have an outer cell wall containing lipopolysaccaride substances, some of which may be endotoxins.

hemocyte: a blood cell or blood corpuscle; a cell specialized to travel in an animal's circulatory system. In humans, the leukocytes (white blood cells) and erythrocytes (red blood cells) are examples of hemocytes.

hemolytic: causing the breakdown or destruction of blood cells.

hyperreactive: a greater than normal response to stimuli; an overreaction. When a response by the body's immune system does more harm than good, the hyperreactivity is called hypersensitivity. Hypersensitivity reactions include anaphylaxis (potentially fatal drop in blood pressure in response to a bee sting, a penicillin injection, or some other allergen), and allergy reactions such as asthma.

legume: any species within a family of plants (Leguminosae) that all have seed cases resembling pea pods. Many food plants, including peas and beans, are legumes. These plants are able to produce their own fertilizer by forming a symbiotic relationship with certain soil bacteria that can extract nitrogen from the air.

leukocyte: a white blood cell. These blood cells are part of the body's immune system. They actively ingest foreign particles in the body and are attracted to areas of injury or infection.

lipopolysaccharide: a class of chemical compounds which are all made up of a starch (polysaccaride) and a fat (lipid). Bacteria that have an outer lipopolysaccharide layer are classified as gram-negative bacteria.

lobar pneumonia: an infection of the lungs by the gram-positive, spherically shaped bacterium, *Streptococcus pneumoniae*. The disease begins with fever, chest pains, cough and blood-stained sputum. After about nine days, it ends with a crisis marked by profuse sweating. During the course of the disease, one or more lobes of the lungs may fill with fluid. Penicillin is effective against the bacteria.

lysosomal enzymes: enzymes (protein molecules that catalyze chemical reactions in the body) found inside a certain class of membrane-bound structures, known as lysosomes, found inside cells. These enzymes are very destructive, and if released from the lysosome, they are able to digest the rest of the cell and destroy other cells.

macromolecule: any very large molecule, especially those made up of repeated subunits. Biological examples include proteins (made up of amino acids) and DNA (or deoxyribonucleic acid, made up of nucleotide bases).

malarial parasite: the protozoan blood parasite, called *Plasmodium*, that causes malaria in humans. The disease is transmitted by the *Anopheles* mosquito in tropical areas of the world. Although they are single-celled organisms, protozoans are much larger than bacteria and have a cell structure like that of the cells of multicellular animals.

meningococcal meningitis: an infection of the membranes that cover the brain, caused by *Neisseria meningitidis*, a round, gram-negative bacterium that grows in pairs. The disease begins with a severe headache and an immovably stiff neck. If the immune system cannot cope with the attack, the bacterial endotoxins (lipopolysaccharide poisons in the bacterial coat) lead to circulatory system collapse (called endotoxin shock). Penicillin, ampicillin, and chloramphenicol are effective in the early stages of the infection.

microbe: a general term that includes all microscopic forms of life, especially the bacteria.

microflora: a general term that includes all microscopic forms of life (bacteria, fungi, unicellular algae) except animal-like single cell organisms such as the flagellated protozoans. Often the term is used to refer to the normally occurring bacteria in the intestinal tract.

mitochondria: subcellular structures (organelles) found in the cytoplasm of both plant and animal cells. These rounded, membrane-bounded organelles contain biochemical machinery that allows cells to burn sugars more completely. Although mitochondria are always found within cells, they closely resemble (and may have descended from) bacteria.

mycetocyte: a specialized cell, found in certain insects, that houses presumably symbiotic bacteria or yeast.

pathogen: any microorganism that can cause disease.

pathogenicity: ability to produce disease. A condition causing disease.

phagocyte: a cell, such as certain white blood cells, that ingests (consumes) microorganisms, other cells, or foreign particles in the body.

phagocytic: action of phagocytes.

pheromone: a chemical substance that certain animals secrete externally and that produces specific responses in other animals.

physiologic concentrations: the amount of a substance that would normally be found in the body; the usual or average concentration of a substance. In contrast, the concentrations might be very different in the presence of disease or as a result of medication.

pyrogen: a fever-causing substance.

reticulo-endothelial cells: cells that form an important part of the body's defense mechanism. They are all phagocytic (ingest foreign particles and cells) and are found in a variety of locations, including the lymph nodes, liver, spleen, and bone marrow.

rhizobial bacteria: bacteria that live symbiotically in the roots of certain plants. Presumably the bacteria obtain shelter and nourishment from the plant while the plant obtains nitrogen compounds, fixed from atmospheric nitrogen by the bacteria.

root nodules: enlarged areas in the roots of certain plants (especially legumes) that contain symbiotic nitrogen-fixing bacteria.

septicemia: a bacterial infection that is being carried throughout the body by the bloodstream; the presence of harmful bacteria in the blood. Septicemia represents a very serious stage in bacterial infections.

spirochete: any of the spiral-shaped bacteria that move by undulation. The best-known spirochete is *Treponema pallidum*, which causes the disease syphilis.

streptococcal infections: these diseases include "strep throat" and skin infections such as impetigo. One strain of streptococcus, when infected with a virus, produces a poisonous protein (exotoxin) and causes scarlet fever. Although the infection itself is usually not serious, the body's own immune response can lead to dangerous situations including inflammed kidneys (glomerulonephritis) and rheumatic fever (resulting in damaged heart valves and arthritis). Penicillin and many other antibiotics are effective against these bacteria.

syphilis: a sexually transmitted (venereal) disease caused by a spiral-shaped bacterium (spirochete) called *Treponema pallidum*. The untreated disease always progresses through two stages followed by a latent period. In less than half the cases, the disease eventually develops into a third stage, tertiary syphilis. Up until this stage the disease can be successfully treated with penicillin. Tertiary syphilis, which is actually due to a developed hypersensitivity and not to the spirochete itself, takes three forms: large ulcers in the internal organs, cardiovascular damage, or neurological damage.

tuberculosis: a chronic progressive disease of the lungs caused by a rod-shaped bacterium, *Mycobacterium tuberculosis*. The initial infection is usually undetected and in most cases the body is able to isolate the bacteria permanently in nodules called tubercules. If the bacteria are not contained, the infection becomes the disease infectious tuberculosis. At this stage the body's own hypersensitivity may contribute to the destruction of lung tissue. A combination of antimicrobial drugs, such as isoniazid, streptomycin, and rifampin, taken faithfully over a one- to three-year period, will generally control the disease.

vascular channels: the pathways taken by blood or other fluids through an organism. In some animals, including humans, the blood usually remains inside blood vessels; in other animals, including the horsehoe crab, the blood sometimes leaves blood vessels and flows directly through the tissues.

vibrios: any of the gram-negative bacteria that have a curved-rod shape and that move with a characteristic wiggle.

Questions and Exercises

1. Write a paragraph summarizing the major point of this article.

2. Prepare a diagram or outline that presents the major topics of this article and illustrates their relationship to each other.

3. Use the information contained in the paragraph on horseshoe crab hemocyte aggregation to write an abstract of that particular research. Use *Biological Abstracts* to find the original article by Bang and compare your abstract with the abstract that accompanies the article. What information did Thomas omit when he wrote his paragraph?

4. In question 1 you should have found it relatively easy to summarize the major point of this article in one paragraph. However, you may sense that your summary, although accurate, is not exactly National Book Award material. What is missing? Two abilities characteristic of experienced writers are well illustrated in this essay: First, experienced writers are able to relate a topic to a broader field. Second, they are able to expand a topic with relevant, colorful detail.

   a) Beginning in the sixth paragraph, Thomas explains how a number of common infectious diseases fit into a pattern of accidental, rather than purposeful, attack on the part of the disease-causing organism. In this explanation, he is relating these diseases to a larger pattern of interaction between microorganisms and humans.

      1) List the bacteria that Thomas mentions, the disease they accidentally cause in humans, and their normal mode of existence.

      2) According to this article, what disease-causing microorganisms could not be included in a list of those that *accidentally* cause diseases?

      3) What other instances can you find in this article to illustrate the way a topic can gain new significance by its relationship to a broader field?

Meet in small groups to compare your lists and to discuss these issues.

b) Throughout the article Thomas uses interesting examples to expand his topics. Identify the main topic in the first paragraph. What example does Thomas use to expand the topic? Locate two other sections in this essay where Thomas expands a relatively straightforward topic with well-chosen examples.

5. Thomas uses colorful writing throughout this essay. Look up and skim through a recent issue of the *New England Journal of Medicine*. Meet in small groups to discuss your impressions. How is Thomas's style typical of other articles in that journal? How is it atypical?

6. In "Germs" Thomas uses the technique of personification; that is, he writes of bacteria as if they behaved like human beings. Find several examples of Thomas's use of personification. Compare lists with your classmates.

7. Choose a concept from your study of science: photosynthesis, seed germination, water pollution, or any other topic that interests you. Draft an explanation of this concept in the style of Lewis Thomas. Use personification and analogy. Consider that your audience includes your classmates and your English instructor, not research scientists.

8. Few research scientists follow Thomas's lead in writing for the general public. More often, journalists report on scientific issues that affect public health and welfare. Friends and relations may ask you to comment on such newspaper and magazine articles. The following assignment will give you some practice in intelligently discussing biological issues:

a) By using the *Reader's Guide to Periodical Literature* or the *New York Times Index*, find a newspaper or popular magazine article published within the last year on one of the following:[1]

1) Recombinant DNA
2) Genetic engineering
3) Antibiotic resistance
4) Viral causes of cancer
5) Increasing the ability of plants to fix atmospheric nitrogen
6) Nutrition (including vitamins, minerals, and diet)
7) Incapacitating diseases (for example, Guillain-Barré syndrome, muscular dystrophy, multiple sclerosis, and so on)
8) Toxic effects of environmental pollutants like insecticides, lead, herbicides, polyvinyl chloride, and so on

1. The editors wish to thank Professors Carol Shilling and Myra Jacobsohn of Beaver College for permission to reprint this assignment.

9) Birth defects caused by environmental pollutants
10) Increased incidence of cancer caused by environmental pollutants
11) Food contaminants (for example, kangaroo meat in hamburger)
12) Development of new vaccines
13) When does life begin?

You may use any newspaper or magazine, from the *National Enquirer* to the *New York Times* or the *Wall Street Journal*. Do not hesitate to use the shoddier journals. Looking up the background may be more work, but the analysis is much more fun. You may also want to look at some of the magazines that push a particular health philosophy, like *Prevention* (which promotes organic foods) or one of the other natural food journals. The articles should be about 700 words or longer. You must record the name of the author (if available) and the title, date, volume number, and page numbers of the publication. Include a photocopy of the article.

b) Summarize the article:
1) What is the subject of the article?
2) Is any background information given? If so, what?
3) What practical applications, if any, does the article suggest?
4) Is the article one that simply reports on new developments, or does it convey the impression that new cures or technological advances are at hand?

c) What background can you find on the subject of the article? Use your textbook, *Bioscience* or *Scientific American* as reference material. Articles appearing in the popular press frequently follow explanations of the topic which have appeared in *Science*, *Nature*, or the *New England Journal of Medicine*. You may also consult these. Do not write more than one typewritten page of background. Attach references (author, title, date, volume number, page numbers).

d) In what ways does the article in the popular press present an accurate presentation of the topic? Or in what ways does it distort the facts or not give any facts? Does the article lead the reader to emotional expectations that are not fulfilled, or does it leap to sentimental conclusions that are not justified?

e) If you conclude that the article focuses on presenting accurate information rather than on biasing the reader's response to the topic, explain why you think that is the case. Refer to specific word choices, specific pieces of information, and the sequencing of information to support your conclusion.

f) If you conclude that the article misleads the reader or reveals a bias, pick out the specific items that are misleading. Is any significant information which might lead the reader to another conclusion missing from the article? How would you explain to someone who is not a biology student what is wrong with the content of the article, with the way the information is presented, or with its conclusion?

g) The summary, background, and analysis should not exceed three pages, and should be in the following format:

    1) Title page
    2) Acknowledgements page
    3) Summary (no more than one page)
    4) Background information (no more than one page)
    5) Analysis of article
    6) Photocopy of article
    7) Bibliography

The Songs of the Whales: A Study of Scientific Writing for Various Audiences

The five articles included in this section are arranged chronologically and span almost ten years of research on the sounds made by whales. This topic has several advantages over most other scientific topics: First, nonscientists can easily understand the concept itself — namely, that whales sing beautiful songs (this fact had escaped scientific scrutiny until recently because the sounds are transmitted through water, not air). Second, the research itself is up to date; the first scientific reports on whale sounds were published in 1971, and research on the nature and meaning of these songs has continued since then. Finally, Roger Payne, who has done much of the research on whale songs, has published articles that are intended both for scientists and for nonscientists. His flexibility shows us how a scientist adjusts his writing style to accommodate to differing audiences.

The sequence of selections begins with a *Newsweek* article, obviously intended for a general audience, announcing Payne's discovery of whale songs and commenting on the incorporation of the newly discovered songs into a musical composition. The second excerpt, from an article written by Roger Payne and his co-worker Scott McVay, is the original description of humpback whale songs published in the journal *Science* and is intended for an audience of other scientists. The third selection, also by Payne, is a more recent (1979) report on the humpback whale song intended to interest the rather general audience that reads *National Geographic*. The fourth selection is especially enlightening for college students since it takes the information from Payne's *National Geographic* article and presents it for the benefit of the more scientifically inclined readers of the publication *Science News*. This type of recasting is similar to the writing tasks students face when they write term papers on scientific topics. The last excerpt, a very technical report again from the journal *Science*, illustrates how other scientists are now expanding upon the original work done by Roger Payne.

As you read these five selections, keep notes on the clues that indicate the intended audience.

We think it is fitting to conclude the selections in this anthology with the whales' songs. Scientists now hypothesize that the songs heard by Ulysses and his crew might have been sung by humpback whales. And so the arts and the sciences come together in the sirens' songs.

A Whale of a Singer

from *Newsweek*

The science section of news magazines is an important source of information to the nonscientist. From the following article reprinted from
Newsweek, general readers could learn that whales sing well enough to
inspire a serious musical composition. *Newsweek*, in fact, scooped the scientific journals by being the first to publish news of Roger Payne's remarkable tape recordings.

It is unusual for scientific research to be publicized in the popular press
before it appears in a scientific journal. But echoes of the whales' songs
came to the ears of *Newsweek* reporters before Roger Payne had published his scientific research report. Probably, the team assigned to science
reporting at *Newsweek* interviewed Dr. Roger Payne directly. They then
put the new information into a general context of whale lore.

A Whale of a Singer

from *Newsweek*

Every schoolboy knows that the great whales of the world's oceans are not
fish at all, but warm-blooded mammals who breathe air just like land creatures and also suckle their young. Now zoologists have discovered that
some species can actually sing — or at least that the sounds they produce
can only be described as songs.

One of the best singers is the humpback whale, a creature about 50
feet long with a bulky body rather like that of a jumbo jet. In style and
function the humpback's song resembles a bird song but is much lower in
pitch and longer-lasting — up to half an hour of elaborate sequences in
infra- and ultra-sound frequencies, as well as audible sound. "The songs
are like no earthly thing — very beautiful," says Roger Payne, a Rockefeller University zoologist who has studied the singing humpbacks for several
years with support from the New York Zoological Society. His interest is
in understanding how undersea animals communicate and his research
turned up an interesting sidelight: in certain layers of the ocean, known as
sound channels, humpback songs can travel thousands of miles without
losing much power.

No one knows how the whales, who have no vocal cords, produce their
haunting songs. Nor does anyone know their purpose, although most likely
they represent no more than an oral calling card, identifying the presence
of a humpback whale, or perhaps of a specific one. "The sounds serve possibly only one function," says Payne. "They allow two whales to converge,

although it may take them days to get together." Soon, however, the humpback song will serve another function: making music for human ears. A composition by Alan Hovhaness, entitled "And God Created Great Whales" and based on Payne's tape recording of the humpbacks, will receive its premier next week as part of the New York Philharmonic's Promenades series.

Questions and Exercises

1. If, as the first sentence of this article says, "Every schoolboy knows," then why repeat the fact that whales are mammals? What does this repetition tell you about the audience for this article?

2. What analogies are used in this article to make the scientific facts more relevant to the reader? What does "calling card" mean?

3. The topics in this brief, popularized article could easily be expanded as the framework for a scientific review paper on singing whales. What would be the major subheadings for each section? What information would be included in each section?

4. Some parts of this article (certain words, phrases, and sentences) would not be appropriate for a more formal scientific review. Identify the inappropriate parts and comment on why they would not be appropriate for that audience.

5. Summarize, in one paragraph, the scientific information in this article. Share your summaries in a small group.

6. Look up Alan Hovhaness in a directory of contemporary musicians. Imagine that you are a *Newsweek* science reporter. Write a memo to your colleagues in the music department to alert them that they might be interested in the new work of this whale of a musician.

7. Imagine that you are a reporter in the music department. Rewrite the entire article focusing on the musical composition by Alan Hovhaness.

Songs of Humpback Whales

ROGER S. PAYNE AND SCOTT MCVAY
from *Science*

With the publication of the article reproduced here, Roger S. Payne and Scott McVay announced to the scientific community that the sounds made by whales were actually organized into reliably repeated sequences and therefore could be compared to the songs sung by birds. Their announcement was unusual in several respects. First, some of the information had already been published in the popular press (for example, in the preceding *Newsweek* article), and their research had also been publicized by their release of a long-playing record, "Songs of the Humpback Whale." Second, probably because of this widespread prepublication exposure, the announcement was presented as an "article" in *Science*, rather than the more common "research report." Each weekly issue of *Science* has two or three articles and approximately fifteen research reports. While the research report announces new findings on a particular problem in scientific research, the article is more like a scientific review, often describing an extensive and ongoing research program. For example, the article after this one in that particular issue of *Science* was by Julius Axelrod, and it explained the work that had won for him the Nobel Prize in Physiology in 1970.

The format and style of an article in *Science* follows the general pattern expected in scientific review articles. Three features of this format and style are especially important. First, review articles, even though they may contain extensive discussions of the research done by a particular laboratory, do not dwell upon the details of methodology. The concentrations of solutions, the speeds of centrifugations, and other details that are important only to other scientists working in the same field are usually omitted from scientific reviews. Second, review articles use descriptive subheadings to divide the information clearly into sections. And finally, review articles, because they are intended for a wider audience than are research reports, avoid using specialized technical terms unless they are defined in the review itself.

Because of the space limitations in the journal *Science*, its articles are not entirely typical of scientific reviews. Most other scientific reviews use the author-date system of citations and give more complete reference information by including the titles of research reports.[1] These other reviews omit footnotes and instead incorporate information directly into the body of the paper. Finally, they typically have an acknowledgments section, while *Science* articles use the last footnote for acknowledgments.

In preparing this article for inclusion in the book, we purposely omitted about one third of the text and most of the eleven figures. The omitted text describes technical details and interpretation of data from the sound spectrograms of singing whales. Without these graphic aids, you may find the rather technical writing in this article even harder to read. Remember that you are not the reader for whom the article was originally intended. You are eavesdropping on a conversation between professional scientists. Strain your ears — that is, read slowly and carefully. Do not, however, dwell on your unfamiliarity with new vocabulary; instead, note a few words to look up later. You may find it useful to read the concluding summary first.

1. The author-date system provides the name of the author and date of publication in the text in parentheses, with full citation at the end in references.

Textbooks are intended to present material that is aimed at the student's level; you are therefore expected to master the information in textbooks. When instructors assign supplementary reading in journals, they do not expect mastery. They expect growing familiarity with the general terms of scientific discussion.

Songs of Humpback Whales

ROGER S. PAYNE AND SCOTT MCVAY

During the quiet age of sail, under conditions of exceptional calm and proximity, whalers were occasionally able to hear the sounds of whales transmitted faintly through a wooden hull (1). In this noisy century, the widespread use of propeller-driven ships and continuously running shipboard generators has made this a rare occurrence. Not until World War II, when research in sonar and antisubmarine warfare fostered major efforts and facilities for listening underwater, did it become generally known that many species of whales are vocal. At this time the first whale recordings were made.

Of the 25 or more species of whales that have been recorded, most are Odontocetes (toothed whales). Their sounds fall into three rough categories: short broad-band clicks, longer narrow-band squeals, and complex sounds (2). The complex sounds usually consist of rapidly repeated clicks. Most authors assume that both clicks and complex sounds serve principally for echolocation and that whistles are primarily for communication. However, there is little direct proof of either assumption (2). There seems to be no evidence that the sort of sound-patterning with which this article is concerned occurs among Odontocetes, but there are good reasons to suppose that it might.

Mysticete (baleen whale) sounds are varied and complex, consisting, for the most part, of lower and longer sounds than have yet been recorded from Odontocetes. The fin whale (*Balaenoptera physalus*) makes very low moans (at a fundamental frequency around 20 hertz) that are monotonously repeated in a regular pattern (3, 4). To date, the most vocal Mysticete that has been studied is the humpback whale (*Megaptera novaeangliae*).

Humpback whales, like sperm whales, are found in all oceans of the world. However, while the sperm whale has been, and remains, the most numerous large cetacean on earth, the humpback has never been very plentiful. The principal concentration of humpback whales is in the Antarctic Ocean (5), where they have probably never numbered more than

34,000 at any one time. However, the intense whaling of the past 40 years has reduced the number of humpbacks there to no more than a few percent of the original numbers.

The International Whaling Commission has called for full protection of the humpback. Yet, even if this moratorium is honored, the number of humpbacks in the Southern Hemisphere seems dangerously low, perhaps too low to provide the pool of genetic variability needed to survive the next natural or man-made crisis.

Though they have also been seriously overhunted in the Northern Hemisphere, small herds of humpbacks appear in a few areas during natural periods of concentration (that is, for feeding, migration, delivering young, and the like). The waters near Bermuda are well known as such an area. Humpbacks are found to the south of Bermuda in considerable numbers during their annual spring migration from winter breeding grounds in the south to summer feeding grounds in the north (2, 3, 6). It is from studies of the herd sojourning in these waters that we have become aware of what we believe to be the humpbacks' most extraordinary feature — they emit a series of surprisingly beautiful sounds, a phenomenon that has not been reported previously in more than a passing way. We describe here one part of the humpbacks' sonic repertoire — a long "song" that recurs in cycles lasting up to 30 minutes and perhaps longer.

History of Recordings

The first recordings of humpback whales that we know of were obtained in 1952 by Schreiber (7) from a U.S. Navy hydrophone installation on the underwater slope of Oahu, Hawaii. Although Schreiber did not identify the species, Schevill (2) subsequently recognized the sounds recorded by Schreiber as coming from humpbacks. Most of the sounds that we describe here were recorded by Frank Watlington of the Palisades Sofar Station at St. David's, Bermuda. Watlington recorded from a hydrophone installation, similar to Schreiber's, deep in the North Atlantic on the slope of Bermuda.

Humpback whales may winter near Bermuda as well as pass nearby during their spring migration to northern Atlantic waters (8). The fortunate location of the broad-band hydrophones used by Watlington made it possible for him to record humpback sounds during spring migrations from 1953 to 1964. The broad-band hydrophone from which all of the recordings analyzed here were made was in about 700 meters of water, about 3 kilometers southeast of the entrance to Castle Harbour. Watlington's hydrophone-preamplifier combination was flat in response ($\pm$ 3 decibels) from 500 hertz to 10 kilohertz, with an amplitude loss of 6 decibels per octave below 500 hertz. A cable from this hydrophone extended to Watlington's office, where the sounds were taped by a Magnecorder, type PT 6-AH, operating at 19.1 centimeters per second. Thus, when whales uttered sounds within range of the hydrophone, Watlington was able to make recordings free of the usual shipboard and cable noises, with the assurance that the whales were not being disturbed by the presence of an observer.

Evidence That Sounds Are Correctly Ascribed to Humpbacks

Schevill and Watkins (9), apparently referring to some of the same sounds from the same Watlington tapes that we have described here, have already pointed out that the sounds come from humpback whales. Additional evidence that this is true comes from observations by Watlington. By using binoculars, he was able, on several occasions, to observe whales blowing in the vicinity of the hydrophones during a recording of "whale sounds." On rare occasions, Watlington was able to verify that these whales were humpbacks by noting the prominent white flippers when the whales breached. However, such observations did not accompany all of the recordings analyzed in detail here.

In addition to the tapes provided by Watlington, we have taken into consideration several hundred hours of recordings made by Payne, who has studied humpback sounds and behavior off Bermuda during the past five springs (1967 to 1971). Payne and Payne (10) have reviewed many of these tapes by noting the form of the sounds in a simple shorthand and, in some cases, by spectrographic analysis. All of our general conclusions about songs are based on considerations of both the Watlington and Payne recordings, but all spectrographic analyses shown here are from the Watlington recordings.

The evidence that Payne's recordings come from humpbacks is as follows: (i) when the sounds (such as those to be analyzed here) that were heard were loud and whales were visible in the area, the whales proved in each instance to be humpbacks; (ii) interposition of a motorboat's wake between identifiable, nearby humpbacks and a hydrophone reduced the intensity of the sounds being recorded (the bubbles in the wake presumably acted as a partial screen); (iii) unfavorable orientation of a hydrophone array in relation to a visible group of humpbacks reduced the intensity of the sounds recorded (one occasion); (iv) pauses in an exceptionally loud series of sounds were correlated with blowing of a nearby humpback at the surface (several occasions) and with a breaching humpback (one occasion); and (v) while drifting in a boat on a very calm sea, Payne went near a pair of clearly identifiable humpbacks and heard one whale emit a complete sequence of sounds, of the sort described here.

In describing the humpback whale song, we will adhere to the following designations. The shortest sound that is continuous to our ears when heard in "real time" will be called a "unit." (Some units when listened to at slower speeds, or analyzed by machine, turn out to be a series of pulses or rapidly sequenced, discrete tones. In such cases, we will call each discrete pulse or tone a "subunit.") A series of units is called a "phrase." An unbroken sequence of similar phrases is a "theme," and several distinct themes combine to form a "song." Finally, a series of songs within which there is no pause longer than 1 minute is termed a "song session." Some sessions last for hours.

In summary: subunit < unit < phrase < theme < song < song session. A diagram is shown in Fig. 1.

The shortest complete humpback song we have yet timed lasts 7 minutes, and the longest more than 30 minutes. Since these two songs are quite different in form and were recorded in different years, they are probably from different whales. But even the same whale, repeating its own song, will show different cycle lengths during a song session. . . . In spite of such variations in length, we call these vocalizations "songs" because they differ primarily in the number of times the phrases of a given theme are repeated. In our sample, the sequence of themes is invariable, and no

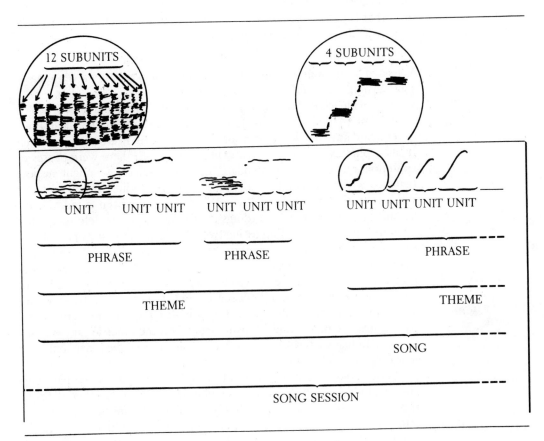

Fig. 1. Diagrammatic sample of whale spectrograms (also called sonagrams) indicating terminology used in describing songs. Frequency is given on the vertical axis, time on the horizontal axis. The circled areas are spectrograms that have been enlarged to show the substructure of sounds which, unless slowed down, are not readily detected by the human ear.

new themes are introduced or familiar ones dropped during a song session. Except for the precise configuration of some units and the number of phrases in a theme, there is relatively little variation in successive renditions of any individual humpback's songs. Yet, although we will not deal with it in detail here, we must not overlook this variation, for it is obviously an important feature of the songs.

Besides the variation among successive songs of one individual, there are often large differences among songs sung by different individuals. This raises the question of whether there is a single, species-specific song pattern, or whether each humpback sings its own pattern. All songs of humpback whales that we have heard consist of the following three main sections: (i) trains of rapidly repeated pulses that often alternate with sustained tones; (ii) many short, high-frequency units, most of which abruptly rise in frequency; and (iii) lower, more sustained notes that are monotonously repetitious in rhythm and frequency and contain many units that fall in frequency. We feel that these three sections constitute a very general, species-specific song pattern. . . .

Evidence That One Whale Is Responsible for a Song

We have been assuming throughout this discussion that any given song or song session is the performance of one whale.

The evidence that a song is produced by one whale and not by two or more in alternation ("duetting") follows. In long samples of sounds: (i) we never heard anything less than a song (if we had ever heard songs in which themes, phrases, or units were absent but in which there were pauses of appropriate length to accommodate the missing piece, we might suspect that two whales cooperate to produce a complete song); (ii) no units, or subunits (excluding what are obviously echoes), have been found to overlap in time; (iii) in some recordings . . . we find two complete songs that differ in average volume (indicating two whales, one near and one distant), each progressing in its own rhythm and form with no obvious relationship to the other. . . . [S]ome of Payne's 1969–1970 tapes include several whales producing sounds at once. In some cases (presumably when the hydrophone was roughly halfway between two whales), two sound sources are at equal volume, but analysis reveals that both sources are rendering complete songs. Neither whale seems to depend on the other for any phrases or notes. In many cases, one of the sources stops while the other continues repeating complete songs.

None of our observations absolutely excludes the possibility that songs are actually duets between whales swimming very close together. (Pairs or trios of humpbacks are frequently observed near Bermuda, and they are often in bodily contact when traveling together.) But if the whales are duetting, they are very precise in their alternation of sounds and unfailingly wait their turn to add their own notes.

Sex of the Performing Whale

On the question of whether songs come from males, females, or both, we have nothing yet to offer. It is possible that there will prove to be significant differences between the vocal apparatus of males and females. However, since we are not really sure that the larynx produces these sounds (though it seems likely that it must be involved), we would not even know what part of a humpback corpse to examine if we had one (and we have never had one). Mature male humpback whales are smaller than mature females, but, because there is so much overlap in size, it is only on very favorable occasions at sea that one could hope to determine the sex of a given whale. In addition, it has been our experience that humpback whales stop singing when we get close enough to distinguish subtle differences in their morphology. [Levenson (6) reports the same difficulty, as does Schevill (2), although Schevill's remarks are restricted to Odontocetes.] It will take a very fortunate occasion indeed to see whether males, females, or both sexes produce the songs.

Other Species

The songs we have described are often sung very loudly (a detailed discussion of the theoretical consequences of this is in preparation); therefore, one need not be within viewing range of the source to record the songs. Although this makes recording easy, it raises the constant specter that we have tried too hard to find similarities between songs recorded on different occasions near Bermuda. It is also possible that we may, in fact, be lumping together vocalizations of more than one species.

As mentioned earlier, there is good evidence that finback whales produce their moans in set patterns, and Cummings and Philippi (13) have evidence of cyclic sounds from what they believe to be a right whale (Eubalaena glacialis). If their species determination is correct, it could mean that singing is a common form of Mysticete vocalization. For this reason, also, we advance the possibility that we may have combined the sounds of a stray right whale or some other species with true humpback sounds. The large number of humpback whales in the vicinity of Bermuda during April and May (the only months from which our analyzed records were taken) and the apparent lack of right whales in that area at the same time (with the exception of one pair that Payne observed 25 miles southwest of Bermuda on 13 April 1970) argue against this concern. Yet the possibility remains that some other species have been included with our data on humpbacks.

Possible Significance of the Song

Schevill (2) notes: "The sonorous moans and screams associated with the migrations of Megaptera past Bermuda and Hawaii may be an audible manifestation of more fundamental vernal urges, for in New England waters and at other seasons we do not hear anything nearly so spectacular from this species." The implication here is that courtship is seasonal. However, there is good evidence, from measurements of embryos collected by whalers, that, even though most successful humpback matings occur during two peak seasons each year, some matings do occur throughout the year (14). Mating, of course, does not always immediately succeed court-ship in all species. Even if some humpback pairs mate year-round, it is quite likely that courtship activities leading to pair formation are seasonal. In this case, the songs may be related to pair formation.

The playful behavior of humpbacks near Bermuda in April and May has suggested to some observers that they are courting. The whales slam their tails on the surface of the water (lobtailing), wave and slap their fins on the water (finning), and frequently and repeatedly jump (breaching). . . . However, since these activities are frequently observed at other latitudes and at other times of year (8, p. 288; 15), they do not seem to be particu-larly linked with singing. If we wish to consider such antics, as well as songs, part of courtship, then we might conclude that the songs are involved with seasonal pair formation, and the acrobatics with year-round mating. Of course, if pair formation occurs year-round, such theories have no meaning.

Winn (16) has heard and recorded humpback songs near Puerto Rico in February, so the songs are apparently sung for at least 3 to 4 months. Thus, if songs are part of pair formation, we would expect it to be a lengthy process lasting from midwinter until well into spring.

In the North Atlantic, this time period (February to May) also corre-sponds to northward migration. Thus, one might imagine that the songs serve as a sort of flock call to hold a loose cluster of individuals together during their long migration. Until there is further evidence, we can only guess what function this remarkable series of vocalizations serves.

Summary

1) Humpback whales (*Magaptera novaeangliae*) produce a series of beautiful and varied sounds for a period of 7 to 30 minutes and then repeat the same series with considerable precision. We call such a performance "singing" and each repeated series of sounds a "song."

2) All prolonged sound patterns (recorded so far) of this species are in song form, and each individual adheres to its own song type.

3) There seem to be several song types around which whales construct their songs, but individual variations are pronounced (there is only a very rough species-specific song pattern).

4) Songs are repeated without any obvious pause between them; thus song sessions may continue for several hours.

5) The sequence of themes in successive songs by the same individual is the same. Although the number of phrases per theme varies, no theme is ever completely omitted in our sample.

6) Loud sounds in the ocean, for example dynamite blasts, do not seem to affect the whale's songs.

7) The sex of the performer of any of the songs we have studied is unknown.

8) The function of the songs is unknown.

References and Notes

1. H. L. Aldrich, *Arctic Alaska and Siberia* (Rand McNally, Chicago, 1889), p. 35; C. Nordhoff, *In Yankee Windjammers* (Dodd, Mead, New York, 1940).
2. For a review of this area see W. E. Schevill, in *Marine Bio-acoustics*, W. N. Tavolga, Ed. (Pergamon, Oxford, 1964), pp. 307–316.
3. B. Patterson and G. R. Hamilton, in *ibid.*, pp. 125–145.
4. W. E. Schevill, W. A. Watkins, R. H. Backus, in *ibid.*, pp. 147–152.
5. N. A. Mackintosh, *The Stocks of Whales* (Heighway, London, 1965), pp. 119, 201.
6. C. Levenson, *Informal Report No. 69-54* (Naval Oceanographic Office, 1969).
7. O. W. Schreiber, *J. Acoust. Soc. Am. 24*, 116 (1952).
8. A. G. Tomilin, *Mammals of the U.S.S.R. and Adjacent Countries*, Volume IX, Cetacea, O Ronen, Transl. (Israel Program for Scientific Translations, Jerusalem, 1967), p. 270.
9. W. E. Schevill and W. A. Watkins, *Whale and Porpoise Voices* (a phonograph record accompanied by a booklet) (Woods Hole Oceanographic Institution, Woods Hole, Massachusetts, 1962).
10. R. Payne and K. Payne, in preparation. [*Zoologica* (N.Y.) 56 (No 4) 159 (1971).]
11. W. B. Broughton, in *Acoustic Behavior of Animals*, R. G. Busnel, Ed. (Elsevier, London, 1963), pp. 824–910.
12. W. A. Watkins, in *Marine Bio-acoustics*, W. N. Tavolga, Ed. (Pergamon, Oxford, 1967), pp. 15–43.
13. W. C. Cummings and L. A. Philippi, *Publication No. NUC TP 196* (Naval Undersea Research and Development Center, 1970).
14. Tomilin (*8*, p. 280) bases his claim (that mating occurs year-round) on 68 humpback fetuses collected during whaling operations in the North Pacific. By extrapolating from embryo lengths, he calculated conception dates and, thus, the number of humpbacks conceived in each month: January, 1; February, 9; March, 12; April, 14; May, 4; June, 3; July, 1; August, 1; September, 12; October, 8; November, 3; and December, 0. Although two periods of increased mating activity are apparent, they are not sharply defined. Yet, even from such a small sample, we see that successful matings have occurred in 11 out of 12 months.
15. W. E. Schevill and R. H. Backus, *J. Mammalogy 41*, 279 (1960); R. G. Van Gelder, *Amer. Mus. Novitates 1992 (1960)*, pp. 1–27; anecdotal observations of many authors.
16. H. Winn. personal communication.
17. Research was supported, in part, by NSF grant GB 5564 and by grants from the New York Zoological Society. We thank M. Konishi, P. Marler, and F. Nottebohm for letting us use their sound analysis equipment and K. Payne and E. D'Arms for helping us with the spectography. We are particularly grateful to Frank Watlington of the Palisades Sofar Station, St. David's, Bermuda, for so generously making tape recordings available to us.

Questions and Exercises

1. Each of the first six paragraphs of the article could be the answer to a question. Write an appropriate question for each.

2. Paraphrase the summary section of this article, eliminating the numbered points to produce your own brief summary of this research on whale songs.

3. Although he is not named as a coauthor, Frank Watlington made an immense contribution to this research. What was his contribution? How was it acknowledged?

4. What is the hypothesis that is being tested in this research? How does this research differ from the more common scientific research that uses a series of experiments in a laboratory setting?

5. This article ends with two statements about what the researchers still do not know. Why do the authors choose to conclude their report in this way?

6. Although many scientific papers are written using third person and passive voice constructions ("The investigators noticed that . . ." or "It was noticed that . . . "), scientists today are increasingly likely to use the straightforward first person and active voice ("We noticed that . . ."). Which convention is used in this paper? When only one of the two authors of this paper is responsible for a particular observation, how is that information expressed? What verb tenses are used in this article and what appears to determine their use?

7. This article is intended for an audience of professional scientists. On what points do you need further explanation? Compare lists with classmates.

8. The nature of the sound spectrogram (or sonograph) is only briefly explained in this article. Using other sources, such as an introductory-level animal behavior textbook (for example, *Animal Behavior* by John Alcock or *Comparative Animal Behavior* by Jack Hailman), seek more information on sound spectrograms. Compare notes with classmates.

9. Using the sources mentioned in question 8, write a brief summary of the place of whales in the animal kingdom. Include examples of other animals sharing the same class and order.
    a) Into what different categories are whales classified?
    b) Relate the categories of whales to the categories mentioned in the introductory part of this article.
    c) Using all the information you have gathered on whales, draft a short essay explaining what whales are, how they are classified, and what types of noises they make. Your essay should be aimed at an audience of curious eleventh-graders.

10. Write a paragraph describing the sound spectrograph. What is its function or, if you prefer, why is it useful? Include a labelled illustration of a spectrograph. Your readers are freshman biology students.

Humpbacks, Their Mysterious Songs

ROGER PAYNE

from *National Geographic*

National Geographic is read in homes and professional waiting rooms throughout the country. Children look at the beautiful, glossy pictures; adults in all walks of life find the articles interesting. In fact, for many people, *National Geographic* is their only contact with research and exploration in science. The following article appeared in the January 1979 issue of the magazine. Although it was written by Roger Payne, one of the authors of the previous article from *Science*, the format and style are quite different from the earlier piece because of the popular audience here addressed.

Payne adopts a friendly, personal style. He notes colorful details ("I sat in the stern sheets . . . "), and refers to the reader as "you" ("When you go out to listen to a humpback whale . . . "). He also writes as if he were telling a story.

In certain respects, however, *National Geographic* articles resemble research reports in scientific journals. For example, the use of subheadings to separate the article into sections is a standard form of organizing material in science writing. And, although accessible to lay readers, the information given is always accurate and represents real scientific research.

Because this article was written nine years after Payne and McVay's original article, many of the questions posed in that original *Science* article have been answered by intervening research. As you read this brief excerpt, identify the questions that have been answered. (*National Geographic* permits us to print no more than 500 words of the original article.)

Humpbacks: Their Mysterious Songs
ROGER PAYNE

At dusk I sat in the stern sheets of our small sailboat, braced against a stanchion and using the last light of day to take a final sight on Bermuda's Gibbs Hill Lighthouse, 35 miles to the northeast.

We were too far from land to return that evening; my wife, Katy, and I would have to spend the night at sea . . .

As night deepened, a familiar feeling came over me, one of loneliness at sea. I felt at one with the other solitary watchers elsewhere on earth — the shepherds, sentinels, and herdsmen who huddled alone beneath these same stars, feeling the night close in around them.

To break the mood, Katy and I got down to work. We brought the boat about onto the other tack and pointed her as high into the wind as we could, so that she nodded gently with the waves. After lowering a pair of hydrophones into the sea, I switched on their amplifiers and listened in stereo through the headphones.

We were no longer alone! Instead, we were surrounded by a vast and joyous chorus of sounds that poured up out of the sea and overflowed its rim . . .

"Humpbacks: Their Mysterious Songs," by Roger Payne, Ph.D. Reprinted from *National Geographic Magazine* 155, 1979 by permission of *National Geographic Magazine*.

I felt instantly at ease, all sense of desolation brushed aside by the sheer ebullience of it all. All that night we were borne along by those lovely, dancing, yodeling cries, sailing on a sea of unearthly music . . .

Humpback whales pass Bermuda each spring on their way north from southern calving grounds near Puerto Rico. During this period the humpbacks fill the ocean with complex and beautiful sounds. Many hours of these sounds were recorded and later analyzed with the help of a friend, Scott McVay, at Princeton University. The analysis showed that humpback sounds are in fact long songs. . . . By song I mean a regular sequence of repeated sounds such as the calls made by birds, frogs, and crickets.

Humpbacks Change Their Tune

Most birdsongs are high pitched and last only a few seconds, while humpback songs vary widely in pitch and last between six and thirty minutes. Yet if you record a whale song and then speed it up about 14 times the normal rate, it sounds amazingly like the song of a bird. . . .

When you go out to listen to a humpback sing, you may hear a whale soloist, or you may hear seeming duets, trios, or even choruses of dozens of interweaving voices. Each of those whales is singing the same song, yet none is actually in unison with the others — each is marching to its own drummer, so to speak.

The fact that whales in Bermuda waters are singing the same song at any given moment is not surprising when you think of how similar two robins . . . sound. But if you collect humpback songs for many years and compare each yearly recording with the songs of earlier years, something astonishing comes to light that sets these whales apart from all other animals: Humpback whales are constantly changing their songs.

Questions and Exercises

1. Find two statements, one from the preceding *Science* article and one from this *National Geographic* article, that contain similar information. You will find more examples if you use the entire article (available in your library) rather than just the excerpt presented here. Compare the style of presentation in each of the two statements. Identify the information that is unique to each of the two articles and relate the nature of that information to the intended audience for each magazine.

2. Read the entire article from which this excerpt was taken and then write a paragraph summarizing the changes in the interpretation of whale songs that occurred between 1971 and 1979. Compare paragraphs with classmates.

3. Using your library, locate Sylvia Earle's companion article on humpback whales in the January 1979 issue of *National Geographic*. Compare her writing style with Roger Payne's. Does she tell a story? Examine the choice of verbs, adjectives, and nouns in each article. Do the

two writers prefer active or passive voice constructions? How long are their sentences? How do they provide context for the reader? What is their purpose in writing? Speculate on a "*National Geographic* style." Draft a letter describing this style to a friend who wants to be a free-lance writer.

A Whale of a Song

JULIE ANN MILLER

from *Science News*

Science News is a brief (sixteen-page) weekly magazine that summarizes recent scientific discoveries. All of the articles are written by science writers, not research scientists, and are generally based on research reports published in leading scientific journals like *Science*. *Science News* does not publish original research articles. However, as the number of original research reports published each year reaches unmanageable proportions, many scientists use this magazine to stay up to date.

Although *Science News* articles are written for the general college-educated public, the style is more businesslike than that of *National Geographic*. *Science News* readers want to be informed, not entertained. Consequently, the style resembles that used in newspaper articles, rather than that of either popular press publications or scientific journals. *Science News* articles are especially useful, however, because they always provide a reference to the original source.

The *Science News* article that follows was written and researched by science writer Julie Ann Miller, using information obtained from the two *National Geographic* articles on humpback whales and a press conference held by the scientists who wrote the articles, Sylvia Earle and Roger Payne. Although lacking the anecdotal details that give color to the *National Geographic* articles, this shorter summary in *Science News* contains all the important points from those articles and some additional information, presumably from the press conference. As you read, compare the style and the information in this article with the previous articles from both *Science* and *National Geographic*.

A Whale of a Song

JULIE ANN MILLER

The song of the humpback whale, nature's loudest, longest and slowest song, is an evolving art form. In addition to being performers, humpback whales seem to be composers, constantly incorporating new elements into their old tune. Roger Payne of the New York Zoological Society and Sylvia A. Earle of the California Academy of Sciences told a press conference of discoveries about the whale's song, and also about its feeding, that indicate an intriguing intelligence.

Rumbling bass passages and squeaky treble phrases, arranged in complex sequences, make up the song of the humpback whale. If the song is sped up fourteen times, it sounds surprisingly like a bird's song. (A recording of whale song at natural tempo and at high speed is included in the January *National Geographic*, along with articles by Payne and Earle.) At its natural speed, the whale song evokes a variety of human reactions. Writer and biologist Richard Ellis describes its "ethereal beauty" and others liken it to an enticing siren's song (see box). But in 1856 Charles Nordhoff reported a whale under the boat uttering "the most doleful groans, interspersed with a gurgling sound such as a drowning man might make."

Occasionally Earle and other researchers have dived near singing, 40-ton whales. "Under water the song was so intense that we could feel the sound as the air spaces in our heads and our bodies resonated," Earle says. Underwater cinematographer Al Giddings described the experience as feeling like "drums on my chest."

When the researchers transcribed numerous whale songs from underwater recordings, they found that all the humpback whales in an area sing the same song although the whales are well out of synchrony in duets or choruses. By analyzing songs collected over twenty years Katy Payne, Roger Payne's colleague and wife, discovered that the songs change progressively from year to year. "The songs of two consecutive years are more alike than two that are separated by several years," Roger Payne says. "For example, the songs we taped in 1964 and 1949 are as different as Beethoven from the Beatles." He points out, "We are aware of no other animal besides man in which this strange and complicated behavior occurs, and we have no idea of the reason behind it." Paralleling some critics of human music, Roger Payne says that the songs of the 60s were more beautiful than those of the 70s.

Because whales only sing in winter, Roger Payne says the researchers' first hypothesis was that the changes reflect flawed memory; the humpbacks simply forget part of the song over the summer and have to improvise in parts each fall. When the Paynes and Earle organized a six-month study to record a full season of songs, they learned that the whales return to their winter grounds faultlessly singing the song of the last season. The variations arise only as the winter progresses; an old phrase gradually decreases in frequency and a new phrase takes its place. Roger Payne observes that the introduction of new material and the phasing out of old in many ways are similar to the evolution of language.

Like human compositions, whale songs have a defined structure. In a given year the humpback whales that winter in Hawaii sing a different song than the whales wintering in Bermuda. But the structure of the song

What song the sirens sang?

Eerie melodies lured mythic mariners to shipwreck on the rocks. The whale song is the fact behind that legend, Roger Payne and Sylvia Earle believe, accepting evidence that whales formerly inhabited the Mediterranean. The researchers explain that the wooden hull of a boat, as the Greeks must have used, broadcasts underwater sounds. To a person in the boat, the song can't be localized; it seems to come from all around. Even being familiar with whale songs, the researchers admit being frightened and awed by hearing them within a boat. "You actually feel the song, it is so intense," Payne says.

and the rules for change are the same. Each song, for example, contains about six themes that follow in the same order. Each phrase contains 2 to 5 sounds. If a theme is deleted, the others stay in order. The researchers have deduced about fourteen simple, predictive laws for the song modification.

Because the laws of composition are the same between two, probably isolated herds of whales, Roger Payne suggests that the whales inherit, genetically or through learning, a set of song rules. "It must be a function of the huge brain to keep track of the changes," he says. In addition, the whales must memorize all the complicated sounds and their order and store the information at least six months. "To me, this suggests an impressive mental ability and a possible route in the future to assess the intelligence of whales," Roger Payne says.

The purpose of the elaborate song so far eludes scientists. They suspect from circumstantial evidence that it is a love song. It is sung only in one season, suspected to be the breeding time, and only by adults. So far all singers that have been sexed are male, but the researchers have been unable to determine the sex of most of the whales they observe.

Linking specific behaviors with the songs is an immediate goal of the research. Roger Payne says that whales are almost always alone and relatively inactive when they start to sing. When more whales appear on the scene, the first stops singing and they all go off in a tumbling melee.

Systematic investigation is a challenge because the scientists find it difficult even to tell which whale is making the sound. Because the whales, like opera singers, breathe surreptitiously at certain points where the breath won't interrupt the song, the researchers identify the singer by listening for a characteristic breath spot while scanning the ocean surface for a spout. (The song is performed entirely by air shuttling within the whale head, so no air is expelled to make the sound.) Once the singer is spotted, following is still a challenge. Earle says that tracking a whale feels like being an ant chasing an elephant.

A clever feeding behavior is the other observation that has brought a high regard for the whale intelligence. Chuck Juarasz of Glacier Bay in Alaska, where some of the humpbacks spend the summer, first observed whales capturing food with a net woven of bubbles. The krill and small fish that are the staples of humpback diet are scattered as in a very thin soup. However, a cylinder of bubbles rising through the depths can concentrate the creatures. Taking advantage of that phenomenon, a humpback whale will swim in a slow spiral from about fifty feet deep to the surface, emitting bursts of air through its blow hole. The whale chooses the angle for its spiral so that many bubbles reach the surface just as the whale does. Surfacing open-mouthed in the center of the bubble circle, the humpback devours its catch.

Earle reports that when she tried to scoop the fast-moving krill with a dip net, she rarely captured a single specimen. But when she scooped within a whale's bubble net, each dip yielded dozens, sometimes hundreds, of krill. To catch fish, the whales blow bigger bubbles than they do to catch krill. Occasionally two or three whales team up to make a single bubble net as large as a hundred feet across.

Payne and Earle look forward enthusiastically to learning much more about the whales. For instance, they would like to be able to identify the songs of individual animals to determine whether each herd has one leading song-changer or whether every humpback is a composer. In the only case where an identified whale was recorded singing twice, months apart, its song had changed in the same way as the song of the herd had changed.

In addition to their songs, the humpbacks produce a variety of seemingly social noises. Future investigations may relate those sounds to specific behaviors. And no whale species besides the humpback is now known to have a song, although others monotonously repeat a low, loud note that, before the underwater din of ship traffic, must have been audible for hundreds or thousands of miles.

The mission of the whale investigators appears to be more than scientific curiosity. It includes a strong concern for the preservation of the whale species. While whales are endangered, Roger Payne says, their mysteries are also endangered. "The whales are symbolic," Earle says. "They help us see ourselves more clearly. Perhaps by preserving them, we will preserve ourselves."

Questions and Exercises

1. Compare the style and format of this article with that of the *Science* article and that of the *National Geographic* article.

2. Locate a newspaper article on a scientific topic (for example, in the weekly science section in the Tuesday *New York Times*). How does it compare in style and format with this article from *Science News*?

3. What details of format and style in this article are characteristic of newspaper articles? Discuss with classmates.

4. For a three-week period, read the science sections in the Tuesday *New York Times*. At the end of that period, write a letter to the editor, either to commend or attack the coverage of scientific topics.

5. Pretend you are a science writer for *Science News*. Choose a topic from a recent issue of *Science*. Draft a news report on that topic in the style of Julie Ann Miller's treatment of whale songs.

6. Pretend that you are a science writer for *Newsweek*. Look through some recent issues of *Science News*. Select one or two items that might make interesting articles for *Newsweek*. Draft a memo in which you suggest to your editor two or three of these topics as possibilities for your next assignment. (Ask a classmate to play editor and to help you decide which topic to use.) Draft an article in the style of the *Newsweek* article on pp. 349–50.

Sound Playback Experiments with Southern Right Whales (Eubalaena australis)

CHRISTOPHER W. CLARK AND JANE M. CLARK

from *Science*

The final selection in this series of articles on whale songs is an actual research report from the journal *Science*. The editors of *Science* set stringent requirements for reports of recent research to the scientific community. The mere inclusion of a researcher's current work in *Science* is a signal that the experiment is important, that it represents one of the small steps through which science progresses. Even though a great many submissions to *Science* are rejected, the editors still must insist on a prodigious degree of condensation before an accepted report can be published. The major function of the research report is an announcement to other scientists that a certain piece of work has been performed. The report presents the methods, results, and conclusions in a form that will seem cryptic to all but its intended audience. The only people who will understand the article fully will be those who work in closely related areas. Scientists in other fields will simply learn that a certain type of work has been done. If they want more information, they can write to the researchers. You should not feel inadequate if you think that you are missing a great deal as you read the Clarks' report.

From time to time, *Science* will publish a major article providing background material on a particular subject, like Payne and McVay's "Songs of Humpback Whales" (pp. 352–59). The editors devote more space to these articles in order to provide sufficient context for scientists working in other fields. If you compare the style of the Payne and McVay article with that of the Clark and Clark research report, you will find many differences. The longer article was probably difficult for you to read, but the shorter one presented here may seem at first glance almost impenetrable to a beginning student.

Why do we reprint the Clarks' article in a general anthology of the arts and sciences? We do so because we want you to become accustomed to gleaning something from a technical article which was not written for you. Even if you never take a science course beyond the introductory ones, you ought to be able to skim through *Science* and learn something about what is current in the world of scientific research. Let us say that you are a journalist assigned to update the *Newsweek* article on pp. 349–50. Whom would you interview? What would you ask them?

As you read the following research report, formulate questions that you might ask the researchers. You might begin by asking the Clarks to state their working hypothesis. What hunch took them on this journey to Patagonia? Because of your own background reading, you might recall that Payne and McVay in their 1971 *Science* article say that the function of the whale songs is unknown. Obviously, other researchers will want to seek the answer to that question. You might also remember from reading the *National Geographic* excerpts that whales sing only during the breeding season, a fact that indirectly suggests that the songs might be important in whale courtship, just as bird songs function in the courtship of birds. The Clarks might very well have hoped to find information to confirm or disprove these hunches. However, the underlying hypothesis of the article is much more cautious: right whales will recognize and respond preferentially to the songs of their own species ("conspecific songs") and will not respond in the same way to other sounds, even though these sounds might be similar. Actually, the results reported here are less than a total confirmation of the hypothesis, but given the difficult circumstances, these results really do, as the Clarks say, "strongly indicate that southern right whales can differentiate between conspecific sounds and a variety of other sounds."

The Clarks tested their hypothesis by measuring the response of southern right whales to recordings of their own species' songs. The researchers then compared this response to the responses evoked by other sounds, including songs from whales of other species. The Clarks carried out these experiments using the southern right whale, a species different from the humpback whale used by Roger Payne. The southern right whales heard the following recorded sounds: water noise; a series of two-second, 200-hertz (Hz) beeps; humpback whale sounds; southern right whale sounds; and imitation right whale sounds. The Clarks measured the whales' responses of singing and swimming.

Although the basic design of the experiment is reasonably straightforward (play the sounds, measure the response), the execution was obviously quite difficult because the subjects were free-ranging whales in their natural habitat. Many irregularities, which would have been intolerable in a laboratory-based experiment using white rats as subjects, are permitted in this difficult-to-control environment. One reason that these uncontrolled variables are permitted here is the fact that the experimenters have allowed for the "worst possible" situation and have still emerged with statistically significant results. You can see an example of allowing for the "worst possible" situation by looking at the bracketed sound scores in Table 1: these scores, although probably the response of just one whale in the group, have been divided equally among all the whales present, since the actual singer could not be determined. Another example is in the procedure itself: all trials began when the whales were swimming away from the loudspeaker, even though swimming toward the loudspeaker was the hypothesized response to southern right whale songs.

When we decided to reprint the Clarks' article, we wrote to them to ask them some of the questions that might also be in your mind. We wanted to know how they became interested in whales and how they actually wrote their research report. We reprint their letter because we think it shows that scientists work hard on their writing as well as on their experiments.

3 November 1980

Dear Elaine Maimon,

. . . Historically, my involvement with whale research has been a combination of serendipity, a fondness for challenging adventures, and a predisposition toward questions on acoustic communication.

In the summer of 1972, I was assisting Dr. Charles Walcott with his research on the affects of magnetism on bird navigation. Dr. Walcott's research facilities are in Lincoln, Mass., just up the road from Dr. Roger Payne's home and laboratory. At that time, Dr. Payne was in the process of converting an old barn into a lab and needed a truck to haul old chicken wire, logs, swallow nests, etc., to the dump. I just happened to own a truck, which Roger spotted, and the rest is history. One night after a marvelous dinner with the Payne family, I was escorted upstairs to the lab, outfitted with headphones, introduced to a full variety of whale sounds, and shown pictures of the dry, dusty, desolate, and nearly uninhabited peninsula Valdes of Southern Argentina. I was enchanted. But there was a hitch. Roger was making me an offer that I couldn't refuse but I had committed myself to pursue a career in biomedical engineering. Having spent a laborious five years as an undergraduate training in biology and

Reprinted by permission of Christopher W. Clark.

engineering for this purpose, it was a difficult choice, medical school or a once-in-a-lifetime adventure with the whales in Patagonia. Needless to say, I chose the whales over medicine and have never regretted the decision.

The article in *Science* was a very small part of my thesis. Yet in a sense, since it was my first attempt at publishing, it was the most difficult. There were in all five drafts. The last one was completed after the review by three scientists (selected by *Science*) from the international scientific community and the earlier ones after criticism by professors at Stony Brook University. It was an ordeal, particularly since it required reducing a tremendous amount of data into a short almost telegraphic piece of writing. The playback experiments were, relatively speaking, a very small part of the research and were done only after two years of intensive observations on the whales. This was something that I had never anticipated or appreciated until writing up the results: All the thousands of hours of labor, from haggling with customs officials in Buenos Aires to making a plot of a whale's swimming pattern, are reduced to a few pages of text. The reader never hears of the sweat that was perspired, the drudgery of analysis, or the frustrations of conforming to the rules of the system. In the end the only motivations were the memories, the love for that wilderness, and a hope that we could have a chance to return to the whales.

The whales that Janie and I studied rely heavily on acoustics for communicating. There are very few distinctive visual displays and none that we could specifically correlate with vocalizations. This is not surprising since their visual world is considerably restricted. In the shallow waters of the bay the turbidity is high and on most days whales can probably only see about 15 m through the water. This might help explain the complexity of the sounds. In general, their vocal repertoire is not a limited number of discrete sound types but is instead a broad continuum with a complex set of rules. What we hope to do eventually is determine exactly what the rules are, how they are maintained in the whales' society, and how the whales use those rules to communicate their emotions, intentions, and feelings to other whales. . . .

Best regards and Cheers,
Christopher Clark

Sound Playback Experiments with Southern Right Whales (Eubalaena australis)

CHRISTOPHER W. CLARK AND JANE M. CLARK

Abstract. A variety of sound recordings were played to southern right whales. Whales approached the loudspeaker and made frequent sounds in response to recordings of other southern right whales, but swam away and made relatively few sounds in response to playbacks of water noise, 200-hertz tones, and humpback whale sounds. Thus it appears that southern right whales can differentiate between conspecific sounds and other sounds.

Playback of sounds to mysticetes has rarely been attempted (*1*). We present here the results of playback experiments which demonstrate that southern right whales (*Eubalaena australis*) can differentiate between sounds made by other southern right whales and a variety of other sounds. The experiments were conducted off the southern coast of Argentina (42°23′S. 64°03′W), where right whales were observed from mid-May through mid-December 1977. The whales spent most of their time swimming or resting at the surface.

The head of each southern right whale is adorned with a distinct pattern of dermal eruptions (callosities) that are colonized by cyamids (whale lice). By photographing these callosity patterns, we could identify individual whales on any given day (*2*). From more than 1000 photographs taken throughout the 15 playback experiments (a total of 19.8 hours), we identified 18 individual whales, some of which were present during more than one experiment.

An array of hydrophones was fixed 124 m in front of our observation hut, and the sounds made by the whales were tape-recorded during all periods of observation (*3*). To determine which whale made a particular sound, the array was linked to a real-time, underwater sound-direction finder (*4*), which indicated in less than 1 second the bearing to any sound between 30 and 500 Hz that was 3 dB (re 0.0002 μbar) louder than the ambient noise.

Five types of sounds were selected for playback to the whales: (i) water noise, (ii) 200-Hz tones, (iii) humpback whale sounds, (iv) southern right whale sounds, and (v) imitation southern right whale sounds (*5*). In the first three experiments, sounds were broadcast from an underwater loudspeaker suspended 3 m beneath a rubber boat. During all subsequent play-

Table 1. Sound scores (A columns) and swimming scores (B columns) for each whale for all the playbacks (first trial data only). The sound score for the selection is the whale's rate of sound production in sounds per minute. In experiments 2, 4, and 6, we could not accurately determine which whale in the group made the sounds. In these cases, the group's sound rate was divided by the number of whales in the group and the result entered once as the sound score (bracketed). The swimming score is the sum of the distances the whale swam toward the loudspeaker, minus the sum of the distances it swam away, divided by the total distance it swam (a negative swimming score signifies that during the playback the whale swam away from the loudspeaker more than it swam toward it).

| | | | Pre-playback | Playback selection | | | | | | | | | |
| | | | | Water noise | | 200-hz tones | | Humpback whale sounds | | Right whale | | Imitation | |
Experiment	Date	Whale	A	A	B	A	B	A	B	A	B	A	B
1	18 July	A	0.00									0.17*	+0.92*
2	18 August	B	[0.00]			[0.00*]	−0.40*			[0.15]	+0.40		
		C					−0.86*				+0.66		
		D					−0.81*				+0.20		
		E					−0.91*				+0.08		
3	24 September	F	0.05			0.00*	−0.35*			1.95	+0.42		
4	4 November	G	[0.00]									[0.35*]	+0.75*
		H											+0.75*
5	6 November	I	0.00					0.00	−0.28	0.80*	+0.79*		
6	8 November	H	0.18					1.22*	−0.12*	1.83	+0.68		
		J	[0.00]					[0.05]	−0.37	[0.07*]	+0.87*		
		K							−0.37		+0.87*		
7	8 November	L	0.18					0.78	−0.49	0.85*	+0.45*		
8	10 November	M	0.08	0.10*	+0.09*					0.25	+0.16		
9	11 November	N	0.00	0.00*	−0.41*					0.83	+0.68		
		I	0.00	0.00*	+0.02*					0.58	−0.18		
10	15 November	P	0.00	0.00	−0.21			0.00*	−0.82*	0.09	−0.09		
		Q	0.00	0.00	−0.21			0.00*	−0.82*	0.18	+0.96*		
		N	0.00	0.00	−0.94					0.00*	+0.67*		
11	27 November	R	0.00					0.00*	−0.41*	0.00	−0.39		
12	29 November	R	0.00	0.00*	−0.24*					0.00	−0.11		
13	30 November	R	0.00							0.00			
14	30 November	N	0.00							0.00*	−0.94*		
15	2 December	S	0.61							2.36*	−0.40*		

*Score is for first selection played in experiment.

backs, the loudspeaker was fixed on the bottom of the gulf, 128 m north of the observation hut (6).

The general procedure for a playback experiment was as follows. We identified each whale, tracked its movements with a theodolite (7), and recorded its sounds for at least 16 minutes (mean, 31 ± 15 minutes) prior to the experiment. We began a playback when the whales had passed and were swimming away from the loudspeaker (8). Two selections were played for equal amounts of time (mean, 11 ± 6 minutes) and were separated by a period of silence (mean, 2 ± 1 minutes) (9). This sequence is referred to as a trial. In each of 12 experiments, a single trial was run. In the three experiments with more than one trial, the same two selections were played in the same sequence for approximately equal amounts of time in each trial: trials were separated by periods of silence (mean, 20 ± 18 minutes) that were longer than the periods separating the selections.

For each experiment, we determined the movement of each whale, its distance from the loudspeaker, and the number of sounds it made (see Fig. 1). We scored the whale's response to a playback selection on the basis of the number of sounds it made (sound score) and its swimming pattern (swimming score). Table 1 lists the sound and swimming scores for all the whales during the experiments (data given are for first trials only).

The distribution in the swimming scores shows a significant difference ($P < .01$, Kruskal-Wallis test) from what would be expected if the playback had no effect on the whales' behavior. However, there were no significant differences ($P > .40$, Wilcoxon's signed-rank test) between sound and swimming scores for the first and second selections in a trial, meaning that the whales were not responding preferentially to the first selection (10). When right whale sounds were played, the sound scores were significantly different ($P < .01$) from the preplayback sound scores and the sound scores for the playback of water noise. The swimming scores when right whale sounds were played were significantly different ($.01 < P < .05$, Mann-Whitney U test) from the swimming scores when water noise, 200-Hz tones, and humpback whale sounds were played.

Behaviorally, this means that during playbacks of right whale sounds, the whales responded by making more sounds and swimming toward the loudspeaker. In response to the three other sound selections, the whales swam away and did not make more sounds. When a whale was exposed to a series of trials on the same day, its responses decreased with increasing exposure to the playback sounds (see Fig. 1) (11).

These results strongly indicate that southern right whales can differentiate between conspecific sounds and a variety of other sounds. To the best of our knowledge, this represents the first instance in which such evidence has been gathered for any species of whale in the wild. We believe that the playback technique presented here would be useful in determining the biological function of the sounds in a whale's acoustic repertoire.

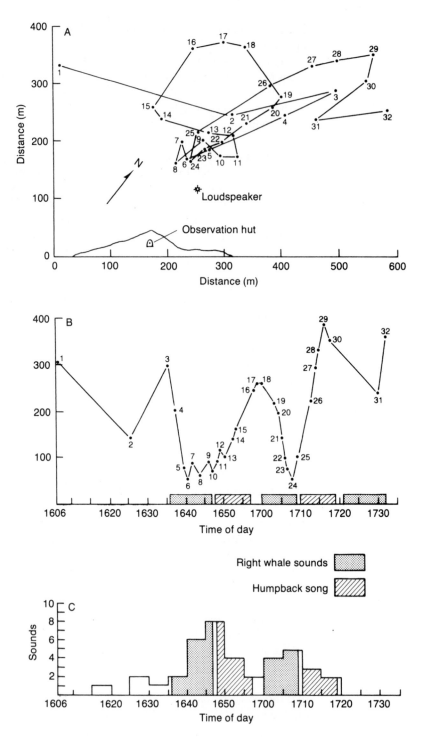

Figure 1. Response of Whale L (experiment 7) to right and humpback whale sounds (5). (A) The path of the whale in the area of the loudspeaker (numbered points represent position of whale ± 0.5 m) (B) The distance of the whale from the loudspeaker. (C) The number of sounds made by the whale per 5-minute interval.

References and Notes

1. W. C. Cummings and P. O. Thompson, *U.S. Fish Wildl. Serv. Fish. Bull.* 69 (No. 3), 525 (1971); ———, *J. F. Fish. Antarct. J. U.S.* 9 (No. 2), 33 (1974).

2. R. S. Payne *et al.*, in preparation.

3. The receiving system consisted of three AQ-17 hydrophones (with amplifiers) and a Nagra IV-S tape recorder or Sony TC-520CS cassette recorder. The system was flat $=$ 3 dB (re 0.0002 μbar) from 50 to 3000 Hz.

4. This device was designed and built by C. W. C. It utilized the phase-time information from a stationary, two-dimensional hydrophone array to compute the direction to the sound. Tests conducted in situ indicate that the system was accurate to within $\pm$ 12° (C. W. Clark, in preparation).

5. The first four selections were tape recordings, whereas the imitation was spontaneous. The 200-Hz recording consisted of a 200-Hz tone lasting 2 seconds and repeated every 10 seconds; 200 Hz is in the midfrequency range of sounds made by southern right whales [(*1*), R. S. Payne and K. Payne, *Zoologica (N.Y.)* 56 (No. 4), 159 (1971); C. W. Clark, personal observation]. A phonograph record [R. S. Payne, *Songs of the Humpback Whale* (CRM Records, Del Mar, Calif., 1970)] provided the humpback whale sounds. Two tapes of southern right whale sounds were used. In experiments 2 and 3, the playback consisted of three low, frequency-modulated sounds lasting a total of 3.4 seconds and repeated every 10 seconds. In all the other experiments, we used a tape of sounds recorded in 1977 from a group of four whales, none of which were resighted during any of the experiments.

6. Sound broadcasting equipment included a Sony TC-800B tape recorder, a crystal microphone, a Realistic MPA-20 amplifier, and a University 30 underwater loudspeaker. Sensitivity curves for the loudspeaker and microphone are not available. However, comparison between the spectral characteristics of the original playback sounds and the rerecorded sounds were made and the rerecorded sounds were judged to be good reproductions of the originals. The tape recorder and amplifier were flat $=$ 5 dB (re 0.0002 μbar) from 50 to 3000 Hz. Signal intensities 1 m from the loudspeaker were estimated as 95 $\pm$ 10 dB (re 0.0002 μbar).

7. This technique, pioneered by R. S. Payne, was accurate to $\pm$ 0.5 m at 1 km. During the first playback experiment, the theodolite was not used. Distances were calculated from photographs in which the whale, boat, and nearby landmarks appeared in the same frame. We estimate an accuracy of $\pm$ 5 m.

8. Water depth at the loudspeaker and hydrophones during the experiments averaged 5.8 $\pm$ 2.0 m. Water depth for the whales averaged 7.8 $\pm$ 4.5 m.

9. There were five exceptions. In experiments 1, 4, 14, and 15, we played one selection only. In experiment 10, we played 10 minutes of humpback whale sounds, 5 minutes of water noise, and 10 minutes of right whale sounds.

10. The results indicate that the responses to the second selection were independent of the responses to the first selection.

11. Whale N (see Table 1) was seen during three experiments when we played the tape of southern right whale sounds. On its first exposure, its response was typical: it swam toward the loudspeaker and increased its rate of sound production. Sixteen days later, it swam toward the loudspeaker but remained silent. Three days after this, it remained silent and swam away, never once turning toward the loudspeaker.

12. We thank C. Walcott and R. S. Payne for help and encouragement during the study, and C. Walcott and D. G. Smith for reading the manuscript. We also thank G. Blaylock, A. Macfarlane, J. Crawford III, and T. W. Clark for field assistance, and S. J. Clark for darkroom assistance. Supported in part by a grant from the National Geographic Society and by facilities and equipment from the New York Zoological Society and the State University of New York at Stony Brook.

15 June 1979: revised 26 September 1979

Questions and Exercises

1. Although the research reports in the journal *Science* do not use sub-headings, they do often follow the official sequence for research reports in other journals. Using this article, place the following subheadings at appropriate locations:

   Introduction
   Methods
      Subjects
      Apparatus
      Procedure
   Results
   Discussion
   References
   Acknowledgments

2. The Clarks explain their research methods in the body of the paper, in endnotes, and in the figure and table. Reorganize this information into a single section on methods. You might use the following sub-headings: subjects, apparatus, procedure.

3. Reread the endnotes. Make categories for their various functions. Assign each endnote to a category. Then meet in small groups to compare your lists.

4. Some might say that it was mere chance that brought Christopher Clark to a study of whales. Was it mere chance? What might have prepared him for his change of interests?

5. In this research report, Figure 1 is presented to show the response of a single whale during a trial. By comparing the results from this whale to the results obtained from other whales (Table 1), decide whether this response is typical. Meet in small groups to compare your decisions.

6. If you were going to repeat this experiment, what equipment would you need? What equipment would you have to build yourself? What does each piece of equipment do? (Explain in simple terms.)

7. The results reported for the playback experiments done on November 15, 1977, as shown in Table 1, do not match the procedures outlined in the article itself. Point out the discrepancies and suggest the probable sequence for the trials run that day. Meet in small groups to compare your reading of the table.

8. In experiments 1 and 4 the playback sound was "imitation southern right whale sounds" rather than a tape recording. Meet in small groups and speculate on the source of this particular sound. In your opinion,

how effective were the imitation sounds compared to the tape recording of genuine right whale sounds?

9. You and three of your classmates are science reporters for *Newsweek*.
Work together to formulate a list of interview questions to pose to
Christopher and Jane Clark.

10. Rewrite the selection as a brief news article aimed at an audience that
has had no more than a high school course in biology. Incorporate
human interest material from Christopher Clark's letter.

Appendix: Acknowledging a Community of Colleagues

One reason for attending college rather than studying on your own is to learn from other people, including your instructors, classmates, and friends. A college campus is a community of scholars — individuals who are connected with each other through intellectual exchange.

Throughout this book we have suggested that you share ideas with classmates because we believe from our own experience that ideas grow through exchange. You may feel some initial reluctance to discuss your work-in-progress with others because you are afraid of "stealing" other people's ideas or of having your own stolen. Professional writers behave quite differently. Look at the beginning and end of any book that happens to be on your desk (including this one) and read the page of acknowledgments (sometimes included in the foreword, preface, or afterword). You will find long lists of people who are thanked for reading and commenting on the stages of a manuscript as it evolves toward a publishable text.

We suggest that you write a page of acknowledgments as a preface to every paper that you submit for a grade. Such a document can be liberating; if you openly give witness to the help you receive, you can feel free to connect your own thinking to the ideas of others. Remember, too, that you have an ethical obligation to acknowledge help, whether it comes from a roommate or from a tutor in your college's writing center.

An expression of gratitude, however, *never* justifies exploitation. You must not seek or accept help with the actual phrasing of sentences. We can think of only two instances when such specific help is legitimate. If you are under contract to a publisher, an editor may be assigned to make some changes in your prose style. If you are working with coauthors, they, of course, may rephrase and reformulate your drafted ideas.

If a friend, classmate, or family member writes any portion of your paper or dictates passages of prose to you, you have acquired a coauthor, whose name belongs with yours on the title page of your paper. Coauthorship is a tricky business (as we well know), and we do not recommend it to inexperienced writers. It is best to gain a sense of your own autonomy as a writer before you synthesize your work with that of others.

If you accept inappropriate help, if you do not acknowledge the help you receive, or if you copy passages from published sources without quotation marks and proper documentation, you are guilty of plagiarism. Some professional authors have been sued by people whom they had gratefully acknowledged in their preface but whose work should have appeared within quotation marks in the published text.

The challenge for you in writing is similar to that posed in other social situations. You must work with other people because conversation is essential to growth, but social interaction always necessitates responsibility and honesty. A university or college campus is a place to practice the art of conversing freely without exploiting anyone.

In the following pages we present sample acknowledgments from many different published works. As you read these testimonies to the social nature of writing, we hope that you will also better understand the collaborative nature of reading. Printed words are not perfect words. The words you read are simply a record of a writer's latest choices. You may be surprised to find that published authors ask colleagues to read their unfinished work, and few writers ever regard any work as finished once and for all. When they publish something, they merely abandon it to public notice. Therefore, when you read the printed page, you are not confronting something closed and complete. As you read, you are a collaborator in the making of meaning.

We begin this section with the preface to a textbook, Peter Gay and R. K. Webb's *Modern Europe to 1815* (Harper and Row, 1973). The two historians explain three different kinds of collaboration. First, they describe the process of coauthorship. Then they thank the scholars whose primary research they summarize. Finally, they acknowledge the ongoing but invisible conversations with their critics, who provided the conditions for the internal dialogue that makes writing possible.

> All histories are works of collaboration, and this history is a work of collaboration in three ways. It is, first, a collaboration between two authors. For fifteen years we were colleagues at Columbia University, working in allied fields with steadily converging interests. We have criticized each other's manuscripts, talked much about historical problems, and in the process have come to a considerable identity of views, if not always precisely the same conclusions, about history. We planned this book together as a whole. With some exchange of jurisdiction, we have independently drafted those sections in which our chief competence lies, but we have

Preface (pp. xiii–xiv) from *Modern Europe to 1815* by Peter Gay and R. K. Webb. Copyright © 1973 by Harper and Row, Publishers, Inc. Reprinted by permission of the publisher.

read and criticized our individual efforts so often and so thoroughly that the book has become a truly joint venture.

We have underscored the collaborative nature of this enterprise in a second way, by acknowledging as far as possible our obligations to other scholars. Even the author of a highly specialized monograph must lean heavily on the work of others; all the more, the authors of a general textbook go to school to many specialists. We have used our footnotes to indicate the sources of quotations in the text, and the essays on selected readings, which we have attached to each chapter, record our main debts. Most works in foreign languages have had to be omitted, even though some of them have been of first importance to us; the authors of such works must be collectively acknowledged. Still, we trust that in these ways we have told the student of history something about the nature of the craft he is engaged with. And our dedication will indicate that such a book can owe a sum beyond reckoning to a historian from an entirely different field, whose contribution is the friendship he gave us and the example — scholarly, critical, humane — he set to all of us in a generation, at Columbia and beyond.

This is a more traditional book than the one we set out to write. We have devoted a considerable amount of space to the lives of ordinary people and to popular taste and culture, but even more to the high culture of our Western past — its painting and building, it religious convictions, and its scientific achievements. This difference is to some extent owing to the still tentative stage in which social history finds itself; many of the old sources and forms are no longer quite satisfactory or convincing, and the promising new materials and techniques have not yet yielded up the results in some fields that will allow authoritative generalizations. We had to reckon as well with the insistent and proper claims of traditional political history — reigns and battles and political struggles. We have tried to turn to account the remarkable results of research in these fields in the past couple of decades, and to go, as far as possible, beyond mere narrative to analysis. We have sought synthesis, not compromise.

There has been a third collaboration, a largely invisible debate with our critics. Of those whom we know and can thank by name for their mixture of severity and encouragement, we want particularly to thank Professors John A. Garraty, Orest Ranum, and Gordon Wright, Dr. Patricia Kennedy Grimsted, and Mr. Christopher Thorne. Ruth Gay collaborated not only as a critic but as a contributor in her own right.

PETER GAY
R. K. WEBB

When Sheila Rowbotham wrote *Hidden from History: Rediscovering Women in History from the 17th Century to the Present* (Random House, 1974), she did not have a coauthor, but she did not work alone. As she wrote, she heard remembered conversations with colleagues. She referred to unpublished papers and dissertations and to published work that friends had recommended. Most important, she was surrounded by that larger community of feminists, living and dead, about whom she wrote.

For ideas, information and help I would like to thank:

Joan Smith whose paper on women's production and the family at the International Socialists' day school on the family in spring 1972 forced me to re-examine my own ideas historically.

Keith Thomas for sending me his articles on the double standard of sexual morality and women in the puritan sects.

Christopher Hill for his talk to the Ruskin History Workshop in 1972 on the family and his talk on 'Sex and Sects' at a meeting of London Workers Education Association history tutors in January 1973.

Hermione Harris, whose interest in spirit possession, prophecy and witchcraft and the relationship of myths and magic to social reality has helped me to think about these subjects.

Edward Thompson for sending me his article on the moral economy of the eighteenth century crowd, Mary Collier's poem and Tom Mann's article on co-operative households and both him and Dorothy Thompson for their criticisms of *Women, Resistance and Revolution* and for letting me read Alf Mattison's letter book and their copies of *Commonweal*.

Gay Webber for lending me her paper on the background to nineteenth century anthropology.

Suzy Fleming for help on the Women's Labour League.

Gloden Dallas for long conversations about socialism and feminism in Leeds before 1914.

Anna Davin for telling me about the conditions of women's work in London in the late nineteenth century.

Florence Exten-Hann and Maurice Hann for giving me their time in remembering socialism, feminism and the trade union movement in Bristol and Southampton in the early 1900s.

Bill Fishman for introducing me to East End anarchism in the same period.

Barbara Winslow for lending me her thesis on Sylvia Pankhurst and the East London Federation of the Suffragettes.

Wilhelmina Schroeder and the Institute of Social History in Amsterdam for allowing me to consult the Sylvia Pankhurst papers.

Sheffield Public Library for letting me use the Carpenter collection.

From *Hidden from History: Rediscovering Women in History from the 17th Century to the Present* by Sheila Rowbotham. Copyright 1974 Random House. Reprinted by permission of Random House, Inc.

Julian Harber and Chris Goodey for help on the shop steward movement during World War I.

Jean Gardiner for the use of her unpublished paper on the effect of the 1914-18 war on women's position in the economy.

Stanmore and West Wickham WEA classes for their accounts of their experiences which range from childhood in the 1900s, dilution and war work to feminism and nursery education in the twenties and the situation of women teachers and clerical workers in the depression.

Ralph Bond for information about Lily Webb and the organization of the unemployed.

Keith Hindel for information about Stella Browne.

Finally for their encouragement, criticism and labour:

Anne Scott and Val Clarke who between them transformed my messy drafts into typewriting.

Richard Kuper, comrade and publisher, who disentangled my anarchical use of tenses and scrupulously made clear his political disagreements while still helping me to say what I wanted to say without imposing his own views.

David Widgery whose patience and sustained interest in my outpourings amazes me and who read the text as it was being written, between snatched Guinnesses when he emerged exhausted from being a housesurgeon and from his own writing and organising.

And to all the women in women's liberation and without, whose action, ideas and organisation while this was being written directed many of the questions I was asking about the past. In particular the Fakenham women who occupied their factory, the London cleaners who went on strike, and the women in the claimants union who in campaigning against the cohabitation clause are confronting patriarchy and the state.

SHEILA ROWBOTHAM

Seymour Papert wrote *Mindstorms: Children, Computers, and Powerful Ideas* (Basic Books, 1980) to report specifically on work that he did in a laboratory setting. However, Papert understood the meaning of that work because of a series of past and present collaborations; one of the most important of those collaborations was with Jean Piaget, the Swiss psychologist who changed the world's view of how children learn. As Papert wrote, he heard Piaget's voice and also those of other imagined readers with whom he wished to continue a conversation.

In this book I write about children but, in fact, most of the ideas expressed are relevant to how people learn at any age. I make specific references to children as a reflection of my personal conviction that it is the

From *Mindstorms*, by Seymour Papert. © 1980 by Basic Books, Inc. Reprinted by permission of the publisher.

very youngest who stand to gain the most from change in the conditions of learning. Most of the children who collaborated with us were of mid-elementary school age. Radia Perlman was the first to explore techniques for working with much younger children, as young as four years of age. Abelson and diSessa have specialized in work with older students of high school and college age. Gary Drescher, Paul Goldenberg, Sylvia Weir, and Jose Valente are among those who have pioneered teaching LOGO to severely handicapped children. Bob Lawler carried out the first, and so far the only, example of a different kind of learning experiment, a kind that I think will become very important in the future. In Lawler's study, a child was observed "full time" during a six-month period so as to capture not only the learning that took place in contrived situations but all the overt learning that took place during that period. I have also been influenced by another study on "natural learning" now being conducted as part of research by Lawrence Miller for his thesis at Harvard. Both Lawler and Miller provided data for a general intellectual position that underlies this book: The best learning takes place when the learner takes charge. Edwina Michner's Ph.D. thesis was a learning study of a very different sort, an attempt to characterize some of the mathematical knowledge that the mathematical culture does not write down in its books.

I have acknowledged intellectual obligations to many people. I have to thank most of them for something else as well: for support and for patience with my too often disorganized working style. I am deeply grateful to everyone who put up with me, especially Gregory Gargarian who had the very difficult jobs of maintaining the organization of the LOGO Laboratory and of entering and updating many successive versions of this book in the computer files. In addition to his competence and professionalism, his friendship and support have made easier many moments in the writing of this book.

MIT has provided a highly stimulating intellectual environment. Its administrative environment is also very special in allowing out-of-the-ordinary projects to flourish. Many people have helped in an administrative capacity: Jerome Wiesner, Walter Rosenblith, Michael Dertouzos, Ted Martin, Benson Snyder, Patrick Winston, Barbara Nelson, Eva Kampits, Jim McCarthy, Gordon Oro, Russel Noftsker, George Wallace, Elaine Medverd, and surely others. Of these I owe a very special debt to Eva Kampits, who was once my secretary and is now Dr. Kampits.

The LOGO project could not have happened without support of a different kind than I have mentioned until now. The National Science Foundation has supported the work on LOGO since its inception. I want also to mention some of the Foundation's individuals whose imaginative understanding made it possible for us to do our work: Dorothy Derringer, Andrew Molnar, and Milton Rose. The value of the support given by such people is moral as well as material, and I would include in this category Marjorie Martus at the Ford Foundation, Arthur Melmed at the National Institute of Education, Alan Ditman at the Bureau for the Education of the Handicapped, and Alfred Riccomi of Texas Instruments. I would also most especially include three individuals who have given us moral and material support: Ida Green, Erik Jonsson, and Cecil Green all from Dallas, Texas. It has been a particularly rich experience for me to work closely with Erik Jonsson on developing a project using computers in the Lamplighter School in Dallas. I have come to appreciate his clarity of thought and breadth of vision and to think of him as a colleague and a friend. His support for my ideas and intolerance of my disorganization helped make this book happen.

John Berlow contributed beyond measure to the writing of this book. He came into the picture as an unusually intelligent editor. At every phase in the manuscript's development, his critical and enthusiastic readings led to new clarity and new ideas. As the project developed he became, for me, more than an editor. He became a friend, a dialog partner, a critic, and a model of the kind of reader I most want to influence. When I met John he was without computer expertise, although his knowledge in other areas provided him with an immediate base from which to generate his own ideas concerning computers and education.

There are many people whose contributions cannot be categorized. Nicholas Negroponte is a constant source of inspiration, in part precisely because he defies categorization. I also wish to thank Susan Hartnett, Androula Henriques, Barbel Inhelder, A. R. Jonckheere, Duncan Stuart Linney, Alan Papert, Dona Strauss and I. B. Tabata. And there are a few people with whom disagreements about how computers should be used have always been valuable: John Seeley Brown, Ira Goldstein, Robert Davis, Arthur Leuhrman, Patrick Suppes. If the book can be read as an expression of positive and optimistic thinking this must be attributed to my mother, Betty Papert. Artemis Papert has helped in so many ways that I can only say: *Merci*.

Everyone concerned with how children think has an immense general debt to Jean Piaget. I have a special debt as well. If Piaget had not intervened in my life I would now be a "real mathematician" instead of being whatever it is that I have become. Piaget invested a lot of energy and a lot of faith in me. I hope that he will recognize what I have contributed to the world of children as being in the spirit of his life enterprise.

I left Geneva enormously inspired by Piaget's image of the child, particularly by his idea that children learn so much without being taught. But I was also enormously frustrated by how little he could tell us about how to create conditions for more knowledge to be acquired by children through this marvelous process of "Piagetian learning." I saw the popular idea of designing a "Piagetian Curriculum" as standing Piaget on his head: Piaget is par excellence the theorist of learning without curriculum. As a consequence, I began to formulate two ideas that run through this book: (1) significant change in patterns of intellectual development will come about through cultural change, and (2) the most likely bearer of potentially relevant cultural change in the near future is the increasingly pervasive computer presence. Although these perspectives had informed the LOGO project from its inception, for a long time I could not see how to give them a theoretical framework.

I was helped in this, as in many other ways, by my wife Sherry Turkle. Without her, this book could not have been written. Ideas borrowed from Sherry turned out to be missing links in my attempts to develop ways of thinking about computers and cultures. Sherry is a sociologist whose particular concerns center on the interaction of ideas and culture formation, in particular how complexes of ideas are adopted by and articulated throughout cultural groups. When I met her she had recently completed an investigation of a new French psychoanalytic culture, of how psychoanalysis had "colonized" France, a country that had fiercely resisted Freudian influence. She had turned her attention to computer cultures and was thinking about how people's relationships with computation influence their language, their ideas about politics, and their views of themselves. Listening to her talk about both projects helped me to formulate my own approach and to achieve a sufficient sense of closure in my ideas to embark on this writing project.

Over the years Sherry has given me every kind of support. When the writing would not work out she gave me hours of conversation and editorial help. But her support was most decisive on the many occasions when I fell out of love with the book or when my confidence in my resolution to write it flagged. Then, her commitment to the project kept it alive and her love for me helped me find my way back to being in love with the work.

SEYMOUR PAPERT

Ernst Mayr's *The Growth of Biological Thought* (Belknap Press, 1982) is a weighty book by an important biologist. However, Mayr began his project in the way that you might begin your own, with reading and note-taking. As Mayr drafted his ideas and consulted with others, his original conception of the book changed. He also accumulated many debts as he consulted with colleagues and accepted help and encouragement from various sources: foundations, libraries, friends, and family. In his preface he gives witness to the organic filaments that link the scientific community.

Much of modern biology, particularly the various controversies between different schools of thought, cannot be fully understood without a knowledge of the historical background of the problems. Whenever I made this point to my students, they would ask me in what book they could read up on these matters. To my embarrassment, I had to admit that none of the published volumes filled this need. To be sure, there is much literature on the lives of biologists and their discoveries, but these writings are invariably inadequate as far as an analysis of the major problems of biology are concerned or as a history of concepts and ideas in biology. While some of the histories of individual biological disciplines, like genetics and physiology, are indeed histories of ideas, there is nothing available that covers biology as a whole. To fill this gap in the literature is the object of this work. This volume is not, and this must be stressed, a history of biology, and it is not intended to displace existing histories of biology, such as that of Nordenskiöld. The emphasis is on the background and the development of the ideas dominating modern biology; in other words, it is a developmental, not a purely descriptive. history. Such a treatment justifies, indeed necessitates, the neglect of certain temporary developments in biology that left no impact on the subsequent history of ideas.

When I first conceived the plan to write a history of ideas in biology, the goal seemed impossibly remote. The first years (1970–1975) were devoted to reading, notetaking, and the preparation of a first draft. Soon it became obvious that the subject was too vast for a single volume, and I decided to prepare first a volume on the biology of "ultimate" (evolutionary) causations. But even this limited objective is a hopelessly vast undertaking. If I have been successful at all, it is because I have myself done a considerable amount of research in most areas covered by this volume. This means that I was already reasonably familiar with the problems and some of the literature of the areas involved. I hope to deal with the biology of "proximate" (functional) causations in a later volume that will cover physiology in all of its aspects, developmental biology, and neurobiology. When a biological discipline, for instance genetics, deals both with ultimate and proximate causations, only the ultimate causations are treated in the present volume. There are two areas of biology that might have been (at least in part) but were not included in this volume: the conceptual history of ecology and that of behavioral biology (particularly ethology). Fortunately, this omission will not be quite as painful as it might otherwise be, because several volumes by other authors dealing with the history of ecology and ethology are now in active preparation.

The professional historian is not likely to learn much from chapters 1 and 3; in fact he may consider them somewhat amateurish. I have added these two chapters for the benefit of nonhistorians, believing that it will help them to see the purely scientific developments of the other chapters with a deepened perception.

I owe an immense debt of gratitude to numerous individuals and institutions. Peter Ashlock, F. J. Ayala, John Beatty, Walter Bock, Robert Brandon, Arthur Cain, Fred Churchill, Bill Coleman, Lindley Darden, Max Delbrück, Michael Ghiselin, John Greene, Carl Gustav Hempel, Sandra Herbert, Jon Hodge, David Hull, David Layzer, E. B. Lewis, Robert Merton, J. A. Moore, Ron Munson, Edward Reed, Phillip Sloan, Frank Sulloway, Mary Williams, and others have read drafts of various chapters, have pointed out errors and omissions, and have made numerous constructive suggestions. I did not always follow their advice and am thus solely responsible for remaining errors and deficiencies. To P. Ax, Muriel Blaisdell, and B. Werner I am indebted for useful factual information.

Gillian Brown, Cheryl Burgdorf, Sally Loth, Agnes I. Martin, Maureen Sepkoski, and Charlotte Ward have typed innumerable drafts and helped with the bibliography. Walter Borawski not only typed preliminary versions but also the entire final copy of the manuscript and of the bibliography and prepared the manuscript of the index. Randy Bird contributed to filling gaps in the references. Susan Wallace edited the entire manuscript and in the process eliminated numerous inconsistencies, redundancies, and stylistic infelicities. All of these people materially contributed to the quality of the final product. It is obvious how great a debt of gratitude I owe to them.

The Museum of Comparative Zoology, through the courtesy of its Director, Professor A. W. Crompton, has provided office space, secretarial help, and library facilities, even after my retirement. Research periods at the Institute for Advanced Study (Princeton, spring 1970), at the library of the Max Planck Institute of Biology (Tübingen, 1970), a senior fellowship of the Alexander von Humboldt Foundation (Würzburg, 1977), a fellowship awarded by the Rockefeller Foundation (Villa Servbelloni, Bellagio, 1977), and a grant (No. GS 32176) by the National Science Foundation have greatly facilitated my work.

Whenever secretarial help was not available, my wife took over, transcribed dictations, excerpted literature, and aided the work on the manuscript in countless ways. It is impossible to acknowledge appropriately her inestimable contributions to this volume.

ERNEST MAYR

On pp. 54–59 of this anthology you read a portion of Helena Curtis's *Biology*, 3rd edition. Before you perused it, a long list of reviewers read and commented on earlier versions. In fact, the edition from which our excerpt was taken was itself a revision of an earlier published version. In the preface, Helena Curtis acknowledges many readers — including students who read earlier editions and sent her ideas for improving the text. Those readers understood that reading, like writing, is a collaborative activity.

As students of biology — whether professionals or amateurs — we are particularly fortunate to be living at a time when almost every aspect of the life sciences brims with new insights and discoveries. I feel privileged to

From Helena Curtis, *Biology*, 3rd edition, Worth Publishers, New York 1979, preface pages vii–ix. Reprinted by permission of the publisher.

be able to introduce newcomers to this subject, and I have tried to convey some of my own enthusiasm and to share some of the excitement that is so much a part of contemporary biology.

I find it remarkable that each new edition of the book requires more work than the preceding one. The entire book must be reconsidered, sentence by sentence, rewritten to a large extent, and also, to some degree, reorganized. The same questions must be answered with each edition: What is modern biology? What do students *have* to know? What should they remember ten years from now? What will still be true?

The most important undertaking of this revision has been to modernize the basic chemistry in the early chapters and to show throughout the remainder of the book how this knowledge of events at the molecular level deepens our understanding of biological phenomena. The goal has been to make the chemistry more coherent, more relevant to biology, but no more difficult. (Some reviewers have, indeed, found it to be easier.)

The Introduction, as before, deals with evolution, the major unifying principle of the life sciences. The historical background and essential ideas of Darwinian evolution provide a perspective that will be useful to students throughout their study of biology. No matter what organization is followed in a particular course, I hope the Introduction will be considered essential first reading.

I am reluctant to march you through a chapter-by-chapter description of the book, even though that seems to be the rule for textbook prefaces. For those who are not familiar with previous editions, such a thumbnail sketch is certainly inadequate, and, after all, the book is right in front of you. For those who are acquainted with the second edition, let me quickly mention the sources of information that guided us in this revision.

First of all, a number of you wrote with constructive criticisms of the book. Second, many teachers prepared detailed reviews of the second edition. A third source of information was the reporting by Worth representatives of conversations with teachers who had used the text. And finally, a number of ideas for improvement had been brewing in my own mind, many of them prompted by my work on new editions of both *Biology of Plants*, Second Edition, coauthored with Peter H. Raven and Ray F. Evert, and *Invitation to Biology*, Second Edition. So a plan emerged that involved a total rethinking of the chemistry, additional emphasis throughout the book on energetics, and a modernized ecology section, with less description and more analysis. And, of course, everything had to be brought up to date.

The overall structure of the book remains basically the same. The levels-of-biological-organization approach is again followed, beginning with atoms and moving to cells, Part I; organisms, Part II; and populations, Part III. For this edition, energetics now appears in a separate section, and the order of the ecology and evolution sections has been reversed. It is within the chapters themselves that a significant amount of restructuring has occurred, resulting, I believe, in a book that is more coherent and more intellectually satisfying.

Acknowledgments

Once again, I have had the benefit of a symbiotic relationship (I hope mutualistic, but perhaps commensalistic and, in a few instances, parasitic) with reviewers and consultants. Robert S. Edgar, University of California, Santa Cruz, and Abraham Flexer have been a continual source of guidance and wise counsel throughout the revision. I am also deeply indebted to Daryl Sweeney, University of Illinois, Urbana-Champaign, for his excellent suggestions and encouragement.

Although it is woefully inadequate recognition for their help, I am, as before, listing those who provided reviews for this edition, together with my thanks for their erudition and generosity:

Roslyn B. Alfin-Slater, University of California, Los Angeles
George T. Barthalmus, North Carolina State University
John W. Batey, Seton Hall University
Dorothy B. Berner, Temple University
Antonie W. Blackler, Cornell University
Walter F. Bodmer, University of Oxford
Richard K. Boohar, University of Nebraska, Lincoln
Charles Brown, Santa Rosa Junior College
Maren H. Brown, Onondaga Community College
Edwin Burling, DeAnza College
John Corliss, Oregon State University
Mary D. Coyne, Wellesley College
Mel Cundiff, University of Colorado, Boulder
Carol Diakow, Adelphi University
Lawrence S. Dillon, Texas A & M University
Mark W. Dubin, University of Colorado, Boulder
David Epel, Stanford University, Hopkins Marine Station
Ray F. Evert, University of Wisconsin, Madison
Ben T. Feese, Centre College of Kentucky
Herbert Friedmann, University of Chicago
John Gapter, University of Northern Colorado
Michael T. Ghiselin, University of California, Bodega Marine Laboratory
Frank H. Gleason, Santa Rosa Junior College
Malcolm S. Gordon, University of California, Los Angeles
James L. Gould, Princeton University
Govindjee, University of Illinois, Urbana-Champaign
Michael C. Grant, University of Colorado, Boulder
Paul B. Green, Stanford University
Alan D. Grinnell, University of California, Los Angeles

Guido Guidotti, Harvard University
Burton S. Guttman, Evergreen State College
Penny Hanchey-Bauer, Colorado State University
Jean B. Harrison, University of California, Los Angeles
Brian A. Hazlett, University of Michigan
Alvin E. Hixon, Daytona Beach Community College
Charles E. Holt, Massachusetts Institute of Technology
George B. Johnson, Washington University
Russell L. Jones, University of California, Berkeley
John Kirsch, Yale University
Richard M. Klein, University of Vermont
Paul Kugrens, Colorado State University
Kenneth O. Lloyd, Memorial Sloan-Kettering Cancer Center
Jane Lubchenco, Oregon State University
Dorothy S. Luciano, formerly of the University of Michigan
R. Davis Manning, University of Mississippi Medical Center
Eugene R. Meyer, New York University
Douglas W. Morrison, Rutgers University, Newark
Todd Newberry, University of California, Santa Cruz
John G. Nicholls, Stanford University
Garth L. Nicolson, University of California, Irvine
H. Frederik Nijhout, Duke University
R. D. O'Brien, Cornell University
John H. Ostrom, Yale University
Jane A. Peterson, University of California, Los Angeles
Keith R. Porter, University of Colorado, Boulder
Gene A. Pratt, University of Wyoming
Carl A. Price, Rutgers University, New Brunswick
Jonathan Reiskind, University of Florida, Gainesville
Edward S. Ross, California Academy of Sciences
Carl Sagan, Cornell University
Thomas K. Scott, University of North Carolina, Chapel Hill
David G. Shappirio, University of Michigan
Lincoln Taiz, University of California, Santa Cruz
Robert M. Thornton, University of California, Davis
Joseph Varner, Washington University
John L. Yarnall, Humboldt State University
Norton D. Zinder, Rockefeller University

I would like to call your attention to the excellent Study Guide prepared by Vivian Null to accompany the text. And with this edition we now for the first time have a Laboratory Manual to be used with the text. It was written by Ray F. Evert and Susan E. Eichhorn of the University of Wisconsin, Madison, and Barbara Saigo of the University of Wisconsin,

Eau Claire. Transparency Masters of some of the illustrations in the book are also available for the first time to adopters.

I feel particularly privileged to be writing for young people; I like their curiosity, their energies, their imaginativeness, and their dislike of the pompous and pedantic. I hope I serve them well.

HELENA CURTIS

We end this series of acknowledgments with the words of another writer whom you have met earlier, John Stuart Mill. In his *Autobiography* he celebrates his intellectual partnership with his wife, Harriet Taylor, née Hardy. The kind of intimate collaboration described here may be possible only in marriage:

> When two persons have their thoughts and speculations completely in common; when all subjects of intellectual or moral interest are discussed between them in daily life, and probed to much greater depths than are usually or conveniently sounded in writings intended for general readers; when they set out from the same principles, and arrive at their conclusions by processes pursued jointly, it is of little consequence in respect to the question of originality, which of them holds the pen; the one who contributes least to the composition may contribute most to the thought; the writings which result are the joint product of both, and it must often be impossible to disentangle their respective parts, and affirm that this belongs to one and that to the other. In this wide sense, not only during the years of our married life, but during many of the years of confidential friendship which preceded, all my published writings were as much her work as mine, her share in them constantly increasing as years advanced.[1]

Their collaboration seems to have been especially close in the writing of *On Liberty*, about which he later wrote:

None of my writings have been either so carefully composed, or so sedulously corrected as this. After it had been written as usual twice over, we kept it by us, bringing it out from time to time, and going through it *de novo*, reading, weighing, and criticizing every sentence. Its final revision was to have been a work of the winter of 1858–59, the first after my retirement, which we had arranged to pass in the

1. Excerpts from *The Autobiography of John Stuart Mill*, Foreword by Asa Briggs. New York: New American Library. Signet Classics. 1964. Reprinted by permission.

South of Europe. That hope and every other were frustrated by the most unexpected and bitter calamity of her death — at Avignon, on our way to Montpellier, from a sudden attack of pulmonary congestion.[2]

. . . .

After my irreparable loss, one of my earliest cares was to print and publish the treatise, so much of which was the work of her whom I had lost, and consecrate it to her memory. I have made no alteration or addition to it, nor shall I ever. Though it wants the last touch of her hand, no substitute for that touch shall ever be attempted by mine.[3]

When the work appeared in 1859, within a year of her death, the dedication read:

To the beloved and deplored memory of her who was the inspirer, and in part the author, of all that is best in my writings — the friend and wife whose exalted sense of truth and right was my strongest incitement, and whose approbation was my chief reward — I dedicate this volume. Like all that I have written for many years, it belongs as much to her as to me; but the work as it stands has had, in a very insufficient degree, the inestimable advantage of her revision; some of the most important portions having been reserved for a more careful re-examination, which they are now never destined to receive. Were I but capable of interpreting to the world one half the great thoughts and noble feelings which are buried in her grave, I should be the medium of a greater benefit to it, than is ever likely to arise from anything that I can write, unprompted and unassisted by her all but unrivalled wisdom.[4]

2. Ibid., pp. 173–174.
3. Ibid., pp. 179–180.
4. *On Liberty*, dedication page.